THE LANDSCAPE
OF MODERNITY

THE LANDSCAPE OF MODERNITY

New York City, 1900–1940

Edited by David Ward and Olivier Zunz

The Johns Hopkins University Press
Baltimore and London

First published in a hardcover edition by the Russell Sage Foundation, 1992
Johns Hopkins Paperbacks edition, 1997
06 05 04 03 02 01 00 99 98 97   5 4 3 2 1

The Johns Hopkins University Press
2715 North Charles Street
Baltimore, Maryland 21218-4319
The Johns Hopkins Press Ltd., London

Library of Congress Cataloging-in-Publication Data

The landscape of modernity : New York City, 1900–1940 / edited by David Ward and
Olivier Zunz.
    p.   cm.
  Originally published: The landscape of modernity : essays on New York City,
1900–1940. New York : Russell Sage Foundation, 1992.
  Includes bibliographical references and index.
  ISBN 0-8018-5609-4 (pbk. : alk. paper)
  1. City planning—New York (State)—New York—History—20th century.
2. Regional planning—New York Metropolitan Area—History—20th century.
3. Central business districts—New York (State)—New York—History—20th century.
4. New York (N.Y.)—Social conditions.   I. Ward, David, 1938–   . II. Zunz, Olivier.
HT168.N5L36   1997
307.1´216´097471—dc21   96-47452
                                                          CIP

A catalog for this book is available from the British Library.

Contents

v

Part IV GOING FROM HOME TO WORK

Part V FIGHTING FOR IDENTITY

Part VI COMPLETING THE LANDSCAPE

Acknowledgments

The Landscape of Modernity is third in a four-volume series sponsored by the Committee on New York City of the Social Science Research Council and published by the Russell Sage Foundation. John Hull Mollenkopf edited *Power, Culture, and Place* (1988) and co-edited, with Manuel Castells, *Dual City* (1991). *Capital of the American Century*, edited by Martin Shefter, is forthcoming.

It gives us pleasure to thank David L. Szanton, formerly of the SSRC staff, and Ira Katznelson and John Mollenkopf, successive Committee chairs, for their leadership and friendship in a most exciting interdisciplinary venture. We have also benefited from suggestions that fellow Committee members, commentators, and other guests offered during the several SSRC workshops that led to this volume. Contributors shared invaluable insights that extended beyond their assigned topics and helped us shape the separate pieces into a coherent whole.

We want also to express our gratitude to Onno Brouwer and his staff at the University of Wisconsin Cartography Lab. for the maps they designed especially for this book. Lisa Nachtigall, publications director at Russell Sage, Charlotte Shelby, and Anna Marie Muskelly, managing editors, have upheld the Foundation's tradition of excellence in production.

D.W. and O.Z.

Madison and Charlottesville
Spring 1992

Notes on Contributors

Daniel Bluestone teaches architectural history and preservation at Columbia University. He is the author of *Constructing Chicago* (1991).

Jameson W. Doig is professor of politics and public affairs at Princeton University. He is the author of *Metropolitan Transportation Politics and the New York Region* (1966), co-author of *New York: The Politics of Urban Regional Development* (1982), and co-author and joint editor of *Leadership and Innovation: A Biographical Perspective on Entrepreneurs in Government* (1987, 1990). In addition to his work on urban development, he has written on ethics, public administration, and police and criminal justice.

Gail Fenske is an architect and an architectural historian. She is currently teaching in the School of Architecture at Roger Williams College. Her most recent project is a book on Cass Gilbert's Woolworth Building.

Robert Fishman is professor of history at Rutgers University, Camden. He is the author of *Urban Utopias in the Twentieth Century: Ebenezer Howard, Frank Lloyd Wright, and Le Corbusier* (1977) and *Bourgeois Utopias: The Rise and Fall of Suburbia* (1987). A fellow at the Wilson Center of the Smithsonian Institution for 1988–89, he has begun a study of urban decentralization in the twentieth century and published "America's New Cities" in *The Wilson Quarterly* (Winter 1990).

Donna Gabaccia is Charles Stone Professor of American History at the University of North Carolina, Charlotte. Her research has focused on the history of Italian migration and the comparative study of immigrant women in the United States. Her major publications include *From Sicily to Elizabeth Street* (1984), *Militants and Migrants* (1988), and two forthcoming volumes on immigrant women, *Seeking Common Ground* and *From the Other Side*.

Nancy L. Green is currently Maître de Conférences at the École des Hautes Études en Sciences Sociales. She is the author of *The Pletzl of Paris: Jewish Immigrant Workers in the Belle Époque* (1986). Her next book will focus on immigrants and the garment industries of New York and Paris from the late nineteenth century to the present.

Deryck Holdsworth is associate professor in the Department of Geography at Pennsylvania State University. In addition to a number of articles on the urban geography of skyscrapers, he is the editor of *Reviving Main Street* (1985), co-editor of the *Historical Atlas of Canada, Vol. III: Addressing the Twentieth Century* (1990), and author of *The Parking Authority of Toronto, 1952–1987* (1987).

Clifton Hood is writing a history of New York City's subways, *Underground Politics: The Rise and Fall of New York's Subways*. He is assistant professor of history at Hobart and William Smith Colleges.

Thomas Kessner, professor of history at the City University of New York Graduate Center, is the author of *Fiorello H. LaGuardia and the Making of Modern New York* (1989), *The Golden Door: Italian and Jewish Immigrant Mobility, 1880–1915* (1977), and with Betty Caroli, *Today's Immigrants, Their Stories* (1982). He has published more than a dozen articles in scholarly journals and received fellowships from the Rockefeller Foundation, the National Endowment for the Humanities, and the American Council of Learned Societies.

Deborah Dash Moore is professor of religion at Vassar College. In 1988–89 she served as research director of the YIVO Institute for Jewish Research and dean of its Max Weinreich Center for Advanced Jewish Studies. An historian of American Jews, she has written two books, *At Home in America: Second Generation New York Jews* (1981), and *B'nai B'rith and the Challenge of Ethnic Leadership* (1981), edited *East European Jews in Two Worlds* (1990), and co-edited *Jewish Settlement and Community in the Modern Western World* (1991). She is currently writing a history of Jews in postwar Miami and Los Angeles.

David Nasaw is a professor of history at the College of Staten Island and Graduate Center, City University of New York. He is the author of *Children of the City: At Work and At Play* (1985), and the forthcoming *Going Out: The Rise and Fall of Public Amusements*.

Keith D. Revell is a graduate student in American History at the University of Virginia and a fellow at the Smithsonian Institution. He is currently completing his dissertation, "Beyond Efficiency: Experts, Urban Planning, and Civic Culture in New York City, 1898–1933."

David Ward is provost and vice chancellor for Academic Affairs and Andrew Hill Clark Professor of Geography at the University of Wisconsin-Madison. His books include *Cities and Immigrants* (1971) and *Poverty, Ethnicity, and the American City, 1840–1925* (1989). He has served as President of the Association of American Geographers.

Marc A. Weiss is director of the Real Estate Development Research Center and associate professor in the Graduate School of Architecture, Planning, and Preservation at Columbia University. He is author of *The Rise of the Community Builders* (1987), co-author of *Real Estate Development Principles and*

Process (1991), and is currently writing *Own Your Own Home: Housing Policy and Homeownership in America*. He is also writing *Prime Property*, a public television series on the history of urban development.

Carol Willis is an architectural historian who specializes in American architecture and urbanism of the 1920s and 1930s. She has curated exhibitions on the work of Raymond Hood and Hugh Ferriss and is currently writing a monograph on the Empire State Building. She teaches in the School of Architecture at Columbia University.

Olivier Zunz is professor of history at the University of Virginia and visiting directeur d'études at the École des Hautes Études en Sciences Sociales. He is the author of *The Changing Face of Inequality* (1982), *Making America Corporate, 1880–1920* (1990), and the editor of *Reliving the Past* (1985).

List of Illustrations

Part I

INTRODUCTION

1

Between Rationalism
and Pluralism:
Creating the Modern City

David Ward / Olivier Zunz

With the amalgamation of the five boroughs in 1898 into a greater city, New York became the most populous city in the world after London. The new metropolitan government and its public agencies faced the challenge of rationalizing a vastly expanded city, with a burgeoning business center in Manhattan and expansive suburbanization. In addition, New York City absorbed a more numerous and diverse flow of immigrants than any other city in the nation. The outcome was a rational and pluralistic metropolis of unprecedented scale.

By the first decade of the twentieth century, New York was already a precursor of those world cities that now anchor global capitalism. In 1901, John Hay, in his eulogy for President McKinley, proclaimed that "the financial center of the world, which required thousands of years to journey from the Euphrates to the Thames and the Seine, seems passing to the Hudson between daybreak and dark."[1] New York was becoming a leading international financial center while remaining both the largest manufacturing center and entrepôt in the United States.[2] These economic functions resulted in a complex assemblage of building types set within a diversified metropolis: a vast array of skyscrapers, department stores, and hotels juxtaposed with residential quarters both lavish and squalid, warehouses and port facilities, factories and sweatshops. Although the region's deindustrialization has altered much of that landscape in recent decades, what was once typical of New York still defines global cities throughout the world. In this volume, then, we retrace the creation of the modern urban landscape in its birthplace, New York City.

In New York, the modern skyline attained its earliest and most extraordinary expression. The New York skyline, and with it the character of the city, was transformed by the construction of dozens of skyscrapers in lower Manhattan. Indeed, for much of the world, its dense lines of skyscrapers are the most graphic statement of modernity. When Le Corbusier, a spokesman for architectural modernism, visited New York in 1930, he celebrated the novelty of that landscape. Although the extreme density of tall buildings on Manhattan was distinct from his modern vision of well-spaced towers, Le Corbusier found his preferred landscape more fully realized in New York than anywhere else in the world. Le Corbusier saw "a vertical city, under the sign of the new times"; and he added in a tone celebratory of modern times: "America, which is in a process of permanent evolution, which possesses infinite reserve of materials, which is animated by an energy potential unique in the world, is surely the country first able to bring to fulfillment, and with an exceptional perfection, this contemporary task" of calling "into service all the techniques of modern times" to build the "radiant city."[3]

Our book neither celebrates that landscape nor assumes that the architectural components of the vertical city or great public works alone can be a complete record of modernity. Indeed, the term "modernity" conveys a myriad of loosely connected meanings—among them the Enlightenment philosopher's faith in secularized knowledge, the nineteenth century poet's search for the ephemeral, and the twentieth century architect's functional designs.[4] Here, we refer to those aspects of modernity directly resulting from the interrelationship of the two great forces that shaped New York: rationalism and pluralism. Neither rationality nor pluralism was new. What was new was their intensity. Whereas nineteenth century America had been a de facto pluralist society with an ideology of assimilation, an aspiration for cultural pluralism intensified just as political, economic, social, and cultural processes were creating a more homogeneous nation. The vigorous search for rationality met with an equally vigorous defense of cultural segmentation.[5]

In this book, we capture the process of adjustment between these conflicting objectives. Within the rough boundaries of New York's political economy, the representatives of corporate capital, real estate, and regulation were building the rational city, the vertical city, and the transport systems essential to its continued vitality. The skyscrapers of the rational city were enmeshed in an extraordinary jumble of neighborhoods and cultural clusters, a microcosm of American diversity.

Corporate capitalism and cultural pluralism in a real sense vied for influence across New York's space and skyline. Their advocates were often at odds with each other. In the tough conflicts for space that ensued among speculators, corporate builders, civic leaders, and immigrant entrepreneurs, we see the competing configurations of modernity. Henry Adams, who witnessed this clash, wrote in 1905 that "the city had the air and movement of hysteria."[6] Although it may be hard to reconcile the seeming certainties of rationality with the seeming chaos of diversity, we argue that these overtly contradictory dimensions are integral parts of the modern experience. The landscape of modernity combined formal and informal economies, tall and small buildings, the service sector and industry, and the deeds of machine politicians and those of reformers.

Vertical and Horizontal Components of the Modern Landscape

A collaboration of social and architectural historians, historical geographers, political scientists, and historians of planning and public policy, this book approaches the relationships between past and present and between form and process from several disciplinary perspectives. Yet it is unified by the authors' common preoccupation with the physical landscape and the complementary perspectives of their individual disciplines. We interpret New York's landscape by linking its key physical and visual configurations to the political, economic, social, and cultural processes of the twentieth century.

In doing so, we take several snapshots of New York that together define the modern landscape. First before the eye is the vertical capitalist city that has captured the imagination of observers like Le Corbusier and that has become part of popular culture. Although some of the key prototypical experiments in the construction of the vertical city were initially worked out in Chicago, lower Manhattan was the site of the world's first major concentration of skyscrapers, the symbol of the modern city.[7] In 1904, Henry James, seeing the spire of his beloved Trinity Church lost amidst tall buildings, deplored the disappearance of the five-story Victorian city.[8] He had only an inkling of the radical transformation still to occur, a transformation driven by high land values, steel-frame construction, and powerful elevators. By 1910, New York had not only outdistanced all other places in the world in the upward extension of its buildings, it had already twice as many tall structures as Chicago would have a full decade later.[9]

Areas transformed by the vertical expansion of the city were the subject of intense debates. Some buildings provided office space for new or rapidly growing corporate enterprises in finance, insurance, commerce, and trade. Others were hotels and luxury apartment build-

Figure 1.1 New York City Boroughs.

Cartography Lab, University of Wisconsin-Madison

ings. Still others served the needs of New York's garment industry as sweatshops piled up on top of one another. This process generated a great deal of heated controversy among corporate builders, garment entrepreneurs, real estate speculators, Fifth Avenue merchants, and planners over the character of the downtown area.

In this volume, Gail Fenske, Deryck Holdsworth, and Carol Willis explore the strategies of corporate builders and real estate speculators. Both builders and speculators wanted to maximize their return on investment. In the process, they created a new aesthetic that combined modern design with new interior arrangements that catered to the requirements of their tenants. Indeed, the vertical architecture of the corporate city resulted from interior as well as exterior constraints.

6

The skyscrapers also reflected the new relationships between the corporations and the thousands of small firms that serviced them. To finance their headquarters, corporate giants provided space for these small firms, which required close proximity to each other and to their corporate clients. The Woolworth company occupied fewer than two stories in its fifty-five-story headquarters building. The Empire State Building's design tightly combined the search for vertical monumentality with that of maximum profitability. A temporary failure because of the Depression, the building turned out to be an extraordinary concentration of well-lit, first-class offices for a great many firms which, in World War II and beyond, would need an anchor in the nerve center of American capitalism.

As new corporate organizations and related smaller firms drew unprecedented concentrations of professionals and clerks downtown, other forces pulled the landscape in different directions. New middle-class neighborhoods expanded, new working-class areas sprang up, and older ones were displaced; phenomena studied in this volume by Nancy Green, Donna Gabaccia, and Deborah Dash Moore. The transformations of the core were also tied to the expansion of port facilities on both sides of the Hudson and the enhancement of railroad terminals, as the waterfront, traditionally connected to the central business district, was now severed from it in the increasing land use specialization. The push and pull of these varied forces created a mosaic of often incompatible and conflicting industrial and residential neighborhoods and an extraordinarily complex but incomplete system of communications.

The sheer dimension and physiographic complexity of the Hudson River and its associated bays limited access to the city center and constricted the development of a regional transportation system. The new mosaic of land uses, the sheer size of the built-up area, and the demand for greater mobility of goods and people required that these limitations be overcome and an elaborate system of connectors be built to meet interregional and internal needs. Great new bridges and tunnels—the longest in the world—were imagined, and some were built. Elevated railroads and subways characterized the expanding transportation network, and a vast web of highways emerged from the mud, sand, and slums of the city.

The extraordinary bridges and tunnels that connect Manhattan to Long Island and the mainland became, like the city's skyscrapers, part of the imagery of the modern city. Since the building of the Brooklyn Bridge, each new crossing from Manhattan island, whether above or below ground, marked an engineering advance. With the completion of the Holland Tunnel in 1927 and the George Washington Bridge in

1931, a crucial phase in the development of modern New York was completed. Commuters to and from new suburban homes west of the city could now bypass the slow Hudson ferry system; and trucking companies were able to compete with railroads in bringing freight from the rest of the continent to New York's factories, shops, and steamship piers.

Politics and Visions

In 1905, Henry Adams had insisted that "the new forces" transforming New York "must at any cost be brought under control."[10] His estimation of the situation was widely shared. Indeed, the historical literature overflows with analyses of the ways in which both political bosses and progressive reformers attempted and failed to control the environment. Tammany Hall and the political and social reformers typically battled over the same ethnically segregated neighborhoods. The overriding need to cope with the new scale of metropolitan life, however, made the conflicts between the old politics of corruption and the new politics of reform less decisive. The big changes that emerged, such as the creation of Greater New York in the last years of the nineteenth century, were the result of hard-won, complex, ad hoc alliances among these contenders for political control.[11]

The newly formed planning agencies eventually set the agenda for debate. With time, even New York's fabled skyline became a partially regulated skyline. A planning tradition—and a new profession—was created in New York City. A complex of these new institutions attempted to redefine the public interest. Their proponents, who wielded considerable political power, promoted advances in urban engineering by balancing the centralizing functions of the city's corporate economy with the diffuse pluralistic realities of a metropolis.

Planning agencies became political forces in their own right. Keith Revell and Marc Weiss analyze the ways planning for the metropolis became, on the one hand, a matter of public discourse and, on the other, a pretext for strengthening an invisible government of experts shielded from electoral politics. The new experts not only mediated among local interests, they also set legal precedents.

Regulating the city also became an integral part of the politics of the growing regulatory state. In looking closely at the 1916 zoning law, the first zoning effort in the country aimed primarily at rationalizing the landscape rather than excluding "undesirables" (like zoning laws elsewhere), Keith Revell and Marc Weiss tell the story of the first planning professionals: how they went about redesigning the cityscape with an ingenious scheme of setback architecture for skyscraper construction, why they buried progressive taxation (with its socialist over-tones), and why they cast the future of the metropolis in an apparently neutral language of public health.

New agencies also constructed most of the public arteries that con-nected sections of the metropolis. Clifton Hood tells of the ways the subway created and revitalized entire neighborhoods. Robert Fishman and Jameson Doig report on the debates over rail and automobile con-nections, and Doig describes the controversies generated by the con-struction of the George Washington Bridge. Creating these links led to new relationships among the city, the state, and private parties. Special-purpose authorities for transport improvements not only rein-forced the growing role of experts in politics, they also mediated among traditional political institutions. These authorities and others created in the 1930s and after would then shape the metropolis for the remainder of the century. By opting for the automobile over rail links by the late 1920s, and promoting a national trend, the Port Authority left a deep imprint on the city. Meanwhile Robert Moses, that master builder, watched the Port Authority at work and learned how to imple-ment his own extensive version of the same program.

It was also clear that these strategies to reduce congestion created new problems associated with decentralization. In fact, although the comprehensive twentieth century plans for the renewal of American cities that were supported by groups of businessmen had begun with the simple idea of beautification, decentralization soon became the predominant trend. In modern New York, the program rapidly became more complex. Planning not just for the city but for the region got under way in the studies that led to the creation of the Port Authority in 1921. A still more extensive and well-publicized regional planning effort was carried forward in the 1920s by the Committee on the Re-gional Plan. With funding from the Russell Sage Foundation, these planners transformed their vision into a set of guidelines for the plan-ning profession. The plan, Robert Fishman shows, involved an extraor-dinary team of professionals and served as the reference point for all the regional planning efforts that would follow.

The ideal behind the regional plan was a balanced system of trans-portation and decentralized industry. The plan's authors understood the peculiarity of New York's industrial base. In their effort to reorder the landscape more rationally, they hypothetically regrouped such ac-tivities as printing and garment manufacturing, which required an un-usually high level of interaction among all parties, in industrial sub-urbs. Despite the planners' efforts, urban growth led to undisciplined suburban sprawl. Nevertheless, the plan's importance as the vision of a group of professionals was more important than their predictive

power. Even though planners failed to see that the railroad corporations would never agree to the regulated coordination of their terminals and interchanges or that urban sprawl would wash away their
effort at "diffuse centralization," the planners made decentralization
an issue that would shape public debates. They also provided a coherent standard by which to judge and criticize suburban sprawl.

Critics of the Regional Plan argued that efforts toward decentralization through improved transportation and zoned land uses created
urban sprawl (which found its ultimate expression in Los Angeles).
These critics, led by Lewis Mumford, preferred a regulated reconcentration of both people and employment in several discrete clusters
within the metropolitan region and, more decisively, an ultimate limit
on the population growth of the region. But while the Regional Planning Association of America (RPAA) was more idealistic than were
pragmatic practitioners, as Fishman notes, both groups took for
granted the necessity for government intervention by public agencies.

Yet, the shift from machine politics to a technocracy was uneven.
In this volume, Clifton Hood and Jameson Doig contrast the limitations of the subway system, eroded as it was from its inception by old
machine politics (saving the fare is a perennial promise at election
time), to the extraordinary engineering, financial, and political success
of the new Port Authority. Furthermore, even the seemingly neutral
language of experts must be understood within its political context. It
reflected the progressives' impatience with national oligopolies and
their fears about the polarization of urban society. The progressives'
intervention by means of the regulatory state began as an effort to
restrain corporate capitalism, but in its mature form fluctuated between the control of corporate entities and the direction of the new
possibilities of abundance.

Pluralism and Contention for Space

In the end, the intensification of land use made possible by the skyscraper and the expanded transportation infrastructure did not produce
the rational city of corporate capitalism; nor did it fully maintain the
variegated neighborhoods that characterize a pluralistic society. In
fact, the debate about how to articulate vertical expansion and integrated transportation systems failed to address the demands expressed
in pluralist politics. At a time when the regional planners were preoc-
cupied with decentralization, the nearby city of tenements developed
along its own lines.

This led to conflict for space. With an unusually high number of
clerical and skilled manual workers moving to the boroughs, Manhat-

tan increasingly and perhaps inevitably became, early in the century, a city of the very rich and the very poor. Underlying these patterns were traces of an older, active, industrial center of immigrants. This is why remnants of overlapping and conflicting landscapes characterize Manhattan in a way not found in other North American cities. Skyscrapers, monumental avenues, warehouses, sweatshops, tenements, pushcarts on crowded streets, when taken together, form a complex association of congested and incompatible commercial, industrial, and residential land uses.

The rivalry for the streets between the rational city and the pluralistic city took many forms. The modern city is inconceivable without electricity. As David Nasaw shows, electricity not only powered the skyscrapers' elevators but also transformed the city's streets in ways that added yet another dimension to urban subcultures. When, at the turn of the century, commercial entrepreneurs made imaginative use of electricity to build places of public entertainment, they contributed to the melting of otherwise segmented communities in a new world of amusement parks, movie houses, and other forms of commercial leisure. Lighting created new public spaces where a variegated people, defined by class and culture, could blend in a new anonymous crowd. Lighting opened up the streets while preserving individual anonymity.

Daniel Bluestone, in turn, shows that those ethnic communities that appropriated city streets for their economic needs met with increasing resistance from a government that differentiated between public and private land uses and codified a geography of specialization. Thus Fiorello LaGuardia's successful fight against pushcarts marked the victory of the homogenizing and rationalizing tendencies of modernity over immigrant culture. Bluestone shows that the New York City streets were a continuously contested and redefined realm. The free use of streets for traffic became but a part of a larger citywide economic planning and program of ethnic assimilation. It was not implicit in the history of the street itself.

The landscape of modernity therefore is a layered patchwork of scenes, not a rational new landscape. Its components were rarely stable, as Nancy Green shows by detailing the first phases of the garment industry's flight from downtown Manhattan to midtown and to suburban locations close enough to provide overnight delivery. We see here how the Lower East Side, one of the world's most densely populated areas, was largely dismantled through industrial decentralization and suburbanization. Ethnic neighborhoods were not just dispersed, they were transformed or re-created with the relocation of the city's industries.

Conflicts for space often translated into conflicts for identity. To

document the process whereby each group worked out residential, oc-
cupational, and cultural strategies of its own, Donna Gabaccia and
Deborah Dash Moore study the residential arrangements of the Italian
and Jewish communities respectively as they were affected by decentralization. The family relationships and friendship networks among
Little Italy residents were partly responses to the investment strategies
of the community's insiders who built most of the new tenements.
The small Italian investors, however, ultimately gave way to more
powerful corporate developers. The forces of large-scale redevelopment
forced many second-generation immigrants to decamp for suburban
neighborhoods.

In these neighborhoods, second-generation immigrants did not necessarily forget the landscape of their youth. Pluralism persisted. Thus
New York's Jews, Deborah Dash Moore explains, re-created the city's
apartment culture, although often embellished by a new suburban art
deco style. A vernacular landscape emerged from the reconcentration
of middle-class Jews in suburbs where they could assimilate apart from
other ethnic groups.

The landscape of modernity, then, is much more than the simple
product of industrial relocation, the real estate market, the architect's
office, the planner's dreams, the government's regulators, and the engineer's system. It is also the product of diverse people shaping neighborhoods. The variegated territory emerges from the competition among
different kinds and visions of modernity.

The Circumstances of Modernity

This book captures a long moment—from the turn of the century to
the 1940s—when the push and pull of homogenizing rationality and
resisting diversity was shaping New York's landscape. But what now
seems a foregone conclusion was far from an inevitable process. The
metropolis was not shaped by abstract, indirect, larger-than-life forces
but by a myriad of actors making a number of specific decisions reflecting their ideals and circumstances. That was true even within the
corporate city. Hence, at the heart of our collective investigation is
the role of human agency. While American reformers dreamed of the
city beautiful and planners conceived of the rational city, poor renters
doubled up to meet payments, and immigrant and native investors
alike cornered sections of the real estate market. Although some of
the large forces transcend individual or local decisions, the shape and
content of neighborhoods is the result of their constant interaction.

New York's landscape was also the product of exceptional circumstances and unusual personalities who knew how to take advantage of singular conditions. Among them is New York's famous mayor of the Depression, Fiorello LaGuardia. While acknowledging the achievements of Robert Moses, New York's famous "park commissioner" turned master builder, who bound the metropolitan area with highways, bridges, parks, and playgrounds, Thomas Kessner forcefully argues that it was LaGuardia, not Moses, who saw the post-Depression programs as a unique opportunity to complete, with a massive infusion of federal moneys, the modern landscape. LaGuardia showed extraordinary skill in controlling Moses—whose bureaucratic power reputedly removed him from accountability—and in outmaneuvering Washington politicians while putting New Yorkers back to work.

The idea that the Depression opened up possibilities for local governments is not new. Robert and Helen Lynd had already noted in *Middletown in Transition* that Muncie, Indiana, had shunned public improvements in the twenties only to transform its environment under the impetus of the federal government's deficit spending to fight the Depression. As the Lynds put it, "It was manna direct from heaven, and Middletown came back for more, and more, and more."[12] Although New York was the only city in the country rich enough to rebuild itself every ten years, government spending did much to complete the modern structure. Once the structure was in place, Moses could dream up his highways and fill many of the blanks.

Conclusion

As we rediscover the original setting in which the modern urban landscape was first imagined and elaborated, we realize that we continue to encounter some of the conflicts and frustrations that characterized it. To be sure, New York City has evolved a great deal since the 1940s. But while the postwar era seemed to suggest that forces of homogenization would without doubt overcome those of fragmentation, homogenization now appears to have been a short-lived parenthesis in American history. Not long ago, in the seemingly homogeneous early 1960s, Nathan Glazer and Daniel P. Moynihan reminded Americans in *Beyond the Melting Pot* that ethnic characteristics were resilient. By looking beneath the surface of assimilation, we could find them.[13] The search beneath the surface is no longer necessary. A new wave of immigrants has forced observers to rethink now obsolete theories of assimilation. Ethnicity is back in full force. The minority population—not only African Americans and Hispanics but also Asians and an array of smaller groups—had increased to become once again a majority by 1987.[14] Today's social landscape is paradoxically closer to the pluralistic mode of the early twentieth century than to the intervening homogeneity of the mid-twentieth century city.

Yet there are significant differences between our age and the early twentieth century. The flurry of public works that marked the construction of the modern landscape has all but disappeared. No bridges or tunnels have been built since the 1960s, and many older facilities are in disrepair. Politicians and planners seem to have lost the ability to conceive of them or to pay for them. With a sinking physical infrastructure, the landscape of modernity appears old indeed. How, then, shall we rebuild a city where rationality and pluralism meet anew? This book shows that the landscape of a huge city is made up of innumerable small units of life where class and culture intersect with economic imperatives. Rationality and pluralism must not cancel each other. Our challenge as citizens remains to find yet another way to create a space that meets and reflects the aspirations of a diverse people.

Notes

1. Quoted in Martin J. Sklar, *The Corporate Reconstruction of American Capitalism, 1890–1916: The Market, The Law, and Politics* (Cambridge, England: Cambridge University Press, 1988), p. 440.
2. *Twelfth Census of the United States (1900)* (Washington, DC: United States Census Office, 1902), 8:998–999; *Statistical Abstract of the United States (1900)* (Washington, D.C.: U.S. Government Printing Office, 1901), p. 126.
3. Le Corbusier, *When the Cathedrals Were White*, Francis E. Hyslop, Jr., trans. (New York: McGraw-Hill, 1964), pp. 34–36.
4. For a convenient summary, see David Harvey, *The Condition of Postmodernity: An Enquiry into the Origins of Cultural Change* (Oxford, England: Basil Blackwell, 1989), pp. 10–38.
5. See Olivier Zunz, "Genèse du pluralisme américain," *Annales: Economies, sociétés, civilisations* 42 (March–April 1987): 429–444; also available as "The Genesis of American Pluralism," *Tocqueville Review* (1987–1988): 201–219.
6. *The Education of Henry Adams: An Autobiography* (1907), Library of America Edition (New York: Viking, 1983), p. 1176.
7. On the issue of the rivalry between Chicago and New York over the design of the first skyscraper, see Winston Weisman, "New York and the Problem of the First Skyscraper," *Journal of the Society of Architectural Historians* 12 (March 1953): 13–21.
8. On this episode, see Leon Edel, *Henry James: A Life* (New York: Harper & Row, 1985), pp. 611–612.
9. See Marc A. Weiss, "Density and Intervention: New York's Planning Traditions," Chapter 3 in this volume.

10. *Education of Henry Adams*, p. 1176.
11. David Hammack, *Power and Society: Greater New York at the Turn of the Century* (New York: Russell Sage Foundation, 1982), pp. 29–105.
12. Robert S. Lynd and Helen Merrell Lynd, *Middletown in Transition: A Study in Cultural Conflicts* (New York: Harcourt, Brace, 1937), p. 120.
13. Nathan Glazer and Daniel Patrick Moynihan, *Beyond the Melting Pot: The Negroes, Puerto Ricans, Jews, Italians, and Irish of New York City* (Cambridge: MIT Press, 1963).
14. On recent social trends in New York City, see John Hull Mollenkopf and Manuel Castells, eds., *Dual City: Restructuring New York* (New York: Russell Sage Foundation, 1991).

Part II

PLANNING FOR NEW YORK CITY

2

Regulating the Landscape:
Real Estate Values, City Planning,
and the 1916 Zoning Ordinance

Keith D. Revell

On July 25, 1916, the New York City Board of Estimate and Apportionment adopted the nation's first comprehensive zoning ordinance. Edward Bassett, the Brooklyn lawyer who chaired the commission that drafted the law, wrote to the members of his handpicked committee to congratulate them on a job well done and to invite them to a dinner in honor of the two men who wrote the ordinance: architect George Ford and statistician Robert Whitten. George Mortimer, president of the Equitable Building Corporation, responded enthusiastically: "While I think we are all to be congratulated, I feel that the real glory to be received from this legislation will perhaps not come until ten years from now, when the general public will be able to appreciate this great accomplishment." George Whipple, professor of Sanitary Engineering at Harvard University, likewise expressed his satisfaction with the work of Ford and Whitten: "I am sure," he emphasized, "that the example of New York City will be followed in many other places in the country." This support from commission members mirrored the response of other interested New Yorkers. Bruce Falconer, attorney for the Fifth Avenue Association, praised the measure even as he made the case for more stringent regulations. A similar verdict came from Benjamin Marsh, representative of the radical wing of the city planning movement. Although the commission could have done more, Marsh remarked, it had "made the most painstaking and careful study of existing conditions of development, use and future needs of New York City, ever made in this country, and probably in the world."[1]

From real estate executives to public health experts, the 1916 zoning ordinance attracted praise as a major step toward salutary government regulation of the built environment. This chapter explores the varied motives of the groups that advocated passage of the ordinance. Supporters of the measure fell roughly into two categories. The first included skyscraper owners, Fifth Avenue merchants, and real estate interests all over the city; they backed the ordinance primarily because they saw it as a way to protect private property. Fledgling city planners, municipal engineers, architects, and public health experts comprised the second group; they pushed for the ordinance because they saw it as a way to control private property for public purposes—that is, as a means to empower a new city planning bureaucracy.

The groups that crafted the 1916 zoning ordinance tried hard to make it appear to be the product of a wide-ranging consensus on the need to regulate the built environment. And, indeed, an impressive array of interest groups supported the measure. But drafting the ordinance required both cooperation and compromise. A long process of negotiation resulted in the exclusion of many planning objectives from the final ordinance. The uneasy alliance between real estate owners and planning reformers gave New York a good first step toward central planning. That step was not followed up, as many reformers had hoped, when the political atmosphere that made the alliance possible changed abruptly in 1918. Before exploring the political environment of regulation and the motivations of the groups that supported it, I will briefly describe the details of the 1916 ordinance.

Comprehensive Zoning

The 1916 zoning ordinance was "comprehensive" because it subjected every piece of real estate in Greater New York City—over $8 billion worth of real property—to three types of regulation: use, height, and area limitations. First, the ordinance divided the city into three use districts—residential, business, and unrestricted. In residential districts, tenants could use new buildings as homes, apartments, hotels, clubs, churches, schools, libraries, museums, hospitals, nurseries, truck gardens, or railroad stations. Whereas this regulation was designed to prevent commercial activities from developing in neighborhoods, it did permit doctors, dentists, artists, hairdressers, manicurists, and dressmakers to set up shop in residential districts, as long as their advertising efforts remained unobtrusive. All other business and manufacturing activities were prohibited. According to George Ford, the ordinance designated two-fifths of Manhattan and about two-thirds of the whole city as residential area.[2]

Buildings in business districts could house all forms of business and industry except those generating objectionable odors or by-products— like asphalt, fertilizer, paint, or soap manufacturing, crematoriums, metal or stone works, or anything involving ammonia or sulfuric acid. The ordinance allowed other types of manufacturing in business districts, but confined them to 25 percent of the total floor space of the building, up to a maximum area equal to the area of the lot. This exception permitted fabricating, altering, and repair areas in larger shops and stores.[3]

Finally, in unrestricted areas, buildings could be used for residential, business, or industrial purposes.[4]

The height limitations of the ordinance were its second and most distinctive feature, producing a form of building known as setback architecture. The ordinance designated five height districts, each establishing a relationship between street width and building height (see Figure 2.1). District One, for instance, allowed the street wall of buildings to be equal to the width of the street; a building could rise to 65 feet on a street 65 feet wide. After that, the building could rise an additional 2 feet for every one foot from the street that it was set back—for instance, rising 20 feet if it were set back from the street line by 10 feet. The most liberal restrictions applied to areas in Manhattan's central business district (CBD), business sections of Brooklyn, and waterfront areas in Queens and the Bronx (see Figure 2.2). Lower restrictions applied to large sections of every borough. Richmond and Queens, where the population was still sparse relative to the CBD, received the most strict height designations (see Figure 2.3). Height districting in the underdeveloped sections of the city suggested that the authors of the ordinance did not want other areas to be built up in the same way as lower Manhattan.[5]

Third, the ordinance created area districts. Area restrictions prevented new buildings from covering their entire sites, mandating open spaces at the rear and sides of the structure—the taller the building, the more space needed on all sides. Although these restrictions left plenty of room in the CBD for bulky buildings, certain area districts provided for rather small structures. For instance, area "E" restrictions applying to interior lots in residential districts made it illegal for the first floor of structures to cover more than 50 percent of the site, with second floors covering only 30 percent of the site (see Figure 2.4). These "villa districts" were located primarily in the upscale residential sections of Brooklyn, and a few parts of Queens, Staten Island, and the Bronx.[6]

The ordinance also included provisions for modification of use, height, and area districts. A Board of Appeals would hear petitions for

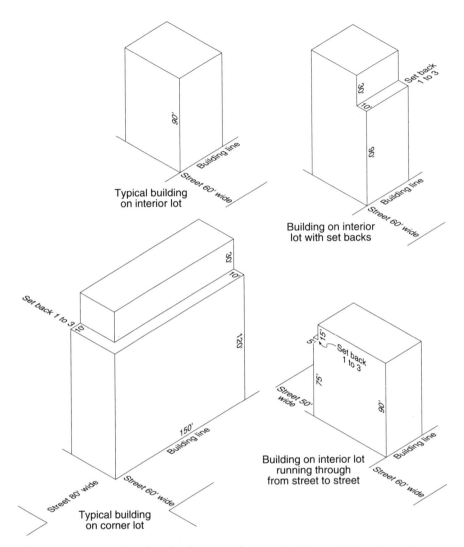

Typical building on interior lot

Building on interior lot with set backs

Typical building on corner lot

Building on interior lot running through from street to street

Figure 2.1 Examples of Setback Principle in a "1½ Times" District. *Source*: Commission on Building Districts and Restrictions, *Final Report* (New York: Board of Estimate and Apportionment, Committee on the City Plan, 1916) [hereafter CBDR, *Final Report*], p. 260.

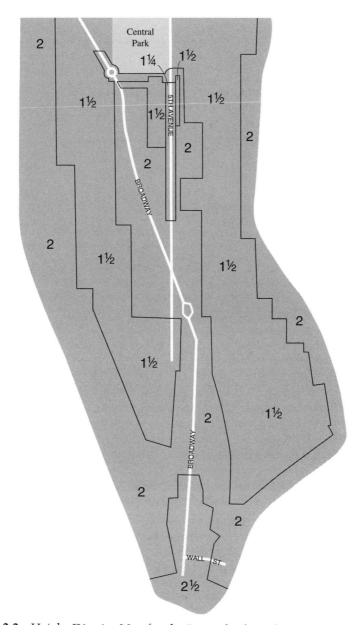

Figure 2.2 Height District Map for the Borough of Manhattan. Height limitations are indicated as a multiple of street width in each district. *Source:* CBDR, *Final Report*, Figure 128.

Figure 2.3   Height District Map for the Borough of Richmond. Height limitations are indicated as a multiple of street width in each district.   *Source*: CBDR, *Final Report*, Figure 131.

changes in the zoning system, emphasizing that the plan was not perfect and that planning experts, real estate owners, and government officials would continue to work together to shape the city's built environment.[7]

The Politics of Successful Regulation

The zoning regulations outlined above emerged from a complex process of negotiation between business interests and planning reformers. Private government groups—the real estate and financial institutions that oversaw much of the city's built environment—worked with appointed officials to define the new powers that municipal bureaucrats should have over private property.[8] The success of these negotiations depended upon the political environment provided by the sponsorship

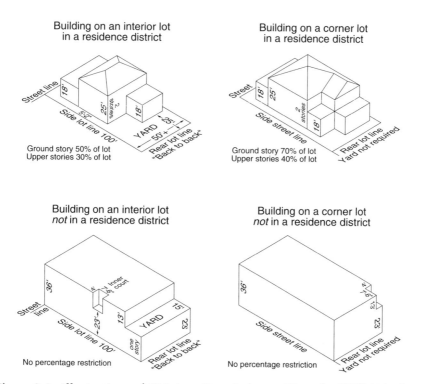

Building on an interior lot in a residence district

Street line
18'
52'
25'
2 stories
18'
YARD
25'
Side lot line 100'
50'+
Rear lot line
"Back to back"

Ground story 50% of lot
Upper stories 30% of lot

Building on a corner lot in a residence district

Street
18'
25'
2 stories
18'
Side street line
Rear lot line
Yard not required

Ground story 70% of lot
Upper stories 40% of lot

Building on an interior lot *not* in a residence district

Street line
36'
4'
6' Inner court
23'
13'
one story
YARD
15'
23'
Side lot line 100'
Rear lot line
"Back to back"

No percentage restriction

Building on a corner lot *not* in a residence district

Side street line
36'
4'
6'
13'
23'
Rear lot line
Yard not required

No percentage restriction

Figure 2.4 Illustrations of "E" Area Restrictions—Note the "Villa" Style in the Upper Left Corner. *Source*: CBDR, *Final Report*, p. 271.

of key city officials during the heyday of progressive politics in New York City.

Two committees developed the zoning regulations. The Heights of Buildings Committee (HBC) began work in 1913 and was dissolved when it completed its study in December of that year. Manhattan borough President George McAneny sponsored the HBC proposal in February 1913 after consulting with Edward Bassett. As a former member of the state's Public Service Commission and a leader in the Brooklyn city planning movement, Bassett had worked with McAneny on the development of the city's subway system. The HBC's report suggested amendments to the state constitution—adopted in 1914—that allowed the city to enforce zoning regulations. With its new constitutional powers, the Board of Estimate created the Commission on Building Districts and Restrictions (CBDR) in 1914 to write the zoning law.[9] The ordinance was completed by the CBDR during the high tide of progressive politics in New York City. Voters swept Fusion Mayor

John Purroy Mitchel into office in November 1913 with the largest plurality ever received by a mayoral candidate in the history of the consolidated city. Fusion candidates also dominated the Board of Estimate. McAneny was elected president of the Board of Aldermen where he continued his oversight of the zoning project.[10] These committees acted as a transitional mechanism, facilitating the transfer of control over portions of the built environment from private governmental organizations to municipal government bureaucrats.

The structure of these committees allowed Bassett, who chaired both the HBC and the CBDR, to create a consortium of private interest groups representing business, civic, and planning concerns with official sanction from the Board of Estimate. Bassett not only helped write the proposal that created the HBC; he also gave McAneny a list of the New Yorkers he wanted on the committee and its technical staff.[11] In effect, Bassett and McAneny provided real estate executives, a few appointed officials, and selected planning advocates with the authority to write public regulations. Insulated from electoral politics, they worked out their disagreements over the purposes and scope of the proposed ordinance.

Although private developers would continue to decide how tall buildings would be and who would rent them, the zoning ordinance placed some control over the height and use of buildings into the hands of public officials. But the ordinance did not change the existing arrangement of space in the city. Height and use districts were based largely on preexisting patterns of development, and their implementation required neither the relocation of industries nor the removal of tall buildings.[12] The ordinance stabilized those patterns, giving official sanction and legal protection to the status quo. At once sweeping and conservative, the zoning ordinance grew out of years of failed attempts to unite private and public efforts to guide the growth of the city's landscape, especially in lower Manhattan.

Addressing Congestion: Spending, Taxing, and Regulating

Lower Manhattan was one of the most crowded areas in the world by the early twentieth century. The Lower East Side contained some areas with over 1,000 people per acre in 1905.[13] The concentration of businesses in the Wall Street area, made possible in part by the ever increasing height of office buildings, brought congestion to wealthier sections of the city as well. For instance, as the most direct route from the Brooklyn Bridge to the financial district, Nassau Street was thick with pedestrians at every hour of the day.[14] The proximity of garment industries to the shopping district brought the rich and poor into frequent contact. Narrow streets, surrounded by ever taller buildings, provided the cramped arenas where ethnic and economic groups mixed.

Plans for relieving the uncomfortable, unsightly conditions in lower Manhattan abounded. In 1904, the Municipal Art Society suggested cutting a series of diagonal boulevards across the tip of the island. From the Williamsburg, Manhattan, and Brooklyn bridges wide streets would speed commuters from Brooklyn and the Lower East Side to downtown locations. In 1907, Mayor George B. McClellan's New York City Improvement Commission proposed a 160-foot-wide parkway connecting Fifth Avenue and the soon-to-be-completed Queensboro Bridge. And in 1910 Mayor William Gaynor, distressed by the congested conditions along his beloved Fifth Avenue, offered to carve a new avenue between Fifth and Sixth stretching from Eighth Street to Central Park.[15]

None of these street-widening projects came to fruition. Several reasons lay behind their failure. Cost was a primary factor. Creating new streets involved the city in lengthy, expensive eminent domain proceedings. The Mayor's Improvement Commission estimated the cost of the parkway to be at least $15 million, and Mayor Gaynor's avenue would have cost $40 million.[16] Although steps were taken to reduce the cost of condemnation proceedings in 1913, little could be done to streamline the political process of creating new streets.[17] Hundreds of existing buildings had to be razed to lay out new thoroughfares—antagonizing legions of real estate owners and disrupting scores of businesses.

Taxation provided another approach to the problem of congestion. Taxation as a solution to overcrowding grew out of the work of the Committee on Congestion of Population (CCP), formed in 1907 by Florence Kelley, Lillian Wald, Mary Simkovitch, and others. Under the leadership of single-taxer turned urban reformer Benjamin Marsh, the CCP attributed the overcrowded conditions of the Lower East Side primarily to the concentration of landownership and its attendant ills: high rents, ramshackle tenements, rich landlords. The CCP's exhibitions on the living conditions in the city's tenement districts inspired several mayoral inquiries into the problem of congestion, and flowered in 1914 with the proposal to untax buildings.[18]

Between 1914 and 1916 Mayor John P. Mitchel's Committee on Taxation considered a proposal that would have practically eliminated the municipal tax on improvements—that is, buildings. The city had always levied real estate taxes on both land and buildings to fill the public treasury. The proposal before the Committee would have lowered the tax rate on the assessed value of improvements by gradually shifting the tax to the assessed value of land over a period of ten years. By 1926, the tax on improvements would be a nominal 1 percent of the tax on land—hence the term "the untaxing of buildings" by which the plan was known. To compensate for the smaller tax base, the city would be compelled to increase the tax on the value of land.[19]

In the eyes of single-taxers, the untaxing scheme offered a multitude of city planning benefits.

> The untaxing of buildings and the corresponding increase of the tax burden upon land values would tend to compel the owners of the most valuable sites, which in general are those nearest the business center of the city, to improve them if vacant, or, if already partly improved, to improve them more fully. It would also tend to do away with the old ramshackle buildings in lower Manhattan and lower Brooklyn and compel their replacement with commodious modern buildings. The whole tendency would be toward the development of a compact, symmetrical city, and consequent great economies in public expenditures for streets, sewers, water mains, transit lines, fire and police protection, public lighting, garbage collection, etc. While, on the other hand, the city might be compelled to acquire more parks and breathing places to take the place of private lands now held vacant, the cost of the park lands to be acquired, as well as the costs of lands for all other city purposes, would be reduced by the partial or complete elimination of speculative values.

Anticipated new construction would hasten the replacement of slums with quality housing, advocates of the proposal insisted. More construction also meant increased competition and hence lower rents. And because new construction required laborers, wages would tend to increase.[20]

Several groups agitated against the untaxing plan. Real estate interests unanimously opposed it, largely because it increased the cost of owning land. Furthermore, the movement for tax reform never escaped its single-tax roots, and real estate owners dwelt on the anti-private-property air surrounding the untaxing campaign.[21]

Many progressives also rejected the untaxing plan. Progressive taxation advocate E. R. A. Seligman joined real estate executives in the fight against the proposal. Seligman and other taxation experts rejected many of the single-tax claims about taxpayer behavior that underlay the city planning benefits of the proposal. After studying the effects of similar proposals in the United States and Canada, they determined that the untaxing of buildings would probably not reduce congestion, decrease rents, or promote more orderly urban development.[22] Rather, it threatened to destabilize the municipal tax base and decrease sorely needed tax revenues by disrupting an already unstable real estate market. Although Seligman thought that a higher land tax of some sort was needed, he vigorously rejected the untaxing plan.[23] His opposition helped lead the proposal to defeat.

A third approach to congestion was promoted by the Fifth Avenue Association. The Association was founded in 1908 by a group of merchants and real estate owners seeking to preserve the genteel appearance and economic value of Fifth Avenue—the city's high-class shopping district. During the late nineteenth century, the garment factories that supplied the shops with their textiles had moved increasingly closer to the retail district. Merchants complained vigorously that garment workers—mostly immigrant, mostly Jewish—invaded the merchants' streets during the lunch hour and drove away their clientele. Garment workers, they said, differed from shoppers, from retail clerks, and from office workers, and those differences changed the character of the retail district below Thirty-fourth Street. Many shop owners moved their businesses north along Fifth Avenue, and with zoning regulations they hoped to prevent the process of invasion and decline from recurring in the new retail area between Forty-second and Fifty-ninth streets.[24]

In the winter of 1911–1912, Manhattan Borough President George McAneny, working with the Fifth Avenue Association, appointed the Fifth Avenue Commission to seek remedies to the invasion problem. The Association diagnosed the problem as a matter of building height. The newest buildings along the avenue were usually loft buildings. These tall, cheaply constructed buildings created a surplus of rentable space. Although retailers used most of the lower floors, the upper stories did not suit the needs of shopkeepers. Building owners then rented out upper floors for other uses—as offices, showrooms, and eventually as factory space. Overbuilding drove down rental rates, creating an invitation for nonretail uses and eventually peopling the district with garment workers. This diagnosis gave the Commission a ready solution. The Supreme Court had found building height regulations constitutional in 1909. The Commission therefore suggested restricting the height of buildings within 100 feet of Fifth Avenue to 125 feet.[25] This measure would have limited "the amount of space permissibly constructible upon a site."[26] Merchants hoped that restricting rentable space would encourage developers to build structures suitable for retail trade, and thus prevent upper stories from converting to office or factory use.

Regulating building height as an approach to the congestion problem linked the efforts of the Fifth Avenue Association to the ongoing debate in the architectural community over the limitation of skyscrapers. At the center of that debate was Ernest Flagg, architect of the Singer Tower. In 1908, Flagg began lobbying for skyscraper regulations based on the design of the Singer Tower, completed the previous year. He struck a balance between height and aesthetics by placing a very tall tower on a smaller base. This allowed the great height desired by many corporations while preserving an aesthetically pleasing cornice line of modest height.[27] The call for regulation of building height along Fifth Avenue allowed Flagg to reintroduce his proposal in 1912. "From the start," wrote Flagg in the *New York Times*, "I have always thought it a mistake to have ever permitted the erection of higher buildings in New York." But, "the door has been left open and the horse is gone." New York would forever be a city of tall buildings, he argued. Therefore, limiting building height would not solve the existing problem. Flagg suggested instead limiting the area of the building that could be tall—as he had done with the Singer Tower; this approach would at least limit the deleterious effects of height by confining height to towers.[28]

The anti-skyscraper emphasis of the zoning movement was apparent from the beginning. In March 1913, George McAneny told the City Club that the "day of the skyscraper is passing." The HBC had been established to explore ways of ending the reign of skyscrapers in the city: "The time was coming," he remarked, "when there would be no more skyscrapers built in this city, and when that type of architecture would be regarded as a curiosity."[29] This theme was picked up by Edward Bassett, who claimed throughout the deliberations of the HBC that tall buildings were "inefficient," that they hurt real estate values, and that they cost more to build than they generated in revenues. Bassett made his attack on tall buildings a keynote of the HBC's final report, although his contentions had been challenged by a prominent New York architect.[30]

The anti-skyscraper perspective did not provide an auspicious starting point for the zoning movement. As Flagg had pointed out, skyscrapers had become a dominant feature of New York's landscape. Imposing regulations that stopped the building of skyscrapers would have antagonized powerful real estate interests. Reversing the effects of height could have cost both the city and private owners millions of dollars.

Almost any type of height regulation could adversely affect the real estate market. Even setback schemes drastically diminished the rentable space of future buildings. For example, had it been built in accordance with the proposed zoning regulations, the new Equitable Building would have lost 483 square feet of space on the second floor, 11,109 square feet on the twenty-third floor, and 36,261 square feet on the thirty-seventh floor.[31] Owners of existing structures that exceeded ordinance specifications had a clear advantage over future buildings which would have to comply with the new regulations. But many planning advocates wanted the new regulations to be retroactive. They viewed lower Manhattan as a planning disaster, and they contemplated enacting regulations that would have forced existing structures to comply with new zoning regulations in order to reverse the effects of overbuilding on the city's downtown. In a tentative report issued in March 1916, the CBDR discussed the possibility of radically replanning New York:

> An ideal districting plan would disregard existing conditions, require the removal of inappropriate buildings and uses, bring back depressed districts to their more appropriate use, sacrifice the vested rights of the individual owner for the improvement and beautification of the district and city. Such a method would seem quite appropriate, for example, if it were a question of preserving the beauty of a public park or boulevard, or securing the removal of an existing factory.

This extreme approach included "lopping off" pieces of skyscrapers that exceeded the height and area restrictions. But after reflecting upon the legal and political uncertainties of the matter, the commission elected to pursue the more conservative option of allowing existing uses to continue.[32]

Bassett knew that the drive for regulation would not succeed under an anti-skyscraper banner. Although he and many of his colleagues continued to believe in the inefficiency of skyscrapers and continued to advocate more stringent regulations, the focus of the zoning debates shifted from the evils of skyscrapers to the benefits of cooperative effort by appointed government experts and real estate owners to guide the city's development.[33] Bassett's chief concerns became satisfying property owners and putting the city's growth in the hands of experts, all in legally defensible form. Real estate owners had the greatest financial stake in property regulations, and they were most likely to bring suit against an objectionable ordinance. Experts could provide a rational framework for future development of the city and protect the community from the careless building practices of private developers.[34]

Drafting an ordinance that addressed the specific needs of the real estate community while laying the foundation for a planning bureaucracy took two and one-half years. By July 1916, both groups had shaped the ordinance to meet some of their concerns.

Motives for Regulation: Protecting Private Property[35]

At least half of the fourteen CBDR members had ties to the real estate industry. George Mortimer was president of the Equitable Building Corporation, vice-president of U.S. Realty, and director of half a dozen other realty companies. Alfred Marling headed a real estate firm and acted as trustee or director of a handful of insurance companies and banks. Other members were involved in real estate through their association with savings banks and trust companies. These men often had extensive experience in public service and undoubtedly thought in terms of the public goals of zoning. Nevertheless, they had a financial stake in regulating the landscape and shaped the ordinance to suit their economic needs.[36] (See Chapter 3 by Marc Weiss in this volume for a discussion of the role of real estate interests in the zoning process.)

Representatives of the real estate industry supported zoning as a way to stop the types of development they thought caused (or exacerbated) the decline in land values. The real estate market in New York City looked very unstable in 1913. The assessed value of taxable land had risen steadily between 1905 and 1911, from $3.107 billion to $4.555 billion (for all boroughs), an aggregate increase of 46.6 percent. However, between 1911 and 1915 the assessed value of land increased by less than 1 percent, from $4.555 billion to $4.563 billion. Brooklyn had actually seen a decrease in the value of its land between 1911 and 1913.[37]

The central business district illustrates the effect of unregulated development on property values. Manhattan had a skyscraper district like none other. In 1914, there were 164 buildings of ten or more stories south of Chambers Street, with an assessed value of over $258 million. On certain streets, the concentration of tall structures turned avenues into canyons. Along New Street, for instance, the average building height was 11.59 stories, while Exchange Place had an average building height of 14.1 stories. The CBD also had several of the tallest buildings in the world, including the forty-story Singer Tower and the fifty-four story Woolworth Building. These large buildings cast large shadows that darkened city streets for much of the day. At noon on December 21 (the shortest day of the year), the Singer Tower cast a shadow 1,127 feet long, whereas the Woolworth shadow was 1,635 feet long. Offices in the shadow of these skyscrapers received little direct sunlight, and that made them less attractive to renters.[38]

The Equitable Building presented even greater difficulties. Although it was shorter than the Singer Tower by 50 feet, it rose straight up from the street (see Figure 6.8 in Chapter 6 by Gail Fenske and Deryck

Holdsworth). Its shadow covered 7½ acres, blocking sunlight from surrounding buildings twenty-one, nineteen, and fourteen stories high, and covering the Singer Tower with its shadow up to the twenty-seventh floor. The Equitable caused problems even before it was built. In 1912, as the old Equitable was torn down, buildings across the street received a burst of sunshine they had never known. "Ever since the demolition of the ruins has approached the ground level," the *New York Times* reported, "property owners and tenants fronting on the block have been impressed with the marked change it has made in the attractiveness of their offices. Such banks as the Fourth National and the Chase National have been flooded with light for the first time in their existence, for the building that has been torn down was one of the oldest of the modern skyscrapers." Several of those bankers promoted the idea that the city should transform the Equitable site into a public park. One citizen even suggested that the demolition of the old Equitable should be the occasion for widening Pine and Cedar streets, as a way to prevent the new structure from covering its entire lot. Cedar Street had an average width of 34 feet from Broadway to Nassau Street, and the new Equitable Building rose fourteen and one-half times the street width. Height and bulk regulations would prevent mammoth structures like the Equitable from rising directly from the curb to the sky, thus permitting more light onto neighboring buildings.[39]

Height restrictions did not prohibit the construction of very tall buildings, as long as they were set back from the street. For instance, a future Equitable Building could rise to only one-third its existing height because it faced a narrow street. But it could include a tower of unlimited height—about half the size of the Woolworth tower—in the center of the building. The Woolworth Building itself could be virtually duplicated, if it were built on a lot facing a park. Height regulations permitted twelve- to fourteen-story apartment buildings on main thoroughfares, and eight- or nine-story buildings on side streets. These structures could be built even higher, but only by setting the upper portions back from the street line. And while towers not covering more than 25 percent of the lot could rise to any height, George Ford anticipated that the regulations would make four- or five-story buildings the norm for the city.[40]

Fifth Avenue merchants also benefited from height restrictions. The 1916 ordinance did not give merchants a flat height limit along Fifth Avenue; but by limiting the street wall of buildings to one and one-quarter times the width of the street, it effectively restricted the heights of buildings in the new retail district (see Figure 2.2).[41]

Merchants also argued for use districting to keep factories out of retail and residential areas. The 1916 ordinance designated most of Fifth Avenue and its side streets as either business or residential sections. Whereas business district regulations did not totally prohibit the use of buildings as factories, the 25 percent rule confined garment manufacturing to a part of future buildings: "The larger type of factory is excluded from business districts," the CBDR reported, "by limiting the floor space that may be occupied for factory use in any one building." This allowed some proximity of factories, showrooms, warehouses, and retail stores, but prevented mixed-use districts from converting to industrial areas.[42]

But the zoning ordinance benefited Fifth Avenue because it was coupled with a merchant boycott of garment manufacturers. When it became clear that the ordinance would not be retroactive, Fifth Avenue merchants launched the "Save New York" campaign—a public relations blitz aimed at forcing garment manufacturers out of the Fifth Avenue district. The Save New York Committee secured agreements from some manufacturers, who promised to move out of the Fifth Avenue area when their leases expired, and exempted them from the boycott. To encourage recalcitrant manufacturers, the Committee obtained the help of lending institutions, which agreed to discourage loans on new loft buildings in the area. And the Committee offered to help relocate manufacturers by putting them in touch with real estate brokers. By July 1916, just as the ordinance was enacted, 95 percent of the garment manufacturers threatened with the boycott had promised to relocate. With the new regulations in place, the avenue could be kept largely free from the types of buildings that contributed to the mixing of garment workers and high-class shoppers.[43]

Other property owners faced the same sort of problems as Fifth Avenue merchants. Neighborhoods changed character as homes were transformed into businesses and businesses gave way to manufacturing. Property became harder to rent, and investments lost their value. The zoning ordinance offered property owners the comfort of knowing what kinds of activity would develop in their neighborhoods, protecting investors from the loss of value due to unpredictable use patterns.[44]

But regulation could be a mixed blessing. Several court cases were filed just after the passage of the ordinance by property owners whose plans had been disrupted by the new restrictions on building use. The owner of a former residence on Fifth Avenue wanted to convert the property into a restaurant—a practice prohibited by the ordinance. When he failed to obtain redress from the courts, he decided to start a boardinghouse, which was permissible in a residential district. And the owner of a building on West Seventy-fourth Street—a residential zone under the new ordinance—wanted to convert the former dwelling into a dry-cleaning establishment. When his neighbors complained, the owner was forced to move his business to other premises.[45] So while stabilizing use patterns preserved property values for some real estate owners, the ordinance also frustrated the plans of other property owners.

Preserving real estate values also attracted mortgage lenders. A long list of financial institutions supported the zoning measure. Life insurance companies, banks, savings and loans, all lent millions to developers—large and small—who relied on the sale value of their property to repay loans. Metropolitan Life, for instance, had $200 million in mortgage loans in addition to $15 million in real estate investments. Walter Stabler, comptroller of the Metropolitan and a CBDR member, claimed that the Metropolitan was "as largely interested in real estate in the city as any corporation and more than any individual."[46] Stable patterns of development helped reduce the risk of bad real estate loans.

Property values were also important for public purposes. Lawson Purdy, president of the Department of Taxes and Assessments from 1906 to 1917, supported the ordinance as a way to protect the taxable value of real estate. For example, the assessed value of land on the south side of Twenty-third Street between Fifth and Sixth avenues had declined from $285,000 a lot in 1911 to $80,000 a lot in 1916. That devaluation meant tax revenues on those lots decreased from around $5,100 to around $1,400. Seen on a citywide scale, individual devaluations signaled financial trouble for the city.[47] Taxes levied on real estate values—on the assessed value of both buildings and land—accounted for the lion's share of municipal revenues. And the assessed value of real estate served as the basis for municipal indebtedness.[48] As one observer remarked, "The city is just as much interested, from the point of view of taxation in the right sort of improvements, as is the property owner himself."[49] For Purdy, the zoning ordinance represented a step toward putting the city on solid financial footing.

Controlling Private Property: Toward Planning

Although economic considerations underlay much of the interest in the zoning ordinance, another segment of the CBDR tried to use concern for preserving the value of private property as a way to gather political support for the larger project of central planning. This group of engineers, architects, and public health specialists thought far beyond protecting skyscrapers or retail stores. Like progressive reformers all over the nation, they hoped to use their political foothold to bring expert knowledge to bear on the pressing urban problems of the day.

They backed the New York City zoning project as a way to force private development along lines specified in a city plan of their own design.

The Board of Estimate Committee on the City Plan undertook the larger task of planning the city. Formed in January 1914 (three months before the legislature gave the Board the power to zone the city), the City Planning Committee was intended as a permanent planning bureaucracy charged with "formulating a general scheme of improvements with which all local improvements can be coordinated."[50] The heart of the Committee lay in its staff, the experts who did most of the technical work for the CBDR: Robert Whitten, George Ford, and Nelson Lewis. They viewed the zoning project as the first step toward realizing a city plan. In 1915, the Committee submitted a tentative plan to the Board which included stringent height and use regulations designed "to drive persons from congested residential districts into the outskirts of the city," and to bar factories from residential and business districts. It had specifications for parks, street layouts, transit facilities, and dock improvements. The staff of the Planning Committee also intended to coordinate municipal services with the city plan, and they won assurances from city authorities that water, gas, and sewer facilities would conform to the objectives of the Planning Committee.[51] With these goals in mind, the technical cabal of the City Planning Committee attempted to incorporate a wide array of planning objectives into the zoning ordinance. The efficient design of public works, provision of municipal amenities, civic beautification, and public health matters were among the chief concerns of the experts who shaped the work of the CBDR.

Nelson Lewis, for instance, viewed zoning as a way to rationalize land use by coordinating population growth with city services like mass transit, water, and sewers. Lewis was a civil engineer with expertise in street pavement and traffic problems. As chief engineer for the Board of Estimate, he served on the Fifth Avenue Commission and the Heights of Buildings Committee and did much of the technical work for the CBDR and the Planning Committee. In 1916, Lewis published *The Planning of the Modern City*, setting forth the principles he thought should guide the great project of municipal direction of private land use. "The economic considerations which should control city planning," Lewis counseled, "are precisely those which should prevail in the design of a house, shop, railway terminal or water-supply system; namely, adaptation to probable or possible increase in demand and capacity to supply that demand." The function of city planning, as Lewis saw it, was protecting the long-term viability of public investments in infrastructure.[52]

Adequate planning for infrastructure investment required zoning. "Zoning is not a substitute for a city plan," cautioned Lewis, "and while the first thing to be done is to determine the general framework or structure of the city, the details cannot be intelligently worked out except in connection with the zoning plan or after use districts, at least, shall have been determined." Lewis looked upon the use and height districts as a way to segregate traffic and predict population distribution. Heavy industrial traffic, Lewis reasoned, moved slowly, whereas vehicles in light industrial or business areas involved faster-moving motor vehicles and hand trucks. Different traffic loads required different types of pavement and gauges of rail. If a planner knew that business areas would not convert to industry, he could make appropriate recommendations for the width of streets and the durability of road surfaces. Similarly, downtown areas with tall buildings needed adequate street area to accommodate rush-hour traffic. "Undoubtedly," Lewis emphasized, "a comprehensive transportation system could be more intelligently planned if those responsible for planning it knew in advance what kind of development would be possible in various districts through which it would pass." Stable population districts also allowed better planning for water and sewer works. And with predictable use and traffic patterns, planners could designate proper locations for parks and public buildings.[53]

Architect George Ford, who served as secretary for the Heights of Buildings Committee and consultant to the CBDR and Planning Committee, likewise saw zoning as a step toward planning the city. After receiving an engineering degree from MIT and studying architecture at the Ecole des Beaux-Arts in Paris, Ford went to work for the prestigious architectural firm of George B. Post and Sons. Although he recognized the importance of efficiency in planning, the Beaux-Arts tradition remained a powerful influence on Ford's vision of the city. He cautioned his colleagues in 1913 that "the reaction from the 'city beautiful' has swung the pendulum too far the other way, and the work has been put entirely in the charge of engineers who, while they have achieved excellent results from a scientific standpoint, have failed to appreciate the vital importance of the social and aesthetic sides of the problem."[54]

Parks, playgrounds, and civic architecture figured prominently in Ford's conception of the well-planned city. Children needed playgrounds for "healthy and normal growth." Parks acted as "lungs for the community." And properly located and designed civic architecture impressed visitors and cultivated civic pride. But these amenities had to be worked out in connection with traffic patterns and population distribution to insure a proper fit between the economic, social, and aesthetic aspects of civic life.[55]

Coordinating private and public development for aesthetic purposes constituted one of Ford's most important goals for the New York zoning effort. "Probably the most useful function the City can exercise along general planning lines," wrote Ford in 1914, "is in the control of the improvement and development of private property. It was with a particular view to making a start toward control by the City of undesirable private development, that George McAneny brought forward the problem of limiting the height, area and arrangement of buildings."[56] Ford believed that the purpose of zoning was civic beautification. "I am convinced," he told his planning colleagues in 1916 after the passage of the ordinance, "that the skyline of New York some 25 or so years from now will be far more wonderful than anything we have yet dreamed of, for the law is full of special provisions which are bound to encourage the erection of towers, mansards, dormers, terracing roofs of a variety and interest far different from anything which this country has yet seen."[57] Ford intended height and bulk regulations to encourage architectural features that would make private architecture part of the city plan.

Zoning also addressed public health concerns, especially the tuberculosis problem. The New York City Department of Health reported 8,601 deaths from pulmonary tuberculosis in 1913 and registered 22,671 new cases of the disease, adding to the 31,212 cases carried over from the previous year.[58] Dr. Adolphus Knopf backed the zoning ordinance as a means to eliminate the conditions that fostered the disease. Knopf was not a member of the CBDR, but he testified before the commission on the need to limit the height of buildings for public health reasons. In his *Tuberculosis: A Preventable and Curable Disease* (1909), Knopf identified the crowded conditions of cities as a leading factor in the spread of the disease: "In our large cities, particularly in the lower strata of air where there is less diffusion of gases, complete change [of air] only takes place when it is sufficiently windy, and when the streets are wide enough and not lined by a row of houses so high that there is almost no sunlight in them." Tall buildings made circulation of air more difficult, trapping the dust that carried the tuberculosis bacilli. Infected individuals carried bacilli-laden dust into buildings, spreading it to other people. "This disease could largely be prevented," Knopf told the CBDR, "if we lived and worked in pure air, in air relatively free from mineral and vegetable dust, and last but not least, if we were to construct the buildings in which we live and labor so as to allow sunlight to enter more freely." Height and bulk regulations would force developers to construct buildings that admitted more light and air into city streets. These structures would assist in the circulation of germ-ridden dust and expose tuberculosis germs to the salutary rays of the sun.[59]

George Whipple, professor of Sanitary Engineering at Harvard University, also helped to make the connection between zoning and public health. Before serving on the CBDR, Whipple had studied the bacteriology of waste water and written on the education of public health officials. On July 2, 1913, Whipple measured the number of dust particles per cubic foot of air from various floors of the Woolworth and Metropolitan Life buildings. The air around the Woolworth Building contained 221,000 dust particles per cubic foot at ground level, 85,000 at the tenth floor, 41,300 at the fortieth floor, and 27,300 at the fifty-seventh floor. At comparable levels, the air around the Metropolitan Life Building had fewer particles—only 173,000 at ground level, 38,000 at the tenth floor, and 24,000 at the fortieth floor. "The lower counts at the Metropolitan Life Building," Whipple speculated, "may possibly have been due to the fact that this building is situated near Madison Square and is more isolated than the Woolworth Building which is located down town in a more crowded section." Whipple's data suggested that tall buildings in crowded areas were more likely to harbor the dust that helped spread tuberculosis.[60]

For Whipple, the zoning ordinance represented a decisive step toward planning a healthier city. "Placing restrictions on the height and bulk of buildings," he reflected, "is virtually public control of the space outside buildings." Controlling that space allowed municipal government to maintain a sufficient amount of sunlight on city streets and adequate circulation of air through heavily populated districts. Placing use restrictions on buildings helped officials control the use of indoor space. Restricting the ways tenants used buildings allowed planners to provide adequate sewer and water services, and to segregate residential sections from the potentially harmful byproducts of industry.[61]

The city planning staff, along with its civic and political sponsors, intended zoning to give the city control over the development of private property. The goals of the Planning Committee reveal what Ford, Lewis, Whipple, Bassett, and McAneny meant by the term "control." The planning cabal envisioned a New York in which each piece of private property was subordinate to a general plan of municipal development. The plan would determine the possible locations and uses of buildings. Stable population patterns would allow fiscally sound, long-term infrastructure investments. And the regulations used to enforce the plan—that is, the zoning ordinance—would discourage unhealthy building patterns. Control, therefore, meant the regulatory power to realize the varied goals of city planning experts, moving the private city toward an era of greater public influence over the built environment.

Stepping Back from Planning

Criticism rained down on the New York zoning effort from the beginning. Ernest Flagg assailed the proposed height restrictions as early as 1914. The height and bulk guidelines were so lenient, he wrote in the *New York Times,* that they would not solve a single problem cited as a reason to limit building heights. Nelson Lewis likewise encouraged the CBDR to go further in limiting the heights of buildings. George Ford reported to his planning colleagues that the law was full of "unduly liberal provisions that tend strongly to defeat the object of the law but which were necessitated by the exceptional economic conditions of New York." And in Cambridge, landscape architect John Nolen chastised George Whipple for supporting restrictions that were too lenient. "I think," replied Whipple, "that he does not fully understand New York conditions."[62]

Clearly, economic conditions forced planning advocates to write less stringent regulations than they desired. The depressed condition of the real estate market proved a great hurdle to more strict limitations. The market slumped in 1911–1912 and did not fully recover until 1923–1924.[63] The real estate interests that backed the ordinance saw value in regulations that promised to end the conditions they felt contributed to the downturn. In this sense, the depressed market helped the zoning effort. But more strict limitations on height and use would have decreased rentable space in future buildings. The first steps toward regulation had to be cautious in order to protect the real estate market from further instability.

Legal considerations also restrained the zoning effort. Bassett took a particularly conservative approach to the possibilities of expanding the police powers to allow increased municipal regulation of the landscape. Nelson Lewis recalled Bassett's conservatism: "The members of the commission, especially its chairman, felt that the zoning idea would be on trial, that cases would inevitably be carried to the courts and that if the plan and resolution were not upheld as reasonable and free from confiscatory provisions, other cities would not be encouraged to undertake zoning." Bassett took the law so seriously because he knew that zoning could be interpreted as "taking" private property, the legitimacy of which rested upon the overall value of zoning to the public. He feared that the courts would miss the broader need for zoning and strike down regulations that appeared unduly confiscatory.

"I sometimes think," he wrote in 1915, "that a sentence should be added to the constitution stating that in the exercise of the police powers of the state every intendment should be taken in favor of the people of the state as against the owner of private property." In the absence of this constitutional mandate, Bassett chose to mollify the language of the ordinance, highlighting its public health orientation rather than its planning objectives. He hoped that once the ordinance received judicial approval, the process of making the regulations more amenable to the goals of planners could continue.[64]

The inability to continue the process of planning presented the greatest obstacle to making the zoning ordinance a more far-reaching piece of legislation. Zoning and planning required political support. Planning advocates intended the City Planning Committee to continue its work as a permanent part of the Board of Estimate, serving as an umbrella organization to sponsor and direct the various projects—like zoning—that would realize the city plan. As planning reformers backed away from specific proposals, like doing away with "inefficient" skyscrapers, the ability to continue the process of planning became *the* important achievement of the zoning law. With the law in place, private property owners would begin to see the benefits of public control of the landscape, and experts could gradually extend their influence over the city's built environment. But political support for planning evaporated during the Hylan administration.

Voters swept Fusion candidates out of office decisively in November 1917. Democratic candidate John Hylan defeated Mayor Mitchel by a larger margin than Mitchel had won by in 1913. The overwhelming Democratic victory ended official sponsorship for many of the reform causes that had flourished during the Fusion years, including planning.[65] On February 1, 1918, the Board of Estimate abolished the City Planning Committee, fired the planning staff, and effectively decapitated the planning project. The new Board took a much narrower view of the Committee's function than the previous administration. With the zoning work done, the Board reasoned, the Committee was no longer needed. The loss of political sponsorship transformed the far-reaching planning project into a narrow zoning victory.[66]

Conclusion

Real estate developers, merchants, skyscraper owners, engineers, architects, and public health reformers cooperated to win the passage of the 1916 ordinance. Their visions of the planned city differed; but each required expanded government power. In 1916, their differences were manageable because the political environment created by progressive politicians allowed both the planning and real estate communities to work out their disagreements. Planning advocates clearly wanted more from the ordinance, but they accepted less restrictive regulations because they anticipated that the continued work of the Planning Committee would allow them to strengthen it over time. The compromise they accepted affected the urban landscape for the next fifty years. In this sense, the progressive reformers who backed zoning succeeded in protecting their vision of the city from the vicissitudes of politics. Central planning, however, never escaped the confines of urban politics.

Notes

1. Mortimer to Bassett, July 27, 1916, and Whipple to Bassett, February 6, 1917, Edward Murray Bassett Papers (John M. Olin Library, Cornell University, Accession 2708; hereafter cited as Bassett Papers), Box 12, File 14; and handwritten, undated memo containing names of future committee members, Bassett Papers, Box 12, File 15. Commission on Building Districts and Restrictions, *Final Report* (New York: Board of Estimate and Apportionment, Committee on the City Plan, 1916; hereinafter CBDR, *Final Report*), pp. 110, 153.
2. Robert M. Haig, *Some Probable Effects of the Exemption of Improvements from Taxation in the City of New York* (New York: Clarence S. Nathan, 1915), p. 20; CBDR, *Final Report*, pp. 233–234; George B. Ford, *New York City Building Zone Resolution: Restricting the Height and Use of Buildings* . . . (New York: New York Title and Mortgage Company, 1917; hereafter *Building Zone Resolution*), p. 5; George B. Ford, "How New York City Now Controls the Development of Private Property," *The City Plan* 2 (October 1916): 3.
3. CBDR, *Final Report*, pp. 234–235; Ford, *Building Zone Resolution*, p. 5.
4. CBDR, *Final Report*, p. 235.
5. Ibid., pp. 236–237, Figures 129–131.
6. Ibid., pp. 238–242, Figures 132–135; Ford, *Building Zone Resolution*, p. 12; Ford, "How New York City Controls Private Property," p. 3.
7. CBDR, *Final Report*, pp. 242–243.
8. See Robert H. Whitten, "The Constitution and Powers of a City Planning Authority," *Proceedings of the Seventh National Conference on City Planning* (1915): 135–143.
9. CBDR, *Final Report*, pp. 1–5.
10. S. J. Makielski, Jr., *The Politics of Zoning: The New York Experience* (New York: Columbia University Press, 1966), pp. 23–24; Edwin R. Lewinson, *John Purroy Mitchel: The Boy Mayor of New York* (New York: Astra, 1965), p. 100.
11. Bassett to McAneny, February 25, 1913; April 26, 1913; and May 9, 1913; Bassett Papers, Box 4, File 65.
12. CBDR, *Final Report*, pp. 12–13.

13. Walter Laidlaw, comp. and ed., *Population of the City of New York, 1890–1930* (New York: Cities Census Committee, 1932), pp. 208–209.
14. See the full-page photograph in Part I of the picture section, *New York Times* (November 24, 1912).
15. Rebecca Read Shanor, *The City That Never Was: Two Hundred Years of Fantastic and Fascinating Plans That Might Have Changed the Face of New York City* (New York: Viking, 1988), pp. 5–16.
16. Ibid., pp. 8, 12.
17. See *Excess Condemnation: A Report of the Committee on Taxation of the City of New York; with a Report Prepared by Herbert S. Swan for the National Municipal League* (New York, 1915).
18. Harvey A. Kantor, "Modern Urban Planning in New York City: Origins and Evolution, 1890–1933." Ph.D. diss. (New York University, 1971), pp. 113–130.
19. Haig, *Some Probable Effects*, p. 11.
20. *Final Report of the Committee on Taxation of the City of New York* (New York: O'Connell Press, 1916), pp. 41–42.
21. *Final Report of the Committee on Taxation*, pp. 17–35. I have explored the taxation issue in greater detail in "Reformers Against Reform: The Ambiguous Position of Progressives in the Campaign to Change New York City's Tax System, 1914–1916." Seminar Paper (University of Virginia, 1990).
22. See Robert Murray Haig, *The Exemption of Improvements from Taxation in Canada and the United States: A Report Prepared for the Committee on Taxation of the City of New York* (New York: M. B. Brown, 1915).
23. *Final Report of the Committee on Taxation*, p. 112.
24. CBDR, *Final Report*, pp. 110–111, 115–116; *Statement of the Fifth Avenue Association on the Limitations of Building Heights to the New York City Commission and the Testimony of the Association's Representatives at a Conference, June 19, 1913*, pp. 36–37.
25. *Statement of the Fifth Avenue Association*, pp. 3–4, 39–44.
26. Ibid., p. 44.
27. Mardges Bacon, *Ernest Flagg: Beaux-Arts Architect and Urban Reformer* (New York and Cambridge: Architectural History Foundation and MIT Press, 1986), pp. 220–223.
28. *New York Times* (November 24, 1912, Sec. V): 9:1–5.
29. *New York Times* (March 30, 1913, Sec. II): 11:1.
30. *New York Times* (June 22, 1913, Sec. VIII): 3:5; (November 16, 1913, Sec. VIII): 3:1–2; (November 23, 1913, Sec. IX): 2:1–3. On Bassett's use of "efficiency," see Olivier Zunz, *Making America Corporate, 1880–1920* (Chicago: University of Chicago Press, 1990), pp. 122–124.
31. *Report of the Heights of Buildings Committee to the Committee on the Height, Size, and Arrangement of Buildings to the Board of Estimate and Apportionment of the City of New York* (December 23, 1913) diagram 6.
32. CBDR, *Tentative Report* (March 1916), p. 9; *Report of the Heights of Buildings Committee*, p. 26; CBDR, *Final Report*, p. 235.
33. CBDR, *Final Report*, p. 6.
34. Edward M. Bassett, "A Survey of the Legal Status of a Specific City in Relation to City Planning," *Proceedings of the Fifth National Conference on City Planning* (1913): 46.
35. My treatment of the importance of real estate and financial interests in

the zoning process has been influenced by the work of Marc Weiss. See Chapter 3 in this volume, and Marc A. Weiss, *The Rise of the Community Builders: The American Real Estate Industry and Urban Land Planning* (New York: Columbia University Press, 1987).

36. William F. Mohr, ed., *Who's Who in New York (City and State,)* 6th Biennial Edition (New York: Who's Who in New York City and State, 1914), pp. 493, 526.

37. Edwin H. Spengler, *Land Values in New York in Relation to Transit Facilities* (New York: AMS, 1968), pp. 142, 143.

38. Haig, *Some Probable Effects*, pp. 31, 34; *Report of the Heights of Buildings Committee*, p. 15; CBDR, *Final Report*, pp. 176–177.

39. CBDR, *Final Report*, p. 177; *New York Times* (November 28: 1:3; December 2: 10:2; and December 3: 14:7, 1912).

40. Ford, "How New York City Controls Private Property," p. 2.

41. CBDR, *Final Report*, Figure 128.

42. CBDR, *Final Report*, pp. 110–120; CBDR, *Tentative Report*, p. 10.

43. Seymour I. Toll, *Zoned America* (New York: Grossman, 1969), pp. 175–179.

44. See *Final Report of the Committee on Taxation*, pp. 283–284, 327.

45. Undated memo concerning "litigation now pending" against the zoning resolution, Bassett Papers, Box 10, File 16.

46. CBDR, *Final Report*, pp. 75–76. *Final Report of the Committee on Taxation*, p. 334.

47. "The Reminiscences of Lawson Purdy," Columbia Oral History Collection (Part III, No. 203), p. 2; CBDR, *Final Report*, p. 166. Tax losses are based on a property tax rate of 1.8 percent; see *New York Times* (March 8, 1914, Sec. VIII): 1:4–5.

48. *Municipal Yearbook of the City of New York* (1913), pp. 33, 44.

49. *Final Report of the Committee on Taxation*, p. 284.

50. *Development and Present Status of City Planning in New York City: Being the Report of the Committee on the City Plan . . .* (New York: Board of Estimate and Apportionment, Committee on the City Plan, 1914), p. 7. *New York Times* (November 23, 1914): 5:6.

51. *New York Times* (November 15, 1915): 7:1–3.

52. Nelson Peter Lewis, *The Planning of the Modern City: A Review of the Principles Governing City Planning*, 2nd ed. (New York: Wiley, 1923), p. 45.

53. Lewis, *Planning of the Modern City*, pp. 48–50, 283; CBDR, *Final Report*, pp. 144, 145.

54. George B. Ford, *Building Height, Bulk, and Form: How Zoning Can Be Used as a Protection Against Uneconomical Types of Buildings on High-Cost Land* (Cambridge: Harvard University Press, 1931), p. v; George B. Ford, "The City Scientific," *Proceedings of the Fifth National Conference on City Planning* (1913): 31–32.

55. *Development and Present Status of City Planning*, p. 59.

56. Ibid., p. 66.

57. Ford, "How New York City Controls Private Property," p. 7. For instance, Article Three, Section Nine, Paragraph C allowed the height of street walls to exceed the street width if they were dormers projecting into a mansard roof.

58. *Two Years of the Home Hospital Experiment: Methods, Results and Comparative Cost of the Combined Home and Hospital Treatment of Families Made Dependent by Tuberculosis, 1912–1914* (New York: New York Association for Improving the Condition of the Poor, 1914), p. 7.

59. S. Adolphus Knopf, *Tuberculosis: A Preventable and Curable Disease— Modern Methods for the Solution of the Tuberculosis Problem* (New York: Moffat, Yard, 1909), pp. 5, 84, 122–123; CBDR, *Final Report*, p. 142.

60. George C. Whipple and Melvin C. Whipple, "Air Washing as a Means of Obtaining Clean Air in Buildings," *Transactions of the Fourth International Congress on School Hygiene* 2 (1914): 228–229.

61. George C. Whipple, "Zoning and Health," *Transactions of the American Society of Civil Engineers* 88 (1925): 603.

62. *New York Times* (May 20, 1914): 12:6; see also (May 27, 1914): 10:7; CBDR, *Final Report*, pp. 146–147; Ford, "How New York City Controls Private Property," p. 3; Whipple to Bassett, February 6, 1917, Bassett Papers, Box 12, File 14.

63. Spengler, *Land Values*, p. 142.

64. Lewis, *Planning of the Modern City*, p. 294; Bassett to Bard, May 18, 1915, Bassett Papers, Box 1, File 183; Bassett to Eidlitz, February 21, 1917, Bassett Papers, Box 2, File 146.

65. Lewinson, *John Purroy Mitchel*, p. 245. Progress in the public health field also came to a halt; see John Duffy, *A History of Public Health in New York City, 1866–1966* (New York: Russell Sage Foundation, 1974), p. 276.

66. *New York Times* (February 2, 1918): 18:1.

3

Density and Intervention: New York's Planning Traditions

Marc A. Weiss

"Make no little plans." Daniel Burnham's famous dictum was written for and about Chicago at the turn of the twentieth century. Yet his large and ambitious vision could equally well have been applied to New York City. Indeed, two of the leading promoters of the 1909 Plan of Chicago, Charles Norton and Frederic Delano, later helped initiate the much grander Regional Plan of New York and its Environs, which played a major role in guiding the infrastructure development of the modern metropolis. New York's regional efforts in the 1920s stood as a direct descendant in a long line of farsighted, massive and highly acclaimed planning efforts, including the 1811 street plan, the creation of the Croton Aqueduct and the water system, the development of Central Park and the park system, the building of the subways, bridges, tunnels, highways, and public housing projects, and many other significant accomplishments. These achievements, while by no means unique in American urban development, were highly influential due to their scale, timing, and level of imagination.[1]

One of the best known of these milestones is the passage in 1916 of the New York City Zoning Resolution, frequently hailed as the nation's first zoning law. New York's actions in publicly regulating private development and land use through zoning were widely imitated around the country, as were its earlier efforts in regulating multifamily dwellings through the 1901 Tenement House Law. The assumption that underlay New York's zoning resolution—that restrictions on the use, height, and bulk of all privately owned buildings differentially applied by "districts" or "zones" was legally permissible under the municipal police powers—helped launch a rapidly spreading wave of zoning laws during the 1920s.[2]

Looked at in the larger context of the evolution of land use regulations in the United States, however, New York's 1916 zoning law was definitely an American pacesetter but not quite for the reasons commonly attributed to it. This is because the primary motivation for zoning on a national basis was the segregation of residential uses from commerce and industry, and especially the creation of exclusive districts for single family houses. Almost all of the many suburban communities that adopted zoning in the 1910s and 1920s had this intention, and most central cities also established zoning fundamentally to help protect certain middle- and upper-income residential neighborhoods. In this sense the first American citywide land use zoning law was passed by the City of Los Angeles in 1908. Los Angeles established, both in legislative and administrative practice and judicially through several key court decisions, the legal validity of regulating and separating land uses for the public purpose of sheltering and nurturing a home environment. New York City essentially adopted and indirectly popularized the Los Angeles model, and applied this approach to winning political support from property owners in zoning certain areas of its outer boroughs.[3]

New York's pioneering zoning law stands as an anomaly in United States urban history because its basic economic, political, and regulatory thrust had its roots in a very different issue than the mainstream of the early twentieth century zoning movement: (1) New York's law was chiefly designed to resolve conflicts among commercial and industrial property owners in the central business districts of Manhattan. Residential regulation, though an important part of the law, was not the principal focus. (2) The main innovation in the New York law was the height and bulk regulations, not the use restrictions. Although New York was not the first city to control building height or even to create height districts (many cities already had statutory limits, and Boston's height regulations by separate zones had been legally upheld by the U.S. Supreme Court in 1909), it was the first city to use public regulation to rationalize and stimulate the growth and development of a central area for modern corporate office buildings, advanced services, and retail trade.[4] The story of zoning in New York is primarily the saga of the growth of Manhattan skyscrapers, which is also the main emphasis of this article.

Thomas Adams, who directed the 1920s New York Regional Plan, wrote in 1931 that "the 1916 zoning law was really a temporary measure based on compromise."[5] Yet the key compromise over height and bulk regulations, which the real estate industry finally recognized in 1916 as necessary to protect the long-term economic viability of commercial property in Manhattan, established a permanent pattern of active public intervention and private involvement to facilitate large-scale development while attempting to create more open space between buildings, and especially to preserve "open space in the sky." The building setback requirements of the original zoning restrictions were later superseded by the more elaborate "tower-in-the-plaza" approach of the 1961 zoning resolution, which encouraged street level open space around high-rise buildings, and then by a rapid succession of density bonuses and special districts in the past three decades, all far more complex than in any other American city.[6]

Since 1916, New York has consistently led the nation by experimenting with more aspects of zoning regulation, a wider variety of administrative processes, and a greater level of interaction between public regulators and private developers in negotiating building form, public amenities, and urban design standards. Only recently have San Francisco, Boston, and a few other places embarked on interventionist methods of central business district development control that rival New York's. But then, no American city has ever approached the level of density or the number of tall buildings that have long existed in downtown and midtown Manhattan.

The Corporate-Commercial City

In many large and rapidly growing American cities in the early twentieth century there were "City Beautiful" plans written by architects, civil engineers, and landscape architects, and sponsored primarily by downtown corporate and commercial interests. These plans were explicitly designed to establish a central business district of commercial office buildings, department stores, hotels, and other related uses while pushing out factories, warehouses, and wholesale markets. The focus of this urban redevelopment planning was on public investment in civic centers, parks, parkways, rail terminals, and waterfront facilities. Its main purpose was reshaping the physical landscape through public works to generate new patterns of accessibility and movement in the city, showcasing the clean and attractive commercial and cultural districts, and attempting to banish the dirty and unsightly city of industry to working-class neighborhoods removed from the central area. The Chicago Commercial Club's 1909 plan by Daniel Burnham and Edward Bennett is a classic of this genre, and many other cities followed a similar path. In each case, from Cleveland to San Francisco, land use conflicts emerged between the commercial and industrial sectors, and this type of central area planning was more successful in some cities than in others.[7]

What makes New York interesting and different is that at the point that most cities were still struggling to assemble a critical mass of tall office buildings, department stores, and hotels that would symbolize the modern downtown, Manhattan was already firmly established as one of the world's leading corporate and commercial centers. This fact explains why New York's zoning law was geared so heavily toward regulating Manhattan commercial real estate when zoning in most communities was more concerned with protecting residential property. It also helps to explain why in New York the height and bulk regulations on commercial buildings adopted in 1916 after nearly two decades of controversial debate were generally supported by key business and real estate interests, whereas in other big cities at that time many comparable business groups strongly opposed height and bulk regulations in proposed zoning laws. New York was already built up with such a great density and volume of large buildings that the corporate-commercial sector turned to public regulation as a necessary measure to facilitate and protect new investment and development without stagnation or chaos, in order to continue growing bigger and taller.

A few statistics give a sense of the contrast between New York and the rest of the country during the period in which zoning laws were first established in most American cities. At the end of 1912, Manhattan had 1,510 buildings from nine to seventeen stories high, and ninety-one buildings between eighteen and fifty-five stories (seventy-one of which were office buildings, with the rest divided between hotels and loft manufacturing buildings). A decade later, during which time new commercial buildings had grown both taller and more numerous, Chicago, the nation's second-largest city with a rapidly expanding downtown, had forty buildings eighteen stories or higher, less than half of Manhattan's total from ten years before. In Chicago's downtown "Loop," where most of the city's high buildings were concentrated, 151 buildings were between nine and seventeen stories, a mere one-tenth of the decade-earlier Manhattan figure. New York not only led the nation in very tall buildings (which in 1912 included a thirty-eight-, a forty-one-, a fifty-one-, and a fifty-five-story office building), but the sheer volume of skyscrapers totally overshadowed any other city. Table 3.1 displays national data for United States cities in 1929, demonstrating that New York had half of all the buildings in America that were ten stories or higher. New York also had most of the tallest commercial structures, from the Woolworth Building, completed in 1913, to the Chrysler Building, which was under construction during 1929.[8]

Table 3.1   Tall Buildings in American Cities, 1929

City	Buildings 10–20 Stories	Buildings 21 Stories or More
Albany, NY	9	2
Atlanta, GA	17	1
Atlantic City, NJ	21	0
Baltimore, MD	36	4
Beaumont, TX	5	1
Birmingham, AL	13	1
Boston, MA	102	2
Chicago, IL	384	65
Cincinnati, OH	24	2
Cleveland, OH	40	4
Columbus, OH	16	1
Dallas, TX	31	1
Dayton, OH	15	0
Denver, CO	9	0
Des Moines, IA	14	0
Detroit, MI	102	19
Duluth, MN	5	0
Forth Worth, TX	11	3
Galveston, TX	5	0
Houston, TX	24	5
Indianapolis, IN	23	0
Jacksonville, FL	14	0
Jersey City, NJ	16	0
Johnstown, PA	5	0
Kalamazoo, MI	5	0
Kansas City, MO	60	2
Knoxville, TN	6	0
Little Rock, AR	6	0
Long Beach, CA	14	0
Los Angeles, CA	134	1
Louisville, KY	17	0
Memphis, TN	23	1
Miami, FL	25	1
Milwaukee, WI	15	1
Minneapolis, MN	32	3
Montgomery, AL	5	0
Nashville, TN	17	0
Newark, NJ	18	3
New Haven, CT	5	0
New Orleans, LA	21	1
New York, NY	2,291	188
Oakland, CA	14	1
Oklahoma City, OK	20	2
Omaha, NE	9	0
Peoria, IL	12	0

Table 3.1 (continued)

City	Buildings 10–20 Stories	Buildings 21 Stories or More
Philadelphia, PA	98	22
Phoenix, AZ	5	0
Pittsburgh, PA	52	15
Portland, OR	25	0
Providence, RI	5	1
Richmond, VA	20	1
Rochester, NY	12	0
Sacramento, CA	7	0
St. Louis, MO	83	3
St. Paul, MN	7	0
Salt Lake City, UT	10	0
San Antonio, TX	21	3
San Diego, CA	8	0
San Francisco, CA	45	8
Seattle, WA	41	2
Springfield, IL	5	0
Stockton, CA	6	0
Syracuse, NY	4	1
Tacoma, WA	6	0
Tampa, FL	11	0
Toledo, OH	6	1
Tulsa, OK	37	2
Washington, DC	20	0
Wheeling, WV	6	0
Wichita, KS	14	0
Wilkes-Barre, PA	5	0
Youngstown, OH	5	0

Source: The American City 41 (September 1929): 130.

One of the driving forces behind New York's 1916 zoning resolution was the Fifth Avenue Association, a group of leading retail merchants, hotel operators, property owners, investors, lenders, and real estate brokers trying to stabilize and reinforce the image of Fifth Avenue between Thirty-second and Fifty-ninth streets as a high-class shopping district. The retail merchants' nemesis was the garment industry, which was steadily moving northward along Fifth Avenue, occupying newly constructed tall loft manufacturing buildings. Arguing that "these hordes of factory employees . . . are doing more than any other thing to destroy the exclusiveness of Fifth Avenue," the merchants turned to the city for the legal authority to control private property through zoning laws, limiting building heights within the district to cut down on the number and size of loft buildings.[9] Zoning under municipal police power regulations, if properly executed, had the advantages of being compulsory on all property owners without the government having to financially compensate these owners.

If the Fifth Avenue Association could have blocked the rapidly spreading lofts by prohibiting light manufacturing in a commercial zone, it would surely have proposed such intervention. By 1913, however, no city, not even Los Angeles, had yet attempted to segregate such uses, and it did not appear to be legally possible. Height restrictions by district, on the other hand, had been declared constitutional by the U.S. Supreme Court in 1909, so the Fifth Avenue Association seized on and vigorously promoted this idea as the means of its salvation.[10]

Fifth Avenue, however, was not really the principal long-term issue. Whereas the Fifth Avenue Association had chosen building height regulation as a method of blocking and redirecting the garment industry's geographic expansion, the main demand in 1916 for regulating the height and bulk of commercial buildings through zoning came from private businesses that leased office space, land and building owners, investors, lenders, insurers, developers, contractors, brokers, lawyers, and others involved in the lower Manhattan real estate market. These real estate and business groups reluctantly agreed that some form of public regulation was necessary, after having opposed commercial height restrictions since they were first suggested in the 1890s.

The 1901 Tenement House Law had imposed height and lot coverage restrictions on multifamily dwellings, but commercial and industrial buildings were still unregulated except by building codes, and the new skyscraper technology had brought much anxiety and uncertainty to the downtown area, where many new tall and bulky buildings blocked the sunlight from older and smaller buildings, causing the latter's property values to drop and in some cases even driving away their tenants. This situation is well illustrated in the accompanying photograph from the 1916 report of the Commission on Building Districts and Restrictions (see Figure 3.1). Though the tenants in the dark buildings could presumably move, and the owners could possibly build a new, taller building, there seemed to be no way to privately ensure that the district would not become strangled by overbuilding and congestion, with each building cutting off the others' sunlight and views, turning the narrow side streets into perpetually dark and impassable canyons. Public regulation was finally perceived by 1916 to be the only viable solution.

Figure 3.1 The *Final Report* of the 1916 Commission on Building Districts and Restrictions used this photo to demonstrate the necessity for zoning regulations in New York City to reduce the density of skyscrapers and allow more light, air, and open space between tall buildings.   *Source*: Avery Architectural and Fine Arts Library, Columbia University.

**Table 3.2   Financial Institutions and Insurance Companies
Endorsing the 1916 New York Zoning Law**

Astor Trust Company
Bank for Savings in the City of New York
Bankers Trust Company
Bowery Savings Bank
Citizens' Savings Bank
Columbia Trust Company
Commonwealth Insurance Company of New York
Commonwealth Savings Bank
Dime Savings Bank of Williamsburgh
Dry Dock Savings Institution
East Brooklyn Savings Bank
Emigrants' Industrial Savings Bank
Equitable Life Assurance Society of the United States
Excelsior Savings Bank
Fidelity Trust Company
Franklin Savings Bank
Franklin Trust Company
German Savings Bank of Brooklyn
Germania Fire Insurance Company
Germania Savings Bank
Globe & Rutgers Fire Insurance Company
Greater New York Savings Bank
Guaranty Trust Company of New York
Harlem Savings Bank
Home Insurance Company
Home Life Insurance Company
Hudson Trust Company
Imperial Assurance Company
Irving Savings Institution
Italian Savings Bank
Jamaica Savings Bank
Lawyers Mortgage Company
Lawyers Title & Trust Company
Liverpool and London and Globe Insurance Company
Long Island City Savings Bank
Manhattan Life Insurance Company
Metropolitan Life Insurance Company
Mutual Life Insurance Company of New York
New York Life Insurance Company
New York Savings Bank
New York Title Insurance Company
North British & Mercantile Insurance Company
North River Insurance Company
People's Trust Company
Postal Life Insurance Company
Royal Insurance Company
South Brooklyn Savings Institution
Sumner Savings Bank

Table 3.2 (continued)

Title Guarantee and Trust Company
Transatlantic Trust Company
Union Square Savings Bank
United States Mortgage & Trust Company
West Side Savings Bank
Williamsburgh Savings Bank

Source: Final Report of the Commission on Building Districts and Restrictions, pp. 75–76.

Construction of the new Equitable Building had demonstrated the difficulty with private methods of control. When the old nine-story building burned to the ground and plans were announced in 1913 for a massive new forty-story, 1.4 million square foot structure covering an entire city block that would "steal" light, views, and tenants from many surrounding buildings, neighboring property owners organized to stop its construction through private negotiations with the property's owner, but failed in their efforts. After the new building was completed, Lawson Purdy, president of the New York City Department of Taxes and Assessments, testified that "the owners of practically all the property surrounding it have asked for and obtained a reduction of the assessed value of their property on proof of loss of rents due to limitations of light and air and other advantages they enjoyed when the Equitable Building was only nine stories high."[11]

Many of the institutions that were concerned with long-term real estate market stability were eager to impose the new regulations by the middle of the decade. Large lenders such as the Metropolitan Life Insurance Company, the New York Life Insurance Company, and the Lawyers Mortgage Company—a pillar of the New York establishment whose president, Richard Hurd, had written the widely admired *Principles of City Land Values* (1903)—supported the building height and bulk regulations (see Table 3.2). Even the Equitable Life Assurance Society, despite or perhaps because of the dispute over its new headquarters, endorsed the proposed zoning resolution. Walter Stabler, the controller of the Metropolitan Life Insurance Company and a member of the Commission on Building Districts and Restrictions, actively encouraged the efforts of the Fifth Avenue Association. Stabler was such a strong advocate for height, bulk, and use restrictions that Edward Bassett, who chaired both the 1913 and 1916 New York zoning commissions and was considered by many to be the leading American zoning expert, dedicated his 1936 book on zoning to Walter Stabler (along with Lawson Purdy and Frederic Pratt). Property, casualty, and fire insurance companies supported the zoning restrictions, arguing that they would bring greater certainty to realty markets and lower the risks of fire and property damage. Title insurance companies, such as the Title Guarantee and Trust Company, also backed the new zoning regulations.[12]

A vital aspect of development in Manhattan was the growth in corporate headquarters as property owners and space users. Many opponents of tall office buildings argued that higher construction and operating costs and a loss of rentable space due to elevators and reinforcing structures meant that these towers were not as economically profitable as was commonly assumed. However, a key factor behind their continued development and rapid growth in height, bulk, and numbers was the prestige value of the building's visual image, which served as a powerful form of advertising for the corporate owners and occupants. Publicity was becoming more important for many large firms, and constructing an elaborate corporate headquarters was one increasingly popular method of displaying to the general public the company's growing wealth and power.[13]

The Politics of Height and Bulk Restrictions

New York's zoning process was unusual not only for the central attention on the issue of building height and bulk in lower and midtown Manhattan, but also because the corporate-commercial sector and the real estate industry generally supported these restrictions. Indeed, the initiative to establish the new public regulations came partly from these business groups. This contrasts with height limitations in many other American cities, where the issue was either less important relative to use restrictions applied mainly to residential areas, or more controversial and unpopular with various segments of the downtown business and real estate communities.[14]

Many cities imposed building height limits beginning in the late nineteenth century when the private "skyscraper" first emerged as a new urban form. Most of the legal limits ranged from 100 to 200 feet. Boston and Washington, D.C., had differential limits for various parts of the city, with the highest buildings permitted in the central area. Other cities, such as Baltimore and Indianapolis, had special restrictions that applied to particular locations. In most cases the height limits were intended mainly to restrict building heights in the downtown area, the only place where land values, transportation accessibility, and corporate image made tall buildings economically feasible or culturally preferable. Much of the early impetus for imposing these restrictions emanated from fears about fire hazards and building safety, concerns about the lack of sunlight and air, aesthetic considerations that preferred the older European city model of smaller buildings of uniform height, and popular desires to avoid excessive urban population density and congestion.

In some cities, such as Chicago or San Diego, downtown business and realty interests were initially against proposed height limits, asserting that restrictions would impede economic growth and civic progress. Such opposition led to compromises that raised the maximum permitted building heights. Once the limitations were in place, however, many of these same interests did acknowledge that the new regulations helped protect the owners of and tenants in smaller existing buildings, stabilizing investments and markets. Particularly during times of real estate recessions, owners of smaller buildings favored height restrictions.

The commercial and real estate sectors in some cities basically supported height regulations from their inception. Los Angeles imposed a 150-foot building height limit in 1906, following San Francisco's earthquake and fire that same year. Civic leaders of southern California's "Riviera" took this action to reinforce Los Angeles' image of safety and serenity in contrast to more intimidating conceptions of city life in their northern California archrival. Boston's Brahmin business elite was content with older traditions of modest building heights, and also wanted to spread private construction across newly filled land in the Back Bay and other areas near the city's center.

Local chapters of the National Association of Building Owners and Managers (NABOM) were very influential in many cities during this period. NABOM was as important in the development of downtown zoning as the National Association of Real Estate Boards (NAREB) was in the evolution of residential and suburban zoning. Throughout the 1920s, many Building Owners and Managers groups strongly opposed urban height limitations, sponsoring and publicizing research studies that argued for the commercial superiority of skyscrapers.[15]

New York City's successful negotiation of a common agreement on building height and bulk restrictions in 1916 stands in contrast to the controversy that surrounded height limitations in many large cities. In Chicago, Philadelphia, Detroit, Cleveland, Pittsburgh, and San Francisco, downtown corporate-commercial and major real estate development and investment interests fought against strict height regulations, often with the local NABOM chapter among the leading organizational members of the opposition coalition. In many cases, opposition to regulating building heights held up the passage of an entire zoning ordinance until some kind of accommodation was made. In Chicago and Pittsburgh, compromises were reached by 1923. In San Francisco, the Downtown Association and the Building Owners and Managers were able to remove all height limitations from the 1921 law, which only regulated land uses. In Philadelphia, Detroit, and Cleveland, opposition from downtown corporations and property owners held up zoning throughout the 1920s, and in Cleveland an ordinance that finally passed in 1928 was quickly repealed two months later. Houston never passed a zoning law, though the downtown lobby eventually supported the idea. Zoning in St. Louis and Los Angeles ran into strong opposition from real estate brokers and developers wanting to build large commercial and residential buildings on wide boulevards that were to be restricted to single family homes. Other cities, including Boston and Washington, D.C., raised their height limits during the 1920s, and Atlanta virtually repealed effective height restrictions by increasing its limits in 1929 from 150 feet to 325 feet with no setback requirements.

What is most interesting about the pattern outside of New York is that the cities with the greatest disagreements about the public control of private building heights were essentially the cities with the tallest buildings. Chicago, Philadelphia, Detroit, Pittsburgh, San Francisco, Houston, and Cleveland, after New York, were the leading cities with buildings twenty-one stories or higher (see Table 3.1). Two factors account for the differences between zoning politics in New York and these other cities. One difference is that New York's law was passed during a period when the real estate market was in a cyclical downturn. Zoning was seen by the main economic actors as a means of stabilizing the city's economy, spreading out property values, and creating incentives for new investment. Major corporate and financial interests were strongly motivated to give this new form of government intervention a chance, and speculative operators who would normally oppose such regulations were in a weak financial and political position due to the real estate recession.[16] By the time New York's example spread and zoning was proposed in other big cities during the early 1920s, their real estate markets were beginning to boom, and property owners, developers, investors, lenders, builders, brokers, corporate tenants, and other major forces all wanted to profit from economic growth without public intervention standing in the way. They wanted to maximize the development potential of their individual parcels while demand was strong. Once the markets collapsed, height regulations once again appeared desirable as a stabilizing factor. This helps explain why Philadelphia, Detroit, and Cleveland waited until the Great Depression before they finally imposed zoning restrictions on their cities.

The second difference is that in New York a complex bargain was struck, establishing what is now a tradition of the city's zoning regulations permitting and encouraging very large-scale private development while still attempting to accomplish certain important public goals. Under the 1916 zoning resolution, New York pioneered a new form of regulation that combined restrictions on height, bulk, and use in one law. Since the issue in lower and midtown Manhattan, other than the Fifth Avenue merchants' conflict with the garment industry, revolved around the problem that tall and bulky buildings blocked sunlight from neighboring buildings and from the streets, the solution was to redesign buildings so that they would allow more space between them and more room for sunlight and open air. This was accomplished through the setback requirements, regulating buildings by volume rather than height alone. Regulating building height and volume in relation to the width of the street and the size of the parcel allowed buildings in some zones to be very tall by requiring progressively stepped-back towers above a certain height determined as a multiple of the width of the fronting street. This approach permitted development while preserving public open-air space because, as buildings went higher, the upper stories drew further back from the streets and lot lines and from surrounding buildings (see Figure 3.2). What was prohibited was *not* tall buildings per se, just bulky, monolithic fortresses covering the entire lot, like the Equitable Building. Such a compromise in 1916 made possible the construction fifteen years later of the world's tallest structure, the Empire State Building, which was legally zoned to soar over Manhattan because it encompassed a very large lot, fronted on relatively wide streets, and utilized numerous setbacks in the building's design.

Why didn't other big cities adopt similar compromises? Eventually, many of them did. It took time for enough people to see the effects of New York's zoning regulations worked out in practice, and during the boom of the early and middle 1920s many private business interests preferred not to rock the boat, wanting only traditional commercial structures and existing government regulations, or no regulations at all. Eventually, most commercial architects, builders, investors, lenders, insurers, corporate tenants, and owners began to accept the new post-zoning New York model of setback skyscraper development and to want to import it to their city or export it to other cities. By the late 1920s, many big cities were changing their zoning laws to adopt "volumetric" controls and the setback system for tall buildings. New York's height and bulk zoning had actually created a popular new aesthetic standard that was beginning to dominate American skylines. Even conservative Boston, which had regulated building heights since 1890 with a flat and relatively low maximum in the downtown area, changed its zoning law in 1928 to permit pyramidal setback towers.

Figure 3.2 The New Yorker Hotel, completed in 1930, is a good example of "sculptured mountain" skyscraper architecture popular in the 1920s and 1930s, encouraged by the building setback requirements of New York City's zoning law. Urban planners, including the authors of the Regional Plan of New York and Its Environs, appreciated the setbacks and argued that high-rise structures should be situated farther away from surrounding buildings and streets than was mandated by the existing zoning. *Source*: Avery Architectural and Fine Arts Library, Columbia University.

60

Part of the motivation for Boston's change was pressure from both local and national corporations for the city to modernize its image, along with the desire by public officials to attract outside capital and to promote new investment in a central business district that was far from booming.[17]

Implementation of the 1916 New York Zoning Law

The imposition of restrictions on the height, bulk, and use of commercial buildings in New York, after more than two decades of sometimes acrimonious debate, was generally received by the real estate industry as an acceptable compromise. Some real estate developers were unhappy with the height limits, and several of them appealed to the city for reductions in property tax assessments on the grounds that zoning had caused a decline in values. The Real Estate Board of New York disagreed, strongly endorsing the ordinance in November 1916 and announcing that it would help the city defend its constitutionality in court.[18]

In February 1917, leaders of the Fifth Avenue Association and other key zoning advocates formed the New York Zoning Committee to mobilize ongoing private sector support for the new law. The Committee worked with the city's Corporation Counsel to protect the legality of zoning, provide technical assistance in its implementation, and publish pamphlets explaining the new regulations to the general public. Frederic B. Pratt, dean of the Pratt Institute and son of one of New York's leading industrialists, chaired the Zoning Committee; Walter Stabler of Metropolitan Life was the treasurer; and Edward Bassett served as general counsel. Within five months the committee had over 100 members and was actively working to maintain public acceptance during the critical early period of zoning implementation.[19] Robert E. Simon, a commercial real estate developer and leader of the New York Zoning Committee, stated in 1918:

Never before in the history of this City has a restrictive measure of so radical a nature, affecting real estate, received so nearly unanimous approval of the real estate interests in the City as did this law. Now that it has been in effect sufficiently long to give it an opportunity to be thoroughly tested, it still has the approval of a vast majority.[20]

A vital factor in this broad support for zoning was the improved condition of the Manhattan real estate market after the law's passage in 1916, reversing several years of declining property values. According to the Central Mercantile Association, investment in new buildings between Canal and Thirty-fourth streets increased dramatically after zoning was initiated. Demand for office space rose significantly in lower Manhattan, particularly after the war, and rents were rising substantially, leading to the boom in construction and real estate prices beginning in the early 1920s.[21]

The new zoning law succeeded in defining Fifth Avenue and the midtown area as an office and retail district, rather than an expanding location for garment manufacturing. The Save New York Committee reported in December 1916 that 205 out of 225 manufacturers between Thirty-second and Fifty-ninth streets and Third and Seventh avenues had agreed to relocate from their current buildings by the time their leases expired. Despite this accomplishment, the Fifth Avenue retailers were concerned that too much light manufacturing was still being permitted under the 1916 zoning use district category for "business." To accelerate the pace of change and protect against future encroachment, in 1923 the Save New York Committee proposed the creation of a "retail" use district category in the zoning law. A retail district would permit the same uses as a business district except that manufacturing would be prohibited within the retail zone. Walter Stabler, Edward Bassett, and Charles G. Edwards, president of the Real Estate Board of New York, were among those endorsing the retail zone amendment.[22]

The Fifth Avenue Association was joined by similar associations representing merchants, property owners, and tenants on Broadway, Thirty-fourth Street, Eighth Avenue, and Forty-second Street in lobbying the Board of Estimate for the retail amendment. These groups were opposed on one side by garment manufacturers and wholesalers fighting to retain the business use designation, and on the other side by elite residents of Murray Hill and portions of Fifth and Madison avenues who wanted to preserve their neighborhoods as residential use districts. Finally in 1929 the Board of Estimate created a retail use district category restricting manufacturing activity to a maximum of 5 percent of the total floor space in any building in that zone (25 percent manufacturing was permitted in "business" use districts under the 1916 zoning resolution). Like all the provisions of the law, it was not retroactive and only applied to new development. At the same time, the Board of Estimate designated much of the area between Twenty-third and Fiftieth streets from Park to Eighth avenues as a retail district.[23]

In the 1920s Fifth Avenue above Thirty-fourth Street solidified as the elite shopping district, surrounded by a steadily increasing amount of new office space for corporate tenants, some of them migrating northward from Wall Street to midtown. As early as 1920 the Heckscher Building, a thirty-two-story office tower, was constructed at Fifth Avenue and Fifty-seventh Street, and S. W. Straus, the leading mortgage bond brokerage firm, built a tall headquarters at Fifth Avenue and Forty-sixth Street. By mid-decade the pace of office construction in the midtown area was rapidly accelerating.[24]

One of the most dramatic effects of zoning was on the architecture of New York's skyline (see Figure 3.2). Bulky rectangular buildings were replaced by (1) ziggurat-style "wedding cake" setback buildings, such as the ubiquitous tall loft structures of the new garment district; (2) buildings that looked like sculptured mountains with numerous imposing setbacks; (3) most prominently, very tall but relatively slender and graceful setback towers. All of these new building sizes and shapes conformed to the zoning restrictions on height and bulk. The Chrysler, Empire State, and other famous buildings of the 1920s and 1930s serve as monuments to zoning's impact on urban design in New York and around the world.[25]

The spread of new midtown office towers was reflected in the height district zoning changes for Manhattan taken by the Board of Estimate between 1916 and 1931. Many of the rezoning actions were designed to permit the development of skyscrapers in areas originally zoned for lesser heights. All but one of the fourteen decisions of this type were in midtown. The biggest change occurred in 1928, when the Board of Estimate rezoned all of Eighth Avenue from Thirty-third to Fifty-sixth streets as a "two times" height district, allowing for very tall buildings.[26]

Occasionally, a zoning conflict was resolved against the wishes of real estate developers. One of the most publicized examples of a developer defeat involved the Equitable Life Assurance Society, principal occupant of the bulky skyscraper in lower Manhattan that had been such an important catalyst for the imposition of height and bulk restrictions in 1916. Equitable intended to relocate some of its clerical staff from downtown to midtown in a new building the firm planned to construct on Seventh Avenue between Thirty-first and Thirty-second streets. The proposed building, nineteen stories without any setbacks, did not conform to the height regulations for that district. Equitable asked for a zoning variance, but the Board of Standards and Appeals denied the insurance company's request in 1922.[27]

The rash of skyscraper development, at first reflecting the widespread acceptance of the zoning regulations as well as the new aesthetic of setback architecture, reached such an unprecedented volume by 1926 that the previous enthusiasm for the 1916 compromise turned into dissatisfaction and controversy. Critics began to voice serious objections to the existing height and bulk regulations permitting too many new buildings that were still far too tall and massive, despite the setbacks and the restrictions. One of the most virulent skyscraper opponents was Major Henry Curran, counsel of the City Club of New York, who denounced the buildings as "monsters" and their spread as a "plague." Curran blamed them for subway crowding and automobile accidents, called for an absolute height limit of six stories on narrow streets and ten stories on wide streets, and recommended that tall building design be regulated by the Municipal Art Commission.[28]

William A. Boring, director of Columbia University's School of Architecture, endorsed Henry Curran's proposed ban on skyscrapers and advocated a special tax on tall buildings. The Committee on Community Planning of the American Institute of Architects (AIA), chaired by Henry Wright, also supported Curran's proposals. Wright suggested in 1927 that skyscrapers should provide public open spaces in amounts proportionate to their cubic capacity, an idea that was later partially incorporated into the 1961 zoning law through density bonuses awarded for plazas surrounding tall buildings. The concern of Henry Wright and his AIA committee for open space was also voiced by the Municipal Art Society. Its City Plan Committee denounced the overdevelopment of skyscrapers and the consequent urban congestion, arguing that "we cannot have a beautiful city without a proper adjustment of spaces to buildings."[29]

By the mid-1920s, even some of the 1916 zoning law's strongest supporters were beginning to call for changes, frustrated with the seeming lack of any real control over the advancing juggernaut of skyscraper construction in Manhattan. Edward Bassett, sharing a platform with Henry Curran at the Municipal Art Society in 1926, agreed that the zoning law should be modified to further reduce congestion in Manhattan by promoting decentralization of commercial development throughout the city and region. Earlier in the year, J. E. Harrington, chairman of the Traffic Committee for the Broadway Association, blamed the excessive number, size, and growth of skyscrapers for transit and traffic congestion and stated that "the Zoning Law in New York has outgrown itself and needs revision."[30]

Edward Bassett joined other critics of skyscrapers in opposing the Board of Estimate's upzoning of the midtown section of Eighth Avenue in 1928 to permit the construction of taller buildings. "The greatest present problem is congestion," Bassett asserted, and while politically "it may be impossible to decrease the cubage zoning limit," he nevertheless strongly argued that "successive Boards of Estimate ought to refrain from establishing new skyscraper districts."[31] Bassett also appeared before the Board of Estimate in 1931 to oppose the height district upzoning of Forty-second Street between Eighth and Tenth avenues. The proposed change had the support of the Forty-second Street Property Owners and Merchants Association, hoping that the new thirty-two-story McGraw-Hill Building would spawn a skyscraper development boom in their district. In 1932, the Board of Estimate passed the zoning map amendment over Bassett's objections. By the late 1920s, Bassett was also frequently denouncing the wholesale granting of zoning variances by the Board of Standards and Appeals. Some of these variances were later overturned in court as being legally improper, and Bassett claimed that the appeals board's actions were corrupting the process of zoning.[32]

Zoning reformers banded together to lobby for changes through the City Committee on Plan and Survey appointed by Mayor Walker in 1926. The Sub-Committee on Housing, Zoning and Distribution of Population was headed by Frederick H. Ecker, chairman of Metropolitan Life. On this subcommittee, Lawson Purdy chaired a study of zoning height and area regulations, and Edward Bassett chaired a study of zoning administration. The Purdy report proposed that height limits generally be lowered and that there be three standard building heights for the entire city, replacing the formula for multiples of street widths. In particular, his report proposed a drastic reduction in building heights along the wide avenues and of the corner buildings on the cross streets. It also recommended other changes to increase open space by trading off increased building height for decreased lot coverage, foreshadowing the 1961 zoning law.[33]

The 1928 *Report of the City Committee on Plan and Survey* endorsed the zoning changes proposed by Purdy's study group, stating that "The time is ripe for amendment and strengthening of the Zoning Resolution which was passed into law eleven years ago." The full committee also supported the establishment of a separate retail use district category, which was endorsed by Bassett's study. In addition, the committee advocated that the Board of Estimate create "an official Planning Board functioning as a permanent city department." Among its many other functions, the proposed planning board would have the authority to review and recommend zoning changes:

This would permit a more constructive approach being made to the zoning of the City than has been the case in the past in the absence of a comprehensive plan. In the final analysis the solution of the problems of congestion and of distribution of population will depend on the principles and methods which are applied to the regulation of building uses and densities, and the relation of these to the street and other open areas of the City.[34]

The new city charter adopted in 1938 finally established a City Planning Commission along the lines suggested by the Committee ten years earlier. The City Committee on Plan and Survey's endorsement of the retail district zoning amendment had a more immediate impact on the Board of Estimate, which passed a compromise version in 1929. However, the committee's proposed changes in height and area restrictions ran into too much opposition from real estate developers and property owners to succeed politically.

Manhattan Borough President Julius Miller and New York City Tax Commissioner George H. Payne were two prominent public officials who opposed new height restrictions. Miller believed that tall buildings were necessary for the city's economic vitality, and that the problems of congestion could be solved without curbing the development of skyscrapers in Manhattan. He proposed alleviating traffic congestion by constructing subways under major crosstown streets, express highways on the riverfront, and tunnels to the outer boroughs. The new City Planning commissioner, John F. Sullivan, appointed by Mayor Walker in 1930 to head a one-man agency with no power over zoning or any other land use matters, also was on the side of supporting skyscraper development. For example, he favored the upzoning of Forty-second Street between Eighth and Tenth avenues, which passed the Board of Estimate in 1932. The opponents of stricter height and bulk limitations mostly prevailed during the renewed zoning debates and controversies of the late 1920s, and the Board of Estimate rejected various amendments recommended by the City Committee on Plan and Survey and other civic groups such as the Municipal Art Society, the City Club, and the AIA Committee on Community Planning.[35]

Thomas Adams, who directed New York's metropolitan regional planning during the 1920s, addressed the Building Managers and Owners Association of New York in 1928 about the Purdy report proposing greater zoning restrictions on height and bulk, and acknowledged that "It may appear that certain details of the recommendations of the Sub-Committee go much further than the Association would approve. . . ."[36] Whereas chapters of NABOM in several other cities were bitterly opposed to any regulations limiting the height of buildings, the New York chapter was generally content with the zoning compromise of 1916 but did not support further reductions in the permitted size of commercial structures.

New Yorkers provided national leadership for building owners and managers in the 1920s: Clarence T. Coley, manager of the Equitable Building, served as NABOM president during 1921–1922; and Lee Thompson Smith, manager of the Sinclair Oil Building, was president of NABOM from 1924 to 1926. During Smith's presidency, NABOM's

Height Limitation Committee launched a sophisticated public relations campaign by sponsoring research that argued for the economic and social benefits of tall buildings and disputed charges that skyscrapers caused congestion or were unsafe. NABOM emphasized that advances in building design, construction, and materials, such as the use of setbacks and lightweight terra cotta that reflected sunlight, mitigated problems of light, air, views, and open space.[37]

Probably the most significant efforts at finding a new compromise formula for zoning to reduce densities and congestion while attempting to satisfy both the real estate industry and its critics came from the Regional Plan of New York and Its Environs, directed by Thomas Adams and involving many of the key architects, planners, lawyers, and community leaders behind New York's zoning law: Edward Bassett, Lawson Purdy, George Ford, Robert Whitten, George McAneny, Frederic Pratt, and numerous others. Thomas Adams was sympathetic to Henry Curran's ideas and the movement against skyscrapers, and, like Bassett, opposed the upzoning of Eighth Avenue in 1928. Adams believed that tall buildings per se were not a problem if land patterns around the skyscrapers were better planned and regulated: "The high building in itself cannot be condemned as unhealthful if there is sufficient space around it to give it light and air; nor as inefficient if there is sufficient space for the people and traffic to serve its needs."[38] He argued that in the debate over height limitations, people must "distinguish between, first, the high building that has ample space surrounding it to meet all its need for light, air and accessibility, and second, the crowded groups of high buildings where these essential elements in land values are destroyed as a result of too intensive concentration."[39]

In several key publications of 1931 (volume 6 of the Regional Survey of New York and Its Environs, volume 2 of the Regional Plan, and volume 2 of the Harvard City Planning Studies) Thomas Adams, George Ford, and their colleagues began to work out ideas for continuing to reduce the bulk of tall buildings through less lot coverage at the street level, greater setbacks of the building's lower stories, and slimmer towers.[40] Adams and Ford discussed limiting height and bulk by regulating the total volume of building space in relation to land mass, citing the architect Raymond Hood's ideas about controlling building volume through a maximum floor-area ratio. Three decades later, New York City adopted a variation of this approach as a new and more effective method of controlling building density while still permitting the construction of skyscrapers.

The Regional Plan Association pointed in particular to New York's and the world's tallest structure, the Empire State Building, completed in 1931, as a model skyscraper with sufficient open space surrounding it on the street level and in the sky. In an important rebuttal to NABOM-type arguments over economic efficiency, Adams and his colleagues argued that the older practice of crowding urban land and commercial districts with tall buildings cheek-by-jowl had given way to new techniques of skyscraper planning and development that were the wave of the future: "The rectangular prism remains the most economical framework for a building. But economy of construction is not true economy if the building is not rentable at a profit. As the best lighted space brings the highest rents, this gives the economic justification for wide setbacks."[41]

Conclusion

By 1931, Edward Bassett was critical of the zoning compromise he had so carefully fashioned fifteen years earlier, and was looking ahead to the next generation of height and bulk restrictions that were widely discussed in New York beginning in 1926:

> The regulation of skyscrapers is undoubtedly the most difficult problem of zoning in every great city. After the zoning plan of New York City had been worked upon for years, it was nearly defeated at a certain stage by reason of a spirited and influential attack on limitation of skyscrapers. The same difficulty has been mainly responsible for the fact that Philadelphia and Detroit have no zoning ordinances today. New York City did not advance very far when it adopted the two and two and one-half times limit with setbacks and 25 percent towers, and there are many who say that with this limit the skyscraper problem was hardly touched, that skyscrapers are being erected as high as they probably would have been without zoning, that the total rentable floor space in the high building blocks has not been affected, and that street congestion is as great as if buildings had been left unregulated. These criticisms are partly true. On the whole, however, the results of zoning have been to give greater access of light and air to separate buildings and to the street. The opportunity of blanketing one building by another has been lessened. Architecturally New York has been greatly improved by zoning. What more can be done? Nearly all will admit that something ought to be done. But to say what ought to be done and to say what can be done are two quite different things.[42]

After a decade of experience with regulating the height and bulk of commercial buildings, New Yorkers were contemplating doing more by the late 1920s. Residential structures received a new set of regulations with the Multiple Dwelling Law of 1929, and ideas for rezoning were being discussed, leading in 1961 to the floor-area ratio concept and new sky exposure planes. With the 1961 zoning law the "wedding cake" setback buildings were shunted aside to herald a new era of modernist architecture with tall "glass boxes" rising straight up from the street, leaving more open space around the buildings to allow sunlight and views on every floor. The concept of "open space in the sky" was brought down to street level as the new zoning permitted a 20 percent larger building in exchange for the construction of a plaza made available for public use. Between 1961 and 1973 virtually every major development project in New York took advantage of the zoning density bonus to build taller and bulkier buildings, constructing over one million square feet of plaza space, more than the total in all other U.S. cities combined. Incentive zoning proved controversial; one study of density bonuses in New York found that for every dollar developers had spent on constructing plazas, they earned an additional $48 from the increased value of the buildings due to the extra rentable space they were permitted to build. Despite much criticism, the city government later initiated many other density bonus trade-offs under incentive zoning, especially through the method of creating special districts. Bonuses were granted both as-of-right and by negotiation and special permit for providing a variety of amenities that included sidewalk arcades; indoor public spaces such as atria, retail stores, museums, live theaters, and dance studios; pedestrian passageways; subway station improvements; and affordable housing. As two expert zoning observers commented in 1979, "It is as pointless to talk about special districts without a focus on New York as it would be to discuss the steel industry and ignore Pittsburgh and Chicago. The New York City Planning Commission, these last ten years, has been cranking out special districts as though they could be used to redeem anemic municipal bonds."[43]

In 1975, New York City instituted an elaborate Uniform Land Use Review Procedure (ULURP), officially incorporating the demand for greater citizen participation through the fifty-nine Community Boards. Despite this and other more recent reforms, including a new charter and land use planning system beginning in 1990, zoning in New York continues to be extremely contentious. Yet each new compromise from 1916 forward has had the essential backing of key corporate and development interests. Zoning has also become increasingly interventionist, adding more layers of complexity to address urban physical problems and conflicts that threaten quality of life, economic stability, and property values. Most contradictory, New York has evolved as an innovative leader in urban planning and zoning, yet with a set of problems substantially different from most other cities. The extremely high levels of population and building density, especially in Manhattan, have required a greater degree of real estate market intervention in order to maintain an adequately functioning metropolis.

Since the 1960s, the "Manhattanization" of central business districts has been an explicit urban planning and economic development policy goal, in many cases the main purpose of large-scale urban redevelopment and renewal projects. Density, intervention, and political controversies about the impacts of downtown commercial development that were pioneered in New York City are being repeated across urban America, and new experiments with sophisticated and complex downtown zoning regulations have spread to numerous cities coast to coast, from Boston and Hartford to San Francisco and Seattle.[44] As these planning debates unfold, interest in the origins of zoning for the modern corporate-commercial city leads one back to the New York law of 1916 and its implementation during the real estate boom and bust of the 1920s and 1930s.

Notes

1. Three useful essays on New York planning are Kenneth T. Jackson, "The Capital of Capitalism: The New York Metropolitan Region, 1890–1940," in Anthony Sutcliffe, ed., *Metropolis, 1890–1940* (Chicago: University of Chicago Press, 1984); John Mollenkopf, "City Planning," in Charles Brecher and Raymond D. Horton, eds., *Setting Municipal Priorities, 1990* (New York: New York University Press, 1989); and Paul Goldberger, "Shaping the Face of New York," in Peter D. Salins, ed., *New York Unbound* (New York: Basil Blackwell, 1988). On Chicago planning, see Marc A. Weiss and John T. Metzger, "Chicago: The Changing Politics of Metropolitan Growth and Neighborhood Development," in Robert A. Beauregard, ed., *Atop the Urban Hierarchy* (Totowa, NJ: Rowman & Littlefield, 1989).
2. On New York's 1916 zoning resolution, see S. J. Makielski, Jr., *The Politics of Zoning: The New York Experience* (New York: Columbia University Press, 1966); Seymour I. Toll, *Zoned American* (New York: Grossman, 1969); Harvey A. Kantor, "Modern Urban Planning in New York City: Origins and Evolution, 1890–1933." Ph.D. diss. (New York University, 1971); Marc A. Weiss, "Skyscraper Zoning: New York's Pioneering Role," *Journal of the American Planning Association* 58 (Spring 1992). The reports of the two zoning commissions are vital documents. See *Report of the Heights of Buildings Commission* (December 23, 1913); and Commission on Building Districts and Restrictions, *Final Report* (New York: Board of Estimate and Apportionment, Committee on the City Plan, 1916; hereafter CBDR, *Final Report*). On height and bulk restrictions for residential buildings before 1916 zoning, see Roy Lubove,

The Progressives and the Slums: Tenement House Reform in New York, 1890–1917 (Pittsburgh, PA: University of Pittsburgh Press, 1963); Richard Plunz, *A History of Housing in New York City: Dwelling Type and Social Change in the American Metropolis* (New York: Columbia University Press, 1990).

3. For analysis of Los Angeles' 1908 zoning law and its effects on the national origins and spread of residential zoning, see Marc A. Weiss, *The Rise of the Community Builders: The American Real Estate Industry and Urban Land Planning* (New York: Columbia University Press, 1987). The U.S. Supreme Court affirmed the legality of Los Angeles zoning in a 1915 decision, *Hadcheck v. Sebastian*, which served as an important precedent for New York's 1916 zoning resolution.

4. The 1909 U.S. Supreme Court decision upholding Boston's height limitation districts is *Welch v. Swasey*. On height regulations in Boston from 1891 to 1928, see Michael Holleran and Robert M. Fogelson, " 'The Sacred Skyline': Boston's Opposition to the Skyscraper, 1891–1928," Working Paper No. 9 (Cambridge: MIT Center for Real Estate Development, August 1987).

5. Thomas Adams, "The Character, Bulk, and Surroundings of Buildings," in Regional Survey of New York and Its Environs, *Buildings: Their Uses and the Spaces About Them* (New York: RSNYE, 1931), p. 119.

6. On the post-1916 evolution, see S. J. Makielski, *Politics of Zoning*; RSNYE, *Buildings*; Norman Marcus and Marilyn W. Groves, eds., *The New Zoning: Legal, Administrative, and Economic Concepts and Techniques* (New York: Praeger, 1970); Jonathan Barnett, *An Introduction to Urban Design* (New York: Harper & Row, 1982); William H. Whyte, *City: Rediscovering the Center* (New York: Doubleday, 1988); Michael Kwartler, "Legislating Aesthetics," in Charles M. Haar and Jerold S. Kayden, eds., *Zoning and the American Dream* (Chicago: Planners Press, 1989); Katherine Kennedy and Mitchell S. Bernard, *New York City Zoning: The Need for Reform* (New York: Natural Resources Defense Council, 1989); Richard F. Babcock and Wendy U. Larsen, *Special Districts: The Ultimate in Neighborhood Zoning* (Cambridge: Lincoln Institute of Land Policy, 1990); special issue: "Real Estate Development and City Regulations," *New York Affairs* 8 (1985); Weiss, "Skyscraper Zoning."

7. George B. Ford, *City Planning Progress in the United States* (Washington, DC: American Institute of Architects, 1917); William H. Wilson, *The City Beautiful Movement* (Baltimore: Johns Hopkins University Press, 1989); Judd Kahn, *Imperial San Francisco: Politics and Planning in an American City, 1897–1906* (Lincoln, NE: University of Nebraska Press, 1979); Weiss and Metzger, "Chicago."

8. Data comes from *Report of the Heights of Buildings Commission*, pp. 15–17; Chicago Real Estate Board, *Studies on Building Height Limitations in Large Cities* (1923), pp. 24 and 26 (map); "A Census of Skyscrapers," *American City* 41 (September 1929): 130. For additional information on New York buildings in the 1920s and 1930s, see Adams, "Character," pp. 54–64; Robert H. Armstrong and Homer Hoyt, *Decentralization in New York City* (New York: Urban Land Institute, 1941), 122–147. Carl W. Condit, *The Chicago School of Architecture* (Chicago: University of Chicago Press, 1964), gives a detailed picture of downtown Chicago buildings from 1875 to 1925.

9. "Statement by Mr. Frank D. Veiller, Representing the Fifth Avenue Association, June 19, 1913," *Report of the Heights of Buildings Commission*, p. 269. The Fifth Avenue Association also published a separate book that included all of its arguments for height restrictions in its neighborhood. See *Statement of the Fifth Avenue Association on the Limitation of Building Heights to the New York City Commission and the Testimony of the Association's Representatives at a Conference, June 19, 1913*. Emanuel Tobier, "Manhattan's Business District in the Industrial Age," in John H. Mollenkopf, ed., *Power, Culture, and Place* (New York: Russell Sage Foundation, 1988), analyzes the growth of loft manufacturing in New York and the land use conflict with commercial properties such as office buildings, department stores, and hotels.

10. "Statement by Frank Veiller," p. 270: "In case the occupancy of the building cannot be regulated either through the factory commission or otherwise, the next best step would be in the limitation of the height of buildings in this zone, thereby diminishing the volume of operatives and making a uniform sky line." New York City's Board of Estimate and Apportionment established a Heights of Buildings Commission in 1913 at least in part at the urging of the Fifth Avenue Association, with the explicit purpose of recommending height regulations on Fifth Avenue above Thirty-second Street.

11. "Statement by Lawson Purdy, President, Department of Taxes and Assessments, May 8, 1916," in CBDR, *Final Report*, p. 168. Purdy in his 1916 testimony, Seymour Toll in *Zoned American*, and Edward Bassett in a speech (Chicago Real Estate Board, *Studies on Building Height Limitations*, pp. 236–237) discuss the efforts of the property owners to privately organize against the Equitable Building. Their accounts conflict on several points, but each of them argues that the failure of these private efforts helped convince the building owners that public regulation would be necessary. Also, one of the leaders of the attempt to stop the new Equitable Building was George T. Mortimer, vice-president of the United States Realty Company that owned two buildings across the street from 120 Broadway as well as several other tall buildings nearby. Mortimer served on both the 1913 and the 1916 zoning commissions, and was a strong advocate for height and bulk restrictions on commercial buildings.

12. "This book is dedicated by the author to Frederic B. Pratt, Lawson Purdy and Walter Stabler," Edward M. Bassett, *Zoning: The Laws, Administration, and Court Decisions During the First Twenty Years* (New York: Russell Sage Foundation, 1936). Richard M. Hurd, *Principles of City Land Values* (New York: Real Estate Record and Guide, 1903). The Lawyers Mortgage Company, which by 1916 had made $465 million in first-mortgage loans on "improved income-producing business or residence property in the most desirable sections of New York City," was so ardently in favor of zoning that it published a handbook explaining the New York zoning resolution through text and maps. See George B. Ford, *Building Zones* (New York: Lawyers Mortgage Company, 1916).

13. When Frank Woolworth paid $13 million in cash to build a nearly 800-foot office tower that became New York's tallest building in 1913, he was warned by his general contractor, Louis Horowitz, president of the Thompson-Starrett Company, that the building might be too costly and not yield an acceptable return. According to Horowitz, Frank Woolworth

replied that "the Woolworth Building was going to be like a giant sign-
board to advertise around the world his spreading chain of five-and-ten-
cent stores. On that basis, of course, his splendid building was a sound
investment." Louis J. Horowitz and Boyden Sparkes, *The Towers of New
York: The Memoirs of a Master Builder* (New York: Simon & Schuster,
1937), p. 2. On early corporate office headquarters buildings, see Kenneth
T. Gibbs, *Business Architectural Imagery in America, 1870–1930* (New
York: Arno, 1984); Mona Domosh, "The Symbolism of the Skyscraper:
Case Studies of New York's First Tall Buildings," *Journal of Urban History* 14 (May 1988): 320–345; Robert A. M. Stern, Gregory Gilmartin,
and John Massengale, *New York 1900: Metropolitan Architecture and
Urbanism, 1890–1915* (New York: Rizzoli, 1983). For more recent office
development, see Tom Schactman, *Skyscraper Dreams: The Great Real
Estate Dynasties of New York* (Boston, MA: Little, Brown, 1991); Karl
Sabbagh, *Skyscraper: The Making of a Building* (New York: Viking,
1989).

14. The discussion in this section draws from a number of sources, including
Weiss, *Community Builders*; Bassett, *Zoning*; *Report of the Heights of
Buildings Commission*; Chicago Real Estate Board, *Studies in Building
Height Limitations*; Theodora Kimball Hubbard and Henry Vincent Hub-
bard, *Our Cities To-Day and To-Morrow* (Cambridge: Harvard University
Press, 1929); George B. Ford, *Building Height, Bulk, and Form* (Cam-
bridge: Harvard University Press, 1931); Norman L. Knauss, *Zoned Mu-
nicipalities in the United States* (Washington, DC: U.S. Department of
Commerce, 1931); RSNYE, *Buildings*; Barbara J. Flint, "Zoning and Resi-
dential Segregation: A Social and Physical History, 1910–1940." Ph.D.
diss. (University of Chicago, 1977); Garrett Power, "High Society: The
Building Height Limitation on Baltimore's Mt. Vernon Place," *Maryland
Historical Magazine* 79 (Fall 1984): 197–219; Marc A. Weiss, "The Real
Estate Industry and the Politics of Zoning in San Francisco, 1914–1928,"
Planning Perspectives 3 (September 1988): 311–324; J. M. Neil, "Paris
or New York: The Shaping of Downtown Seattle, 1903–1914," *Pacific
Northwest Quarterly* 75 (January 1988): 22–33; Holleran and Fogelson,
"'Sacred Skyline'"; Charles M. Nichols, *Zoning in Chicago* (Chicago:
Chicago Real Estate Board, 1923); Toll, *Zoned American*; Wilson, *City
Beautiful*; Houston Chamber of Commerce, *What Other Cities Say
About Zoning* (Houston: Chamber of Commerce, 1946); Weiss, "Sky-
scraper Zoning." Though Cleveland did not have a zoning law during the
1920s, it did have a 250-foot height limit. The proposed zoning would
have lowered this limit, which is one reason why downtown business
and real estate interests opposed the zoning bill.

15. On NABOM, see Earle Shultz and Walter Simmons, *Offices in the Sky*
(Indianapolis: Bobbs-Merrill, 1959); annual *Proceedings of the National
Association of Building Owners and Managers* and their other publica-
tions, including *Buildings* and *Skyscraper Management*. On NAREB and
zoning, see Weiss, *Community Builders*. NABOM is now the Building
Owners and Managers Association International, and NAREB is now the
National Association of Realtors. An influential, widely discussed, and
NABOM-inspired book of the period was W. C. Clark and J. L. Kingston,
*The Skyscraper: A Study in the Economic Height of Modern Office Build-
ings* (New York: American Institute of Steel Construction, 1930). Clark

was a vice-president of S. W. Straus, the mortgage bond firm that financed the development of many skyscrapers, including the Chrysler Building, and Kingston was a commercial architect with Sloan & Robertson. The authors chose a hypothetical example of a site near Grand Central Station to demonstrate that a seventy-five-story building yielded a greater return on investment than smaller structures, thus arguing for skyscrapers as the most economically efficient use of urban land in districts with high property values. The best efforts to critique Clark and Kingston's pro-skyscraper arguments were by George Ford, *Building Height*, and Thomas Adams, "Character, Bulk, and Surroundings of Buildings." For further debate, see Chamber of Commerce of the United States, *Economic Height of Buildings* (Washington, DC, 1927).

16. An excellent statement of the cyclical economic imperative behind New York's 1916 zoning is by Frank Lord, vice-president, Cross & Brown Company, Real Estate and Insurance, *Commission on Building Districts and Restrictions* (March 29, 1916), pp. 149–150. For a broad analysis of how economic timing affects planning and policy initiatives, see Marc A. Weiss, "The Politics of Real Estate Cycles," *Business and Economic History* 20 (1991): 127–135.

17. Carol Willis, "Zoning and Zeitgeist: The Skyscraper City in the 1920s," *Journal of the Society of Architectural Historians* 45 (March 1986): 47–59, gives a good picture of the changes in architectural style and conceptions of urban design that followed the 1916 New York building height and bulk regulations. See also Robert A. M. Stern, Gregory Gilmartin, and Thomas Mellins, *New York 1930: Architecture and Urbanism Between the Two World Wars* (New York: Rizzoli, 1987); Paul Goldberger, *The Skyscraper* (New York: Knopf, 1981); Jonathan Barnett, *Urban Design*; Carol Herselle Krinsky, "Architecture in New York City," in Leonard Wallock, ed., *New York: Culture Capital of the World, 1940–1965* (New York: Rizzoli, 1988). On Boston's late 1920s conversion, see Holleran and Fogelson, "'Sacred Skyline.'"

18. *New York Times* (November 22, 1916): 1:12; (November 5, 1916): 3:4; (May 6, 1917): 4:1.

19. *New York Times* (February 25, 1917): 8:4; (August 5, 1917): 4:4; (February 2, 1919): 1:6.

20. *Real Estate Record and Builders Guide* (June 1, 1918; hereafter *Record and Guide*): 697.

21. *Record and Guide* (September 15, 1917): 329; (October 27, 1917): 531–532; (February 8, 1919): 171; (June 28, 1919): 861; (November 15, 1919): 493–494. *New York Times* (January 25, 1917): 1:13; (September 23, 1917): 8:2; (June 29, 1919): 9:18.

22. *New York Times* (December 31, 1916): 3:5; (May 27, 1923): 9:2; (October 14, 1923): 10:1; (March 23, 1924): 11:2; *Record and Guide* (May 26, 1923): 655–656.

23. *New York Times* (November 7, 1924): 1:1; (December 7, 1924): 11:1; (January 3, 1926): 10:4; (May 4, 1926): 1:16; (November 11, 1928): 13:1; (January 21, 1929): 1:1; (April 19, 1929): 1:8; *Record and Guide* (April 27, 1926): 6.

24. *Record and Guide* (February 21, 1920): 241; (September 25, 1920): 427.

25. See Willis, "Zoning and Zeitgeist" and *Record and Guide* (June 1, 1918): 697.

26. City of New York, Board of Estimate and Apportionment, Building Zone Amendment, Amendments 44 (June 28, 1919): 70; (July 11, 1919): 264; (November 23, 1923): 309; (April 4, 1924): 378; (March 6, 1925): 421; (June 12, 1925): 611; (June 17, 1926): 718; (March 31, 1927): 787; (September 29, 1927): 803–805; (November 17, 1927): 853; (March 8, 1928): 903; (September 27, 1928); *New York Times* (September 29, 1928): 18.

27. *Record and Guide* (July 29, 1922): 134.

28. *New York Times* (June 17, 1926): 25; (November 10, 1926): 29; (December 5, 1926): 4:2; (May 22, 1927): 12:4; *Record and Guide* (May 14, 1927): 8.

29. *New York Times* (June 18, 1926): 15; (May 13, 1927): 29; (July 9, 1926): 33.

30. *New York Times* (December 12, 1926): 2:21; (January 10, 1926): 11:1.

31. *Record and Guide* (January 21, 1928): 6; *New York Times* (April 18, 1927): 39; (June 7, 1927): 12; (June 17, 1927): 41; (January 15, 1928): 11:2.

32. *New York Times* (June 13, 1931): 29; (November 8, 1931): 11:1; (October 26, 1927): 51; (January 15, 1928): 11:2; (February 21, 1928): 27; (September 30, 1928): 12:2; (May 5, 1929): 12:16; (May 22, 1930): 5; (March 24, 1930): 20; *Record and Guide* (October 27, 1928): 6.

33. *Report of the City Committee on Plan and Survey* (New York, 1928), pp. 51–52.

34. Ibid., pp. 3, 8–9; *New York Times* (April 11, 1928): 1; (June 6, 1928): 1; *Record and Guide* (October 20, 1928): 6, 8.

35. *New York Times* (November 16, 1926): 1; (May 16, 1928): 26; (June 13, 1931): 29; (November 8, 1931): 11:1.

36. *Record and Guide* (October 20, 1928): 6, 8.

37. *Record and Guide* (July 12, 1924): 8; (June 20, 1925): 10; *New York Times* (May 1, 1927): 11:2; (June 19, 1927): 10:1; (January 15, 1928): 14. On NABOM, see note 15.

38. *New York Times* (July 4, 1926): 8:3.

39. *New York Times* (May 2, 1928): 24.

40. RSNYE, *Buildings*; Ford, *Building Height*; Regional Plan of New York and Its Environs, vol. 2, *The Building of the City* (New York: RPNYE, 1931).

41. RPNYE, *Building of the City*, p. 192.

42. Edward M. Bassett, "Control of Building Heights, Densities and Uses by Zoning," in RSNYE, *Buildings*, p. 367.

43. Clifford L. Weaver and Richard F. Babcock, *City Zoning: The Once and Future Frontier* (Chicago: Planners Press, 1979), p. 125; Jerold S. Kayden, *Incentive Zoning in New York City: A Cost-Benefit Analysis* (Cambridge: Lincoln Institute of Land Policy, 1978). See note 6 for additional references on the evolution of New York zoning since the 1940s.

44. For example, see Babcock and Larsen, *Special Districts*; Terry Jill Lassar, *Carrots and Sticks: New Zoning Downtown* (Washington, DC: Urban Land Institute, 1990); Mike E. Miles, Emil E. Malizia, Marc A. Weiss, Gayle L. Berens, and Ginger Travis, *Real Estate Development Principles and Process* (Washington, DC: Urban Land Institute, 1991).

4

Joining New York City to the Greater Metropolis: The Port Authority as Visionary, Target of Opportunity, and Opportunist

Jameson W. Doig

When the final wires had been spun and the giant bridge stood ready for use, it seemed to symbolize much that was good and graceful in a world now gone awry. In his dedication address, Franklin Roosevelt caught the spirit that infused the crowd gathered at the Hudson River on that autumn day in 1931: This was an immense project, FDR pointed out, which demonstrated the impact that "skill and scientific planning" could have in surmounting large obstacles, as well as the benefits of "constructive cooperation" across state lines, and the great value of leadership by citizens who approached public projects with "high and unselfish devotion." Because of this marvelous combination, the George Washington Bridge had been completed "six months ahead of schedule and at a cost well below the original estimate." Roosevelt then drew from this experience a lesson that he would soon apply at Albany and then in the nation's capital:

> To my mind, this type of disinterested and capable service is a model for government agencies throughout the land. Their methods are charting the course toward the more able and honorable administration of affairs of government—a course they have proved can be safely steered through political waters with intelligence and integrity at the helm.[1]

The object of Roosevelt's warm embrace was the Port of New York Authority, whose commissioners and staff had developed plans for the large project, worked out a way to surmount the financing problems that had confounded earlier efforts to overcome the Hudson River barrier, and gathered enough political support among the citizens of two states and their wary elected leaders to carry the project through. It was a model of cooperative effort and of skillful planning and execution—set in dramatic contrast to earlier attempts to bring the two states together to solve regional problems of transportation, water pollution, and commercial development. Those efforts had been laced with conflicts and recriminations, and had been marked by false starts and very modest results. And in 1931, as the Great Depression cast a gloomy light across most human endeavors, and the efforts of government institutions and other cooperative activities across the nation were faltering and failing, the Port Authority's success was especially striking.

Governor Roosevelt's enthusiasm for the Port agency was widely shared among editorial writers, business leaders, and civic associations in the bi-state region and beyond. Created in 1921 as a joint venture of New Jersey and New York State, the Port Authority had been endowed with little real power and had been frustrated in its initial efforts to improve the region's inefficient transport system. Now, however, it was famous, and—as Archibald Macleish wrote in a long and thoughtful essay—it was "one of the most interesting and potentially one of the most formidable political agencies America has yet produced."[2] Indeed, Roosevelt and some of his associates could see the possibility of applying "the Port Authority model" to problems of water power, housing, and regional development across New York State, and perhaps across America.

The purpose of this chapter is to explain how the Port Authority scrambled from its unpromising beginnings to the state of high praise that Roosevelt awarded to the agency ten years later. A final section comments on the impact of this successful bridge project on suburban development in the New York region, on the evolution of the Port Authority in later decades, and on the growth of the "public authority movement" in the New York region and across the nation.

Creation of an Open Script:
Julius Henry Cohen and the Authority Idea

We should begin in the years before there was a Port Authority, for here—in the temper of the times, and in the creative imaginings of one man—we find a crucial part of the explanation for the Port agency's early difficulties and for its later triumphs and limitations.

During the years 1900 to 1915, the "temper of the times" in the bi-state New York metropolis meant commercial rivalry and political conflict—between city and town, between machine politician and reformer, between those who identified with the world commercial center of Manhattan and the outlanders in New Jersey, where New York's dominance was associated with wrongful imperialism. The story of the Port Authority begins in this rivalry and contention, as it was played out in the search for strategies of economic development, and for local advantage in using commercial trade as an engine of economic growth.

New York City's rise to the first rank of world cities, and much of the economic expansion that extended into the New Jersey and New York suburbs, were crucially linked to international and coastal trade. By 1915, nearly half of the nation's international commerce passed through the Port of New York, and a vast system of steamship companies and railroad lines converged on the port. A complex array of rail and marine terminals in both states generated thousands of jobs directly tied to the transport system, and thousands more in retail commerce, home and office construction, and industrial development.[3]

The economic advantages linked to vigorous international, coastal, and intraregional trade were not evenly distributed across the cities and towns of the metropolis, and, indeed, there was a sharp contrast between the benefits provided to New Jersey and to her sister state. Manhattan was the dominant center for corporate decision making and office activities associated with maritime commerce, and most of the thriving marine terminals were located along the shores of Manhattan and Brooklyn. On the western side of the Hudson were found hundreds of miles of railroad track, which ran across New Jersey to large rail terminals on or near the Hudson shore in Jersey City, Hoboken, and smaller towns. The modest economic vitality generated by the railroads in New Jersey was far outstripped by the activity and impact on the New York side.

For some political and business leaders in Jersey City, Newark, and elsewhere in northern New Jersey, vigorous economic development in their part of the wider region seemed much more likely if marine cargo and railroad freight could be attracted from Manhattan and Brooklyn terminals to piers constructed along their own shores; and both public criticism and legal action were directed toward that goal. In 1916, New Jersey interests appealed to the Interstate Commerce Commission, arguing that the historic system of setting rates for freight delivery in the New York region was biased against New Jersey's economic rights.[4] If successful, the New Jersey suit would require the railroads to charge lower rates to deliver goods at North Jersey piers; this differential charge might encourage shippers to vastly increase their use of New Jersey marine terminals, and thus fuel economic expansion across the cities and suburbs of that underdeveloped state.

New Jersey's suit was at once challenged by New York's political leaders and by some of its business interests, who wanted to maintain the rate advantage that had historically been theirs. They prepared to battle the upstart before the ICC and then in the courts.

Rivalry and conflict—but these were not the only tempers of these times. Some of New York's business leaders and their political allies resisted the view that competition among factions within the New York region was the best route to follow. They adopted a wider perspective, based on values that are often associated with the Progressive Era: the need for efficiency in economic relationships, and for government action that is helpful in attaining a vigorous and efficient economy. In a complex, highly interdependent metropolis, one implication of these values is that rational, regionwide planning and action might be required in order to provide transportation facilities that are essential to a vital, expanding economy—and that this sort of regional action might require that *public officials* take a central role. However, another implication is that not every government will do: The common, everyday officials who occupied the political stage in New York City and across the River were objects of distrust, for those officials seemed uninterested in using government's powers to achieve broad regional efficiency. Instead, they appeared to focus mainly on "what's in it for me"—what policies would most help their own local citizens, and perhaps help line their personal larders too.[5]

To these New Yorkers, the New Jersey suit offered not only danger but opportunity—an opportunity to reach beyond the direct issue of rate differentials and to grapple with the large problems of inefficiency and congestion that had long burdened the port and its bi-state region, and which were in fact accurately portrayed in the New Jersey challenge. The initiative in thinking about this broader possibility was taken by the Chamber of Commerce of the State of New York, which had a long history of campaigning for improvements in docks, streets, and other transport facilities in New York City, and for more centralized power to ensure that such advances were carried out.[6] Some of the Chamber's leaders saw the transport problem in regional terms, consistent with their own wide business interests.[7] The Chamber turned to its counsel, Julius Henry Cohen, and asked him to explore possible ways to meet the regional problem.

Before 1916, Cohen had given very little thought to port competition or freight rates and perhaps even less to New Jersey. However, Cohen and other leaders of the Chamber soon visited the Port of London Authority, which had been created in 1908, and Cohen took that title, applied it to New York, and urged that a bi-state port authority be created to undertake the effort needed to rationalize the rail and port system in the region. Most discussions of the origins of the Port of New York Authority, as it came into Cohen's mind and from his pen, limit the evolution of his thinking largely to the experience in Great Britain.[8]

Figure 4.1   Congestion at Manhattan Freight Terminals, 1920.   *Source:* Port Authority of New York and New Jersey.

Cohen's thinking, and his ability to influence the shape of future developments, had other and deeper roots as well. Cohen was born in 1873 and grew up in lower Manhattan, where his father, a tailor, was active in the local Tammany club. Julius Henry attended a night law school, and by 1900, he was active in reform politics on the West Side. In 1904, he was named chairman of the Legislative Committee of the reform-minded Citizens Union; in that post, which he held for more than ten years, Cohen became familiar with important issues and political figures in the city—including Alfred E. Smith, as Al evolved in 1911 to 1916 from machine politician to reformer.[9]

Meanwhile, Cohen also served as counsel for the garment industry, and in 1910, he and Louis Brandeis (who represented the laborers) devised a treaty—called the "Protocol of Peace"—which brought an end to an acrimonious industrywide strike. Here we find an early model for the Port Authority; for the Protocol created several independent boards, which were charged with reviewing differences between management and labor "objectively" and proposing solutions. The Protocol continued to govern management-worker relations until 1915 and, during those years, an industry that had been riven by strikes and walkouts found some harmony. In these years, Cohen also had a major role in developing a program of arbitration to resolve business disputes, rather than relying on the courts.

Through these activities, Cohen had by 1916 developed a distinctive perspective on public policies and on ways to grapple with social conflict. He believed that government power should be used in order to meet important social problems, and that public programs should be developed and carried out mainly at local and state levels, rather than by the national government. Also, based on his experience with machine politics in New York City, he preferred that government programs be insulated from the vagaries and potential corruption of party politics. More generally, Cohen was a strong believer in finding ways to resolve disagreements through *cooperation*, and he thought that the route to a healthy economy would often be found in cooperative planning, rather than by relying on vigorous competition in the marketplace.

The ICC suit landed on Cohen's desk in the summer of 1916, and as he looked into the recent history of relationships between the two states, he found his inclination to seek a cooperative solution reinforced. The effort to grapple with water-pollution problems, for example, illustrated the limited value of alternative strategies. For more than a decade, New Jersey and New York had been attempting to reduce pollution in the New York harbor and nearby bays, but during most of those years the two sides had focused on court battles over which side of the harbor deserved most of the blame. In 1916, no positive steps had yet been taken to meet the pollution problem—and the end of litigation was nowhere in sight.

Using his contacts in the reform movement—which included New York City Mayor John Purroy Mitchel, the state's governor, Charles Whitman, and the Republican governor of New Jersey, Walter Edge, who shared the Progressive desire for "business efficiency" in government—Cohen persuaded the two states to take an initial step toward cooperation in the spring of 1917. A bi-state study commission was created and charged with finding some way of meeting the port-development and related regional problems of the two contending partners.

The two governors appointed commissioners who were willing to work together; they in turn named Cohen as counsel to the commission. Less than two years later, in December 1918, Cohen emerged with a draft proposal for a Port of New York Authority that was a regional planner's dream: a bi-state agency would be created and given the power to issue regulations governing construction by governmental bodies and by private industry in a large port district; it would also be given the power to block state actions that were inconsistent with plans (that it would devise) for the "comprehensive development" of the port area—a region which would embrace seventeen counties and more than a hundred communities in the two states. Moreover, if the two states could be persuaded to suspend litigation over water pollution, the Port Authority might then be given responsibility for regulating water quality as well as land development in the region. Through this agency, the growth potential of the metropolitan area could be shaped and controlled harmoniously.[10]

Cohen's brainchild would be a bi-state agency whose commissioners would be appointed by the governors for six-year overlapping terms; its actions would not be subject to gubernatorial veto or other direct controls; and if it were able to generate its own revenues via self-supporting projects, the states could not use the traditional power of the purse to control its programs. In addition, if the Port Authority were unable to meet its total costs through its *own* revenues, it might be authorized to "borrow money upon the credit of the states."

With these safeguards to its independence, coupled with its substantial regulatory powers, the new agency would be an exemplar of the reformer's vision: insulated from intraregional jealousies and the many vagaries of politics, the Authority's skilled staff of engineers and planners would analyze, monitor, and shape the modernization of the port and the economic growth of the surrounding region, guided only by principles of efficiency and the public interest.[11]

During the three years before Cohen submitted his report, the problems of congestion and inefficiency in the Port of New York had reached intolerable proportions. In 1916–1917, the heavy flow of goods bound for the European war had generated recurring breakdowns in the traditional system of transferring freight from the New Jersey rail terminals to lighters, which were floated across the harbor to ocean freighters on the New York side; on some occasions, loaded rail cars had backed up across New Jersey and as far west as Pittsburgh. Then, early in 1918, severe weather led to ice in the harbor, which blocked the lighters delivering coal to New York City. Cohen's proposal offered a way to end conflict between the states, and the organization he proposed might be able to construct the regional rail system which now seemed essential to replace that ancient lighterage pattern. Therefore, Cohen's proposal was greeted with enthusiasm by major business groups, the large metropolitan newspapers, and some political leaders on both sides of the Hudson.

However, once his initial draft was exposed to the light and heat of local and state political forces, many of its crucial provisions could not survive. Cohen's problems began early in 1919, when the governors and legislative leaders from both states met with Cohen and his colleagues in Albany. Most of the discussion was devoted not to the idea of creating a wide-ranging Port Authority, but to a narrow, separate question: Would the two states agree to cooperate to build a tunnel under the Hudson River for motor vehicles?[12] When discussion finally turned to Cohen's Port Authority treaty, he found the legislative leaders were suspicious of his offspring. A legislative commission was appointed, and Cohen's text was submitted to its tender mercies.

In a series of public and private meetings during the next two years, state officials and their local counterparts raised the banner of "democracy" and urged that proper standards of "public accountability" be applied to the offending document. So the Port Authority idea was hammered through three successive drafts before it emerged, a much weakened animal, and was approved by the two states in the spring of 1921. All of its regulatory powers had been stripped away; and the agency began life in 1921 with great regional scope—across seventeen counties in two states—but with no capacity to use tax revenues and essentially no other powers. However, the formal political insulation provided in Cohen's early draft still survived: the Port Authority would be controlled by a six-member board, three to be chosen by each governor for six-year terms. And the bi-state compact did give the Port Authority the abstract ability to "purchase, construct, lease and/or operate any terminal or transportation facility" within the port dis-

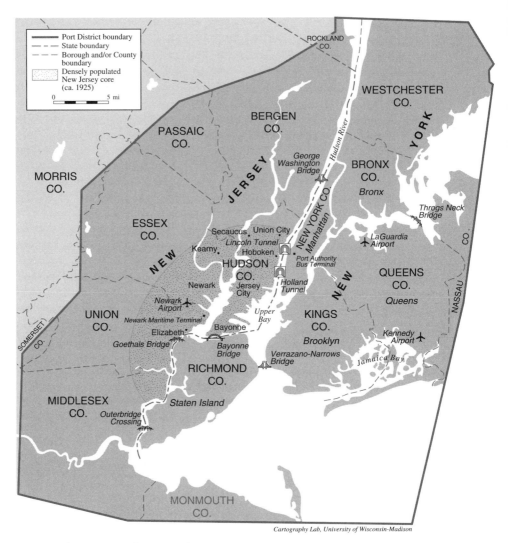

Figure 4.2 The Port of New York District (created in 1921).

trict, and to "borrow money and secure the same by bonds." It was an open script, given to a toothless giant.[13]

Uses of an Open Script:
Regional Visions and Targets of Opportunity

That was the first step—the creation of an institution of metropolitan scope. In the complex political terrain of the New York area, however, there would be several missteps—and a dose of serendipity—before the Port Authority would add any significant political and economic power to its banner of regionalism.

The compact provided the new agency with a wide field of potential action. The open character of the Authority's mandate was understood by the six commissioners who were appointed to the Port Authority in the spring of 1921, for almost all of them had been members of the bi-state study commission; and they appointed Cohen as the Authority's counsel, which ensured that there would be at least one restless imagination on hand to think about political and legal strategies to advance the Port agency's cause. But there was also a specific regional task built into its legislation and its legislative history. The Port Authority was required to turn its attention in its first months to the question of what physical plan should be undertaken to overcome the congestion and cost involved in handling rail and waterborne freight on both sides of the harbor; it was also expected to consult extensively with the public and to negotiate with the railroads in the hope that this plan might gain widespread support.

In order to tap regional sentiment, the Port Authority created an advisory committee of business and civic associations in the summer of 1921, identified 114 organizations from all parts of the metropolis to be included on the committee, and held meetings with the entire group and with subcommittees from various areas. The agency also met with local public officials across the region during the summer and fall of 1921, and it began discussions with the twelve rail corporations. In these meetings, the Port agency drew on the array of rail-improvement ideas its staff had been developing since 1917, and it added more rail spurs wherever they were favored by local sentiment.

In December 1921, the Port Authority announced its "Comprehensive Plan for the Development of the Port District." The plan called for an extensive system of railroad tracks throughout the bi-state region, a rail-freight tunnel from New Jersey under the upper bay to Brooklyn, a separate rail tunnel to carry freight under the Hudson to a new rail line in Manhattan, and unified marine terminals.[14] The improved rail system would, the Port Authority announced, stimulate industrial and

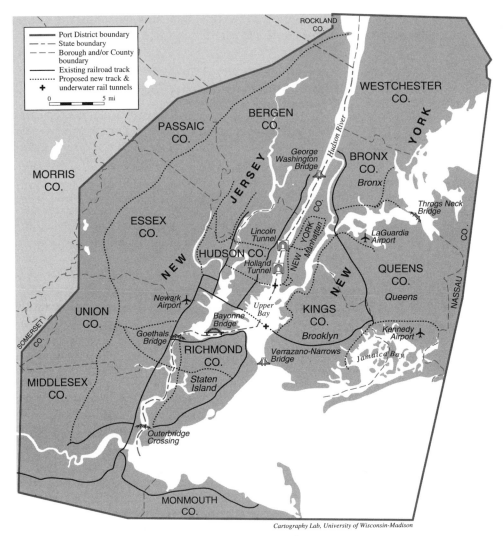

Cartography Lab, University of Wisconsin-Madison

Figure 4.3 Port Authority Railroad-Freight Belt-line System (proposed, December 1921).

commercial growth not only in the central business district but in outlying areas as well.[15]

To carry out any part of this plan would require active cooperation by the region's dozen rail lines, and during the fall of 1921 the Port Authority's staff began intensive consultations with representatives of the railroads. These negotiations continued sporadically until the early 1930s. But the long and the short of it was that all these efforts were for naught. There were times in the early 1920s and again in the late 1920s when the Port Authority thought it might be able to persuade the railroads directly—or through the coercive power of the Interstate Commerce Commission—to join forces in cooperative action, but no significant agreements were ever reached. A decade after the Port Authority had been created, the rail-freight system was as costly and as inefficient as it had been in 1921. The great hopes of Julius Henry Cohen and his colleagues for a vastly improved rail system, which would stimulate economic growth across the region, were but ashes.[16]

However, the Port Authority was not an agency limited to reconstructing the railroad-freight system of the metropolis. It was an enterprise with a formal mandate as wide as all "terminal, transportation and other facilities of commerce." Which meant that the Port Authority's leaders could look beyond the railroad problem and seek other projects—other ways to improve the "planning and development" of the extensive bi-state region around the Port of New York.

Julius Henry Cohen served as the Port agency's counsel—and soon after Al Smith was reelected governor in November 1922, Cohen began working with him to develop legislation that would apply the "public authority concept" to water power and to public housing. It is likely, therefore, that in time Cohen would have pressed his Port Authority colleagues to shift their energies from the great railroad project and send the bi-state agency into greener pastures. But in 1922 and 1923, most of his associates at the agency were "railroad men," and the prospects for agreement with the rail executives seemed promising. So neither Cohen nor his colleagues were fully alert to a political movement that was growing in the wilds of New Jersey—and that would soon envelop the Port Authority and turn it in a very different direction.

This new political movement had its roots in another project spawned in the railroad era. Ever since the 1880s, the Austrian-American bridge designer Gustav Lindenthal had been seeking support for his own scheme to improve the efficiency of regional transportation in the New York-New Jersey area. The centerpiece of Lindenthal's plan was an immense bridge which would span the Hudson River and land in mid-Manhattan; the span would carry twelve railroad tracks, funneling the railroads from New Jersey over the river and then connecting them with rail-to-ship terminals along Manhattan's waterfront. In its early version, Lindenthal's railroad bridge entered Manhattan at Twenty-third Street. A revised plan, announced in 1921, moved the bridge uptown to Fifty-seventh Street; and in a modest bow to the growing use of motor vehicles, he added twenty automotive lanes to his dozen railroad tracks.[17]

Lindenthal was one of the world's great bridge engineers, and his striking proposal caught the imagination of New Yorkers who measured the eminence of their city by the size of its wondrous construction projects. But its cost was equally striking—$200 million or more; neither the railroads nor elected officials were eager to add that sum to their existing burdens. The city's leaders were also dismayed at the thought of massive freight trains and twenty lines of automotive traffic plowing into Manhattan's central business district.

The fledgling Port Authority studied Lindenthal's plan in 1921 and rejected it in favor of the rail-freight system adopted in December of that year. That did not dissuade its creator, who denounced the Port Authority as shortsighted and mounted a campaign to gain business and governmental support for his great project. Out of this effort, much to Lindenthal's distress, arose a campaign for a very different Hudson crossing—a bridge that *would* be built, that would shape the future of the Port Authority and of suburban development in the northwest sector of the region, and that would influence the thinking of Franklin Roosevelt as he completed his term as governor and prepared to go to Washington.

In designing his combined rail-vehicular bridge, Lindenthal had hired as his chief assistant Othmar Ammann, who had worked with him earlier on the Hell Gate railroad span. As Lindenthal carried his campaign for the Fifty-seventh Street bridge forward, through the fall and winter of 1921 and then into the summer and fall of 1922, Ammann concluded reluctantly that the political and financial obstacles confronting the proposal were too formidable, at least in the near term. He appealed to Lindenthal to reduce the size of the project, and to move it north of the business district, but Lindenthal refused. Finally, reluctantly, Ammann left Lindenthal and struck out on his own.[18]

Ammann had been trained in Switzerland and, like Lindenthal, had come to the United States in search of opportunities to build wide bridges over America's great rivers and bays. Arriving in New York in 1904 at the age of twenty-five, Ammann had worked on several bridges under the supervision of Lindenthal and other senior engineers, but he had never designed or supervised construction of a single span, large or small. Now, in the winter and spring of 1922–1923, Ammann began to devise a set of political and engineering strategies aimed at accomplishing an immense and complex task—the creation of a great suspension bridge across the Hudson, with a center span twice as wide as any yet constructed.[19] And in the course of this effort, he would vault into the front ranks of bridge builders of the nineteenth and twentieth centuries.

Ammann's first and crucial step was to conceive of a very different kind of span across the Hudson—a bridge which would be oriented to the new automotive age, serving only motor vehicles and light-rail transit. A crossing of this kind, which would not be connected with the railroad system, could be built far north of congested mid-Manhattan and its dense system of railroad tracks. Ammann's preference was to cast the bridge across the river six miles north of Fifty-seventh Street, between 179th Street in Manhattan and Fort Lee on the western shore. This decision had several beneficial effects:

1. The span could be much lighter than a bridge designed to carry loaded freight cars, and the construction cost would therefore be a fraction of Lindenthal's total.
2. A bridge at Fort Lee would rise atop the Palisades and cross to a high point on the Manhattan shore, far enough above the Hudson to clear all ship masts. Thus, the burden that Lindenthal faced, building long approaches from the low shores at Fifty-seventh Street so the bridge deck would be high enough for ship clearance, would be eliminated. With these two advantages, Ammann estimated that his bridge would cost only $25 million, compared with $200 million or more for the Fifty-seventh Street span.
3. Ammann's bridge would not face the fervent opposition of Manhattan business leaders, and he would not be compelled to persuade a dozen railroad corporations to use the bridge—an essential element to make Lindenthal's scheme financially viable.

Coupled with these advantages was one important problem: Would there be enough automobile and truck traffic to justify (and pay tolls to finance) a crossing this far north? In the winter and spring of 1923, Ammann studied the patterns of ferry traffic—which at busy periods often required travelers to wait two or more hours to cross the river—and he consulted with the staff of the recently formed Committee on the Regional Plan. He also dug into earlier history, and he found a 1910 report that advocated a bridge at 179th Street as a crucial step in creating a regional park system as well as improving access for work, residences, and shopping.[20]

Ammann's analysis indicated that a toll bridge at Fort Lee would be heavily used for travel to work and recreation by the 2.5 million who lived near the bridge.[21] In addition, it would serve as an important link between New England/Westchester roads and western points, providing a northern bypass for autos and trucks around the region's congested core.[22] With these major flows of traffic, Ammann concluded that his bridge could be self-supporting.

The engineering and financial questions had been resolved, at least to Ammann's satisfaction. But two difficult issues still remained:

> First, who would be willing to undertake the project? Could a private corporation build the bridge? (A group of private investors had recently, in 1922, developed plans to construct a tunnel under the Hudson at 125th Street; perhaps they could be persuaded to invest in a bridge instead.) Or should Ammann ask the two state Bridge and Tunnel Commissions, then struggling to make progress with the Canal Street tunnel project, to take on the task? Or could the Port Authority, despite its recent commitment to a "comprehensive plan" that focused almost entirely on railroad-freight problems, be persuaded to throw its energies into a very different kind of enterprise?
>
> Second, would the cities and towns in the region and the leaders of the two contentious states join together to support a cooperative plan to build a bridge across the Hudson? The recent experience of the tunnel commissions, whose efforts were often delayed by conflicts between Jersey City and New York factions, and the attempts to solve the region's water pollution problem, which were still mired in litigation, suggested that the political path to a bridge at Fort Lee would not be easy.

The central role in exploring these issues was taken by Ammann. Ammann was a political novice and a taciturn man, reluctant to engage in political campaigning. However, he knew George Silzer, a Democratic politician who was elected governor of New Jersey in the fall of 1922, and who was interested in developing a record of accomplishment as governor.[23] The two men worked out a strategy that would serve both their interests: Ammann would travel across Bergen and other North Jersey counties, and into Westchester and the Bronx, explaining the engineering advances that at last made a bridge of such great size feasible, and organizing local political support for his trans-Hudson crossing.[24] Meanwhile, Silzer would speak publicly about the advantages of a bridge to connect Manhattan to the "high, healthy" suburbs of North Jersey.

The governor would also use his personal influence with the Port Authority's commissioners to persuade them that their goals need not be limited to solving the railroad freight problem: the Authority might, in addition, take action to meet the growing problem of vehicular congestion in the bi-state region. The long lines of automobile and truck traffic, which waited sometimes for hours for ferries between North Jersey and Manhattan, was a notable example of this congestion; a bridge at 179th Street, Silzer pointed out, would make a great contribution toward meeting this interstate problem. Silzer and Ammann also suggested that the Port Authority make a more modest contribution to improving transport in the region by building two smaller bridges that would connect Staten Island to nearby New Jersey cities.[25]

Ammann's political activities extended for more than two years. He met with business groups and civic associations on both sides of the Hudson, and with state senators and newspaper editors, seeking support for his bridge at 179th Street—while he also fended off those who favored a tunnel at 110th Street or 125th Street. He continued to work with the Committee on the Regional Plan, analyzing traffic conditions and the advantages of a bridge that would bypass the congested center of the region.[26] He and Governor Silzer also met with officials at the Port Authority, where they found a modicum of enthusiasm for adding motor-vehicle projects to their other work—although some were reluctant to divert the agency's energies from the railroad issue, where success seemed elusive but almost at hand.

In the spring of 1924, the Authority's leaders took the first step into the automotive age, agreeing to build a pair of bridges to join Staten Island to New Jersey; but they turned down Ammann's offer to design those spans.[27] Finally, early in 1925, Ammann's extensive organizing effort bore fruit: The Fort Lee project now had wide support on both sides of the Hudson, and the Port Authority at last agreed to take responsibility for the project. In March, the two state legislatures authorized the bi-state agency to undertake that task—constructing the world's longest-spanning bridge at Fort Lee and 179th Street. And Ammann, who had been unemployed since the spring of 1923, was asked to join the Port Authority as bridge engineer.[28]

There, in the summer of 1925, he took charge of the bridge-building effort, organized a dedicated staff, brought the George Washington Bridge into existence well ahead of the target date and under budget, and so deserved a large measure of acclaim, as Governor Roosevelt

Figure 4.4 The George Washington Bridge, 1931. *Source:* Port Authority of New York and New Jersey.

noted in his dedication address in October 1931:

> Behind this mighty structure, that seems almost superhuman in its perfection, there is an inspiring background of that high intelligence. It is only fitting that we should for a moment today pause to congratulate Mr. O. H. Ammann, the Chief Engineer, and indeed the entire staff of The Port of New York Authority who are responsible not only for the design of this bridge but for its speedy and successful execution.[29]

For Ammann, then, the Port Authority served as Opportunity. If that agency had not been at hand, a somewhat empty vessel of railroad hopes and plans and unrequited love, it is not clear that he could have constructed a viable strategy to carry out his grand engineering project.

We might instead have a series of tunnels through the Hudson mud and perhaps a Port Authority of quite different cast.

The Impact of the Bridge and Its Port Authority

What Julius Henry Cohen, Othmar Ammann, and their colleagues had wrought by 1931 was a great bridge, completed earlier than expected and at a lower cost, *and* an organization whose strong reputation derived largely from that striking accomplishment.[30] The impact of the George Washington Bridge on the New York region and on the fortunes of the Port Authority was immense, and it flowed in several directions.

First, there was the influence of the span on suburban development in the vast open land extending out from Fort Lee and on traffic congestion in the central portion of the region. As soon as the state legislatures at Albany and Trenton authorized the Port Authority to construct the Fort Lee bridge, real estate developers and other civic boosters across northern New Jersey recognized what the giant span would mean for residential and commercial development in their area. The bridge would displace a set of ferries (which were then the only way to cross the Hudson within the New York region), sharply cutting travel time to Manhattan and points east. Although the Holland Tunnel would be completed earlier, in 1927, the Port Authority's bridge would be nine miles further north, away from the congested core, and so it would be attractive to residents and other travelers bound to and from Bergen, Morris, Rockland (New York), and other northwestern counties. The new bridge would also be of great value to truckers delivering goods into and out of New England, Westchester, and the Bronx, who would be glad to be able to reach the rest of the continent via a bridge well north of the congested center of the region—instead of threading their way down Manhattan's crowded thoroughfares to Canal Street, where the Holland Tunnel would head into the Hudson River mud, to emerge onto busy Jersey City streets.

The hopes of developers and local officials were fulfilled; throughout the 1930s and 1940s, the George Washington Bridge had a profound effect—attracting those who worked in New York's business district to seek homes in the northwest suburbs, and turning rural valleys of Bergen and points north and west into suburban enclaves of the middle class. The bridge also improved the efficiency of truck travel from New York City, Westchester, and New England to locations west of the Hudson—the Trenton area, Philadelphia, Bethlehem and Pittsburgh, Chicago and Detroit—and in that way strengthened the competitive advantage of truckers as they sought to attract freight traffic from the faltering railroads.

Second, by carrying out this complex project with striking effectiveness, the Port agency demonstrated that it was *more* than just a planning agency, and perhaps *better* for some important tasks than any other government institution. Its success with this project placed the Port Authority's leaders in a strong position when they argued that the Holland Tunnel should be removed from the jurisdiction of the competing bi-state agencies (the Bridge and Tunnel Commissions, which had planned and carried out that complex effort) and brought into their own domain. Indeed the Port Authority's record appeared particularly strong when compared to that of the Holland Tunnel builders, who had begun their project in 1919, found their early efforts marred by bickering and political conflict, and completed the task in the fall of 1927—years behind schedule and far over budget.[31]

Even before the George Washington Bridge was completed, Julius Henry Cohen had grasped the significance of this comparison. In terms of effective regional planning and efficient action, surely the Port Authority's record was stronger. Moreover, to keep the Holland Tunnel and the bridge in separate hands would risk the possibility of destructive competition between the two—each trying to attract traffic by lowering tolls below its competitor's level. And if future tunnels and bridges were the responsibility of the Port Authority, the earnings from the Fort Lee bridge and the Holland Tunnel could be used for those crossings, rather than requiring legislative appropriations. So the Port Authority's counsel turned reasonable opportunist, urging that his agency be given jurisdiction over all trans-Hudson vehicular crossings. As the bridge moved toward completion, the governors and legislatures on both sides of the Hudson finally agreed with Cohen and his colleagues, and, early in 1931, the two states permitted the Port Authority to take control of the Holland Tunnel and its growing toll revenues; they also agreed that the Authority would have monopoly power over all interstate crossings that might in the future be constructed between New Jersey and the Empire State.[32]

This "merger," as it was called, provided the Port Authority with the toll revenues of the Holland Tunnel—millions of dollars a year, even in the Depression—the largest single source of toll income from vehicular traffic in the nation. In the short run, this ensured that the Port agency would not go into bankruptcy—a distinct possibility otherwise, as the Authority found itself loaded down with debt from bonds issued to finance the Staten Island bridges, which produced little revenue, and the George Washington Bridge, which would produce no revenue until late in 1931, and only a modest stream in 1932 and

1933.[33] The Holland tolls also permitted the Port Authority to begin a third Hudson crossing, the Lincoln Tunnel to mid-Manhattan, before the bi-state agency sank into the doldrums of the deeper Depression years.[34]

Looking still further ahead, the merger meant that the Port agency could, once the Depression and World War II had ended, apply the combined net revenues of the Holland Tunnel, the George Washington Bridge, and the Lincoln Tunnel to new opportunities in the wide field of "terminal and transportation facilities"—opportunities that might be discovered or created anywhere along the shores or inland reaches of the hundred cities and towns and the seventeen counties that comprised the port district.

Moreover, in developing the Fort Lee project, the Port Authority established a pattern of cooperative relations with the Committee on the Regional Plan which would be of value to both organizations in the short run and in later years. As noted earlier, Ammann had begun to consult with the Committee's planners in 1923, and, throughout the 1920s, he and other Port Authority staff members worked with the evolving Regional Plan staff on the development of regional highway and rail systems. The Port Authority benefited, since its proposals were endorsed by an "objective" group of planners; and the Regional Plan team, in turn, was able to indicate that its efforts were influential in shaping the Port Authority's thinking and its important projects.[35] Later, when the Port Authority cast an admiring gaze on the region's airports, it again turned to the Regional Plan staff for support. Their endorsement of the Port Authority's argument that the three major airports should be controlled by a single regional agency helped wrest those air terminals from Newark's city commissioners and from Robert Moses and his City Airport Authority, which was rendered stillborn.[36]

It does not stretch our understanding of causal connections too far, perhaps, to argue that the Port Authority's successful effort in devising and carrying out the George Washington Bridge was crucial to all that followed: to its ability to escape bankruptcy and failure in the 1930s, to its capacity to attract "entrepreneurial" planners and project developers to its staff in the 1940s and beyond, and to its great successes in redeveloping old airports and piers at Newark, Hoboken, and LaGuardia, and in developing gigantic new projects at Idlewild (now Kennedy Airport) and Elizabeth (home of the largest containerport on the East Coast).[37] Even the 110-story boxes that grace lower Manhattan owe much to their more graceful metal cousin that spans the Hudson upriver. So do the thousands of jobs that early and continuing investment has generated at these many facilities, especially at Kennedy

Airport (the largest employment center in Queens) and the Newark/ Elizabeth seaport and airport facilities (the largest employment generator in that section of New Jersey).[38]

The impact of the George Washington Bridge can be extended still further. As FDR's dedication address of 1931 suggested, the Port Authority's success in that project had been inscribed in his own thinking. In that same year, he built upon an idea first devised by his predecessor as governor, Al Smith, working with adviser Cohen, and drafted legislation to create a Power Authority, which would develop the state's hydroelectric potential. Traveling then to Washington, Roosevelt used some of the Port Authority's distinctive elements—its multiheaded board, its "businesslike" ethos, and its loosely defined, open-ended mandate—in setting forth plans in 1933 for a Tennessee Valley Authority.[39] A few years later, his proposal that cities create local housing authorities also built on the Port Authority model.[40]

Meanwhile, Robert Moses had sat and watched, throughout the 1920s, as Al Smith and Julius Henry Cohen devised ways to expand the Port Authority's reach, and to create state agencies for housing and water power that were based on the Port Authority design; and Moses had seen how the struggling infant had grown in ten years to a healthy cub, using its vague mandate and its potential toll revenue to reach out for new challenges, where the need was great and the opposition weak. By the early 1930s, Moses was prepared to use what he had learned, and during the next several decades he employed the authority model as a crucial vehicle in shaping highways and recreation and other activities throughout New York City and across much of New York State.[41]

In retrospect, it can be argued that the Port Authority's decision to go forward with the George Washington Bridge and the Staten Island spans set it on a trajectory that would exacerbate the problems of planning and development in the city and its region. The Authority's bridges and tunnels would encourage travelers from the western suburbs to enter Manhattan by automobile, and thousands who worked in the center city would, in the coming decades, search for housing in the thinly developed reaches of the metropolis, away from the network of commuter rail lines. The result, in time, would be suburban sprawl, greater use of automobiles for transport into the region's core, deterioration of rail services, and increased traffic congestion in and near the central business district.[42]

In the 1920s, however, the George Washington and the array of other regional highway improvements were viewed more positively. The number of automobiles and trucks traveling in the bi-state region expanded sharply throughout the decade, and to the Regional Plan staff and others, that expansion was seen as beneficial in stimulating economic growth across the metropolis. The Hudson River crossings were essential projects in facilitating this favorable pattern.[43] Indeed, the bridge at Fort Lee would be especially helpful, since it would encourage suburban growth in the undeveloped northwestern counties while providing a bypass for trucks and automobiles with destinations outside the congested center.[44]

To Ammann and the Port Authority planners and to the Regional Plan experts, the future would not arrive on rubber tires alone; rather, it seemed likely to hold a harmonious mix of rail and road facilities, which would stimulate and serve an expanding and efficient regional economy. Thus the George Washington span was designed so that a light rail track could be added on a lower deck; if local authorities then agreed, rail service on the bridge could be connected with the North Jersey trolley system and with New York's subway system.[45] Meanwhile, the Port agency was active during the years 1927 to 1931 in a regional effort to improve suburban rail transit operations; and throughout the 1920s it continued its activities to improve the efficiency of rail freight operations.[46]

Those rail plans foundered on the rocks of the Great Depression, railroad intransigence, and the American love for the automobile. So the Port Authority was left with half a loaf—its "skill and scientific planning" yoked to the demands of the automotive age. During the 1930s and beyond, that partial loaf seemed far better than none, however; not only did it permit the agency itself to thrive, but the George Washington span and its other bridges and tunnels appeared certain as well to aid transportation efficiency and economic growth in the vast bi-state metropolis. That was, at least, the expectation of the region's planners, and of the general public, in those early years of the automotive revolution.

Acknowledgments

I acknowledge with thanks comments on an earlier draft by Eugenie Birch, David Billington, Roger Gilman, Pendleton Herring, Josef Konvitz, Edward Olcott, Lynne Sagalyn and Leonard Wallock, and by the members of the Social Science Research Council's Conference on New York's Built Environment, especially Robert Fishman, Olivier Zunz, and David Ward. My thanks also for the research assistance of Alexis Faust and Valerie Kanka, and financial support from the Alfred Sloan Foundation.

Notes

1. Franklin D. Roosevelt, governor of New York State, address delivered at the dedication of the George Washington Bridge, October 24, 1931.
2. Archibald Macleish, "Port of New York Authority," *Fortune* (September 1933): 22ff.; the quotation is on page 119.
3. For a more detailed summary of the developments discussed in these paragraphs, see Jameson W. Doig, "Entrepreneurship in Government: Historical Roots in the Progressive Era." Paper prepared for the Annual Meeting of the American Political Science Association, 1988, pp. 11–15.
4. The traditional system required that all pier delivery points in the region be subjected to the same railroad charge, regardless of actual cost of delivery to various local areas. However, the *real* cost to deliver transcontinental goods to New York City locations was much higher, for those goods had to be floated from the North Jersey rail terminals across the Hudson (or across New York Bay) to Manhattan and Brooklyn piers.
5. What the urban reformers sought, as Robert Wiebe comments, was "scientific government," with "efficiency rather than moral purity its objective"; this sort of government action "would bring opportunity, progress, order, and community" (Robert H. Wiebe, *The Search for Order, 1877–1920* [New York: Hill & Wang, 1967], pp. 170–171). On the developments in the New York region summarized in the next several paragraphs, see Doig, "Entrepreneurship in Government," pp. 15–38, and Erwin W. Bard, *The Port of New York Authority* (New York: Columbia University Press, 1942), Chapter 1.
6. On the work of the Chamber in earlier decades, see David C. Hammack, *Power and Society: Greater New York at the Turn of the Century* (New York: Russell Sage Foundation, 1982), 188ff. The congestion at the region's freight terminals is illustrated in Figure 4.1.
7. For example, the Chamber's president, Eugenius Outerbridge, operated manufacturing plants in Trenton and Passaic in New Jersey and an import-export firm in Manhattan.

    One might argue that the Chamber's efforts in the story summarized in this chapter, and in earlier decades, were largely motivated by a desire for government action that would "produce new investment in the built environment capable of generating private profit and of expanding the market value of real estate." See the discussion of business-government relationships in capitalist societies, in Susan S. Fainstein and others, eds., *Restructuring the City* (New York: Longman, 1983), especially Chapter 7 (the quotation is on p. 252). But other factors also shaped the Chamber's actions, for example, a belief that an efficient transport system was better than an inefficient one—better for economic vitality generally, better for the citizen's sense of easy communication and mobility, perhaps better as a matter of general morality.
8. In Britain, Cohen studied not only the London port agency but also the Liverpool port authority (called the Mersey Docks and Harbour Board), which had been created sixty years earlier, and which in its organization was much closer to Cohen's design for the New York agency. For discussions of the impact of British experience on Cohen's ideas, see Robert G. Smith, *Ad Hoc Governments* (Beverly Hills, CA: Sage, 1974), Chapter 2, and Bard, *Port of New York Authority*, p. 27.

9. On Cohen's work as a reformer and his other activities, see Doig, "Entrepreneurship in Government," pp. 16–38, and Julius Henry Cohen, *They Builded Better Than They Knew* (New York: Julian Messner, 1946).

10. For an extended discussion of Cohen's 1918 plan and how it evolved into the 1921 compact, see Doig, "Entrepreneurship in Government," pp. 43–87, and Bard, *Port of New York Authority*, pp. 25–34.

11. In Cohen's view, the need for a unified approach, insulated from local jealousies, could readily be appreciated by examining the close economic ties among the parts of the metropolitan region, as those ties had evolved historically. In the late nineteenth century, Manhattan had experienced "phenomenal economic development" which outgrew available space; "many industries and more people migrated from the island to New Jersey." As "arms grow from a starfish," Cohen wrote, separate towns "have grown up . . . whose life was given by and centers at the harbor of New York; who are so closely connected with it that the Federal Census Bureau unites them in one 'Metropolitan District' . . ." J. H. Cohen, "The New York Harbor Problem and Its Legal Aspects," *Cornell Law Quarterly* 5 (May 1920): 375–376.

    Cohen noted that a similar perspective had been taken by the ICC in 1917, when it rejected New Jersey's plea to separate its side of the harbor and to set lower freight rates for shipments bound for North Jersey piers: "Historically, geographically and commercially New York and the industrial district in the northern part of New Jersey constitute a single community." Interstate Commerce Commission, *New York Harbor Case* (December 1917), as quoted in Cohen, "New York Harbor Problem," p. 376.

12. Each state had created a bridge-and-tunnel commission, and the two commissions had agreed upon a route under the Hudson between Canal Street and Jersey City. The estimated cost for the tunnel was $12 million, and the issue at hand was whether each state would supply half that total in state appropriations, so the two commissions could hire a staff and begin work. Officials from the two states finally agreed to provide the needed moneys.

    The different dimensions of the tunnel project and the Port Authority scheme are suggested by Cohen's whispered comment to a colleague during the long discussion of funding the tunnel: "It seems to me they are discussing the matter of one trouser button and buttonhole to save us from disgrace, while we are here to discuss an order for a whole suit of clothes" (Cohen, *They Builded Better Than They Knew*, p. 261).

13. See Figure 4.2 for the boundaries of the Port Authority's domain, the Port of New York District.

14. See Figure 4.3. The physical plan was probably strongly influenced by the rail-belt project developed by William Wilgus in 1908ff., although the Port Authority reports do not refer to this heritage. See the discussion of Wilgus by Robert Fishman in Chapter 5 of this volume, and Josef W. Konvitz, "William J. Wilgus and Engineering Projects to Improve the Port of New York, 1900–1930," *Technology and Culture*, 30 (1989): 398–425.

15. For example, a new rail line around Jamaica Bay in Brooklyn would "open up new territory for commercial and industrial development," as would new rail lines near Newark Bay and in the Hudson-Bergen sector. As the agency explained, it had projected "plans for future development as far ahead as the process of reasoning could foresee, so that each part of the

port in the development of its local projects and its growth might properly coordinate them with the whole." Port of New York Authority, *Report with Plan for the Comprehensive Development of the Port of New York* (December 21, 1921): 14, 30, 31.

16. For detailed materials on these negotiations and related developments, see Bard, *Port of New York Authority*, Chapters 2–6, and Jameson W. Doig, *Empire on the Hudson* (1993, forthcoming), Chapter 4.

Some members of the Port Authority staff maintained a continuing interest in the plan and, years later, still thought that this phoenix might yet rise. In 1941, when a defense preparation committee was formed in the New York region, and the agency's chief planner, Walter Hedden, was appointed to the committee, he commented to his young assistant, Roger Gilman: "Now maybe we can get the funds we need to construct the railroad tunnel under New York Bay!" The tunnel was the linchpin and the most expensive part of the Comprehensive Plan (Interview, Roger H. Gilman, October 27, 1990).

17. Lindenthal was born in Austria in 1850, came to the United States in 1874, and first proposed a railroad bridge over the Hudson in 1888. In 1902 and 1903, he was bridge commissioner for New York City, during which time he completed the Williamsburg span and planned the Queensboro and Manhattan bridges. In 1907, he began work on the Hell Gate Bridge, which crosses the upper East River, joining the rail lines of New England and Westchester to the Long Island Railroad and then to Pennsylvania's continental rail system. Completing the Hell Gate in 1917, he turned his full attention to the Hudson River problem. On Lindenthal's career, see David P. Billington, *The Tower and the Bridge* (New York: Basic Books, 1983), pp. 122–128 and passim; Rebecca Read Shanor, *The City That Never Was* (New York: Viking, 1988), pp. 135–149; Tom Buckley, "A Reporter at Large: The Eighth Bridge," *The New Yorker* (January 14, 1991): 37–59.

18. Ammann set down his views on the conflict in a letter at the end of 1923:

". . . The giant project for which I have been sacrificing time and money for the past three years, today lies in ruins. In vain, I as well as others have been fighting against the unlimited ambition of a genius who is obsessed with illusions of grandeur. He has the power in his hands and refuses to bring moderation into his gigantic plans." (Othmar H. Ammann to Rosa Labhardt Ammann, December 14, 1923; translated by Margot Ammann, 1988).

19. The discussion of Ammann's thinking and strategies is based on the author's article, "Politics and the Engineering Mind," *Yearbook of German-American Studies*, vol. 25 (1990), pp. 160–175, which draws upon letters and other documents discovered in the New Jersey State Archives in 1987–1988.

20. "A bridge at this location will connect the park system of New York City with the proposed . . . Interstate Palisade Park. . . . The great highway and park system planned to extend from Fort Lee, New Jersey to Newburgh, New York, can best be made available to the immense population of the metropolitan district by a crossing of the river at 179th Street." That early report viewed the bridge as being used for highway and trolley service, with connections to "the trolley system of New Jersey." (New

York Interstate Bridge Commission, *Report of 1910*, quoted in O. H. Ammann, "Study of a Highway Bridge Across the Hudson River . . . ," typescript, December 15, 1923, p. 22.) Ammann submitted his report to Governor Silzer on December 15, and Silzer forwarded the report to the Port Authority.

21. Ammann counted those living in the Bronx, Westchester, and Manhattan north of Central Park, together with the "large and fast growing suburban and industrial centers," such as Paterson, Passaic, and Hackensack, in North Jersey (O. H. Ammann, "Proposed Hudson River Bridge . . ." [December 18, 1923], p. 1).

22. Referring to Figure 4.2, the core includes the portion of New Jersey bounded by Secaucus, Kearny, Newark, and Elizabeth, extending eastward to the Hudson River and associated waterways, together with Manhattan below Fifty-ninth Street.

Ammann's preference for locating the bridge at Fort Lee, and his view that it could be a crucial part of a circumferential route for cars and trucks, apparently preceded the Committee on the Regional Plan's similar position. Ammann had selected the site by early 1923. In May of that year, Harold Lewis of the Regional Plan group published an article, "Highway Routes in the New York Metropolitan Region," in the magazine *American City and County*, pp. 483–484; a diagram on p. 483 shows several crossings of the Hudson, including one at Edgewater, just south of Fort Lee. However, the text emphasizes an "inner circumferential road" which crosses the Hudson at Nyack, fifteen miles north of Fort Lee. The Regional Plan's 1925 report, "Some Preliminary Suggestions for the Relief of Highway Congestion . . . ," indicates that the group's engineering staff made a study of a Fort Lee bridge in 1924; the report includes a diagram (p. 11) of what appears to be Ammann's bridge, without acknowledging Ammann. The proposed Nyack crossing has disappeared.

23. Silzer had been a legislative leader at Trenton during Woodrow Wilson's first year as governor in 1911. Like Wilson, Silzer hoped to parley a record of accomplishment into a successful campaign for other public offices.

24. Because of ship traffic on the Hudson, bridge piers could not be placed in the river, and therefore the center span would need to be as wide as the river—which would make it twice the length of any bridge span in existence.

25. These spans would link upper Staten Island to Elizabeth in Union County, and lower Staten Island to Perth Amboy in Middlesex County, which was Silzer's home and political base. Local groups had urged for several years that such bridges be constructed. (See Figure 4.2 for the location of the Goethals and Outerbridge crossings.)

26. In his speeches and commentaries, Ammann placed his proposed bridge in the context of the "larger problem of transportation in and through the great Metropolitan district of New York," which, he argued, required improved rail facilities as well as highway improvements to meet the "phenomenal development of the passenger automobile, motor bus and motor truck." Moreover, he pointed out, the pattern of transport demand was continually being altered by the "rapid development of new centers of population and industry."

Citing the work of the Regional Plan, Ammann argued that the New York region, embracing parts of three states, "must be regarded to-day as a social unit, the various parts depending upon each other in their economic struggle and development." As its population continued to grow, therefore, the Hudson River would be crossed by a network of rail transit tunnels, by three or four vehicular tunnels—and by three or four great bridges. So a span at Fort Lee would be followed by several offspring! O. H. Ammann, "The Problem of Bridging the Hudson River . . . ," given at a meeting of the Connecticut Society of Civil Engineers, February 19, 1924, as published in the Society's *Fortieth Annual Meeting* proceedings (1924), pp. 5–26; quotations on pp. 6–7, 12–13. The same arguments are found in his other speeches.

27. Since these would be its first projects, the Port Authority concluded that they should be awarded to "an engineer of long established reputation." This was the explanation given to Ammann by the Port Authority's chief engineer (correspondence, Ammann to Silzer, April 17, 1925). The job of designing what are now the Goethals and Outerbridge crossings went to Waddell & Hardesty, a firm led by the prominent engineer J. A. L. Waddell.

28. It is worth noting that the Port Authority's discussions of the role of these new vehicular bridges, as set forth in its reports in 1924–1926, lack the kind of broad framing found in Ammann's reports (for example, in his 1924 speech quoted above). To the Port agency in those years, these new bridges were needed as "highways . . . for trade and commerce and the passage of people to and fro"; legislation was passed, and the Authority would undertake the task. Discussion of the broad transportation and economic-development needs of the New York region are explored with enthusiasm in its reports, but linked to the great rail projects of the Comprehensive Plan, not to the Hudson and Staten Island motor bridges. See, for example, the Port Authority's *Annual Report* (January 15, 1926), pp. 13–20, 40–41; quotation is on p. 13.

The broader question touched upon here is whether the Port Authority abandoned its early rail plans too readily, tossing them aside as soon as lucrative vehicular projects were within its grasp. Bard's careful analysis leads him to conclude that the Port agency fought hard to persuade the railroads to implement the plan, but that by 1926, finding failure there, it began to shift its primary interest to bridge building; even then, it pressed forward with a railroad-freight terminal in Manhattan, an important element of the plan, and put it into operation in 1932. Bard, *Port of New York Authority*, pp. 114–122, 185.

On this issue, Carl Condit's views are more disparaging; arguing that the Comprehensive Plan was potentially of great benefit, he concludes that the Port Authority's leaders "quickly lost interest in the railroads and turned to the construction of transharbor arteries for automotive vehicles, which offered an immediate, abundant, and ever increasing revenue from tunnel and bridge tolls" (Carl W. Condit, *The Port of New York* [Chicago: University of Chicago Press, 1981], p. 131). However, Condit does not discuss the evidence in Bard's volume or in other sources, and he provides no evidence to support his views on the motivations of Port agency officials.

My own conclusion, based on review of the documents and interviews with several men who joined the agency between 1931 and 1936, is that its leaders continued to view the railroad-freight plan as the more important task for the Port Authority throughout the 1920s, although their optimism about the possibility of carrying it out in the near future dwindled in 1926 and beyond. (See Doig, *Empire on the Hudson*, Chapter 4, pp. 29–62.) From this perspective, the narrow treatment of the bridges in the Port Authority's annual reports in the mid-1920s, compared with Ammann's broad exploration of regional dynamics, may be understandable.

29. Franklin D. Roosevelt, governor of New York State, address delivered at the dedication of the George Washington Bridge, October 24, 1931.

30. Under Ammann's supervision, the Port Authority had also completed three smaller spans between Staten Island and New Jersey—the Goethals and Outerbridge, opened in 1928, and the Bayonne, finished in 1931. The efficient completion of these three projects added to the reputation of the agency and its bridge engineer. Ammann also won an award for the Bayonne Bridge, which was the longest arch bridge in the world.

31. See Bard, *Port of New York Authority*, pp. 187–188.

32. See Bard, *Port of New York Authority*, pp. 188–193, and Doig, *Empire on the Hudson*, Chapter 5.

33. When the Staten Island bridges were begun in the mid-1920s, the Port Authority's planners expected that they would provide an efficient bypass from central New Jersey to the Holland Tunnel (via rural Staten Island roads, avoiding the congested Elizabeth-Newark area). However, by 1932 New Jersey had constructed the toll-free Pulaski Skyway and an expanded network of highways that tapped central New Jersey. The Staten Island bypass was no longer attractive from most points, and with the onset of the Depression, traffic counts fell below a break-even point. (See Bard, *Port of New York Authority*, pp. 206–208.)

34. In 1931, the two states authorized the Port Authority to begin the Lincoln Tunnel. The bond market collapsed before bonds were issued for the project, and the agency then appealed in 1933 for federal funds. The Public Works Administration rejected the plan to finance a two-tube tunnel but agreed in September 1933 to loan funds for a single tube. Under Ammann's direction, the first tube of the Lincoln was opened in December 1937. (Bard later recalled traveling in Manhattan in the mid-1930s and hearing the sounds of construction for the Lincoln, which "seemed to be the only construction going on in the City" in those years; interview, September 1984.) The second tube was not completed until 1945.

35. See Chapter 5 by Robert Fishman in this volume.

36. See J. W. Doig, "Regional Conflict in the New York Metropolis: the Legend of Robert Moses and the Power of the Port Authority," *Urban Studies*, 27 (April 1990): 209–219.

37. Of course, the Port Authority's capacity to go forward with the George Washington Bridge and the later projects also depended on decisions made at the Authority's creation, especially the open-ended mandate provided by the compact, and the agency's power to float bonds to finance its projects.

38. Some of these efforts as well as the projects that the Port Authority avoided—especially its failure to rescue the region's commuter rail lines as they headed toward bankruptcy in the 1950s—generated much criticism as well as applause. See, for example, Annmarie H. Walsh, *The*

Public's Business: The Politics and Practices of Government Corpora-tions (Cambridge: MIT Press, 1978), Chapters 4, 7, 8, and passim; Michael N. Danielson and Jameson W. Doig, *New York: The Politics of Urban Regional Development* (Berkeley: University of California Press, 1982), Chapters 4–7 and 10.

39. FDR's proposed Tennessee Valley Authority would be headed by a three-person board of directors and would be a "corporation clothed with the power of government but possessed of the flexibility and initiative of private enterprise"; it would be charged with "the broadest duty of plan-ning for the proper use, conservation, and development" of the Valley (Franklin D. Roosevelt, message to Congress, March 1933).

40. As did the plans for public authorities that were created in Australia, Thailand, Israel, and other nations during the decades after World War II. On the various impacts of the Port Authority summarized in the text, see Walsh, *The Public's Business*, p. 27 and passim, and Jameson W. Doig, " 'If I See a Murderous Fellow Sharpening a Knife Cleverly . . .': the Wilsonian Dichotomy and the Public Authority Tradition," *Public Administration Review* 43 (July/August 1983): 292–304.

41. Moses also borrowed the services of Ammann from the Port Authority. On loan to Moses' Triborough Bridge and Tunnel Authority during the 1930s, Ammann designed the Bronx Whitestone Bridge and supervised construction of that span and the Triborough Bridge. He then retired from the Port Authority in 1939 and established a private consulting firm. In the 1950s he returned as consultant to the Port and Triborough agencies, designing the second deck of the George Washington Bridge, the Throgs Neck span over the upper East River, and the Verrazano-Narrows Bridge, which was completed in 1964, a year before his death.

   In his massive and persuasive biography of Moses, *The Power Broker* (New York: Knopf, 1974), Robert A. Caro discusses the strategies used by Robert Moses in making use of the public authority model. Caro does not, I think, sufficiently credit the impact that the Port Authority's activities in its first dozen years had on Moses' thinking.

42. See Robert C. Wood, *1400 Governments: The Political Economy of the New York Metropolitan Region* (Cambridge: Harvard University Press, 1961), pp. 123–144, and Jameson W. Doig, *Metropolitan Transportation Politics and the New York Region* (New York: Columbia University Press, 1966), Chapter 2.

43. Thus the Regional Plan leaders, addressing the issue of vehicular projects in the region, said in 1923:

   "There can be no questioning the urgency of the need for more bridges and tunnels across the Hudson. . . . The prosperity of five counties in New Jersey should be immensely promoted, and their prosperity should react more helpfully on Manhattan Island—and also on the Bronx, lower Westchester County, and Queens County—if the improvement of circu-lation across the river is combined with the comprehensive planning of the undeveloped areas in New Jersey that would thereby be brought into close and direct physical connection with Manhattan." (Testimony of Thomas Adams, speaking also for F. A. Delano and Nelson Lewis, at the Port of New York Authority's hearing on future vehicular crossings of the Hudson River [December 5, 1923]; the first sentence quoted above refers to both vehicular and rail projects, the second only to vehicular crossings.)

The Regional Plan position in 1927 is also positive: "The motor vehicle has become the chief factor in highway traffic and a main essential of all plans for the future must be to make adequate provision for the growth of this form of transportation." Regional Plan of New York and Its Environs, *Regional Survey*, vol. III, *Highway Traffic* (1927), p. 38.

These views were consistent with the national attitude: "The rapid rise in motor-vehicle registrations created a booming optimism, a national faith in technological progress" (Kenneth T. Jackson, *Crabgrass Frontier* [New York: Oxford University Press, 1985], p. 162, commenting particularly on the 1920s).

44. Even before the Canal Street tunnel opened in 1927, it was clear that additional vehicular traffic at this point would exacerbate traffic congestion in lower Manhattan that was already nearly intolerable. The 179th Street bridge would divert some of the growing stream; and to traffic planners of that era, the next step would be to deconcentrate Manhattan-bound traffic further with tunnels at 40th Street and perhaps at 110th Street, allowing trucks and autos to enter the Island close to their destinations and then move efficiently to parking and off-loading areas.

45. As Ammann commented soon after the span was completed: "There can be little doubt . . . that with the growing up of a large population contiguous to the bridge the more efficient and economical transportation of people by electric rail service will become a necessity" O. H. Ammann, "George Washington Bridge: General Conception and Development of Design," in American Society of Civil Engineers, *Transactions*: 97 (1933), 21.

46. Its freight rail efforts are discussed earlier in this essay; its passenger rail studies are summarized in Bard, *Port of New York Authority*, pp. 128–132. The Port Authority's activities on rail transit continued despite the opposition of Al Smith, who as governor opposed the Port Authority's involvement. The agency's commissioners argued, in defense of their continued efforts, that the Port compact gave the bi-state unit jurisdiction over all means of transportation, and that "no adequate or effective interstate transportation development" could take place without taking "full account of passengers as well as freight . . ." Port Authority, resolution adopted June 11, 1928, as quoted in its *Annual Report* (February 1929), pp. 64–66.

5

The Regional Plan
and the Transformation
of the Industrial Metropolis

Robert Fishman

In ten weighty volumes of maps, surveys, statistics, detailed architectural drawings, and earnest prose, the Regional Plan of New York and its Environs (1929–1931) presented itself to the world as the sober product of practical economics, rigorous social science, and disciplined planning theory.[1] Funded by more than a million 1920s dollars from the Russell Sage Foundation, the plan remains the most thorough and ambitious single project in the history of American planning. Yet, at the heart of this massive effort was a vision of an ideal twentieth century metropolis that was as much an "urban utopia" as the contemporary plans of Frank Lloyd Wright and Le Corbusier.[2]

The future that the plan proposed for the New York region in the years from 1929 to 1965 was summed up in the word "recentralization." In the 1960s as in the 1920s, Manhattan would remain the region's vital center. Easily accessible by an upgraded and expanded mass transit system from even the remotest corners of the "environs," Manhattan's centrality as the nation's financial, corporate, and cultural capital would be enhanced by purging the island of its slums, industrial sites, and other "inappropriate uses." The ground thus gained would be used for art deco towers and luxury apartment blocks. Manhattan would be rebuilt as the world's ultimate "downtown."

At the same time, the planners were convinced that the New York region's economic well-being rested ultimately on maintaining its status as the nation's premier industrial region. As Thomas Adams, general director of the plan, expressed it:

> The leading forces that create great cities have been seen to be their industries and means of communication. The efficiency of industry and of the transportation that ministers to it, lies at the root of prosperity in the city. All else is secondary from an economic point of view.[3]

In eight wonderfully detailed volumes of the *Regional Survey*, the planners studied specific industries and their needs. They concluded that the region's industrial health could be sustained only by a massive and coordinated effort to improve the infrastructure in what was termed the "industrial zone," that is, the outer boroughs and New Jersey within a twenty-mile radius of lower Manhattan.

In precisely those industrial/working-class areas that would in fact by 1965 become tragic loci of decay and deindustrialization, the plan called for massive investments in new rail and mass transit lines, highways, and shipping piers. The industrial zone would thus enjoy the most efficient and best-coordinated rail and shipping network in the world, a network specifically adapted to the needs of small manufacturers that the plan regarded as the key to the region's prosperity. Manufacturing would be encouraged to relocate to the industrial zone from congested areas in Manhattan—in 1922, as the planners learned, more than 420,000 workers were still employed in factories located in Manhattan south of Fifty-ninth Street[4]—and in these new locations industry would be freed from Manhattan's congestion while enjoying even better access to the region's wealth of labor and markets. The plan thus envisioned the gentrification of Manhattan and the reindustrialization of the region as a single coordinated project.

Population in the twenty-two counties in three states, which the plan defined as "New York and its environs," was predicted to double from 10 million people in 1929 to 21 million in 1965. (In fact the region's population in 1965 was 17.4 million.) Nevertheless, sprawl would be discouraged by mass transit facilities that would keep not only workers' housing but also most middle-class housing within the core and industrial zone. Beyond the twenty-mile radius of the industrial zone, land not previously developed was mostly reserved for agriculture, private estates, or recreational facilities. Even after population had exceeded 20 million, three-quarters of the region's 5,500 square miles would be preserved as undeveloped farm or park land.[5]

The Regional Plan was the last embodiment of a specter that had been haunting American reformers since the 1890s: the progressive city. The plan's most profound influence was its detailed embodiment of a metropolitan landscape where, in Walter Lippmann's terminology,

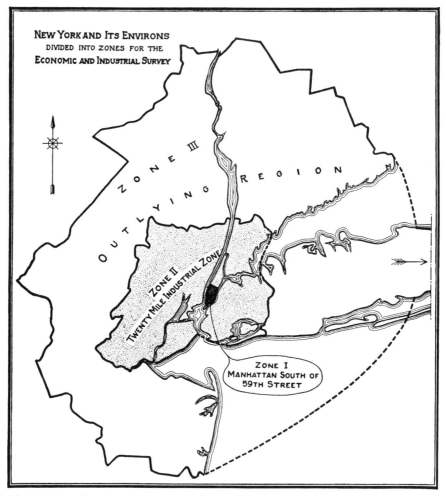

NEW YORK AND ITS ENVIRONS
DIVIDED INTO ZONES FOR THE
ECONOMIC AND INDUSTRIAL SURVEY

ZONE III

OUTLYING REGION

ZONE II
TWENTY MILE INDUSTRIAL ZONE

ZONE I
MANHATTAN SOUTH OF
59TH STREET

Figure 5.1 The Three Zones. *Source:* The Regional Survey. vol. 1, "Major Economic Factors."

"mastery" had replaced "drift." By uniting the region's technical, financial, and philanthropic elite around a set of detailed proposals, the plan would constitute the equivalent of a regional government. The plan was thus addressed to those who had taken up Lippmann's challenge to transcend localism and to devise "administrative methods whereby the great resources of the country can be operated by some thought-out plan."[6]

Indeed, so many of the plan's proposals were later built by Robert Moses or by the Port Authority that some scholars have suggested that these titans were in fact merely carrying out the plan's purposes. In this view the plan and its backers constituted New York's original "growth coalition" that has guided the region's development since the 1920s.[7] This interpretation, however, overlooks the fundamental divergence between the plan's overall program for the region (especially its careful balance between rail and auto transportation) and the aims of those who selectively adopted some of its recommendations in a very different context.

For example, the Regional Plan Association (the successor group to the Committee on the Regional Plan) has recently taken credit for its 1920s advocacy of a Narrows crossing between Staten Island and Brooklyn, a crossing that was finally achieved in 1964 by Robert Moses' Triborough Bridge Authority and the Port Authority as the Verrazano-Narrows Bridge. But the plan's original proposal was for a freight-rail subway tunnel that would be a key link in an ambitious program to revitalize both rail and mass transit in the region.[8] The Verrazano-Narrows Bridge, when built, served automobile and truck traffic only, and facilities for a subway link were carefully and consciously excluded.[9]

This points to a fundamental paradox in the plan's influence. The "landscape of modernity" that the plan proposed was still organized around a vision of a tightly centralized industrial metropolis based on rail transportation. Nevertheless, the specific proposals that were actually implemented were almost all highway projects, usually magnified in scale and purged of their rail and mass transit components. This selective implementation promoted an automobile-based suburbanization, and helped to create the conditions for the neglect and abandonment of the "industrial zone."

In the 1920s, the plan had indeed united a remarkably broad coalition of business leaders, politicians, and philanthropists around a detailed program for New York's future as a rail-based centralized industrial metropolis. Such people are usually regarded as powerful. Why then did the region develop along quite different lines, and what does this tell us about the real forces that created New York's "landscape of modernity"?

Like every vision that looks to the future, the Regional Plan had its roots firmly planted in the conditions and concerns of the recent past. It can trace its lineage back directly to the *locus classicus* of progressive city planning: Daniel H. Burnham and his protégé Edward H. Bennett's "Plan of Chicago" (1909).[10] Charles Dyer Norton, the inspiration and driving force behind the New York plan, had begun his business career in Chicago. As president first of the Merchant's Club and then the Commercial Club of Chicago, he had been instrumental in persuading Burnham to undertake the project and had also been invaluable in raising money to finance it through contributions from the city's business elite. Although the New York plan eventually "out-Burnhamed Burnham" in its scale and ambition, the Chicago plan set the ideological parameters within which the New Yorkers later functioned.[11]

Burnham understood that the modern centralized city required massive coordination to achieve an efficient infrastructure and to create the boulevards and the great urban monuments he believed a great metropolis required. With Haussmann's Paris as his inspiration, Burnham in effect posed the question: How to achieve a Haussmann-like control over the great city and its hinterland without a prefect of Chicago? And without an authoritarian state to back up the prefect?

Burnham's answer was to create, outside of all political or corporate frameworks, a comprehensive plan that would spell out all the necessary forms of coordination and investment for the region. This plan would then gain the general support of the urban business elite. Through them it would be publicized and praised in newspapers; its images would become familiar to citizens; it would even be taught in the schools. A general consensus, achieved outside the usual political channels, would mold the actions both of elected politicians and of corporate leaders. In this way the design would set the agenda for massive, harmonious rebuilding. The plan itself would be the substitute for the absent prefect. This, for Burnham, was "Democracy."[12]

Charles Dyer Norton brought Burnham's vision to New York when, after service in the Taft administration, Norton was called to Wall Street in 1911 to be vice-president (and later president) of the First National City Bank. In early 1914, reform Mayor John Purroy Mitchel appointed Norton a member of the "Advisory Committee on City Plan," formed to continue the work of the Heights of Buildings Commission, whose 1913 recommendations would result in the pioneering zoning resolution of 1916. The Heights of Buildings Commission had concluded that specific problems raised by influential business groups—most notably the Fifth Avenue merchants' complaints about the "invasion" of their elite shopping street by garment workers' lofts—could be solved only by citywide zoning districts and a citywide plan. Norton, in Burnham's spirit, came to see that even the best New York City zoning plan could not deal adequately with issues of population and industrial distribution that necessarily touched the whole region.[13]

As an outsider to the complex mosaic of New York politics, Norton turned instinctively to a Burnham-style regional plan that would transcend all local political boundaries, address fundamental concerns of urban form, and set the agenda for reordering the world's largest and richest metropolitan region.

> From City Hall a circle must be swung which will include the Atlantic Highlands and Princeton; the lovely Jersey Hills back of Morristown and Tuxedo; the incomparable Hudson as far as Newburgh; the Westchester lakes and ridges, to Bridgeport and beyond, and all of Long Island.[14]

He concluded, "Let some Daniel H. Burnham do for this immense community what Burnham did for Chicago and its environs. . . ."[15] But, as Norton soon realized, the New York elite was far too fragmented for there to be an equivalent of the Commercial Club of Chicago, and the planning itself was already too professionalized for there to be the equivalent of a Daniel Burnham.[16] Norton turned from business clubs to prestigious foundations as a source of funding, and began to assemble an authoritative team of experts to substitute for the authority of a charismatic individual. The Russell Sage Foundation, already known for underwriting the Pittsburgh social survey (1907) and for building the model community of Forest Hills Gardens in Queens (1911), agreed in 1921 to fund the project.[17]

After Norton died in 1923, his position as chairman was filled by his old Chicago colleague Frederic Delano, a consulting engineer, Federal Reserve Board commissioner, and former railway executive. A team of social scientists under the direction of Columbia economist Robert Haig was ready to begin an elaborate social and economic survey of the New York region on which the plan was to be based. Meanwhile, a distinguished group of planners, which included Harlan Bartholomew, Edward H. Bennett, George B. Ford, John Nolen, and Frederick Law Olmsted, Jr., was already formulating proposals for various parts of the region. Overall coordination was in the hands of Thomas Adams, once an enthusiastic disciple of Ebenezer Howard and the Garden City movement and now a bland proponent of "practical," business-oriented planning.[18]

The plan began from the same problem which had concerned the members of the "Advisory Committee on City Plan": how to free Manhattan from "inappropriate" industrial uses, while retaining for the region the vitality of Manhattan's industrial base. As the plan's economists soon realized, New York's prosperity depended not on large mass-production industries or on corporate or financial employers but on the multitude of small businesses who derived unique advantages from the very congestion of the region:

> . . . the area is the paradise of the small manufacturer. The average
> number of employees per factory in the United States is 43, here it
> is a little over two-thirds of that number. In many lines of industry
> a small firm may conduct a national business without the owner
> traveling more than a few blocks in any direction. Supplies, related
> industries, financing, space in lofts or old buildings, labor at the door,
> styles or ideas, all in the very locality, and buyers who come regu-
> larly from all over the country at not distant hotels, all make it
> possible for the small fellow to exist.[19]

These small manufacturers, however, were forced to pay high rents
for cramped space in congested streets in the older manufacturing districts or move to the outskirts where access to wholesale markets,
transportation, and labor was slow and uncertain. Under these circumstances many manufacturers were tempted to leave the region entirely.

The Regional Plan's answer to this dilemma was termed, in one of
Thomas Adams' characteristically woolly phrases, "diffused recentralization."[20] This meant a coordinated effort to "diffuse" manufacturing out of Manhattan and then to recentralize it in specially
planned districts in Brooklyn, Queens, the Bronx, and New Jersey.
Although these districts would be miles rather than blocks away from
Manhattan's wholesale markets, the rail links to Manhattan would be
so efficient that little convenience would be lost. Moreover, the new
districts would have room for expansion, and far better freight connections to national and world markets. With improved mass transit,
employees from throughout the region could reach their jobs more
quickly than before.

The key to this scheme was rail transportation. The plan was fortunate to find a visionary engineer whose ideas exactly met their needs.
This was William J. Wilgus, best known as the engineer who created
the city's masterpiece of railroad engineering, the Grand Central Terminal.[21] Wilgus possessed not only the progressive zeal for order and
efficiency, but also a superb technical understanding of how a coordinated system of electrically driven rail transportation could unify a
vast centralized region. The same imagination he applied to creating
the intricate multilayered structure of Grand Central he now applied
on a regional scale. If the plan represents an alternative future for New
York, then William Wilgus was surely its alternative Robert Moses.

As early as 1908 Wilgus had begun to concern himself with the
rationalizing of the region's freight network. The great port which had

given birth to the city was now proving to be an even greater barrier to the region's communications. Almost all freight entering or leaving the region had to be unloaded at least once at chaotic docks, put aboard car ferries or lighters, floated across the congested waters of the harbor and then unloaded again at one of the terminals of the twelve trunk-line railroads that served the region. The terminals on the New Jersey side of the Hudson were a nightmare of chaos, congestion, and delay; those on the Manhattan side were worse. During World War I, the system virtually collapsed, crippling the whole American war effort.

The particular genius of Wilgus' plan was to transform a seemingly intractable situation into so logical and well-organized a transportation system that it not only solved the problems of freight congestion but also gave tremendous advantages to manufacturing within the region. Wilgus proposed two concentric rail beltways around the region. An "Outer Belt Line" would cut congestion by enabling freight bound for outside the region to bypass the core; a complex "Inner Belt Line" requiring new bridges and tunnels would carry rail freight efficiently around the heart of the region without the need for cross-harbor flotations. The inner loop, moreover, would be operated cooperatively by all the railroads that would direct freight along the most cost-effective routes, not the ones that gave them the maximum profit. As a good progressive, Wilgus believed that a more efficient and rational system would serve the best interests of both the railroads and the region as a whole.[22]

In the Regional Plan the "industrial zone" is defined by the inner belt line, especially by those areas where rail transportation could be coordinated with piers for ocean-going shipping. The zone includes both manufacturing sites and separate-but-adjacent residential districts, because the planners assumed that most working-class and lower-middle-class families would continue to live in relatively high densities close to their work. The plan envisioned small manufacturers clustering in the Bronx, Queens, and Brooklyn. Large-scale industry would favor New Jersey with its more direct access to the rest of the country. The plan proposed a grandiose "industrial city" for the Hackensack Meadowlands which would combine expansive sites for large plants with all the advantages of a site only five miles from midtown Manhattan.[23]

Wilgus, moreover, did not neglect rapid transit for people. Once again he cut through the welter of competing private companies and public authorities by advocating a single public authority to operate all rapid transit in the region. Operations would be financed not only by fares but also by property taxes and general tax revenues. Commuter trains and subways would share the new facilities of the inner

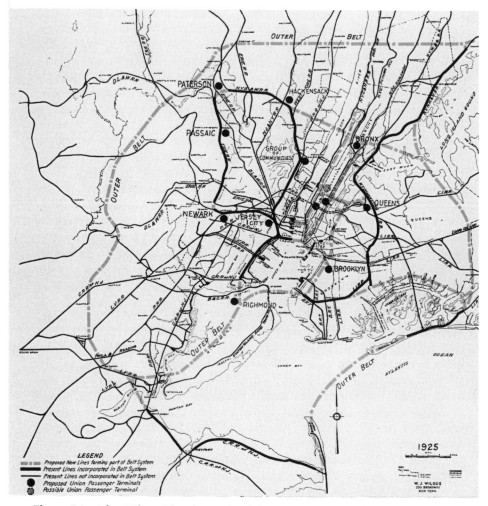

Figure 5.2 The Wilgus Plan for Rail Beltways. *Source:* The Regional Survey, vol. 4, "Transit and Transportation."

and outer belts, and new branch lines would be built to handle the region's expanding population. The system would not only bring workers to their jobs in the industrial zone but would also vastly improve service into Manhattan.

Such improvements would be vitally necessary, for the plan foresaw Manhattan not only retaining but augmenting as well its cultural and commercial dominance over the rest of the region. The plan was conceived when Manhattan was at its peak as the office, shopping, entertainment, and even manufacturing center for the region. A survey taken in 1924 found that 2.2 million people entered Manhattan on a typical business day—23 percent of the population of the whole region. When, on such a typical day, one combined those residing in Manhattan south of Fifty-ninth Street with those who worked or visited there, the total came to 2.9 million people, or 30 percent of the region's total population.[24] These staggering numbers included points of especially intense congestion, such as the 175,000 people who worked in the garment center,[25] or the 44 legitimate theaters with 56,000 seats located within a 1,000-foot radius of the corner of Broadway and Forty-second Street.[26]

Far from challenging this degree of concentration, the plan argued that such numbers would at least double by 1965 as the population of the region doubled. They believed that office and other service employment would more than compensate for lost manufacturing jobs, and they tried to ensure that Manhattan would maintain its supremacy as the retailing and entertainment center for the region. By 1965, they predicted, 4.5 million people would enter Manhattan each business day and 7 million residents, commuters, and visitors would be found each workday between the Battery and Fifty-ninth Street.[27]

Wilgus' mass transit system was specifically designed to handle such unprecedented crowds. Commuter trains or subways would travel on all the new links of the inner and outer belt lines as well as on many other new branch lines. For example, the rail tunnel from Hoboken to Fifty-ninth Street in Manhattan would also carry commuters to a new passenger terminal on Fifty-ninth Street. Within Manhattan, the elevated lines would be replaced by new subway lines, and these lines would carry not only subway traffic but also suburban trains to deliver commuters as close as possible to their destinations.[28]

To save Manhattan from self-suffocation, the planners argued that skyscrapers should not be allowed to cluster together as they had in the financial district or midtown, but must be spaced out at regular intervals to prevent crowds from overwhelming the facilities at any given point. More imaginatively, they proposed to separate pedestrians and shops from street traffic by a network of second-story arcades—skyways, in current terminology. While pedestrians moved unimpeded above, crosstown streets would tunnel under north-south avenues, permitting a continuous traffic flow. Taxis or trucks wishing to unload would pull into parking areas under the arcades, allowing traffic to flow unimpeded.[29] Meanwhile, as the garment lofts, the kosher slaughter houses, and other "inappropriate" uses left the island to be replaced by financial and corporate services, Manhattan would emerge as the world's ultimate downtown, a region of modern office towers and luxury apartments for the elite, and a mecca of shopping and entertainment to draw the masses from around the region.

In contrast to these massive development plans for both the core and the inner industrial zone, the planners were most concerned in the outer zone to maintain the quiet and open space that was already there. The plan was deeply hostile to any "mass suburbanization" that might have lured the working and lower middle classes from their "natural" position in the industrial zone. The plan's section on housing is filled with accounts of failed "premature" subdivisions that attempted that strategy. The planners were especially concerned about subdivisions that "invaded" territory they had reserved for upper-class estates. Thomas Adams distinguished sharply between "the erection of houses for well-to-do people on plots of an acre or more"—this he regarded as "a most desirable form of development"—and "the subdivision of country estates into small lots for the erection of small houses. . . ." The latter was "unwholesome and uneconomic" because it led to "wasteful and disorderly spreading of houses, [which] is one of the primary causes of the worst evils of city growth."[30] Thus, each of the three zones in the plan would retain its distinct identity: the still rural quiet of the outer zone; the productive bustle of the inner industrial zone; and, in the core, a sleek art deco wonderland.

We must now resist the temptation to linger further on the details of the plan and attempt instead to deal with its fate—that is, with the powers that really determined the future of the region. Although the plan certainly called for large expenditures, one cannot doubt its practicality on those grounds alone. By 1965 the region had expended far greater sums on other goals. Nor could the planners be accused of harboring impractical social goals. Indeed, they were so close to the views of business leaders that Lewis Mumford could charge that the plan was

conceived first of all in terms which would meet the interests and prejudices of the existing financial rulers: indeed . . . its aim, from the beginning, was as much human welfare and amenity as could be

Figure 5.3 The Sleek Art Deco Wonderland: The Proposed Chrystie-Forsyth Parkway for a Rebuilt Lower East Side. *Source:* Regional Plan, vol. 2, "Building the City."

obtained without altering any of the political and business institutions which have made the city precisely what it is.[31]

Mumford was certainly right that the makers of the plan were more than willing to allow an elite consensus to substitute for democratic decision making. But he and the makers of the Regional Plan were both mistaken to believe that any such consensus existed. Ironically, the crucial opposition to the plan would come not from parochial political bosses or "the masses" but from among the "financial rulers" who refused to play their part in the civic harmony the plan proposed. As we shall see, the railroads had perhaps the most to gain in the long run from implementation of the plan, yet they used their veto powers to block its progress. At the same time, other "financial rulers" deeply involved in suburban land speculation and home financing sought to profit from developments that profoundly altered "the political and business institutions which have made the city precisely what it is."

The plan's reception revealed the limitations of "the Burnham Method" for controlling regional development, and with it the weaknesses in progressive thought of the late 1920s. Its proponents saw so clearly the vital need for order and coordination, but their reliance on elite consensus and the authority of social science left them with no real power to discipline those organizations who through greed or inertia were "out of control." There is an element of pathos in Wilgus' declaration that

> In some way the diverse elements in our midst, comprising as they do twelve trunk lines, three major and several minor traction systems, a variety of trucking interests, many water carriers, four hundred organized communities, three states and the nation, must be brought into harmony for the common purpose. Self-preservation demands it.[32]

The inability of the Regional Plan to pursue "the common purpose" was mirrored at the national level where Herbert Hoover's hopes to harmonize the national economy through the voluntary actions of trade associations would lead to a far worse case of disorder. The future lay with those more willing and able to grasp directly the levers of state power.[33]

The real test of the Regional Plan came in the attempts to implement the restructuring of the rail network. Not only was this restructuring a necessity if recentralization were to succeed, but success would provide a vital example of regional cooperation. Despite the difficulty of the task, the planners were in a strong position because their efforts were being advanced by an agency that not only shared the plan's progressive agenda but also possessed real governmental powers, the Port of New York Authority.[34] Unfortunately, a plan for railroad reorganization required the cooperation of the region's railroads. The twelve trunk-line railroads achieved a rare level of agreement through their concerted refusal to cooperate with the Port Authority. Their opposition effectively vetoed not only the inner loop but also the whole revitalization of transportation for the inner zone that Wilgus and the Regional Plan sought. As Wilgus had feared, the habits of competition through exclusive use of terminal facilities outweighed for the railroads all the benefits of a rational plan.[35]

Unable to overcome the railroads' opposition, the Port Authority in the mid-1920s made a crucial decision to abandon its initial rail orientation and to concentrate on providing bridges and tunnels for automobiles. The Port Authority's projects, moreover, were only one part of an uncoordinated but ultimately revolutionary program of road and bridge building undertaken by the highway departments of the three states and by other special authorities, most notably Robert Moses' Triborough Bridge Authority. The result was a massive tilt toward the automobile and the truck in the regional transportation system.

Ironically, one source for major highway projects was the Regional Plan itself, which had undertaken as part of its work to identify major traffic bottlenecks and to compile proposals for new roads for the region. Perhaps most importantly, the plan through its "Graphic Survey" maps propagated the ideal of a coordinated, comprehensive regional highway network. Nevertheless, this highway network was always intended to be subordinate to a centralized rail system that would continue to define the region. The plan's highway emphasis fell on creating a "metropolitan loop highway" that would for most of its length run adjacent to Wilgus' rail loop, a telling indication that the planners still saw highways as subordinate to rails. Many roads later built as superhighways appear on the plan's maps as boulevards or as joint highway/rail facilities. For example, the plan advocated the 178th Street (George Washington) Bridge both as a highway connection and—on a separate rail deck—as a link in the inner rail belt to carry both passengers and freight.[36]

The authors of the plan saw only dimly the impetus that the automobile would give toward decentralization. We can now perceive clearly that whereas rail systems favor locations close to the regional hub where rail lines converge—that is, the plan's industrial zone— highways turn previously inconvenient areas in the "outlying region" into better sites than the congested core. As the case of New York illustrates, this fateful shift from rail to highway was not a case of

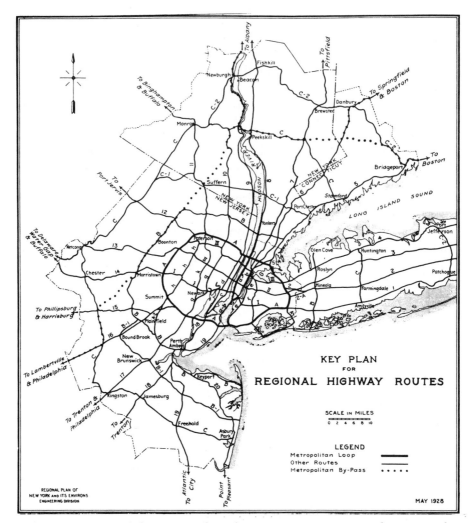

Figure 5.4 Proposal for Regional Highway Routes. *Source:* The Regional Plan, vol. 1, "The Graphic Regional Plan."

an outmoded technology being replaced by a more efficient, modern technology. Wilgus' plan demonstrates that rail technology had potential at least as great as the innovations that created the superhighways.

The great strength of the highway system was that where the rail system was controlled by private corporations whose structure and ethos were inherited from the nineteenth century, roads were constructed under newly organized public or quasi-public authorities. The former could draw directly on the public purse; the latter could act entrepreneurially to combine public funds with private loans. Under a buccaneer like Robert Moses or a powerful bureaucracy like the Port Authority, the quasi-public agency secured virtual freedom from public control. Highway technology was thus pushed to its limits, while the possibilities for rail transportation remained unfulfilled.

The great weakness of the rail system was its bondage to increasingly sclerotic organizations that felt neither the necessity nor the promise of breaking ingrained patterns of competitive behavior to act cooperatively. They and the public mass transit agencies were incapable of the level of urbanistic thinking displayed in the Wilgus plan. Ironically, the harmony that Wilgus sought was finally found only in the "grave" of a universal bankruptcy that saw all of the region's freight railroads merged into Conrail in the 1970s. By then the inner industrial zone was in ruins. Thus, the railroads slowly strangled the centralized industrial metropolis as unconsciously as they had created it.

If the failure of the rail network was the Regional Plan's first great miscalculation, the second was surely the plan's belief that most residents would be content to live in high-density neighborhoods close to their work. The planners' class bias is evident here, but so is their misunderstanding of the economics of suburbanization. Despite their elaborate surveys, they completely failed to appreciate the depth and breadth of the appeal of the single family suburban house. More importantly, they failed to understand the powerful forces that had assembled to make this aspiration a reality.

The twenties, the decade of the Regional Plan, also saw a crucial shift in the resources of large financial institutions toward home mortgages. As industrial corporations began to finance their own operations through retained earnings, the banking system sought new customers for its funds among lot and home purchasers. The suburban developer functioned as a kind of middleman for the banks, arranging for mortgages for his customers which he immediately sold at a discount to large institutions. These mortgages were still the short-term balloon mortgages or high-interest second mortgages whose inadequacy led directly to disaster during the Great Depression. Nevertheless, the twenties opened that crucial pipeline between "the financial rulers" and the individual homebuyer that would fuel the suburban housing revolution.[37]

The collapse of the homebuilding industry in the 1930s offered a brief, tantalizing hope that the future might match the Regional Plan. As Gail Radford has shown, housing reformers within the New Deal sought to direct capital away from suburban housing and the private mortgage market toward nonprofit or limited-profit corporations that would build cooperative rental housing either in blighted areas within the cities or in New Towns safely beyond them.[38] Such a shift would have favored the goals of the Regional Plan; indeed, the plan published in 1933 a slim volume on *The Rebuilding of Blighted Areas* with detailed plans for extensive new construction throughout the industrial zone.[39] Despite these hopes, the New Deal followed its usual course of propping up and rationalizing the failed structures of the 1920s. The National Housing Act of 1934 set up the Federal Housing Administration and a network of savings-and-loan institutions that could draw mortgage money both from small savers and from large institutions. A far more reliable pipeline was now in place to advance the building of suburban homes and the decentralization of the urban population.[40]

In this context, we can now appreciate the irony of the famous controversy in 1932 between Lewis Mumford and Thomas Adams over the Regional Plan. Mumford charged that Adams and the plan had sold out to real estate interests by advocating high population densities (and thus high land values) in the core and industrial zone. But Mumford shared Adams' concern to limit the spread of the metropolis and to maintain the open character of the outer zone. For Mumford (following Raymond Unwin and Adams' old mentor Ebenezer Howard) the solution was first to establish a greenbelt around the built-up areas of the metropolis to stop suburban sprawl, and then to decongest the urban areas by moving people and industry to compact New Towns in the outer zone. These New Towns, for which a prototype existed at Radburn, New Jersey, would be carefully planned and distributed to maintain the area's rural character. In fact, the industrial zone would indeed be decongested, but by a method Mumford opposed as vehemently as Adams: the tide of "spread city" suburbanization that would eventually engulf not only Radburn but so much of the outer zone.[41]

The shift from rail to highway and the revitalization of suburban housing thus each contradicted the basic assumptions of the Regional Plan. Moreover, the two functioned together as strongly interacting forces that together gave momentum to decentralization. Firms were pushed out of the old industrial zone by congestion and deteriorating rail service at the same time that they were drawn to the periphery by cheap land for expansion, by better roads for trucking, and by a work force now itself moving to the suburbs. As more jobs moved, the market for suburban housing was strengthened. The dream of a dense, efficient, prosperous industrial zone as the heart of a recentralized region was lost.

In 1942, the Regional Plan Association published a short report ironically entitled *From Plan to Reality*.[42] Despite the title, this and other reports showed that whereas the region's population had grown 26 percent since 1925, its built-up areas had increased 56 percent. Twelve million people in 1940 occupied almost as large an area as the plan had forecast for a population of twenty-one million in 1965.[43] Moreover, one could see trouble ahead in significant population declines not only for Manhattan but also for such prime industrial zone locations as Jersey City and Newark. David Johnson, the Regional Plan's most thorough and sympathetic historian, concludes that by 1941 the plan was obsolete.[44] One might go further and argue that by 1941 the centralized industrial metropolis was itself obsolete.

Notes

1. For bibliographical details of the *Regional Plan* and *Regional Survey*, see the general bibliography at the back of this volume.
2. For the context of the Regional Plan, see Peter Hall's comprehensive and definitive *Cities of Tomorrow: An Intellectual History of Urban Planning and Design in the Twentieth Century* (Oxford, England: Basil Blackwell, 1988), and my *Urban Utopias in the Twentieth Century: Ebenezer Howard, Frank Lloyd Wright, and Le Corbusier* (New York: Basic Books, 1977).
3. *Regional Survey*, 6:131.
4. *Regional Survey*, 1:10.
5. *Regional Plan*, 1:317. For figures on the region's population, see David A. Johnson, *The Emergence of Metropolitan Regionalism: An Analysis of the Regional Plan of New York and Its Environs.* Ph.D. diss. (Graduate Field of City and Regional Planning, Cornell University, 1974), p. 236.
6. Walter Lippmann, *Drift and Mastery: An Attempt to Diagnose the Current Unrest*, (orig. ed. 1914); new edition with introduction and notes by William E. Leuchtenburg (Englewood Cliffs, NJ: Prentice-Hall, 1961), p. 85.
7. Michael Heiman, *The Quiet Evolution: Power, Planning and Profits in New York State* (New York: Praeger, 1988), and John H. Mollenkopf, *The Contested City* (Princeton, NJ: Princeton University Press, 1983), pp. 71–72.
8. For a discussion of the plan's proposal and the subsequent controversy, see Johnson, *Emergence of Metropolitan Regionalism*, pp. 396–419.
9. Michael N. Danielson and Jameson W. Doig, *New York: The Politics of Regional Development* (Berkeley: University of California Press, 1982), pp. 200–204.
10. Thomas S. Hines, *Burnham of Chicago: Architect and Planner* (New York: Oxford University Press, 1974), Chapter 14.
11. For a profound account of planning theory from Burnham through 1945, see M. Christine Boyer, *Dreaming the Rational City: The Myth of American City Planning* (Cambridge: MIT Press, 1983).
12. Daniel H. Burnham, "A City of the Future Under a Democratic Govern-

ment," *Transactions of the Town-Planning Conference, Royal Institute of British Architects* (October 1910): 369–378.

13. Johnson, *Emergence of Metropolitan Regionalism*, pp. 113–121; for background on New York zoning, see Chapter 2 by Keith Revell and Chapter 3 by Marc Weiss in this volume.

14. Norton memorandum of November 27, 1915, quoted in Johnson, *Emergence of Metropolitan Regionalism*, p. 118.

15. Ibid.

16. For the fragmentation of the elite, see David C. Hammack, *Power and Society: Greater New York at the Turn of the Century* (New York: Russell Sage Foundation, 1982) and for the professionalization of planning, see Boyer, *Dreaming the Rational City*, Chapters 4 and 5.

17. Johnson, *Emergence of Metropolitan Regionalism*, pp. 121–141.

18. Ibid., Chapter 5. For Adams, see Michael Simpson, *Thomas Adams and the Modern Planning Movement: Britain, Canada, and the United States, 1900–1940* (London: Mansell, 1985).

19. *Regional Survey*, 4:188.

20. *Regional Plan*, 1:150.

21. For Wilgus, see especially Josef Konvitz, "William J. Wilgus and Engineering Projects to Improve the Port of New York," *Technology and Culture* 30 (1989): 398–425.

22. *Regional Survey*, 4:171–175. The Wilgus plan is similar in outline to the one advanced in the 1920s by the Port Authority, despite sharp differences over particulars, such as the Narrows Tunnel between Brooklyn and Staten Island that Wilgus supported and which the Port Authority vetoed. More research is necessary to determine who is the true originator of the concept.

23. *Regional Survey*, 4:150–157.

24. *Regional Survey*, 4:36–39.

25. *Regional Survey*, 1B:12.

26. *Regional Survey*, 4:55.

27. Ibid., p. 14.

28. Ibid., pp. 168–169.

29. *Regional Plan*, 2:413–416.

30. *The Graphic Regional Plan*, pp. 387–388.

31. Lewis Mumford, *New Republic* (1932), as reprinted in Carl Sussman, ed., *Planning the Fourth Migration: The Neglected Vision of the Regional Planning Association of America* (Cambridge: MIT Press, 1976), p. 255.

32. *Regional Survey*, 4:176.

33. For Hoover, see Ellis W. Hawley, "Herbert Hoover, the Commerce Secretariat, and the Vision of an 'Associative State,'" *Journal of American History* 61 (1974): 116–140. By contrast, see Mollenkopf, *Contested City*, for an important account of the impact of those who knew how to use the power of the state on the cities.

34. Jameson W. Doig has documented the Port Authority's role in the 1920s in Chapter 4 of this volume and in his "Entrepreneurship in Government: Historical Roots in the Progressive Era." Paper prepared for the Annual Meeting of the American Political Science Association, 1988.

35. Erwin W. Bard, *The Port of New York Authority* (New York: Columbia University Press, 1942), Chapters 1–6. I thank Jameson Doig for permitting me to see the relevant chapters in his forthcoming definitive history

of the Port Authority, *Empire on the Hudson*, that will tell the complete story of the Port Authority and its "railroad plan."

36. *Regional Plan*, 1:200.
37. Leo Grebler et al., *Capital Formation in Residential Real Estate* (Princeton, NJ: Princeton University Press, 1956), Parts A and B.
38. Gail Radford, "Modern Community Housing: New Responses to the Shelter Problem in the 1920s and 1930s." Ph.D. diss. (Department of History, Columbia University, 1989).
39. Clarence Arthur Perry, *The Rebuilding of Blighted Areas* (New York: Regional Plan of New York and Its Environs, 1933).
40. Kenneth T. Jackson, *Crabgrass Frontier: The Suburbanization of the United States* (New York: Oxford, 1985), Chapter 11.
41. Both Mumford's polemic and Adams' response are reprinted in Sussman, *Planning the Fourth Migration*. For Radburn, see Daniel Schaffer, *Garden Cities for America: The Radburn Experience* (Philadelphia: Temple University Press, 1982).
42. Regional Plan Association, *From Plan to Reality: Three* (New York: Regional Plan Association, 1942).
43. Forbes B. Hays, *Community Leadership: The Regional Plan Association of New York* (New York: Columbia University Press, 1965), p. 88.
44. Johnson, *Emergence of Metropolitan Regionalism*, p. 505.

Part III

BUILDING
THE VERTICAL CITY

6

Corporate Identity and the New York Office Building: 1895–1915

Gail Fenske / Deryck Holdsworth

The steel-framed office building dramatically altered the urban character of New York at the end of the nineteenth and the beginning of the twentieth centuries. The dimensional changes it effected in the city's fabric were found in the new verticality of the skyline, visible from afar, but also along important commercial thoroughfares such as Broadway, Wall Street, and Park Row, as large edifices housing the headquarters of major enterprises replaced earlier rows of narrow buildings housing small-scale commercial activity. The swiftness with which the new urban landscape emerged startled observers; its outward appearances, however, were but the final ramifications of the intensive round of economic restructuring responsible for the change.

On one hand, the agents of New York's transformation from a midnineteenth century city, with an extended villagelike character, to a twentieth century skyscraper city were the large-scale commercial enterprises, whose presence was announced by larger and larger business buildings identified with company names. On the other hand, scores of smaller commercial and professional firms, although less readily identifiable on the urban scene, played an equally important role. They were interrelated with the large-scale enterprises through numerous social and economic connections, and their demand for office space close to key sites and key enterprises influenced the shaping of the emerging skyscraper city.

The concentration of business in lower Manhattan can be attributed to the city's dominant position in world trade and finance. In the second half of the nineteenth century, New York functioned as a key link in the Atlantic trade economy, and, as a consequence, became the world's busiest port. Merchant exchanges specializing in commodities such as coal, cotton, oil, iron, and produce, as well as several financial exchanges, helped drive this trading system. Specialized insurance services served the exchange market from adjacent office buildings, many gravitating to William, Nassau, and other streets north of Wall Street. By the end of the nineteenth century, the stocks and bonds that financed the nation's major industrial enterprises were traded in the New York Stock Exchange, and merchant bankers, stockbrokers, and lawyers sought space on or near Wall and Broad streets, where the capital investment market had centralized. New York was also an industrial city in its own right, and as one of the key hubs of ocean freight and national rail systems was in an excellent position to serve an increasingly national wholesale and retail market. For these reasons, the city provided a desirable location for the headquarters, or, at the very least, the sales offices of large-scale commercial enterprises. Business concerns of importance found it imperative that they establish an office in lower Manhattan, to effectively compete for a share of the national or international marketplace.

The skyscraper is typically correlated with the appearance of large-scale enterprise on the American economic scene. The revolution that took place in the work force—the massive influx of white collar labor to implement, manage, process, and record the flow of information and decisions to national and global markets—engendered big buildings with vast accumulations of floor area. This, in turn, supported the networks of communications that characterized modern business life.[1] New York's emergence as a skyscraper city cannot be fully explained, however, unless the agents of change are specifically identified and their requirements for space and image are properly characterized. Requirements for space and image engendered building programs that were more complicated than initially met the eye. Major enterprises that built landmark headquarters, for instance, typically functioned as landlords over the smaller commercial or professional concerns, which already depended on them, directly or indirectly, for economic sustenance. They generally assumed this role, however, only after occupying rental space as tenants in a speculative office building at a key location in lower Manhattan's business district. Developers of speculative building projects, in turn, sought major enterprises as anchor tenants and competed with landmark headquarters for the smaller concerns. Case studies of skyscrapers built by large-scale enterprises primarily for the purpose of image—the American Surety, Singer, Metropolitan Life Insurance, Woolworth, and Bankers Trust companies—as well as examinations of other skyscrapers built primarily for speculative purposes—the Trinity, U.S. Realty, City Investing, Hudson Terminal, and Equitable buildings—show that both helped define critical phases of the transformation of lower Manhattan. Both were enmeshed in the changing morphology of lower Manhattan's business district, whose irregularly shaped parcels and complexities of land ownership often inhibited lateral expansion and made vertical expansion inevitable.

The building programs of the large-scale enterprises that constructed landmark headquarters followed a recurrent scenario. After initially staking out a foothold or an operating base, usually a room or suite of rooms in a large office building in lower Manhattan, the businesses relocated a number of times, usually in response to the need to house a larger staff. Then, once they had garnered the financial clout to undertake their own building projects, they planned head offices. The time at which a decision was made to construct a landmark headquarters varied in each company's history, but generally construction was proposed in sequence with major organizational changes. Changes included internal expansion and departmental reorganization, market dominance or competitive advantage, and enhanced reputation as an "honest" economic institution. Once it decided to build its own head office, the enterprise began to take an active role in reshaping the urban environment. Often, it expanded its head office through a piecemeal construction program, fashioning a landmark image and forging a corporate identity in the process.

A large-scale enterprise's evolving building program generally resulted in increased visibility on the urban scene. Visibility was achieved through the sheer scale and lavishness of construction—ornate and stylistically up-to-date office blocks and conspicuous crested towers stood out from the "standard," typically speculative, steel-framed office building construction—but also through siting the new construction such that it had high exposure to urban crowds. Becoming a highly visible architectural presence in the city marked a critical turning point, for now the enterprise began to exercise some control over its urban surroundings. It exerted this control visually—as a dominant structure in its setting, it radiated its influence outward—as well as demographically, because its building program typically entailed adding office space many times in excess of its own requirements, so that as a landlord, it incited shifts in the social and economic composition of an urban district.

An enterprise's interests in achieving increased visibility with a landmark headquarters and in assuming the role of a landlord over tenants went hand in hand. Such a two-pronged building objective was already evident in some of New York's earliest headquarters for commercial enterprises, including the New York Tribune Building (designed by Richard Morris Hunt and built between 1873 and 1875), which loomed over its four- and five-story surroundings in contemporary views of the city. The top two stories of the New York Tribune Building were occupied by the newspaper, whereas the lower seven stories were rented to tenants.[2] The prototype for the developments that would follow, however, was the American Surety Building (Figure 6.1). The American Surety Company opened its first office at 160 Broadway in 1884. When it required larger quarters, it purchased 100 Broadway in 1892, at the corner of Broadway and Pine, and in 1894 it retained Bruce Price as architect.[3] Price proposed a twenty-story, 303-foot tower that, at the time of its completion in 1895, rose over three times higher than its surroundings, and dominated skyline views.

Price's design departed from earlier designs for tall buildings in a number of ways. It was the first office building in New York to utilize a complete steel frame, and among the first to employ the caisson method of constructing foundations, both of which were necessary for its unprecedented height.[4] Price also emphasized that he had designed the American Surety Building as a "campanile," calling it a new concept in skyscraper design.[5] Campanile meant that the structure was to be seen in the round, from near and distant points in the city, by contrast with earlier office buildings that had been designed with street facades only, and viewed as discrete units in a street wall. Price utilized Renaissance detailing for all four elevations, alternating vertical groups of windows with vertical rusticated strips, so that they resembled fluted pilasters. Price expended considerable effort in creating visual interest on the otherwise flat elevations. Heavy rustication strengthened the tower's corners and vigorously projecting stringcourses, cornices, and cheneaux enlivened its crown.

Although Price's tower was at the forefront of structural design in New York office buildings and stylistically distinctive, it immediately created problems for surrounding landowners. Cornices at the fifteenth and nineteenth stories of the tower projected over the Schermerhorn Building—a T-shaped building that fronted 96 and 98 Broadway immediately south and also extended through the block to 5 Pine Street at the tower's eastern side. The Schermerhorn Building was owned by the Astor estate, and when a plan to have the American Surety Company lease the Schermerhorn ran into difficulty in 1895, John Jacob Astor announced plans to build a 300-foot, twenty-one-story office building on the site of the T-shaped building, including buying out the multiyear leases of the 135 tenants of the Schermerhorn, and sending shivers down the spines of the American Surety Company executives and developers, who now realized that "it was

Figure 6.1 American Surety Building, 100 Broadway, 1896. Bruce Price, architect. *Source: American Architect and Building News* LIII (August 15, 1896).

foolish for persons to put up a tall building without making permanent provision for light and air."[6] The threat of a "spite skyscraper" forced the American Surety Company to sign a ninety-nine-year lease on the adjacent property, and from the time of the American Surety Tower's completion, the firm occupied space in the adjacent Schermerhorn Building.

In a mere twenty-five years, the American Surety Building was surrounded by a "huge pile of more colossal structures," its mechanical equipment was worn out, and its offices, once regarded as spacious and rentable, were now inadequate. Consequently, in 1919, the company bought the Schermerhorn Building, demolished it, and rebuilt on the entire site (now with a floor area twice that of the tower).[7] The company occupied the top five stories of the new building and leased the remaining space to financial, legal, and industrial concerns.[8] Although the tower was occupied by others, it continued to function as the company's symbol nonetheless, appearing on its letterhead and in its annual reports throughout the ensuing decades. And whatever neighbors to the north, south, and east might do, the westward view over Broadway to the graveyard of Trinity Church guaranteed some amount of air and light.

The offices in Price's tower were marginal to the company from the beginning as work environments. But the company's decision to retain the tower long after it ceased to serve the company's needs only underscored its value as a symbol. Once it was leased to tenants, it functioned as an architectural monument that paid for itself. Speculative uses provided the financial mechanisms for creating an imposing company image on the urban scene. The addition of large amounts of space increased a building's sheer size and, consequently, the concern's seeming impressiveness. Furthermore, speculative uses contributed to the financing of construction with a quality and sumptuousness that surpassed typical steel-framed office building construction.

The American Surety Company therefore was responsible for both restructuring its urban surroundings and for commissioning the architect Bruce Price to design an imposing corporate symbol. Its tower exerted a forceful presence on the skyline, but the complex as a whole had to accommodate itself to the local irregularities of existing construction and to the vagaries of land economics in the heart of New York's business district. The Singer and Metropolitan Life Insurance companies restructured urban space in a similar fashion. Their head office complexes were built in a sequence and form that recalled the American Surety Company's project, but they departed from the pattern in significant ways. In contrast to the American Surety Company, each ultimately developed coherent architectural relationships among the various parts that comprised their complexes, despite protracted and piecemeal building processes.

Isaac M. Singer got the idea of producing a commercially viable sewing machine in Boston in 1850, and by 1855, the Singer Company established its base of operations in New York.[9] In 1890, the company began acquiring property for a headquarters along lower Broadway, and by 1896, it commissioned the architect Ernest Flagg to design a new ten-story head office building, the Singer Building, at 149, 151, and 153 Broadway, the corner of Liberty Street. The company occupied the top four stories. During 1898 and 1899, the company expanded its quarters to the west and erected a fourteen-story addition at 85-89 Liberty Street, the Bourne Building, also designed by Flagg. The Bourne Building's more assertive commercial character contrasted with the domestic character of the original head office, which recalled a French *hôtel*. In 1906, Singer decided to expand and unify the complex with additions and to construct a forty-seven-story landmark tower. The lower office block was extended in two directions—north along Broadway, creating a new frontage of 132 feet, and west along 91-93 Liberty, creating a new frontage of 238 feet. To draw together the various blocks that comprised the complex, the original ten-story structure was reconstructed to a height of fourteen stories and crowned with a mansard roof which aligned the cornice lines and, consequently, imposed a new coherence on the complex (Figure 6.2).[10] These decisions marked a crucial turning point in the Singer Company's conception of its head office. Now the *hôtel*-inspired headquarters, with its sculpturally rich ornamental scheme, dominated the corner at Broadway and Liberty. Its facade, showing a new monumentality, had increased in size and scale as a result of the additions, and at its center stood the building's principal entrance, "one of the most imposing and elaborate in the city," which had been shifted from Liberty Street to Broadway, and, consequently, emphasized the headquarters' prestigious Broadway address.[11]

The Singer Company's grandiose building program was hardly a knee-jerk response to pressing spatial needs. When completed, most of the complex was leased to tenants. The president of the company occupied the thirty-fourth story of the tower, but otherwise all of the offices in the forty-seven-story tower were taken by various professional and commercial interests. These included a disproportionately large number of lawyers and a number of offices housing industrial concerns.[12] The Singer Company's acquisition of property along lower Broadway began after it rose to a clear position of world dominance over its competitors in the sewing machine industry. Singer was the first American business to establish branch offices abroad, and, given

Figure 6.2 Singer Tower, 149 Broadway, 1908. Ernest Flagg, architect.
Source: King's Views of New York, 1909.

its ambitions in the international marketplace, it is perhaps logical that it decided to undertake its energetic building program in 1890, when it controlled 80 percent of the world market. It began international marketing efforts in 1861, with sales offices in Glasgow and London, and opened its first factory outside of the United States in Glasgow in 1867. After the turn of the century, the Singer Company was boasting in its trade advertisements about its stability in markets around the world. It built the tower and increased the size of its complex during its final phase of foreign expansion. Particularly significant to the Singer Company's effort was its development of the Russian market. Between 1902 and 1914, Singer's ventures in Russia increased its international sales by 44.7 percent and accounted for at least three-quarters of its profits.[13]

The Singer Company indulged in a lavishness of construction during the early phases of its project, with Flagg's skillful adaptation of the residential idiom of the French *hôtel*, but it was in the final phases of the project, with the erection of the tower, that the company made its most imposing mark on the urban scene. The tower seemed to grow out of some undefined point at the middle of the base of the building and its design, an audacious hybrid, combined exposed engineering with an ornate crown. Flagg's crown drew its imagery from a number of sources: the tower of the Singer Manufacturing Company's Kilbowie factory in Scotland, probably the clock tower of the Gare de Lyon in Paris, and from the Second Empire mansard roof treatment and ornamental scheme of an important Parisian civic building, Visconti and Lefuel's "new" Louvre (1852–1857).[14] The chief drawback to the Singer complex was that its imposing facade could never be fully appreciated. It could only be perceived from awkward angles in visual fragments, due to the relatively narrow proportions of Broadway's width to the clifflike scale of its street walls. The tower provided some recompense, because it captured the view of the pedestrian from points south along Broadway, and it loomed before the face of the traveler approaching the complex along Liberty Street.

The view of the Singer Tower from the north along Broadway, however, would be immediately blocked by the construction of the forty-three-story City Investing Building in 1908, a speculative office building that rose adjacent to the Singer complex, even before the tower was completed (Figure 6.3). The potential fate of the American Surety Building thus became the actual fate of the Singer Tower; the entire Singer complex occupied only a third of the block, the company had not secured the balance of the block's property, and now it found its speculative rental space competing with some thirteen acres of new office space in what was hailed as the "largest single office building

Figure 6.3 Singer Tower and City Investing Building Under Construction, Broadway, 1907. *Source:* Courtesy of the Library of Congress.

in the world."[15] The quality of the Singer space paled by comparison; the few elevators in its slim tower were slow because of so many stops, and the interior spaces of its lower block were small and irregular with lots of corridors and inflexible plans resulting from projecting bays and dormers.[16] Yet the prestige of the building and its location on Broadway kept it rented in good times, and Singer Tower still had advertisement value.

The American Surety and Singer companies restructured urban commercial space along lower Broadway, undertaking a program of spatial intensification in the heart of New York's already heavily built business district.[17] The Metropolitan Life Insurance Company, by contrast, fled the business district to a site bordering Madison Square, then still predominantly a residential district. As a result, it escaped a number of the business district's problems, such as escalating property values, crowded services, and, as seen in the two examples above, the problem of securing adequate viewing angles and light sources. The Metropolitan Life Insurance Company, like the Singer Company, established itself in New York before it decided to build its own head office complex. It was incorporated in 1868, and initially rented two rooms at 248 Broadway. The following year, it moved to 319 Broadway, at the corner of Pearl Street, to rent larger quarters. In 1874, Metropolitan Life decided to purchase a building of its own "that would be another mark of an established and successful company." It acquired the seven-story Constant Building at Park Place and Church Street, and commissioned Napoleon Le Brun to renovate it for the company's own use, as well as for use by money-producing tenants.[18]

By the end of the 1880s, the Metropolitan Life Insurance Company had grown to such an extent that it decided to build its own head office. It chose at this time to purchase the Madison Square site, far north of the business district. For an insurance company to remove itself from the other insurance companies clustered in the business district might have seemed outlandish at the time, but the decision proved wise, as the company's subsequent requirements for space, as well as its subsequent record of financial growth, would show. Ground was broken for an eleven-story building in 1890, designed by Napoleon Le Brun & Sons, and the company occupied the building in 1893. Its design, which followed precedents set by the earlier arcaded office buildings in New York, utilized Italian Renaissance-derived features to evoke the character of an urban palazzo. Soon the company found the original building inadequate, and, in 1895, it decided to commission a twelve-story addition to be constructed adjacent to the original building, to the northwest, along Twenty-fourth Street.[19] A company historian later noted that the addition was "filled at once," implying a rapid pace of growth within the corporate offices.[20] In reality, however, the company was mixing its own expansion with its role as a landlord for tenants. Vice-president Haley Fiske reported to Metropolitan Life's board of directors in 1894 that the competition for space was stiff between the company's expanding clerical staff and the tenants to which the company had already made commitments.[21]

Metropolitan Life's clerical staff continued to expand, from approximately 530 in 1893 to about 1,080 in 1897. To accommodate this growth, the company repeatedly added space to its home office complex. Between 1898 and 1901, properties on the remainder of the block bounded by Madison and Fourth avenues, and by Twenty-third and Twenty-fourth streets, were acquired (on which stood the National Academy of Design and the Lyceum Theatre), with the exception of the Parkhurst Presbyterian Church, and the company expanded its offices to occupy the new building sites.[22] Napoleon Le Brun & Sons' design, with its regular bays, had the advantage of extensibility in virtually any direction—an architectural strategy well suited to the piecemeal land acquisition process. When completed in 1905, the building occupied virtually all of the block, except the site of the church, and its crowning cornice encircled the entire composition.[23] That year, the company bought a sizable lot on the adjacent block to the north and began construction on a new sixteen-story annex to house its printing department.

Additional space was needed in 1905, and Metropolitan Life found it most cost-effective to enlarge the home office building still again, the alternative being the unsavory prospect of purchasing tenants' leases. The Parkhurst Presbyterian Church, holding out at the corner of Madison and Twenty-fourth Street, was bought and demolished. Pierre Le Brun, of Napoleon Le Brun & Sons, designed a fifty-story, 700-foot Italian Renaissance-inspired and white marble-clad version of the Campanile of St. Mark's, Venice, at the suggestion of the company's president, John Rogers Hegeman, and construction began in 1906.[24] The tower, completed in 1909, was also built for the purpose of image (Figure 6.4). "Mr. Fiske called it an advertisement that didn't stand the company a cent because the tenants footed the bill."[25] The tower functioned equally well as an advertisement for the tenants, to the further advantage of Metropolitan Life, which saw it incorporated into a range of letterheads and logos.[26] Even after it erected the tower, the company continued to expand, demolishing the church's second home, which was now in the company's path—the Madison Square Presbyterian Church (McKim, Mead & White, 1906)—and developing the balance of the block to the north by 1940.[27]

Figure 6.4 Metropolitan Life Insurance Company Tower on Madison Square, 1909. Napoleon Le Brun & Sons, architects. *Source:* Courtesy of the Library of Congress.

The Metropolitan Life Insurance Company's decision to move its head office to Madison Square, where property values were lower, and where it would have plenty of room for expansion, coincided with an administrative policy of aggressively taking over smaller insurance companies. The company absorbed ten smaller life insurance companies between 1893 and 1904, and another thirteen between 1907 and 1918.[28] This period of intensive corporate expansion coincided with its energetic building program, which culminated with the construction of the tower. Furthermore, just before the tower project was begun, the company emerged unscathed from the famous 1905 New York State Armstrong Insurance Investigation. The investigation censured the white collar crimes and the unchecked growth of the "Big Three": the Mutual, Equitable, and the New York Life Insurance companies. The Metropolitan Life Insurance Company proclaimed itself an honest commercial institution and called its tower a "plea for righteousness and purity in business corporations."[29] The company immediately profited from its new standing. Between 1906 and 1913, the company's ordinary insurance department, which accounted for about half of its total business volume, gained 50 percent more business than the similar departments in the Big Three combined. By the time its tower was completed in 1909, the Metropolitan Life Insurance Company was known as the world's largest insurance company.[30] Like the Singer Company, it had international offices, which it managed until the 1920s from the Madison Square complex.

The Singer and Metropolitan Life Insurance companies followed a piecemeal process in realizing their headquarters complexes, down to the erection of the towers. As the complexes advanced, the mechanisms used to finance them seemed to take on a life of their own, setting up a financially impelled chain of acquisition, demolition, and construction. The sparks that set the processes in motion and the fuel that kept them propelled were changes in the organizations themselves, particularly the expansion of markets or the acquisition of potential competitors. The changes seemed to prompt the need to assert an increasingly higher profile in America's commercial capital, regardless of the utilitarian requirements for space. To build a tower was the most obvious manifestation of this need. The towers were attention-grabbing cynosures, but they were also wholly dependent on the less visually assertive head office complexes. The low masses of the complexes isolated the towers from surrounding skyscrapers, providing them with maximum exposure in city views.[31] Moreover, the lower offices, in all likelihood, were a source of revenue for the extremely expensive tower undertakings. It was widely known by contemporaries that an "economical" speculative office building was about sixteen stories high and filled as much of the site as possible. Tall, narrow towers required caissons during construction and sophisticated systems of wind bracing, both of which were costly.[32] Besides, the confined tower plans were virtually useless from the companies' point of view. Expensive, exotic icons, the towers actually had very little to do with an enterprise's day-to-day business operations.

If the low-office-block-plus-tower arrangement of the Singer Company's and the Metropolitan Life Insurance Company's headquarters can be regarded as typical for the head office species, then the Woolworth Building represented a major aberration. The F. W. Woolworth Company's landmark headquarters was not constructed in separate, identifiable stages, but all at once (Figure 6.5). Frank Woolworth also intended that the building be seen all at once, like the completed Metropolitan Life complex, and, consequently, chose a site adjacent to City Hall Park. He wanted to capture an entire urban audience by surprise with his seemingly sudden decision to build a gigantic and extremely visible Gothic skyscraper, the height of which topped all earlier records, and he did.

Woolworth conceived his head office building as an imposing urban monument and his tower as skyline feature. In both aspects of his project, he utilized the familiar formula of mixing head office space with rental space for tenants, although in this case the proportion of space to be occupied by the head office diminished considerably. The F. W. Woolworth Company's headquarters filled only the Woolworth Building's twenty-fourth story and part of its twenty-third story. It occupied less than two stories in a building with fifty usable stories, although the twenty-two stories of the tower were much smaller in dimension than the twenty-eight stories in the lower block. The tower was not well suited to the needs of the F. W. Woolworth Company's head offices, nor to any but the smallest of companies' for that matter, since its offices were among the last occupied when the building opened in 1913.[33] The lowest four stories of the Woolworth Building were taken by the Irving National Bank, which had been part of the venture from the start. For the most part, the building was comprised of speculative office uses. The small head office requirements of the Woolworth Company can be ascribed to its decentralized administrative hierarchy, which Woolworth set up in 1908. The company had regional headquarters in a number of major cities, including Boston, Chicago, Philadelphia, and Omaha.[34]

Woolworth had plenty of time to plan the spectacle of the building's construction, having had company offices in the immediate vicinity of the building site since 1886. That year, he rented a "desk room," to serve as a buying office, at 104 Chambers Street. The following year,

Figure 6.5 Woolworth Building on City Hall Park, 1912. Cass Gilbert, architect. *Source:* Courtesy of the Library of Congress.

he rented an office at 321 Broadway, and, in 1888, he moved to the Stewart Building, at the corner of Broadway and Chambers Street. His office faced Chambers Street and looked out over City Hall Park. Before the end of the year, he moved to the opposite side of the building, overlooking Reade Street. When he incorporated his company in 1905, however, Woolworth returned to the Chambers Street side of the building with its view of the park, on which bordered the future site of the Woolworth Building, at the southwest corner of Broadway and Park Place.[35] Woolworth studied the activity around City Hall Park. He watched urban crowds spill over the Brooklyn Bridge toward the business district, the construction of the lower Broadway subway line, and the efforts by the Municipal Art Society and others to plan City Hall Park as New York's civic center, a focal point for government offices.[36]

Woolworth commissioned the architect Cass Gilbert in 1910 to design Woolworth's head office project after rising to a clear position of dominance over competitors, incorporating the company, and expanding its operations abroad. He opened his first successful five-and-ten-cent store in Lancaster, Pennsylvania, in 1879. Before he incorporated his company in 1905, Woolworth had purchased several five-and-ten-cent stores as well as chains from a number of competitors. In 1909, the year before he began acquiring parcels for his project, Woolworth opened his first store overseas in Liverpool, England. Within two years, he opened twelve stores in England.[37] Woolworth began construction on the building's foundations in 1910, but this did not deter him from continuing to enlarge the site, which, by early 1911, included the entire Broadway block front, a feat in the eyes of New York real estate dealers. Gilbert, with a series of proposals, increased the scale of the design accordingly.[38] The enlargement of the project occurred just before the F. W. Woolworth Company underwent its 1911 merger, which involved the acquisition of four sizable five-and-ten-cent chains, causing it to nearly double in size.[39] Although the project increased in size as the construction progressed, the Woolworth Building was still conceived as a single building operation and financed accordingly. Woolworth refused to rely on the pay-as-you-go financial methods adopted by the Singer and Metropolitan Life Insurance companies, choosing instead to set up the Broadway Park Place Company to help finance the building's construction. When construction was completed, Woolworth bought back the shares from the Broadway Park Place Company, consequently owning the building outright, and letting the company collect the tenants' returns on his investment.[40]

The Woolworth Building project started out as a twenty-story office block adjoining a taller thirty-story tower, based on the Victoria Tower, Houses of Parliament, a civic tower that Woolworth had suggested as a model. When Woolworth enlarged the site, Gilbert retained the idea of a civic Gothic tower, but sought a new model for the building's compositional scheme, casting back to medieval Flanders in search of a theme. Gilbert had observed that in the major cities of Flanders, Gothic civic buildings, particularly the *hôtels de ville*, celebrated the success of the city's mercantile trade. Such a celebration of commerce on an urban scale, he must have assumed, found a parallel in contemporary New York.[41] In his choice of the *hôtel de ville* as a compositional motif, Gilbert, like Price, Flagg, and Le Brun, was only acting in the spirit of the time. All were seeking an appropriate architectural character for America's newly powerful commercial enterprises.

The Woolworth Building's composition, with its central tower projecting from a lower block—although a block of proportions considerably more grandiose than those of the Singer and Metropolitan Life Insurance complexes—was enriched with Gothic elements and details appropriated from a diversity of other civic and ecclesiastical sources besides the *hôtel de ville*, including the Perpendicular Gothic facades of the Houses of Parliament and the Flamboyant Gothic tracery of the Cathedral towers at Reims, Antwerp, and Malines.[42] The contradictions of such a bold use of imagery borrowed from civic and ecclesiastical sources for a commercial office building were emphasized by the building's siting—at the northern boundary of the business district, with direct access to the Broadway subway line on one hand, and at the corner of City Hall Park, New York's municipal government nexus, on the other. The ambiguities of the Woolworth Building's siting were reflected in its tenancy, which included manufacturing, engineering, railroad, and publishing concerns, but also a vast number of lawyers. For a short time, the city's federal courtrooms were housed in the building's twelfth story.[43]

The Banker's Trust Company, by comparison with the Singer, Metropolitan Life, and the Woolworth companies, chose to build its own head office relatively early in its history—after leasing space for only six years in the immediate vicinity of its chosen building site.[44] Moreover, Banker's Trust's strategy for choosing a site had less to do with the familiar issues of visibility and room for expansion than with the desire to be near the Stock Exchange. The company's stated intention was to erect a "monument" at "the vortex of America's financial life, namely, where Wall, Broad, and Nassau Streets meet."[45] The rapidity of the company's growth was attributed to its powerful directorate, not the least of whom was J. P. Morgan, but there were other influential factors as well. In 1908, the company began pursuing international business with the establishment of its foreign department, and it took over the Mercantile Trust and the Manhattan Trust companies in 1911 and 1912.[46] The takeover activity occurred while the head office tower was under construction.

In 1909 the new home of the Banker's Trust Company was announced as a sixteen-story tower on the site of the old seven-story Stevens Building, an L-shaped office building fronting on Wall Street and also Nassau Street, the corner being occupied by the needlelike eighteen-story Gillender Building. The Banker's Trust Company had decided to lease the land, so expensive was the purchase price of land on the block.[47] Soon thereafter, the Gillender site was acquired, making it possible to build a more imposing square building on the prominent corner with its principal entrance on Wall Street.[48] As usual, the company's plan was to lease a sizable percentage of the tower to tenants.[49] Banker's Trust retained Trowbridge & Livingston in the same year to design a freestanding thirty-one-story steel-framed tower, which in basic concept recalled Bruce Price's design for the American Surety Building. Encased in granite, the tower's vertical rows of windows, contained by pilasters, extended from the Ionic colonnades that demarcated its base to the engaged Ionic colonnades that encircled its crown. Topped with a solid geometric stepped pyramid, the whole had an air of vaultlike gravity and permanence (Figure 6.6).

After the tower was completed, the Banker's Trust Company continued to expand, but it also continued to lease space in its tower to tenants, choosing to occupy the first three stories only. As the Federal Reserve System diminished the necessity for bankers to have their "own" reserve system, Banker's Trust began to function more like a commercial bank. It began operating a securities department in 1918 and a bond department in 1919, which included wire offices to Chicago and to eleven other cities in the East and Midwest. As part of this expansion, the firm developed New York branch offices.

In each of the case studies analyzed above, the restructuring of urban space by corporations constructing landmark headquarters involved not just changes in the skyline, but the reshaping of ground-level plots and the simplification of street facades as well. City blocks comprised of perhaps a dozen discrete buildings providing a variegated facade became more uniform and more monolithic. The footprints of corporate office buildings expanded to monopolize increasingly larger areas on their particular blocks. Such a pattern of urban change was also followed by at least a half-dozen speculative office complexes that were built around the same period. Their impact on the city, along

Figure 6.6 Banker's Trust Building, Wall Street at Nassau Street, 1912. Trowbridge & Livingston, architects. *Source: King's Views of New York, 1915.*

with the corporate head office construction, hastened the critical attitude toward massive building schemes and, in turn, precipitated the Zoning Resolution of 1916. The promoters of these giant speculative office structures sought anchor tenants, firms that wanted to be close to the key sites, but did not want to develop their own head office space.[50] They also sought the same lawyers, accountants, stockbrokers, and industrial agents that corporate head office developers yearned for as tenants to underwrite their buildings. In the heady decade that opened the twentieth century, hardly a day went by, it was claimed, that a company did not announce a decision to move its head office, or a major sales office, to New York.[51] So congested was the Wall Street area that there was talk of a shift of development north to Canal Street, but as the opening of elevated railway lines made the trip from Forty-second Street to Wall Street fifteen minutes instead of an hour, the demand for Wall Street offices continued. "Steel frames and elevators made it possible to accommodate within a quarter of a mile of the Stock Exchange an office population which without them would have needed all the available space for three times that distance."[52]

Many of the key sites in the vicinity of the Stock Exchange were along lower Broadway. Just north of Trinity Church, Harry S. Black, president of the Fuller Construction Company, replaced the old five-story Trinity Building (1852) during 1904 and 1905 with a twenty-story office block. The new Trinity Building, designed by the architect Francis H. Kimball, was 40 feet wide and 270 feet deep. It was essentially one row of thirteen offices facing Trinity churchyard, with a corridor and banks of elevators on the northern edge. Then, in 1906, Black proposed building an addition, also designed by Kimball—the U.S. Realty Building—directly north of the Trinity Building. Black used the caissons of the Trinity Building and exploited a relocated Thames Street as little more than a light well, adding another twenty stories and 260,000 square feet of office space in the vicinity. About 70 percent of the space was rented immediately to "four bankers, thirteen attorneys, besides brokers, engineers and trust and other companies." The ground floor was occupied by the "Carnegie Trust Company and the newly formed National Copper Bank."[53] Both of these buildings rose from the sidewalk as no-nonsense speculative buildings, just like the City Investing Building, which fully exploited the site to the north of the Singer Building (Figure 6.7).

The Hudson Terminal complex, another bulky speculative development, designed by Clinton & Russell and completed in 1908, loomed over its neighbors at Church and Cortlandt streets. The developers of the Hudson Terminal had as their major tenant various subsidiaries

Figure 6.7 Trinity Building, 111 Broadway, 1905, and U.S. Realty Building, 115 Broadway, 1906. Francis H. Kimball, architect. *Source: King's Views of New York*, 1909.

of the newly formed, Morgan-dominated, United States Steel Corporation: American Steel Hoop, American Steel and Wire, National Tube, American Steel and Tin Plate, National Steel, American Bridge, Shelby Steel Tube, United States Steel Products and Exports, and Lorain Steel. The subsidiaries leased four full stories in the highest single annual rental agreement in the city.[54] And yet the president and other executives of U.S. Steel operated out of the Empire Building, at 71 Broadway immediately south of Trinity Church, where presumably they were closer to the critical actors on Wall Street.

Immediately to the south of the Empire Building at 71 Broadway, the American Express (63 Broadway) and Adams Express (59 Broadway) companies rebuilt their sites (twenty-one and thirty-two stories respectively) to take advantage of the demand for space in key locations on Broadway. To the east of Broad Street, two separate buildings at 43 Exchange Place and 43 Wall Street were reconstructed—43 Exchange Place in 1903 to a height of twenty-six stories and then the United States Trust Company at 43 Wall Street during 1906 and 1907. As the U.S. Trust Building (also designed by Kimball) was constructed, the rear walls of 43 Exchange Place were knocked out to make a combined twenty-six-story tower fronting on both Exchange Place and Wall Street that offered 5,000 square feet per story at the node around the Stock Exchange.[55] The escalating pace of rebuilding narrow lots after the turn of the century made the squabble between the American Surety Company and Astor over a cornice line seem minor by comparison.

Such intensive construction activity fueled debates about height and light, which came to a head with the criticism of the proposed Equitable Building, documented in the Heights of Buildings Commission's 1913 report. When fire destroyed the eight-story Equitable Insurance Building in 1913, an entire block bounded by Broadway, Pine, Nassau, and Cedar became available. Thomas Coleman du Pont financed a new forty-story building, designed by D. H. Burnham & Company, that extended straight up from the sidewalks (Figure 6.8).[56] It provided 1.2 million square feet of rentable space, with 30,000 square feet in each of the upper stories. It also cast long shadows over surrounding buildings. Owners of buildings that once towered over the eight-story Equitable reportedly offered du Pont $2.5 million to keep the new building at the same height, but he chose instead to maximize his profits.[57] The widespread reaction to the intrusive nature of this building made it a target of the movement to fix the height and bulk of buildings, and ultimately facilitated the passing of the 1916 Zoning Resolution. The Equitable entered the same market in which the Woolworth and City Investing buildings were keenly seeking tenants,

Figure 6.8 Equitable Building, Broadway between Pine and Cedar streets, 1915. D. H. Burnham & Company, architects. *Source: King's Views of New York*, 1915.

and although the Equitable Life Insurance Company took 125,000 square feet of floor space, a depression led to high vacancies—until World War I broke out in Europe. Then J. P. Morgan & Company took an entire floor to coordinate the buying of munitions for the Allies and quickly "inland manufacturers of everything that fighting soldiers needed, brokers, lawyers and a host of others signed up for space."[58]

The Trinity, U.S. Realty, City Investing, Hudson Terminal, and Equitable buildings resulted from patterns of land purchase, design, construction, and occupancy as rich and complex as those of the American Surety, Singer, Metropolitan Life, Woolworth, and Banker's Trust buildings. For both kinds of skyscrapers—those built primarily for speculative purposes and those built primarily to house a head office and secure an image—the search for tenants large and small was critical to whether the buildings were successful as financial ventures or not. Corporations that sought to build for long-term accommodation of their own head office staff had a more relaxed attitude toward their building ventures than those who built strictly for speculative purposes. Speculators often ceased planning new buildings in times of oversupply and low rents. The building industry's journal observed in 1911: "Of late years it has been banks, insurance buildings or individual investors like Mr. Woolworth who have been erecting the skyscrapers; and inasmuch as they can afford to accept a smaller return on their investment, they are making the operations of speculative real estate companies in this field increasingly difficult."[59]

The story did not end once a tenant list had been established, backed up with signed leases. Leases were often yearly leases, occasionally five-year leases, and tenants were shameless in their lack of loyalty to the building owner or the location. The volatile market for rental space meant that any slight variation in rental costs, in the perception of the acceptable office standard in terms of light, heat, air, and services, or in the opinion of a desirable location could lure customers to a new set of office spaces among the millions of square feet of floor space available.[60] Even when the Delaware, Lackawanna & Western Railroad became a prime tenant of the new West Street Building in 1908—taking four floors in a building filled with coal and iron agents, railroad and steamship concerns—it still participated in the broader rental market. In 1913, its foreign freight department leased four rooms in the executive office story of the New York Produce Exchange, and its general eastern freight office took space in the Woolworth Building.[61]

The restructuring of New York's urban environment was not just a matter of changing the skyline. The landmark towers that were so conspicuous in skyline views were rarely of any true functional use to their corporate builders—this was shown time and time again, whether by the American Surety Company, which never made full use of, and eventually vacated, its tower; by the Singer Company, which hardly occupied its tower; by the Woolworth Company, which had difficulty leasing its tower; or by the Banker's Trust Company, which refused to take space in its tower before opening ancillary offices in midtown. The only justification for the towers was an enterprise's augmented visibility on the urban scene. Whereas there is no simple explanation for why some enterprises sought such visibility as opposed to others, familiar themes were advertising and public relations, establishment of a physical presence for an unmaterial business such as insurance, and the assertion of an individual ego, as in the cases of John Rogers Hegeman and Frank Woolworth.[62] In general, the visibility afforded by the towers expressed, and ultimately, legitimized a newly powerful commercial order (Figure 6.9). The unabashed appropriation of a form typically reserved in earlier civilizations for ecclesiastical or civic purposes vividly conveyed the dominance of commercial affairs in American life.

It was not just the towers, however, that remained for the most part unoccupied by their corporate builders. As a rule, the corporations used only a fraction of the offices that they financed and built. Their

Figure 6.9 Lower Manhattan Skyline, 1912. *Source: Master Builders of the World's Greatest Structure, 1913.*

role as agents of change in the metropolis was contingent upon their ability to finance and construct office buildings that would be occupied by others. It was the others—a shifting population—whose workplaces were responsible for the demographic makeup of the city's commercial districts. Consequently, while the large-scale enterprises functioned as agents of physical change, the construction program that they proposed would not have been feasible without the sweeping, less easily defined, social changes that gave rise to the white collar work force and its attendant spatial requirement for housing paperwork. The same held true for speculative builders orchestrating the shaping of the urban environment. It was the intersection of corporate capital and property capital with the design and engineering fields that translated the national and global restructuring of industry and trade into the tangible built environments called New York skyscrapers. And without a large army of agents, brokers, and directors—and their white-collar work force in turn—in search of space, the built changes the corporations and the speculative builders proposed would have been impossible. Nor would corporate enterprise have been able to assert itself as powerfully as it did on the urban scene. Such a scale of construction in all probability would not have been carried out without the range of tenants who helped to finance it.

Notes

1. Jean Gottman, "Why the Skyscraper?" *Geographical Review* 56 (April 1966): 190–212; Harry Braverman, *Labor and Monopoly Capital: The Degradation of Work in the Twentieth Century* (New York: Monthly Review Press, 1974).
2. Sarah Bradford Landau, "Richard Morris Hunt: Architectural Innovator and Father of a Distinctive American School," in Susan R. Stein, ed., *The Architecture of Richard Morris Hunt* (Chicago: University of Chicago Press, 1986), p. 58.
3. "Home Office Buildings of Distinction," *The Spectator: The Business Newspaper of Insurance* CXXIX (November 17, 1932): 13, 26.
4. Carl W. Condit, *American Building* (Chicago: University of Chicago Press, 1968), p. 119; "Home Office Buildings of Distinction," p. 13, states that "for the first time the method used to construct a river bridge pier was applied to a building."
5. Barr Ferree, "A Talk with Bruce Price," in Adolf K. Placzek, ed., *Great American Architects Series*, No. 5 (New York: Da Capo Press, 1977 reprint of May 1895–July 1899 editions), pp. 75–78.
6. "The Real Estate Field," *New York Times* (May 6, 1895): 12; "Mr. Astor's Proposed Building; Some Think He Would Make Terms with the Surety Company," *New York Times* (May 7, 1896): 2; "The Real Estate Field," *New York Times* (May 10, 1896): 14.

7. "Home Office Buildings of Distinction," p. 13. The original American Surety Building was renovated, with many of the tenants remaining through the renovation.

8. The nineteenth story was occupied by the executive offices, the twenty-third by lunch rooms for the officers (private dining rooms) and employees (one for men, one for women), and the twenty-second and twenty-fourth "preserved as recreation spaces for employees to promenade during their mid-day recess." "Home Office Buildings of Distinction," p. 26.

9. Mira Wilkins, *The Emergence of Multinational Enterprise: American Business Abroad from the Colonial Era to 1914* (Cambridge, MA: Harvard University Press, 1970), pp. 37–39.

10. Mardges Bacon, *Ernest Flagg: Beaux-Arts Architect and Urban Reformer* (New York and Cambridge, MA: Architectural History Foundation and MIT Press, 1986), pp. 209–212, 374 n. 5.

11. "Tallest Skyscraper to Stand on Broadway," *New York Times* (February 22, 1906): 1.

12. Robert Bruce Davies, *Peacefully Working to Conquer the World: Singer Sewing Machines in Foreign Markets, 1854–1920* (New York: Arno Press, 1976), p. 334. Of 637 Singer tenants who were listed in the 1929 New York City telephone directory, 145 (or 23 percent) were lawyers; 119 (19 percent) were in industrial, engineering, or mining sectors; and 108 (14 percent) were in the financial services sector.

13. Wilkins, *Emergence of Multinational Enterprise*, pp. 38–45; Fred V. Cartensen, *American Enterprise in Foreign Markets: Studies of Singer and International Harvester in Imperial Russia* (Chapel Hill: University of North Carolina Press, 1984), pp. 13, 23; Davies, *Peacefully Working to Conquer*, pp. 42–44, 100, 334–336.

14. Bacon, *Ernest Flagg*, pp. 216, 227.

15. So pronounced the picture postcards of the day. See also *King's Views of New York* (New York: Manhattan Postcard Company, 1926), p. 14.

16. Earle Shultz and Walter Simmons, *Offices in the Sky* (New York: Bobbs-Merrill, 1959), pp. 64–65.

17. A similar pattern of development can be documented for the Standard Oil Company at 26 Broadway, the head office complex for the Rockefeller empire. A nine-story building of 1886 quickly became obsolete and six more stories were added in 1896, as well as a slim nineteen-story addition on the lot to the north. In 1922, a huge landmark addition was made to the south, the Carrère and Hastings design being constructed in four stages as tenants surrendered their leases. See R. A. M. Stern, G. Gilmartin, and T. Mellins, *New York 1930: Architecture and Urbanism Between the Two World Wars* (New York: Rizzoli International Publications, 1987), pp. 539–540.

18. Marquis James, *The Metropolitan Life: A Study on Business Growth* (New York: Viking Press, 1947), p. 59.

19. "Manhattan's Highest Skyscraper," *Real Estate Record and Builder's Guide* LXXIX (January 24, 1907): 169, 173.

20. James, *Metropolitan Life*, p. 129.

21. Metropolitan Life Insurance Company, Board of Directors, Minutes, 1894, p. 260.

22. James, *Metropolitan Life*, p. 129.

23. Each addition needed its light court, so although the design of the exterior conveyed the impression that the Metropolitan Life company occupied the entire block, there were a total of six internal light courts, which took some 15 percent of the space on upper floors. See floor plans in *The American Architect* XCVI (October 6, 1909): 127.

24. Kenneth Turney Gibbs, *Business Architectural Imagery in America, 1870–1930* (Ann Arbor, MI: UMI Research Press, 1984), p. 136.

25. James, *Metropolitan Life*, p. 174; Gibbs, *Business Architectural Imagery*, p. 136.

26. Olivier Zunz, *Making America Corporate, 1870–1920* (Chicago: University of Chicago Press, 1990), p. 123.

27. In 1908, "the indoor staff numbers 2,468 clerks and 427 employees in the Printing Division and other mechanical departments. The clerical force is made up of 1,533 women and 935 men." *The Metropolitan Life Insurance Company: Its History, Its Present Position in the Insurance World, Its Home Office Building and the Work Carried On Therein* (New York: The Metropolitan Life Insurance Company, 1908), p. 33. James, *Metropolitan Life*, p. 326.

28. James, *Metropolitan Life*, pp. 207–208.

29. William Henry Atherton, *The Metropolitan Tower: A Symbol of Refuge, Warning, Love, Inspiration, Beauty, Strength* (New York: The Metropolitan Life Insurance Company, 1915), p. 6.

30. H. Roger Grant, *Insurance Reform: Consumer Action in the Progressive Era* (Ames, IA: Iowa State University Press, 1979), pp. 38–43; Gibbs, *Business Architectural Imagery*, p. 138.

31. "Skyscraping Up To Date," *Architectural Record* 23 (January 1908): 74–75, as cited in Robert A. M. Stern, Gregory Gilmartin, and John Montague Massengale, *New York 1900* (New York: Rizzoli International Publications, 1987), p. 173.

32. George Hill, "The Economy of the Office Building," *Architectural Record* XV (April 1904): 313–327; Cecil C. Evers, *The Commercial Problem in Buildings* (New York: Record and Guide, 1912), pp. 177–198.

33. Tenant list dated 1913, Cass Gilbert Collection, New York Historical Society.

34. John K. Winkler, *Five and Ten: The Fabulous Life of F. W. Woolworth* (New York: Robert M. McBride, 1940), pp. 149–150. By contrast with Woolworth, J. C. Penney moved his head office to New York from Salt Lake City in 1913 but never participated in the downtown office market. The company occupied the eighteenth floor of the Masonic Temple Building at 71 West Twenty-third Street, moving in 1914 first to 16 East Thirty-third Street and then to two rooms at 345 Fourth Avenue. The company moved again in 1920 to three floors of 370 Seventh Avenue, and finally built its own building at 330 West Thirty-fourth Street in 1926. Information on J. C. Penney's early days courtesy of the company's corporate archives in Dallas, TX.

35. "Frank W. Woolworth," in B. C. Forbes, *Men Who Are Making America*, 2nd ed. (New York: Forbes Publishing, 1918), p. 432; Winkler, *Five and Ten*, pp. 70–72, 146; Gail Fenske, "The 'Skyscraper Problem' and the City Beautiful: The Woolworth Building." Ph.D diss. MIT, 1988), pp. 148–150.

36. "F. W. Woolworth Invests His Millions in Towering Broadway Structure," *New York City American* (February 22, 1911), in scrapbook, Cass Gilbert Collection, New-York Historical Society. *Woolworth Building (Highest in the World)* (New York: F. W. Woolworth Company, 1912), a rental brochure, stresses the location of the Woolworth Building at New York's civic center and indicates graphically the prevailing assumption that the federal post office would be demolished so that the Woolworth Building would be fronting the park.

37. Leo L. Redding, "Mr. Woolworth's Story," *World's Work* (April 1913): 660; "Woolworth," in Forbes, *Men Who Are Making America*, pp. 432–433.

38. "New Woolworth Building on Broadway Will Eclipse Singer Tower in Height," *New York Times* (November 13, 1910): 7; "A Realty Triumph in Assembling Plot," *New York Times* (January 22, 1911): 7. For an analysis of the evolution of Gilbert's design, see Fenske, "The 'Skyscraper Problem' and the City Beautiful," pp. 175–183.

39. "Woolworth," in Forbes, *Men Who Are Making America*, pp. 432–433; Winkler, *Five and Ten*, pp. 174–175.

40. "F. W. Woolworth Leaves $65,000,000," *New York Times* (April 9, 1919): 11; "Hard to Borrow on New York Realty, Says Woolworth," *New York American* (September 19, 1911), in scrapbook, Cass Gilbert Collection, New-York Historical Society; John Tauranac, *Elegant New York* (New York: Abbeville Press, 1985), pp. 13, 15, 23.

41. Cass Gilbert, "Tenth Birthday of a Notable Structure," *Real Estate Magazine* XI (May 1923): 344–345.

42. Fenske, "The 'Skyscraper Problem' and the City Beautiful," p. 183.

43. "Two-thirds of Woolworth Building Space Leased," *Wall Street Journal* (February 9, 1914), in scrapbook, Cass Gilbert Collection, New-York Historical Society.

44. The company began at 143 Liberty Street in 1903, but moved to larger quarters at 7 Wall Street that same year; Edward Ten Broeck Perine, *The Story of the Trust Companies* (New York: Putnam's Sons, 1916), p. 225.

45. Perine, *Story of the Trust Companies*, p. 225.

46. Perine, *Story of the Trust Companies*, pp. 222–226.

47. "New Office Building for Wall Street; Sixteen Story Structure, Costing $1,500,000, to Go Up on the Stevens Site," *New York Times* (July 7, 1909): 16.

48. Nearby were the Sub-Treasury across Nassau Street to the west, the telling four-story head office of Morgan & Sons on the southeast corner, and the Stock Exchange on the southwest.

49. Of the 133 Banker's Trust tenants who were listed in the 1929 New York City telephone directory, 35 (or 26 percent) were lawyers, and 31 (or 23 percent) were in financial services.

50. A case in point is the Pittsburgh-based Westinghouse empire, which had executive and sales offices at 165 Broadway in the City Investing Building. Companies represented in that building included: Westinghouse Acceptance Corporation, Westinghouse Air Brake Co., Westinghouse Commercial Investment Co., Westinghouse Electric Elevator Co., Westinghouse Electric International Co., Westinghouse Electric and Manufacturing Co. (executive and sales office), Westinghouse Lamp Co., Westinghouse Machine Co., Westinghouse Traction Brake Co., and

Westinghouse Union Battery Co. *Directory of Directors in the Pittsburgh District* (Boston: Bankers Service Company, 1918), p. 431.

51. "The decision of the management of the Union Pacific Railroad to move a large proportion of its executive staff to New York is an interesting illustration of a tendency which of late years has been comparatively rare. During the abounding days of 1901 and 1902 almost every morning newspaper chronicled the leasing of a large group of offices in New York to some Western corporation which had decided to move its executive staff to New York." "Surplus Office Space," *Real Estate Record and Builders Guide* LXXXVIII (October 21, 1911): 590.

52. Editorial, *American Architect and Building News* LXXIV (October 12, 1901): 1.

53. "U.S. Realty Building," *Record and Guide* LXXIX (May 4, 1907): 860.

54. "$240,000 a Year for Rent; Subsidiary U.S. Steel Companies to Pay the Highest Rate in the City," *New York Times* (August 18, 1907): 1.

55. Tauranac, *Elegant New York*, p. 14.

56. Sally A. Kitt Chappell, "A Reconsideration of the Equitable Building in New York," *Society of Architectural Historians Journal* XLIX (March 1990): 90–95; Sandy Hornick, "Letters," *Society of Architectural Historians Journal* XLIX (December 1990): 468.

57. These included the gigantic Trinity and U.S. Realty buildings across Broadway, and also the Hanover Bank, the American Surety Company, the American Exchange National Bank, the Fourth National Bank, and the National Bank of Commerce buildings. Shultz and Simmons, *Offices in the Sky*, p. 79.

58. Shultz and Simmons, *Offices in the Sky*, p. 80.

59. "Surplus Office Space," p. 590.

60. Subcategories of rental markets developed that were clustered in different areas of lower Manhattan. For example, coal agents located near the waterfront, shipping lines near Bowling Green, oil companies near the Rockefeller empire on lower Broadway, newspapers and magazines along Park Row near City Hall, insurance companies near the intersections of William Street, Nassau Street, and Maiden Lane.

61. Sharon Irish, "A 'Machine That Makes the Land Pay': The West Street Building in New York," *Technology and Culture* XX (April 1989): 376–397. Executive Committee Minutes, Delaware, Lackawanna & Western Railroad (December 23, 1913, and March 27, 1913), record collection at Arents Research Library, Syracuse University, New York, NY.

62. Gibbs, *Business Architectural Imagery*; Morton Keller, *The Life Insurance Enterprise* (Cambridge, MA: Harvard University Press, 1963), pp. 38–39.

7

Form Follows Finance: The Empire State Building

Carol Willis

The Empire State Building is the quintessential monument of the golden age when New York reigned as the unchallenged leader in sky-scraper design and construction. A study of the forces that shaped it is the story of all high-rises of the period. At once typical and extraordinary, it was a work of genius in which the operating intelligence was not a brilliant designer, but the *genius loci* of the capital city of capitalism (Figure 7.1).

In both its unmatched height and speed of construction, the Empire State culminated the frenzied development of the 1920s when over 100 buildings of twenty or more stories were added to the Manhattan skyline. Erected in less than eleven months and soaring 1,250 feet above the street, some 200 feet higher than the Chrysler Building, the world's second-tallest tower, it was in every respect extraordinary. Yet, it was also a typical speculative office building in which the interior plans and external form were determined by the principle of cost and return. The Empire State thus offers a case study through which to understand the forces that shaped Manhattan's booming business districts in the decade before the Great Depression.[1]

The entire project was a spectacular demonstration of modern engineering and managerial efficiency. The developers signed contracts in September 1929, just weeks before the Wall Street Crash, and the demolition of the old Waldorf-Astoria Hotel began on October 1, 1929. Excavations were finished by March 17, and the first steel columns set on April 7, 1930. At the peak of operations, 3,500 workers employed on the site constructed a story a day, and in March 1931, the tallest building on the planet was completed forty-five days ahead of schedule and

Figure 7.1 View of the Empire State Building and Midtown Manhattan from the RCA Building, June 17, 1948; Charles T. Miller, photographer. *Source:* Courtesy of the New York Historical Society.

under budget. The opening ceremonies on May 1 were attended by such dignitaries as Governor Franklin D. Roosevelt, Mayor Jimmy Walker, and former Governor Alfred E. Smith, the president of the Empire State Corporation; the date was symbolic, for leases on office rentals were annual, traditionally signed on the first of May.

Speed of construction was only one way the Empire State was extraordinary. Its most obvious distinction, of course, was its 102 stories—85 floors of offices and the equivalent of 17 more in the essentially ornamental "mooring mast." This great height was a reflection of the unusually large site (197 × 425 feet), which allowed for the heroic proportions of the tower within the legal limits of the zoning formula. Even more important to the visual impression of the building was its simplicity of form and splendid isolation. In the 1920s, as today, skyscrapers generally sprouted in clusters like the group around Grand Central Terminal or the concentration around Wall Street, but for a mile of midtown between Madison Square and Forty-second Street, the Empire State stood—and still stands—alone.

Despite its singularity, the Empire State was a typical investment property, like the vast majority of high-rises in New York and elsewhere. Literature on skyscrapers generally distinguishes two categories: corporate headquarters and speculative buildings. In a 1930 article, architect Timothy Pfleuger explained that speculative buildings were constructed as investments for revenue in rental alone, while the corporate structures were designed "to house and advertise a business, in which case the owner often conceded a decrease in revenue for special architectural appeal."[2] Many of New York's tallest or most famous skyscrapers were built as headquarters—monuments on which a proud owner like Frank W. Woolworth or companies like Seagrams and Chase Manhattan Bank could justify certain extravagances. Yet the Empire State was neither a symbol of corporate identity, nor an expression of an overarching ego.

The first blueprint for every speculative building is a balance sheet that figures the maximum return on investment. The idea of "maximum return" does not mean the cheapest alternative, but rather the choice that will pay back the highest profit for the money spent. As Cecil C. Evers noted in his standard work, *The Commercial Problem in Buildings*, "The ultimate test of a value of a building is its earning capacity and not its cost."[3] In the Empire State, the height, overall massing, fenestration, and facade treatment were governed first and foremost by this standard. While specific conditions, especially the size of the site and its zoning restrictions, also affected the building's form, no factor was more important than economic determinants.

The role of market forces on commercial architecture, while seemingly obvious, has been slighted in writings on the skyscraper. Architectural historians have tended to focus their studies on formal and stylistic issues and on the skyscraper as a signifier of cultural values.[4] Urban historians and geographers have raised other questions, such as where tall buildings were located (the spatialization of capital) and how corporations used these new structures to promote business, organize their functions, and house the growing white collar work force. The increasing number and height of skyscrapers have been seen as a function of structural changes in the nation's economy and the history of corporations.[5]

Skyscrapers should be understood not simply as containers expanding to accommodate corporate needs, but as businesses themselves. The majority of high-rises built in the 1920s—and in every decade—were speculative. Even among New York's loftiest towers (generally the most prestigious and expensive), a large proportion were purely rental properties. In 1932, of the city's thirty-six tallest buildings (counting only those over 500 feet), twenty-nine were office buildings (most of the others were hotels); of these, only nineteen bore the name of a corporation, whereas *all* rented out major portions to tenants.[6] Some corporations sold their headquarters, treating them, in effect, as real estate investments. The quip that "the business of New York is real estate" imparts more than a grain of truth. The millions of square feet of space constructed in periods like the 1920s, 1960s, and 1980s represent a significant sector of the city's economy.

New York skyscrapers of the twenties shared a characteristic form that can be seen in the Empire State, Chrysler, Bank of Manhattan, Irving Trust, and dozens of other more anonymous buildings known only by their addresses. The stepped-back massing of the lower stories surmounted by a slender tower was in broad terms determined by the restrictions of the 1916 zoning law. Within the legal parameters, the economics of maximum return further pared the form. The distinctive morphology of skyscrapers of the twenties and of the streetscapes and skyline of New York was less the invention of architects and engineers than the product of zoning law and economic logic.

In his famous 1896 essay, "The Tall Office Building Artistically Considered," Louis Sullivan pronounced the canonic phrase of modern architecture, "form follows function."[7] This article argues that in commercial architecture, where the function of buildings is to make money, the axiom that best describes skyscraper design is "form follows finance."

Site, Height, and Light: Planning the Empire State Building

That the world's premier skyscraper should rise on the southwest corner of Fifth Avenue and Thirty-fourth Street was, in a way, as accidental as it was audacious. The initial proposal for the site was for a bulky and quite banal fifty-story block of mixed loft and office space. The decision to transform the project into a "class A" office building and to pile it up eighty-five floors evolved only after the first developer defaulted and sold his contract to a syndicate, which at first continued with the original plans. The change of program was clearly influenced by the feverish speculation and often phenomenal profits that fired the New York real estate industry in the late 1920s. Midtown, where lots were larger and land less expensive than in the financial district, was the hot new territory. Development in the Grand Central zone spilled over onto scattered sites on Madison, Lexington, and Fifth avenues, and the whole east–west axis of Forty-second Street. The investors in the Empire State believed that their tower could polarize a new center further south.

But if, as the saying goes, "the three most important factors in real estate are location, location, location," the Empire State had several disadvantages. Midway *between* the major train stations, and *near* several subways and elevated lines, it was not *on* any. Furthermore, Fifth Avenue between Twenty-third and Forty-second streets was not an office area, but principally a low-rise shopping district lined with fashionable stores that traded on a lively, but leisurely street life. The tallest building in the immediate vicinity was the Internal Combustion Building, completed in 1928, which, though it occupied a full half-block site, truncated at twenty-eight stories.[8]

The typical pattern of urban transformation from low-density residences to intensive commercial use was grossly exaggerated in the history of the Empire State's site. Still farmland in the early nineteenth century, by the 1850s, this area of Fifth Avenue was graced with elegant homes and spired churches. On the block that would house the tower stood the adjoining Astor mansions where New York's social elite, the "Four Hundred," were so lavishly entertained. By the 1870s, however, the residential character of the quarter was already giving way to commercial uses.[9] The first significant violation of the avenue's former scale was the thirteen-story Waldorf Hotel, built on the southern half of the Astors' block in 1893.[10] In 1897, the much taller Astoria Hotel was constructed, and the two buildings were joined to become the Waldorf-Astoria, the world-famous center of elegance and epicurism. By the mid-1920s, many jazz-age New Yorkers considered the old Victorian pile a bit musty, and it began to suffer financially. Unable to resist the temptation of the skyrocketing value of their land, the owners announced that they would build a new, modern hotel on a full-block site uptown on Park Avenue.

In December 1928, the *Real Estate Record and Guide* reported the sale of the Waldorf-Astoria to the Bethlehem Engineering Corporation, Floyd Brown, president, and published a rendering of a fifty-story building proposed for the site.[11] The price of $14 million (nearly $17 million with additional expenses of leases, etc.) was the highest recorded that year. Designed by the architects Shreve and Lamb, the proposed building was a rather stunted tower with a massive base and multiple setbacks; the lower twenty-five floors were to be devoted to shops and lofts, the top twenty-five to offices.[12] The bulky, mixed-use structure was to contain nearly 2 million square feet (Figure 7.2).

Brown, who was trained as an architect and had developed other large projects, may well have intended to construct this building, or perhaps expected to sell his plans to another investor.[13] A month earlier, he had paid $100,000 "earnest money" for an option on the property and contracted to pay $2,500,000 in two cash installments. Although he met the first payment, he defaulted on the second.[14] On April 30, 1929, the day before the payment deadline, a syndicate was formed to buy out Brown's contract and to develop the site; it was organized by Louis G. Kaufman, the president of the Chatham and Phenix National Bank and Trust from which Brown had borrowed $900,000 for the first payment on his contract.[15]

Such mid-deal changes in ownership were common in speculative construction, whether due to failures to secure financing or to opportunistic profit taking. In *Skyscrapers and the Men Who Build Them* (1928), William A. Starrett (one of the partners in the firm that built the Empire State) outlined the standard process.[16] First, a developer would locate a property (preferably a corner site) suitable for a larger building and would secure an option by putting up sufficient money to hold the lot for a year or by paying a deposit, "earnest money," on a contract of sale. He would then hire an architect to prepare an impressive rendering that was sent to the newspapers along with a press release. This publicity often attracted real estate brokers who knew, or hoped to find, a major client interested in such a building. If a buyer appeared, the speculator could cash in for a quick profit. The plans for the Chrysler Building were sold in this manner. Some sites changed hands four or more times before being built upon, making it possible, as Starrett noted, "to turn a profit without turning a spadeful of earth."[17]

For a developer who continued with the project, the next step was to negotiate a sufficient number of leases for lending institutions to be approached for construction money. The three standard sources of funds were savings banks, insurance companies, and bond houses. Savings and loans offered the best rates (about 5 percent or under), but their policies were conservative, and they only lent up to 50 or 60 percent of the value of the completed structure. The second-lowest rate was offered by insurance companies (around 5½ percent) which, like the banks, would not lend either the full value of the property or the total cost of construction. The last option, bond houses, charged higher rates but would fund the entire project. Buildings were financed by selling bonds to the public at a rate of return of about 6 percent, while charging the developer a fee on the sum.[18] Bond houses that specialized in building issues had developed in the 1890s, and by the 1920s had become the most common method of financing. They helped to fuel the overheated real estate market and contributed significantly to the problem of overbuilding, since they facilitated a vast amount of construction that would not otherwise have found financing.[19]

Speculators played a leading role in the construction boom. From 1920 to 1930 the amount of office space in New York increased by half, from 74 million to 112 million square feet, and by 1935, another 26 million square feet contracted around the time of the Crash came to completion.[20] Whereas the physical growth of Manhattan's business districts was a response to the demand for space in the prosperous peacetime economy, much of the new construction was by speculators who undertook their projects without anchor clients or major leases negotiated. Individual developers seemed to have had unlimited confidence either in the resilience of the market or in their own superior sales skills, for even the oversupply of office space in 1926–1927 did little to quell the frenetic construction of the last years of the decade.[21]

Thus the potential for high returns, the small sum needed to initiate a deal, and the relative ease in securing financing for construction fired the burgeoning speculative market. Earnest money of $100,000 was all that Floyd Brown needed to set in motion a project for which he intended to borrow $25 million. When his plan for a fifty-story building failed, the next developers enlarged the scheme, and the $100,000 became the catalyst for an investment of $50 million.

The new owners had deeper pockets. After quickly raising over $5 million from a syndicate of investors organized under an affiliate of his bank, Louis Kaufman contacted Pierre S. du Pont and John Jacob Raskob. These longtime friends, who were closely associated as executives of the interlocking directorates of the du Pont interests and General Motors, numbered among the country's richest men. They were interested, and on August 28, 1929, Raskob sent a letter of understanding to Kaufman that outlined their proposed participation in the financing.[22]

The interim corporation at first proceeded with plans along the lines of Brown's original project; but during the discussions with Raskob in the summer of 1929, an important change of program was explored: transforming the project from a middle-range, mixed-use building into a very tall "class A" office tower. Raskob's letter to Kaufman had attached a sheet of figures that compared the projected costs and income of two alternatives, a fifty-five-story and an eighty-story building.[23] The first option was to have contained 29 million cubic feet, cost $45 million, and generate a rental income of $5,120,000 (with 10 percent vacancy), thus producing a gross return on total costs of 11.4 percent. The eighty-story alternative (simply the first building with another twenty-five stories piled above in a tower 80 × 240 feet) would produce an additional 330,000 square feet of rentable space, producing an overall income of $6,300,000, a gross return of 12.6 percent. The figures used in estimating the rental rate ($3.25 per square foot and $4.00 for the tower) and operating costs ($.75 per square foot) were both for office space. Such numbers, though very preliminary figures, were persuasive arguments for greater height.[24]

An eighty-story building would be a clear contender for the title of world's tallest, and this factor surely influenced the decision about height. In later years, associates described Raskob as the chief proponent of supreme height and recalled his boasts of planning "the biggest and highest building in the whole world."[25] At this early stage of the project, however, Raskob's tone was extremely circumspect.[26] In his August 1929 letter to Kaufman he wrote:

> Our present tentative feeling is that we should be able to build a building, the cubical content of which will be about 34,000,000 feet at $1.00 per cubic foot including all charges of every kind such as interest, cost of demolition, architect and builder's commission, fees paid for securing mortgages, rental fees, etc. etc. which would mean a total cost of not more than $34,000,000, which added to the land cost of $16,000,000 would give a total cost of $50,000,000.[27]

Financing in place, Empire State, Inc., was officially incorporated on September 5, 1929.[28] The directors of the corporation were Pierre S. du Pont, John J. Raskob, Louis G. Kaufman, and Alfred E. Smith, along with Ellis P. Earle, August Heckscher, and Michael Friedsam. Former New York Governor Al Smith, a close friend of Raskob's, who had been the chairman of Smith's unsuccessful presidential campaign in 1928, was signed on as the corporation's $50,000-a-year president.

Figure 7.2 Sketch for a proposed 50-Story Building for the Waldorf-Astoria Site. *Source:* Published December 29, 1928 in *Real Estate Record and Guide.* Photo by Carol Willis.

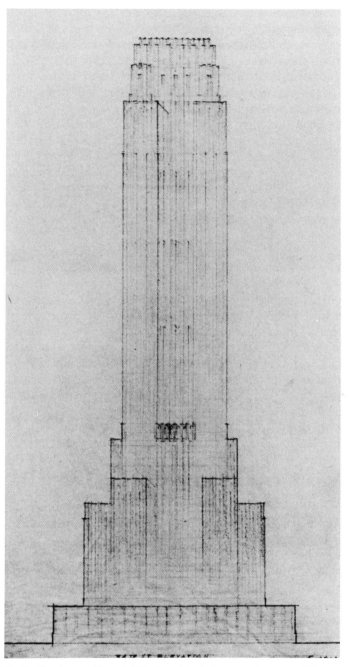

Figure 7.3 Preliminary Sketch, "Scheme K," Empire State Building, Late September or Early October 1929. *Source:* Photo by Carol Willis.

What had begun as a plan for a large, but anonymous, mid-rise loft and office block had, through a series of small steps and tentative decisions, been transformed into an enterprise designed to capture the attention of the world. From the time the corporation was formed, the project became all bombast and hyperbole. The present analysis, however, turns away from the hype in order to understand the logic of the business decisions and their influence on the building's design.

The Empire State had to be big: the high price of the land (about $200 per square foot) demanded a building with a high rental income, and the large site made a very tall structure viable within the limits of the zoning law. The strategy for development was to create an almost autonomous scale, "a city within a city" in the favorite phrase of the period. The building was designed to house 25,000, a floating population of some 40,000, and a maximum of 80,000. As one writer for *Fortune* observed, "It was a very spectacular gesture. If [the owners] were right they might . . . fix the center of the metropolis. If they were wrong they would have the hooting of the experts in their ears for the rest of their lives."[29]

The initial parameters set by the directors (the budget of $34 million, 34 million cubic feet) were the key determinants of the building's final form.[30] How did the developers arrive at these numbers? By a search for the highest rate of return on investment. To calculate the gross return on equity, the standard formula was to divide the anticipated income from rents by the total costs of building (construction, financing, taxes, overhead, etc.). Construction was at market rates; the $1.00 per cubic foot first estimate for the Empire State was not far from the reported final costs of $1.03.[31]

The vexing variable in the equation was the estimate of annual rental income. In theory, one simply calculated how many square feet of rentable space could be constructed with the available budget (16:1 was the rule of thumb for cubic feet necessary to produce one square foot of rentable floor area), then multiplied this number times the average rental rate (less 10 percent for vacancies).[32] Repeating this formula for bigger and smaller buildings provided comparative rates of return. The problem lay in correctly judging market rents. There was no comparable model for the Empire State, as real estate expert Hamilton Weber noted with anxiety in his report to the corporation.[33] Under the formula, the first rough estimates had suggested a gross return on equity of approximately 12.6 percent. In September 1930, around midpoint in construction, *Fortune* reported that the owners estimated their return would be about 10 percent.[34] This was considered rather low for speculative development generally, but for a very tall building on high-priced land, it was about average.[35]

These initial figures were based on standard real estate formulas, not on specific building plans. Indeed, from the acquisition of the property through the formation of Empire State, Inc., the plans for the building had been *entirely financial, not architectural.* The different schemes were described only in numbers—stories, cubic feet, operating costs and projected income, etc. No drawings were included or referred to in these reports. Raskob's letter of August 28 noted that one of the next steps would be choosing an architect to prepare a design.

The architectural firm hired was the same one that had developed the original mixed-use scheme for Brown. In 1929, Richmond H. Shreve and William F. Lamb were joined by Arthur Loomis Harmon to become Shreve, Lamb & Harmon. All three were veteran skyscraper designers who had built a number of the city's towers, including, in 1926, the New York headquarters for General Motors (Raskob's corporation).[36] Using their earlier studies, the architects could quickly sketch a structure that would rise more than half again the height of their first scheme.

The directors moved quickly to sign on their team. Most important was the builder, or general contractor. This company would manage the entire operation, promising for a fixed fee to deliver to the owners a finished building, "on time and on budget." The contractor was responsible for purchasing materials, letting subcontracts, supervising construction, financing the work month to month, as well as many other contingencies.[37] Only a limited number of builders had sufficient experience with this scale of operation and the capital necessary to cover the enormous costs of equipment, labor, and so on.

After interviewing the principals of five major firms, the board awarded the contract to Starrett Brothers and Eken.[38] The decision was not based on competitive bidding (i.e., the lowest price offered), since other considerations carried greater weight, especially a proven record of efficiency and speed. Starrett Brothers (as the firm name was commonly abbreviated) could point to several recent successes, including the extremely complex construction of the Bank of Manhattan Company, a sixty-five-story tower on a tight mid-block site on Wall Street that was just being completed in record-breaking time. At his interview, Paul Starrett, the firm's president, promised to deliver a finished building in just eighteen months. He asked a flat fee of $600,000. He was offered the job for $500,000, which was accepted after some changes in the insurance and financing arrangements.[39]

While Shreve, Lamb & Harmon were responsible for the three-dimensional form of the building—its mass and height—the Starretts were the architects of an equally important fourth dimension: time.

"Time is money" applies literally in commercial properties. The running costs of interest and taxes for the Empire State were estimated to be $10,000 a day.[40] The rapid production schedule of eighteen months meant that the owners could market their office space for annual leases signed in May and therefore could begin collecting rents in 1931. Speed of construction became a vital part of the building program. To streamline the design process, the owners, architects, and builders met regularly and also worked closely with consultants on technical problems such as foundations, elevators, wind-bracing, plumbing, and ventilation.[41] These planning meetings occupied four weeks and produced the complete technical, planning, and economic requirements for the project.[42]

The guidelines developed by the committee became the basic blueprint of the building. As William Lamb, the building's chief designer, explained in an article in *Architectural Forum:*

> The program was short enough—a fixed budget, no space more than 28 feet from window to corridor, as many stories of such space as possible, an exterior of limestone, and completion date of May 1, 1931, which meant a year and six months from the beginning of the sketches.[43]

The first three criteria, he emphasized, determined the building's massing and height, the last two, the key features of the facade.[44]

Working with this program, the architects, together with the engineers, builders, and rental agent, began to search for the most efficient and profitable design. During September and October they developed several different versions of massing and height, each supported by forecasts of costs. Their seventeenth version, "Scheme K," was adopted at a meeting of the executive committee on October 3, 1929 (Figure 7.3). Although there were several subsequent changes, including the precise number of stories and the addition of the mooring mast, this scheme established the building's basic massing, plan, and proportions. In an article on the building's general design, Lamb made a point of contrasting Scheme K with the previous version, Scheme J; he reproduced the elevations and plans of both in order to show how the bulk and complexity of the base section had been reduced, light courts removed, and the tower made more integral.[45]

Lamb also described how the programmatic stipulation that "no space [be] more than 28 feet from window to corridor" affected the office plans, circulation spaces, and service core:

> The logic of the plan is very simple. A certain amount of space in the center, arranged as compactly as possible, contains the vertical

circulation, toilets, shafts and corridors. Surrounding this is a perimeter of office space 28 feet deep. The sizes of the floors diminish as the elevators decrease in number. . . . The four groups of high-rise elevators are placed in the center of the building with the low-rise groups adjoining on the east and west sides so that, as these drop off, the building steps back from the long dimension of the property to approach the square form of the shaft, with the result that instead of being a tower set upon a series of diminishing setbacks prescribed by the zoning law, the building becomes all tower rising from a great five-story base.[46]

The massing of the Empire State was thus a direct expression of its floor plans. The setbacks signaled the floors where the elevators terminated, whereas the height was limited to the core area needed for elevators. The precise location of the setbacks at the twenty-first, twenty-fifth, and thirtieth floors was also affected by the New York zoning law; this important parameter is discussed later. The present focus concentrates on the internal arrangement of space and, thus, the outward expression of form (Figure 7.4).

In the 1920s, as today, the first task of the skyscraper architect was to establish the plan of a typical upper floor (which is to say, all the upper floors, since in a tower they would be virtually identical). Current market opinion about what constitutes quality space greatly influences layouts. In the 1980s, market preference was for huge open areas of 20,000 to 30,000 square feet or larger that could then be subdivided by work-station cubicles.[47] In the 1920s, the ideal rental building was designed to be divided up into suites that comprised many small, individual offices. Private offices were generally about 9 or 10 feet in width and had a working window, usually from 4 to 5 feet wide and 6 to 7 feet high. The maximum distance from window to corridor wall ideally measured no more than 25 to 30 feet, although 20 feet was increasingly becoming popular.[48] No office space was rented without a window (at least for executives) (Figure 7.5).

The quality of light distinguished a "class A" office building from inferior space—a difference that translated directly into dollars. As the skyscraper architect Harvey Wiley Corbett explained: "It is better business to construct less building, and have shallow offices well lighted, than to have more building with deep spaces poorly lighted. In other words, it is better to have less space—less capital investment—permanently rented at a high figure than too much space partially rented at a low figure."[49] Thus, for the Empire State, the principle of cost and benefit dictated a ring of offices no more than 28 feet deep surrounding a compact core of circulation.

Skyscraper interiors were not constructed as offices, but as generic

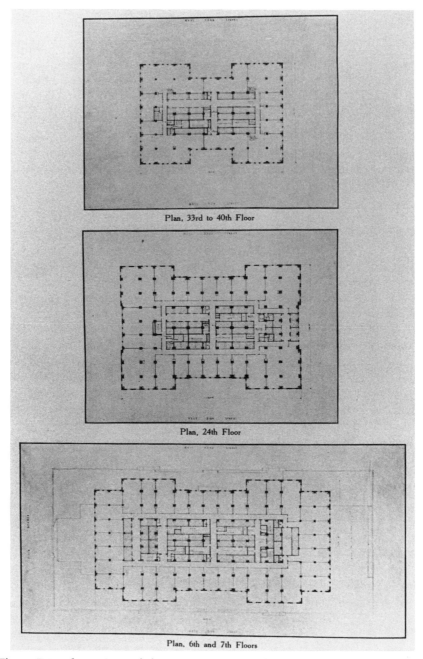

Plan, 33rd to 40th Floor

Plan, 24th Floor

Plan, 6th and 7th Floors

Figure 7.4 Floor Plans of the Empire State Building. *Source: Architectural Forum*, January 1931. Courtesy of Avery Architectural and Fine Arts Library, Columbia University.

Figure 7.5 Empire State Under Construction; Note the Relation of Structural Columns and the Pattern of Fenestration. *Source:* Courtesy of Avery Architectural and Fine Arts Library, Columbia University.

space that was to be subdivided and finished after a specific amount of space was leased by the tenant; nevertheless, the floor plan with its windows and structural columns had to be designed for easy division into an optimum number of individual offices. Structural columns were generally placed two office widths apart (around 18 to 20 feet) and hidden as much as possible within the walls.[50] The dimensions of the ideal office, each with its opening, and the placement of columns thus determined the pattern of piers and windows of the facade. Even the trough, the three-bay recession in the north and south faces, was conceived from this "inside-out" rationale, for its multiple angles provided more coveted corner-office layouts—eight to twelve per floor.[51] Thus as Shreve quipped: "Finance dictates the fenestration; rent rolls rule the *parti*."[52]

The height of the Empire State, while influenced by the "race into the skies," was also an economic decision. The banner year 1929 saw the construction of the seventy-story Bank of Manhattan Company and the seventy-seven-story Chrysler buildings, while other even taller towers were announced, but never started.[53] There was, of course, enormous advertising value attached to holding the title of "world's tallest," and Empire State, Inc., exploited this aspect unremittingly in its publicity. The observation deck was designed to steal away the paying crowds from the Woolworth Building's top and other aeries (and, indeed, it proved to be a major source of revenue during the Depression). The value of record-breaking height clearly justified some extra expenditure, but the erection of several speculative office towers of sixty-five to seventy-five stories during these years make clear that very tall towers were also profitable. The eighty-five floors of the Empire State made sense economically.

At some point in the construction of every skyscraper, the law of diminishing returns sets in—that is, the rents for the additional stories do not cover the costs. Taller towers need extra foundations, wind-bracing, mechanical systems, and so on. By far the greatest price of height, though, lies in the requirements of efficient vertical circulation.[54] While elevators are expensive to build and to run, their major cost accrues in the vast amounts of unrentable space they consume for their shafts. Quality office space demands strict standards of elevator efficiency, both in terms of speed and minimal waiting time. Since adding floors to a tower requires more service, floor space for offices on all floors below must be sacrificed. The optimal *economic* height of a skyscraper is therefore different from its maximum *engineering* limits. In the 1920s, towers of 1,500 feet and higher were considered by most engineers to be structurally feasible, but while many articles discussed such soaring spires, no actual projects were initiated.

The issue of the most profitable height for tall buildings was studied by a committee of architects, engineers, and contractors and published in 1930 in *The Skyscraper: A Study in the Economic Height of Modern Office Buildings*.[55] Under the auspices of the American Institute of Steel Construction, these experts analyzed the relative costs of a series of eight office buildings ranging in height from eight to seventy-five stories. The hypothetical site was a corner lot with the dimensions of 200 × 405 feet (20 feet shorter than that of the Empire State) a block south of Grand Central Terminal. All the models conformed to current zoning laws and building codes, and estimates of land and construction costs were based on current market rates.

The committee determined that the sixty-three-story building returned the maximum rate on the original investment. While various factors contributed to this conclusion, including the cost of elevators, mechanical systems, and so on, by far the most important factor was the price of land, because it represented such a large portion of the total investment. Based on current costs, the experts calculated that a sixty-three-story building promised a return of 10.25 percent; by comparison, fifty stories would bring only 9.87 percent; seventy-five stories, 10.06 percent.[56] The report also noted that the higher the value of land, the taller a building must rise to reach the point of maximum economic return. If the value exceeded the $200 per square-foot figure they used for their hypothetical site, the economic height of a building would also rise.[57]

The land and lease buyouts for the Empire State were slightly more than $200 per square foot.[58] Years later, Robert C. Brown recalled that Andrew Eken of Starrett Brothers and the architects had reported that seventy-five stories would be the most economical height for the building and that eighty-eight stories would require an additional bank of elevators.[59] In fact, the commercial office tower occupied only the lower eighty stories, since the top five floors were reserved for the corporation and were serviced by the elevators for the observation level. When the directors weighed the costs of a less-than-profitable extra five (or ten) floors, the benefits of supreme height must have seemed worth the cost. The addition of the "mooring mast" (supposedly for dirigibles, though the engineers knew the technology to be very problematic!) was the *coup de grâce* that stretched the tower from 1,045 to 1,250 feet, ensuring a commanding authority over its competitors.

While in theory there are many ways to stack more than 2 million square feet of floor space on about two acres of land, in New York in the 1920s, there was generally one *best* solution. Alternatives were limited by a number of variables, including office layout, elevator service, and available budget, and the imperative of speed discouraged innovations or complicated engineering that would slow the design or building process. In addition, one *external* force definitively shaped New York high-rises: zoning.

The passage in 1916 of New York's first zoning legislation changed the rules of the game for skyscraper design. In addition to dividing the city into zones of use (business, residential, and unrestricted), the law introduced a new concept—the zoning envelope—into the vocabulary of urbanism. Designed to protect some measure of light and air for Manhattan's canyons, the zoning envelope was a formula that limited and defined the height and bulk of tall buildings. In the laissez-faire period before 1916, buildings generally rose straight up from the lot lines for twenty, thirty, and even forty stories, as did the Equitable Building of 1915. The new code demanded that after a maximum vertical height above the sidewalk (usually 125 or 150 feet), a building must be stepped back as it rose in accordance with a fixed angle drawn from the center of the street. A tower of unlimited height was permitted over one-quarter of the site. These restrictions produced the characteristic "setback" massing of New York high-rises between 1916 and 1961 (when the zoning law was changed to encourage the modernist "slab" tower and plaza).

The code's limitation of the area of the tower made large sites particularly attractive for development because they allowed shafts of profitable proportions. The generous dimensions of the Empire State's lot, 197 × 425 feet, meant that its tower could expand to 100 × 212 feet; by contrast, the lot of the Chrysler Building could support a tower of only half that area. For skyscrapers on small or medium-size lots (typically around 100 × 200 or 200 × 200 feet), the slender tower limited the number of elevators that serviced the upper stories and meant that floors below generally filled the zoning envelope. The massing of the Bank of Manhattan Company or Cities Service Building, both on constricted downtown lots, have bulky bases and multiple setbacks that illustrate how developers pressed the legal limits. The ideal of symmetry was often sacrificed to gain additional rental space, as the massing of 500 Fifth Avenue, Shreve, Lamb & Harmon's other New York tower of 1930, clearly demonstrates (Figure 7.1, left foreground). Both the logic of the zoning envelope and the economics of development thus argued for big buildings on large sites. However, given New York's high land costs and the typical pattern of divided ownership of characteristically small Manhattan lots, large building sites were very difficult to assemble.[60]

The 1916 zoning law created a new dimension of public space *around and above* buildings. No longer did private property extend infinitely into the heavens—only a quarter of it did. Economics shaped the solids, zoning the space. Between the outer limits of the zoning envelope and the zone of public space, however, was an ambiguous area in which private property reduced the building's mass in its own economic self-interest.

The Empire State offers one of the best expressions in form of the interplay between zoning and economics, for while the building's general massing was determined by the legal envelope, its ultimate form was tailored by economics. Under the code, the lower section would have been permitted to rise sheer above the sidewalk to a height of ten floors on Fifth Avenue and sixteen on Thirty-Fourth Street. Instead, after only five stories, it set back a full 60 feet on the east and west sides. The resulting effect of a low base was praised by architectural critics for establishing a more human scale at the pedestrian level. However, the major reason for the setback was economic, for it shielded the lower-floor offices from the noise of the street and created a zone of sunlight and quiet that would fetch higher rents than deep, loft-type space. Likewise, the setbacks below the thirtieth floor were trimmed back to maintain the shallow, 28-foot perimeter of quality space defined in the building program. Particularly at its base and top, then, market forces placed stricter limitations on the form of the building than did the zoning law.

If, as suggested earlier, in economic terms there was one *best* solution for any high-rise on a given site, then why didn't all buildings on comparable sites take the same shape? Program and the particular needs of specific clients were important factors in the logical design of massing and height.[61] So were variations in rental markets and limitations of financing. Developers held varying opinions about what type of space or floor plan brought the highest return.[62] Some were more willing to pioneer in new areas or to innovate with design or engineering. Since construction costs and financing were fairly standard, the volume of a building was a direct function of how much money the developer was able to borrow and prepared to spend. Then, too, some speculators were more optimistic than others and willing to take greater risks to win an extra margin of profit; the role of human nature should not be discounted.

Every skyscraper poses a slightly different economic and design problem. The complex equation of the Empire State was perhaps best stated in a 1930 article in *Fortune:*

> These various elements fixed the perimeter of an oddly shaped geometric solid, bounded on one side by 83,860 square feet of land, on the other by $35,000,000, on the other by the law of diminishing

returns, on another by the laws of physics and the characteristics of structural steel, and on another by the conical exigencies of the zoning ordinances, and on still another by May 1, 1931.[63]

A design with these disparate dimensions could not be planned by the architects alone. A team of experts—which included the owners, the builders, architects, structural and mechanical engineers, elevator experts, and rental agents—was required to collaborate, first to define the problem, then to solve it.

Affected by specific conditions of site, budget, program, schedule, or other factors, every New York high-rise was, in a limited sense, unique. Yet, like snowflakes, skyscrapers of the 1920s looked very much alike. Their similarities were essential, the differences superficial. Owners and architects, of course, endeavored to distinguish their buildings, but this individualization was generally achieved on the facade through the choice of materials and ornament, rather than through any radical rethinking of form. Exterior materials could be limestone, colored brick, terra cotta, and, later, metal and glass.[64] Windows could be aligned in various vertical patterns, as was the preference in the 1920s, or stress horizontals. In the 1950s, under the influence of the International Style, the same steel skeletons were wrapped with horizontal window bands or glass curtain walls that emphasized the airy space within rather than the solidity and weight of stone.

Underneath their decorative skins, these buildings displayed a basic uniformity that was the product of the formal parameters set by the zoning law and the economic formulas of maximum return. This consistency in design began after the passage of zoning in 1916, and continued until the zoning ordinance was revised in 1961. The buildings of this period, especially those of the pre-Depression decade, constituted a distinctive type that contemporaries often referred to as the "setback style" or the "New York School," but which recent historians have begun to call "art deco." As this essay has suggested, the "style" was far more than an aesthetic of surface decoration. Rather, it was the logical resolution of both market and regulatory forces, a kind of "inside-out" design process, and a complex equation of estimated costs and returns.

For all the careful considerations of economics that affected its design, the Empire State proved to be a financial disaster for one unavoidable reason: the Great Depression. Had the business community continued to thrive, it could perhaps have absorbed the 26 million square feet of new office space that came onto the market in the years following the Crash. Yet, the overbuilding in midtown was severe. Rockefeller Center, the tour de force of urban design that covered three full blocks from Forty-eighth to Fifty-first streets between Fifth and Sixth avenues, began construction in 1931 on a projected 7 million square feet of rental space, and through the thirties it became the Empire State's most awesome competition. Leasing was extremely slow; in 1932, only slightly more than a quarter of the space was rented, and through the Depression the building received the nickname the "Empty State."[65]

The Empire State was, and will remain, an unrepeatable achievement. Its rapid erection, just twenty-one months from the acquisition of the site to tenant occupancy, is inconceivable today given the added layers of governmental reviews and different labor standards; the process of constructing a building of comparable scale, such as the recent full-block development of midtown's Worldwide Plaza, would consume at least five years. Current popular and professional opinion has turned against great height, and community boards and preservation groups can often marshal sufficient power to stop projects they consider out of scale with the existing neighborhood. Today the old Waldorf-Astoria Hotel would be protected against demolition, the design of a tower rising above it would have to be approved by the Landmark Preservation Commission. Zoning has changed too. Under the present law, a new tower would be considerably smaller; built "as of right" its FAR (floor-area ratio) could not exceed 15, that is, fifteen times the area of the lot. With a total area of 2,158,000 square feet, the Empire State has an FAR of approximately 25.[66] This economic fact, far more than its 1981 designation as a city landmark, should protect the noble tower for many years to come.

A contemporary of Sullivan, the critic Barr Ferree, observed in 1894: "Current American architecture is not a matter of art, but of business. A building must pay or there will be no investor ready with the money to meet its cost. This is at once the curse and the glory of American architecture."[67] Economic determinants do not preclude aesthetic choices. The Empire State demonstrates that economics, fully understood and skillfully manipulated, can produce masterworks.

Notes

1. The design and construction of the Empire State were superbly documented in numerous articles written by the major figures involved in the project. In 1930–1931, *Architectural Forum* published an important series of articles, and dozens of others appeared in both professional and popular magazines. Two general books on skyscrapers are of particular value: Col. William A. Starrett, *Skyscrapers and the Men Who Build Them* (New York: Scribners, 1928) and Paul Starrett, *Changing the Sky-*

line (New York: Whittlesey House, 1937); these brothers were principals of Starrett and Eken, the general contractors for the Empire State.

The Avery Architectural and Fine Arts Library at Columbia University has a rich archive of Empire State material, including blueprints, construction photographs, and material collected by the Empire State's publicity office, including scrapbooks of clippings and other ephemera.

As part of their holdings of the financial records of Pierre S. du Pont and John J. Raskob, both major investors in the Empire State, the Hagley Museum and Library in Wilmington, Delaware, has important material on the building's history. I am indebted to the Center for the History of Business, Technology, and Society for a Hagley-Winterthur Fellowship, which afforded me the concentrated use of their collection, and to the generous assistance of the administration and staff.

2. Timothy L. Pfleuger, "The Modern Office Building," *Architectural Forum*, 52 (June 1930): 785.

3. Cecil C. Evers, *The Commercial Problem in Buildings* (New York: The Record and Guide Company, 1914), p. vi.

4. For a discussion of the historiography of the skyscraper in architectural history and a concise bibliography, see Rosemarie Bletter, "The Invention of the Skyscraper: Notes on Its Diverse Histories," *Assemblage* (February 1987): 110–117.

5. See Olivier Zunz, "Inside the Skyscraper" in *Making America Corporate: 1870–1920* (Chicago: University of Chicago Press, 1990), and Gail Fenske and Deryck Holdsworth, "Corporate Identity and the New York Office Building, 1895–1915," Chapter 6 in this book.

6. These numbers are based on the list of "New York's 100 Highest Buildings" in W. Parker Chase, *New York Nineteen Thirty-Two: The Wonder City* (1932; reprint ed., New York: New York Bound, 1983), p. 151.

7. Both Sullivan's exact words ("form ever follows function") and their import have often been misinterpreted. The streamlined phrase was better suited to the polemics of the Modern Movement's doctrine of "functionalism"—an aesthetic with both moralizing and formalizing motivations that held that a building's design should be a simple, truthful expression of its internal program and structure. Sullivan was little concerned with the plans of his office buildings; his phrase referred to the expressive message of the facade—its aspirations to loftiness and its status as a symbol of modern business culture.

8. Chase, *The Wonder City*, p. 215.

9. M. Christine Boyer, *Manhattan Manners: Architecture and Style, 1859–1900* (New York: Rizzoli, 1985), pp. 32, 48–50.

10. Boyer, *Manhattan Manners*, p. 227, and Robert A. M. Stern, Gregory Gilmartin, and John Massengale, *New York Nineteen-Hundred* (New York: Rizzoli Intl., 1983), pp. 254–261.

11. "Waldorf-Astoria Hotel in the Year's Largest Sale: Celebrated Hostelry Is to Be Replaced by Fifty-Story Office Building Representing Investment of Approximately $25,000,000," *Real Estate Record and Guide* 122 (December 29, 1928): 7–8. Other articles announcing the sale of the Waldorf-Astoria and plans for a fifty-story office building on the site appeared in the *New York Times* (December 23, 1928), section XI–XII: 1, and in Charles F. Noyes, "Two Experts' Views of Realty Prospects for 1929," *Real Estate Record and Guide* 123 (January 5, 1929): 9.

12. Several sources called the project an office building, but William F. Lamb described this first design as a "loft-type" building in his article, "The Empire State Building: The General Design," *Architectural Forum* 53 (January 1930): 7. Paul Starrett also described Brown's scheme as a loft building in *Changing the Skyline*, p. 285.

13. According to his obituary, Floyd de L. Brown was an architect and builder. Born in New York, he first attended the Ecole des Beaux Arts, then received his degree in architecture from Columbia University. In 1918, after working in several New York firms, he organized the Bethlehem Engineering Corporation, of which he was president; his company designed and developed the National Broadcasting Building (711 Fifth Avenue), a project that Paul Starrett claimed had earned Brown $1 million. Obituary: *New York Times* (November 8, 1955): 31.

14. Apparently, Brown badly misjudged the market with this loft-type design, for this area of midtown was already glutted with vacant loft space. See the *Regional Survey of New York and Its Environs*, vol. VI (1931), pp. 97–98.

15. The precise nature of Brown's deal and what happened to him afterward is not entirely clear. His option with the Waldorf-Astoria Realty Corp. of November 21, 1928, required a payment of $2,500,000 in two installments. Chatham & Phenix loaned Brown money for his first payment. Kaufman certainly knew that Bethlehem Engineering Corp. would not be able to make the second payment of $1 million on May 1, 1929. On April 30, 1929, the Enyan Corp. (which subsequently became the Waldorf-Astoria Office Building, Inc., and then Empire State, Inc.) was formed to purchase the agreement, buy the site, and erect a large office building. Kaufman was the major investor in this syndicate, which included eleven other wealthy businessmen connected with the Chatham & Phenix Bank. Brown's name does not appear in any subsequent list of investors. Hagley Museum and Library, Longwood Papers, 229–15, Empire State, Inc., 1937, folder 32, IX.

16. Starrett, *Skyscrapers*, p. 110ff.

17. Starrett, *Skyscrapers*, p. 110.

18. Starrett, *Skyscrapers*, p. 115ff.; see following note.

19. According to Shultz and Simmons, in the late 1890s, the growing market for large commercial buildings (structures of a scale that required mortgages exceeding the borrowing capacity of most individuals) stimulated the development of bond houses that specialized in financing construction. These institutions divided a mortgage into denominations of $100, $500, and $1,000 and sold them to the public. The principal was paid back through the income of the property, and the building itself secured the loan. The bond houses charged commissions of 5 to 10 percent, sometimes even 20 percent, on the loan. Bond houses became the most popular method of financing buildings in the 1920s; during 1925, $675 million of real estate bonds were sold in the United States, which was a more than tenfold increase over the previous five years. Earle Shultz and Walter Simmons, *Offices in the Sky* (New York: Bobbs-Merrill, 1959), pp. 144–147.

20. The major part of this volume was added in midtown. These statistics and conclusions are based on the analysis by Emanuel Tobier in "Manhattan's Business District in the Industrial Age," in John Hull Mollen-

kopf, ed., *Power, Culture, and Place: Essays on New York City* (New York: Russell Sage Foundation, 1988), pp. 77–105; sections on the office market, pp. 86, 99–100. The expansion of new commercial space, especially loft buildings, was comparable to that of the office sector.

21. For an account of the building boom of the 1920s in New York and nationally, see Shultz and Simmons, *Offices in the Sky*, pp. 153–163.

22. Du Pont and Raskob agreed to supply $5 million in cash and to guarantee a part of the second mortgage of $12,500,000; together they provided a total of $6,250,000 of a budget that was raised to $50 million. The mortgage of $27,500,000 was lent by Metropolitan Life Insurance. Letter sent by Raskob to Kaufman (August 28, 1929), Hagley Museum and Library, Longwood Manuscripts, 229–15, Box 1 of 5, File 26, I.

23. Whereas Raskob is often cited as the person who pressed to make the building the world's tallest, there is no document that states this directly; associates such as Hamilton Weber who credited him with the idea joined the project after the events discussed here. From the limited correspondence that exists for this period (May to September 1929), it does seem that Raskob was the leader in the drive for great height. Letter from Raskob to Kaufman (August 28, 1929), op. cit.

24. The estimated construction costs were the same for both buildings, even though tall buildings were more expensive to build; one might therefore suspect that the person who devised the comparison wanted to tilt the figures toward the taller building.

25. Recollections of Hamilton H. Weber, the rental agent for the Empire State; quoted in Theodore James, Jr., *The Empire State Building* (New York: Harper & Row, 1975), p. 45.

26. The only reference to the scale of the project came in Raskob's remark at the end of the letter: "I appreciate the opportunity you have given us in this matter and particularly in the privilege of being associated with you and your group in the doing of something big and really worth while. I am sure it will be the most outstanding thing in New York and a credit to the city and state as well as to those associated with it." In the context of the entire letter, Raskob's comment seems to me to express optimism, but hardly a hubristic compulsion to erect the world's tallest tower.

27. Letter from Raskob to Kaufman, Longwood Manuscripts.

28. Copies of the documents of incorporation are in the du Pont Papers at Hagley Museum and Library, Longwood Manuscripts, 229–15, bound volume, Empire State Inc., Box 5.

29. "Paper Spires," *Fortune* 1 (September 1930): 58.

30. These figures changed several times in the fall of 1929; for example, in November, the estimate was $35 million; the cubage also vacillated between 34 and 36 million.

31. The contract from Starrett Bros., signed in November 1929, was for $27 million (plus their fee of $500,000); the first figure divided by 34 million cubic feet equals about $.79. The *Fortune* article of September 1930 reported costs ranging from $.50 to $.85 per cubic foot (p. 58). The figure of $1.03 quoted by Shultz and Simmons probably included other costs, such as interest, commissions, mortgages, etc. Shultz and Simmons, *Offices in the Sky*, p. 168.

32. Harvey Wiley Corbett reported the 16:1 ratio in an essay, "New Stones for Old," in the *Saturday Evening Post*, Part 3 (May 15, 1926): 6–17. The

Empire State achieved a ratio of 16.11:1, according to *Fortune;* "Paper Spires," p. 122.

33. Weber later became the rental agent for the Empire State; letter from Hamilton H. Weber to Robert C. Brown (October 21, 1929), Hagley Museum and Library, Longwood Manuscripts, 229–15, Box 1 of 5, Folder 26, I.

34. "Paper Spires," p. 122. The first figures were the ones used in a table appended to the letter of August 28, 1929, from Raskob to Kaufman.

35. According to Wallace K. Harrison, in the pre-World War II era, a 10 percent gross return on equity in office buildings was considered to be "a minimum inducement for capital investment" and served as a base from which to compute the form, bulk, and height of a building. Wallace K. Harrison, "Office Buildings," in Talbot Hamlin, ed., *Forms and Functions of Twentieth Century Architecture,* vol. 4 (New York: Columbia University Press, 1952), p. 161.

36. Before establishing their own practice in 1924, Shreve and Lamb had worked in the office of Carrère and Hastings, where they had designed major office buildings, such as the Standard Oil (1921) and Fisk buildings. Their firm's other skyscrapers included the Lefcourt-National Building (1928) and 500 Fifth Avenue (1930); projects outside New York included Carew Tower, Cincinnati (1930) and R. J. Reynolds Tobacco Company Building in Winston-Salem (1930). Harmon had worked independently until 1929; his best-known building was the Shelton Hotel (1924).

37. For a description of the responsibilities of general contractors, see Starrett, *Skyscrapers,* p. 87.

38. Paul Starrett, president of Starrett Brothers and Eken, desperately wanted the Empire State commission, which he regarded as a fitting climax to his forty-year career in the construction industry. In 1922, he had resigned from his long tenure as president of the George A. Fuller Company, the country's largest builder, and joined in partnership with his brother William A. (Bill) Starrett and a younger associate, Andrew J. Eken. Paul Starrett described his interview for the Empire State commission in *Changing the Skyline,* pp. 289–292.

39. Ibid., pp. 289, 292.

40. "Paper Spires," pp. 119, 122. The article also noted that the carrying charges on the two mortgages were estimated at $2,132,500.

41. The collaboration was by all reports exemplary; Paul Starrett called it the most harmonious in his experience, and in articles both Shreve and Lamb praised the changing professional role of architects as members of a team. Starrett, *Changing the Skyline,* p. 293, and William F. Lamb, "The Empire State Building: The General Design," *Architectural Forum* 54 (January 1931): 1. Also see the comments of R. H. Shreve in "The Empire State Building Organization," *Architectural Forum* 52 (June 1930): 771–774.

42. Lamb, ibid., p. 5.

43. Ibid., pp. 1–4.

44. The need for speed of construction dictated several important decisions about the facade treatment, in particular the metal window framing and limestone panels that were specially designed for speed of construction.

45. Lamb, "Empire State Building."

46. Ibid., p. 5.

47. William Pedersen, "Considerations for Urban Architecture and the Tall Building" in Lynn S. Beedle, ed., *Second Century of the Skyscraper* (New York, 1988), p. 163.

48. For discussions of office plans in the 1920s, see Arthur L. Harmon, "The Design of Office Buildings," *Architectural Forum*, 52 (June 1930): 819. In another article, Detroit architect Albert Kahn cited 26 to 28 feet as a maximum depth for office space and noted that offices 20 feet deep "now prove to be in greater demand." Albert Kahn, "Designing Modern Office Building," *Architectural Forum*, 52 (June 1930): 775.

49. Harvey Wiley Corbett, "New Stones for Old," *Saturday Evening Post* 198 (May 15, 1926): 17.

50. Harmon, "The Design of Office Buildings," p. 819.

51. Clyde A. Mann, "The Economic Considerations Involved in the Empire State Building," *Real Estate Record and Guide* (August 16, 1930): 9.

52. R. H. Shreve, "The Empire State Building Organization," *Architectural Forum* 52 (June 1930): 771–774.

53. For example, the first plans for the new Metropolitan Life Building in late 1929 proposed an 80- or 100-story tower (depending on the source), and the real estate broker Charles Noyes announced plans to erect a 100-story building. Counting stories can be ambiguous, since not all the upper floors were usable. Advertised by its agents as "77 stories," the Chrysler Building had its highest floor on 69. The Bank of Manhattan Building had 60 stories and 10 more "floors" of utility penthouses.

54. Efficiency was measured in the number and speed of elevators, and related to travel time, especially waiting time, which for a "class A" building was not supposed to exceed twenty-five seconds. Kahn, "Designing Modern Office Building," p. 776 (see note 48).

55. W. C. Clark and J. L. Kingston, *The Skyscraper: A Study in the Economic Height of Modern Office Buildings* (New York: American Institute of Steel Construction, 1930). Shreve served on this committee.

56. Clark and Kingston, *The Skyscraper*, Table 2, p. 25.

57. A rule of thumb in development held that land and building costs should be at least equal (and usually the building's value was greater). Only with the sixty-three-story structure was the total cost assignable to the land equaled and exceeded by the cost of the building. Clark and Kingston, *The Skyscraper*, pp. 25, 29.

58. Clyde A. Mann, "The Economic Considerations Involved in the Empire State Building," *Real Estate Record and Guide* (August 16, 1930), p. 9. Mann noted that in 1930, the lot was valued at $20 million, or nearly $250 per square foot.

59. Notes by Robert C. Brown made in response to questions posed by lawyers in regard to a lawsuit of 1937; Hagley Museum and Library, Raskob files, Acc. 473, File 743.

60. A recent *New York Times* article demonstrated the persistent difficulty in assembling multiple sites by noting that "seventeen years after abandoning its vision of a second Rockefeller Center east of Times Square, the Durst Organization has apparently given up trying to assemble one last major parcel on the Avenue of the Americas, and will content itself with building one-story shops." David Dunlap, "Commercial Property: Holdouts," *New York Times* (February 28, 1990): 10:7.

61. In fact, while there were several skyscrapers of the twenties constructed on lots of almost identical dimensions, none approached the scale of the Empire State. Two insurance company headquarters on Madison Square Park occupied full-block sites of 198 × 425 feet. The new building for New York Life, completed to the designs of Cass Gilbert in 1928, was a strangely stunted tower sandwiched in a heavy setback base that rose to a height of only 34 stories. The towerless North Annex for Metropolitan Life never grew beyond 32 stories, although when first announced in late 1929, a tower of 80 to 100 stories was projected. Although these mid-rise structures did not inspire awe, they were, in fact, well suited to the special operations of their companies, which required large open areas for clerical workers and floor space for file storage, rather than a multitude of individual office cells. It should be noted that each company already owned the land on which it was building. There is a good discussion of these buildings in Robert A. M. Stern et al., *New York 1930*, pp. 535–537 and 542–544.

62. An important factor in this decision was the size of the total floor area, which had bearing on whether the space was rented by one client or broken up into many individual suites. See Walter H. Kilham, Jr., "Tower Floor Plans of New York Skyscrapers Compared," *American Architect* 138 (October 1930): 30–31, 76–78.

63. "Paper Spires," p. 119.

64. Curtain-wall glass had not been sufficiently perfected in the 1920s, but in any case, until 1937 the building code required fireproof (i.e., masonry or metal) spandrels.

65. Rental figures from the report to stockholders of Empire State, Inc., 1932, Hagley Museum and Library, Longwood Manuscript, 229–15, Box 1.

66. Department of City Planning, telephone interview, March 1990.

67. Barr Ferree, "Economic Conditions of Architecture in America," *Proceedings of the 27th Annual Convention of the American Institute of Architects* (Chicago, 1893), p.231; quoted in M. Christine Boyer, *Manhattan Manners: Architecture and Style, 1850–1900* (New York, 1985), p. 27.

Part IV

GOING FROM HOME TO WORK

8

Subways, Transit Politics, and Metropolitan Spatial Expansion

Clifton Hood

The New York subway straddled the nineteenth and twentieth centuries. The first route, the Interborough Rapid Transit Company's line, was conceived during the industrial depression of the 1890s, yet opened in the new century, at a time of prosperity and optimism. The subway was constructed by thousands of largely Irish and Italian immigrant laborers who worked mainly with their hands, not with machines, yet it became the world's fastest rapid transit railway and a symbol of technological progress. It broke the transportation barriers of the industrial metropolis and stimulated the settlement of northern Manhattan and the Bronx. This immense physical expansion prompted planners to view the subways as an instrument for achieving the efficient city, where population would be dispersed from the overcrowded core, and where residential neighborhoods would be segregated from manufacturing and commercial districts.

But although the subway helped give rise to the modern city, it was embedded in a highly competitive political structure that had been erected in the nineteenth century. The purpose of this chapter is to examine the relationship between transit politics and metropolitan spatial expansion. Operated by private companies and regulated by government commission, New York's subway was plagued by disputes over monopoly and route expansion during the progressive era. At the end of World War I, however, a financial emergency spawned by inflation made the subway the focus of more intense partisan and press conflict than before. As controversies erupted over the rate of fare, route expansion, and other issues, rapid transit became highly politicized. The politicization of the subways contributed to the adoption of a newer and seemingly nonpolitical transport technology, the automobile, that assumed transit's longstanding function of stimulating urban growth.

The subway's fiscal crisis deepened during the Depression. Even though Mayor Fiorello H. LaGuardia brought the city's three separate subway lines under direct municipal control in 1940, rapid transit continued to be defined as a business that was supposed to support itself, rather than as a vital public service entitled to public subsidies. As the deficits mounted in the late 1940s, a group of conservative businessmen and realtors sought to create a special district government that would make the subways self-supporting and stop the political fighting. Established in 1953, the New York City Transit Authority insulated the subways from normal governmental channels, reduced the accountability of top elected officials, and made economy the highest priority. In so doing, the New York City Transit Authority set the stage for future financial disaster and physical deterioration.[1]

New York's original subway was built in response to two critical problems that emerged during the nineteenth century, rapid urban growth and awkward geography. By 1900, the city had 3,437,000 inhabitants and ranked as the world's second-largest city. New York's geography was poorly suited to its explosive development. The city is an urban archipelago that sprawls across several big islands; that is divided by formidable waterways like the upper bay, the Hudson River, and the East River; and that centers on the splinter-shaped island of Manhattan, thirteen miles long and two miles across at its widest point and with only twenty-three square miles of territory.[2]

This combination of extraordinary population growth and arduous geography made urban transport a high priority (see Figure 8.1). By 1890, New York City boasted the world's most comprehensive mass transit system. With 94 miles of elevated railways, 265 miles of horse railways, and 137 miles of horse omnibus lines, New York had more total mileage than London, even though the British capital contained nearly three times more residents. New Yorkers averaged almost 300 mass transit rides per capita in 1890, compared to only 74 rides for each Londoner.[3] But New York's transit network was nevertheless inadequate. The elevated railroads were already overcrowded in 1890, and the construction of new routes or extra storage yards was precluded by space limitations, especially in the financial district on the island's southern tip. Moreover, the els were too slow to stimulate the development of northern Manhattan.

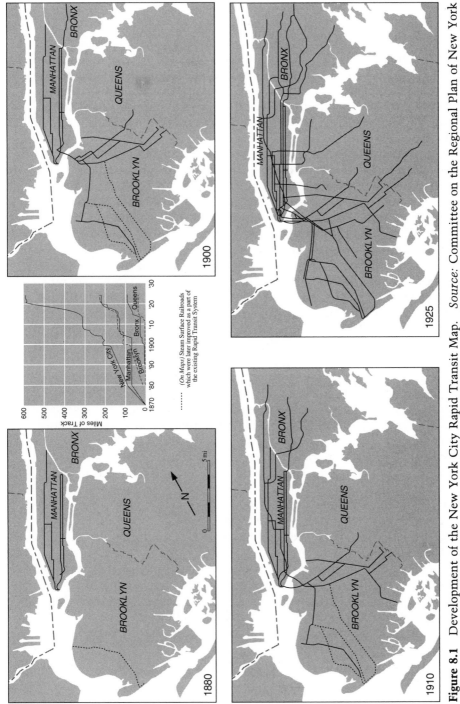

Figure 8.1 Development of the New York City Rapid Transit Map. *Source*: Committee on the Regional Plan of New York and Its Environs, *Regional Survey of New York and Its Environs*, vol. IV, *Transit and Transportation* (New York: Regional Plan of New York and Its Environs, 1928), p. 41.

193

The solution required an underground railway. On January 31, 1888, Mayor Abram S. Hewitt, the son-in-law of merchant Peter Cooper and a wealthy iron manufacturer, proposed the construction of an advanced rapid transit railroad. Hewitt envisioned a railroad that would go from City Hall in southern Manhattan to the annexed district beyond the Harlem River and be capable of fantastic speeds of forty or fifty miles per hour.[4]

Hewitt claimed that state-of-the-art rapid transit would ensure that New York retained its position as the dominant metropolis in North America. New York was running out of space to house its residents, and only high-speed, high-capacity transport could spur the development of the unsettled territory on the Upper West Side, in Harlem, and on Washington Heights as new neighborhoods for the middle class and the skilled working class. Hewitt contended that rapid transit would broaden the municipal tax base and underwrite vital public works—wharves, docks, new streets—needed to guarantee the city's supremacy over rival seaports like Boston, Philadelphia, New Orleans, and Baltimore. He predicted that rapid transit would promote "the future growth of this city in business, wealth, and the blessings of civilization" and confirm "its imperial destiny as the greatest city in the world."[5]

Hewitt's sweeping view of rapid transit's priority had ramifications for the relationship between government and business. Previously, transit had been regulated by franchises: the municipality granted a private company the right to use a public right-of-way, and the company owned, built, and operated the route. Although this franchise system had not seriously impeded the omnibuses, horse railways, or elevated railways, Mayor Hewitt understood that his rapid transit railway would be another matter, due to its great cost. Accordingly, the mayor advanced an idea for combined government and business development, later known as the Hewitt formula, whereby the municipality would finance and own the line and a private company would build and run it.[6]

Although the Tammany-dominated Board of Aldermen rejected Hewitt's plan, his conclusion that subway financing required a different framework was prescient. For when the Rapid Transit Commission of 1891 followed the tradition of minimal government by soliciting bids in December 1892 for a 999-year contract for the private construction and operation of an underground railway, investors proved to be wary of this risky project and did not make one serious bid for it.[7]

This impasse was resolved when one of New York's most powerful business organizations, the Chamber of Commerce of the State of New

York, adopted the Hewitt formula. The merchants who led the Chamber of Commerce thought that "real rapid transit" would solve two problems. Mayor Hewitt had already identified one problem, the unification and development of the metropolitan economy through the settlement of northern Manhattan and the annexed district. The second problem involved traffic congestion. Manhattan's long, narrow shape funneled trolleys, lorries, and carriages onto busy north-south arteries where speeds averaged no more than five miles per hour.[8]

In 1894, the Chamber of Commerce drafted a bill incorporating the Hewitt formula. This measure easily passed the Republican-led legislature and was enacted in law in May 1894. The Rapid Transit Act of 1894 gave the Chamber of Commerce power over subway planning, primarily to prevent Tammany Hall from siphoning off municipal funds. Five of the eight members of the new commission were prominent businessmen; four of these businessmen-commissioners were named in the act itself, and the fifth, serving ex officio, was the president of the Chamber.[9]

Six years later, the Rapid Transit Commission (RTC) selected financier August Belmont as the franchise holder. The president of his own investment bank and the American agent for the Rothschilds, Belmont signed a contract (known as Contract No. 1) on February 21, 1900, to build, equip, and operate the railway for a period of fifty years, renewable for another twenty-five years.[10] Inaugurated on October 27, 1904, New York's first subway, a twenty-two-mile-long route of the Interborough Rapid Transit Company (IRT), went up the east side from City Hall to Grand Central Terminal, then across Forty-second Street to Times Square on the west side, and then up Broadway through the Upper West Side to Ninety-sixth Street, where it divided into two branches that continued into the Bronx (see Figures 8.2 and 8.3).[11]

The Interborough was the first subway in the world with a separate set of tracks for permanent, two-way express service. At speeds that reached forty miles per hour, the expresses became the fastest urban transport mode in the world. Three times faster than the els and six times faster than the trolleys, the subway remade the face of the city. Along with Penn Station and Grand Central Terminal, the subway pulled retail businesses like department stores north to midtown from their old cluster south of Twenty-third Street. The IRT also transformed Times Square into a spectacular entertainment district. Its legitimate theaters, vaudeville palaces, restaurants, nightclubs, and, later, its movie houses depended on the subway to carry huge numbers of passengers to their doors. Equally important was the fact that the IRT was open twenty-four hours a day, giving Times Square a reputation as a place that never closed.[12]

Figure 8.2 Construction of the Interborough Rapid Transit Company Subway, Broadway and Forty-second Street, February 9, 1903. *Source:* Municipal Archives, New York City Department of Records and Information Services.

Figure 8.3 Interborough Rapid Transit Company, City Hall Subway Station, c. 1904. *Source:* Municipal Archives, New York City Department of Records and Information Services.

The express trains unleashed the largest housing boom in city history. As late as 1900, one-third of the building lots on the Upper West Side—a huge area of approximately 200 blocks that stretched from Fifty-ninth Street to 110th Street and from the Hudson River to Central Park—were unimproved. The far west side—from Amsterdam Avenue to the river—had been particularly neglected due to poor transport. By drastically reducing commuting time, the IRT stimulated the construction of housing and retail stores there. The Upper West Side, close to midtown and lower Manhattan and offering short journeys to work, became an upper- and middle-class district with luxury apartment buildings. Broadway replaced Columbus Avenue (along the route of the Ninth Avenue elevated) as the Upper West Side's premier shopping boulevard, and areas along the IRT express stops—like Sherman Square, at Seventy-second Street—became commercial hubs.

Land on the Upper West Side had already been subdivided, but the southern Bronx was so distant from the built-up area that much of its property was still held in large, unbroken parcels as farms, country estates, or charitable institutions. Speculators like Charles T. Barney, the president of the Knickerbocker Trust Company and the brother-in-law of William C. Whitney, assembled huge tracts and had an unusually great impact on the spatial patterns that unfolded there. Due to the economic pressures on speculative builders and the existence of a ready market for low-income housing, the most common form of building in the Bronx became the new law tenement, a relatively high-quality structure offering better living conditions than the squalid old law tenements of Greenwich Village and the Lower East Side. For sixteen to twenty dollars per month, residents could rent a brand-new apartment containing two bedrooms, a combined living room-dining room, a kitchen with hot water and a gas range, and an interior toilet and bathtub. Although the poorest New Yorkers could afford neither the rents nor the time for commuting, the Bronx was a possibility for most semiskilled and skilled workers. Thousands of New Yorkers migrated to the Bronx after 1904 and settled in solidly ethnic neighborhoods like East Tremont and West Farms.[13]

From 1905 to 1920, the population of Manhattan above 125th Street increased 265 percent to 323,800 and the population of the Bronx grew 150 percent to 430,980.[14] These new neighborhoods funneled more and more riders into a subway that was already overflowing. The subway had been designed to hold 600,000 passengers daily, but its average daily traffic surpassed the 300,000 mark in November 1904 and its planned maximum capacity of 600,000 as early as October 1905.[15]

In March 1905, a committee of the Rapid Transit Commission (RTC) unveiled a proposed $250 million expansion program for new subways intended to relieve this overcrowding. But August Belmont, satisfied with the company's 8 percent profit and heeding the industry maxim that "the profits are in the straps," flatly rejected this plan. The RTC, which had counted on cooperating with the Interborough rather than confronting it, thus found itself in deep trouble. Even though the RTC had been conceived as a new institutional response to the problems of the industrial metropolis, the concentration of private economic power revealed its shortcomings. The Rapid Transit Act of 1894 prohibited the city from launching its own subway, and, in effect, gave the IRT control of an important service. The RTC's futility was accentuated when the Interborough Rapid Transit merged with the Metropolitan Street Railway on December 22, 1905. The Interborough thus eliminated its only rival for control of the island's transit lines, became unchallenged master of its street and elevated railways and New York's only subway, and won veto power over new underground railways.[16]

Strong press reaction against the Interborough-Metropolitan merger strengthened the hand of municipal reformers who wanted to replace the Rapid Transit Commission with a powerful regulatory commission. Many progressives saw rapid transit as a means of achieving two major goals, antimonopoly and urban dispersal. First, they were alarmed because the IRT wielded monopoly power over a vital service under the terms of a "cast-iron" contract that did not allow for adequate regulation. Second, they sought improved transportation so that immigrants could escape from crowded urban slums to new neighborhoods on the outskirts. By 1910, Manhattan was among the most congested urban districts in the world. Forty-nine of every 100 New Yorkers lived in Manhattan, which had an average population density (161 people per acre) far above that of Brooklyn (32.5), the Bronx (15.6), Queens (3.8), and Staten Island (2.2). In Manhattan's most thickly packed neighborhood, the Lower East Side, population densities exceeded 700 people per acre. In addition to residential crowding, 70 percent of New York's factories were concentrated below Fourteenth Street in Manhattan. This industrial metropolis was a chaotic landscape where residences were intermingled with cigar shops, garment factories, and laundries, and where the streets were jammed with children, pushcarts, and vehicular traffic.[17]

The progressives launched a campaign to abolish the Rapid Transit Commission as a first step toward imposing tougher restrictions on the Interborough Rapid Transit Company. In May 1907, Governor Charles Evans Hughes and his reform allies succeeded in replacing the Rapid Transit Commission with a potent new regulatory body, the Public Service Commission (PSC).[18]

The PSC's strategy for mastering the IRT revolved around a 1908 proposal for new subways. This Triborough system, as it was called, would have 144 miles of track in Manhattan, the Bronx, and Brooklyn (see Figure 8.4). Instead of being conceived as part of a unified system, these Triborough routes were laid out as a separate network that would be run by an independent private operator with no physical or corporate ties to the IRT. The reason for this design was that the PSC regarded competition between the Triborough and the Interborough as its main regulatory device.[19] Although these progressives had moved beyond laissez-faire doctrines, most preferred a market solution to more active state encroachment and resolutely opposed municipal operation. The PSC insisted on competition even though it would divide the transit system into two parts, require riders to pay a double fare, and sacrifice scale economies. Triborough revealed the tension that existed between the reformers' goals of antimonopoly and urban dispersal. The PSC could not push its Triborough lines far beyond the edge of settlement because its independent subway might go bankrupt if they did not have enough traffic. With relatively little mileage slated for undeveloped areas, Triborough would not deconcentrate Manhattan's population.[20]

But the fatal flaw of the Triborough strategy was its dependence on the private sector. When the Public Service Commission asked in September 1910 for bids to build and manage Triborough, not a single offer was made. Investors feared potentially ruinous competition with the Interborough.[21]

So long as the Public Service Commission had pursued its unsound Triborough plan, August Belmont was convinced that there was "no danger of competition in the building of subways."[22] In November 1910, however, President William McAdoo of the Hudson & Manhattan Company proposed his own subway. A lawyer and entrepreneur who had moved from Tennessee to New York in the early 1890s and become wealthy on Wall Street, McAdoo had recently opened two underground railway tubes that ran below the Hudson River between New Jersey and New York. Now he wanted to push his Hudson & Manhattan subway deeper into Manhattan and to the Bronx and Brooklyn. Reformers hailed McAdoo's plan for a bi-state, regional transit system that would provide competition with the IRT.[23] But August Belmont neutralized this threat by submitting an expansion program that compelled the Hudson & Manhattan to withdraw its proposition rather than attempt competition with the IRT in the credit markets.[24]

Yet Belmont's monopoly was soon broken. In January 1911, the Brooklyn Rapid Transit Company (BRT) joined the negotiations for new subways. The entry of the BRT enabled Manhattan Borough Presi-

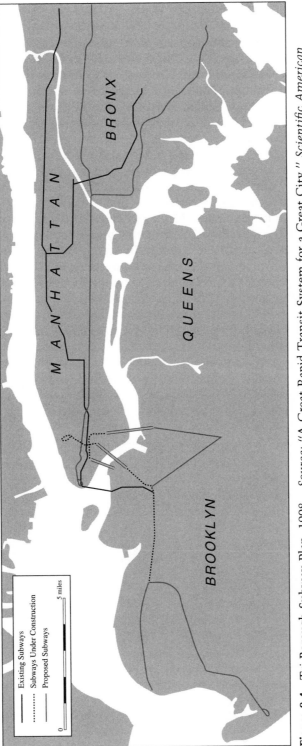

Figure 8.4 Tri-Borough Subway Plan, 1908. *Source:* "A Great Rapid Transit System for a Great City," *Scientific American* 103 (December 17, 1910): 478.

dent George McAneny to advance a new approach to subway building. An ex-newspaper reporter who had assisted Carl Schurz with civil service reform and who had served as president of the progressive City Club, McAneny championed the new profession of city planning and sought to rationalize the urban environment. To McAneny, rapid transit was essential for replacing the chaotic industrial metropolis with a new more efficient city where the population would be dispersed to lower density districts on the periphery and where residential neighborhoods would be segregated from business and manufacturing zones. Subways would carry the residents of this ideal city from their homes on the outskirts to jobs in the core.

Unlike many progressives, McAneny did not draw moral distinctions between business and government and deemphasized the antimonopoly strain of reformist thought. Instead of opposing cooperation with the Interborough, McAneny hoped to integrate the IRT and the BRT in his program. He wanted to create two huge systems, each complete in itself, that would multiply the city's total rapid transit mileage, particularly in the outlying districts. McAneny's ideas were adopted by the Board of Estimate and by the Public Service Commission. On March 19, 1913, the PSC and the two corporations agreed to forty-nine-year pacts, known as the dual contracts, that doubled the

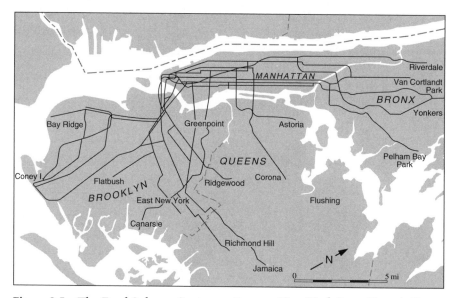

Figure 8.5 The Dual Subway System. *Source:* New York State Transit Commission, *New Subways: Proposed Additions to Rapid Transit System to Cost $218,000,000* (New York: n.p., 1922), p. 17.

Figure 8.6 Looking East Along Queens Boulevard from the Rawson-Thirty-third Street IRT Station, Queens, New York, January 12, 1917. This subway station, which was finished yet unopened, was built as part of the dual subway contracts of 1913. Within ten years of this photograph, this entire area—including parts of Long Island City, Sunnyside, and Woodside—was completely built up. *Source:* Robert L. Presbrey Collection.

length of the existing rapid transit network, increasing its single track-age from 296 to 619 miles (see Figure 8.5). As with the 1904 IRT, the dual contracts extended beyond the built-up section, penetrating new territory in Brooklyn, the Bronx, and, for the first time, in Queens (see Figure 8.6).[25]

The dual system triggered development in the outer boroughs. Before 1913, what is now Jackson Heights, in Queens, consisted of open fields where crops grew and where there were only three roads. Although the Queensboro Corporation started to acquire land there in 1909, Jackson Heights began to boom when the IRT's Corona (now Flushing) line arrived in 1917. By 1925, Jackson Heights was an exclusive (and restricted) bedroom suburb offering upper-middle-class amenities like garden apartments, a golf course, and tennis courts. Other neighborhoods along the new subways experienced similar growth, including Elmhurst and Corona, in Queens, and Brownsville and Canarsie, in Brooklyn.

The dual contracts decentralized New York City. Its total population grew by 45 percent from 1910 to 1930, but the number of people who lived in Manhattan declined by nearly 20 percent in that time. Manhattan's population density decreased from 161 people per acre in 1910 to 128.9 in 1930. During that period, the percentage of city residents who lived outside of Manhattan increased from 51 to 73 percent.[26]

At first, rapid transit planning for the 1920s followed the course of the dual contracts. Planners continued to advocate the rationalization of urban growth through city planning and to conceive of new subways as part of the BRT and IRT systems. For instance, in July 1920, Chief Engineer Daniel L. Turner of the New York State Office of Transit Construction Commissioner proposed a mammoth plan of 830 track miles of extensions to the BRT and IRT. Although Turner confined these lines to New York City, he later amplified his vision of—in his words—"suburban rapid transit" in the transit volume of the *Regional Plan*, which he cowrote. There, Turner foresaw the construction of the subways beyond the city limits into New Jersey.[27]

Turner's vision did not become reality. One reason for this failure was the rise of the automobile in the 1920s as a competing transport mode. Widely regarded as the embodiment of technological modernity because of its novelty, and viewed by many government officials and planners as neutral and nonpolitical because of its pattern of individual ownership, the automobile assumed mass transit's old function of stimulating new settlements on the outskirts.[28]

The positive appeal of the automobile was not the only reason for the failure of Turner's dream of suburban transit. His vision of rationalizing the city through subway construction was not accompanied by the development of new political structures for rapid transit. At the same time that semi-independent government corporations like the Port of New York Authority and later Robert Moses' Triborough Bridge Authority were building vehicular bridges, tunnels, and highways across state and local boundaries, the New York subway was becoming mired in partisan politics and in regulatory conflicts.

The intensification of subway politics was largely accomplished by Mayor John F. Hylan, a fiery demagogue who was allied with publisher William Randolph Hearst and who served two terms in City Hall, from 1918 to 1926. Hylan exploited the deep popular antipathy against the subway corporations by launching a populist crusade to save the "people" from the "interests." Accusing the Republican-controlled state regulatory commission of being secretly in league with the subway companies, Hylan denounced its proposals to reorganize the transit system through financial concessions to the companies and to extend the IRT and BRT subways as cynical exercises in "traction manipulation and traction chicanery" intended to bamboozle the public, save the bondholders, and raise the nickel fare.[29]

Hylan's critique of the Transit Commission's bailout attempts gained credence from the unanticipated results of the dual contracts. The dual contracts had sought to unite business and government in a community of interest. They had instituted an intricate profit-sharing agreement for dividing each subway company's gross annual revenues: First, the corporation would receive a preferential payment for fixed costs and profits, based on current earnings; then, the municipality would recover its charges for interest and sinking fund; and then, the company and the municipality would split the remainder in half.[30]

But this profit-sharing plan rested on a foundation no firmer than expectations of continued revenue increases. The strong prewar performance of the Interborough, which had made profits close to 20 percent and dividends as high as 15 percent, led the municipal negotiators to assume that the new subways would earn large surpluses too.[31] Wartime inflation undermined these calculations by reducing the companies' real income. In 1919, Interborough President T. P. Shonts complained that a ton of coal had gone from $3.22 to $6.07 and that labor costs had increased by $6 million, while the contracted nickel fare controlled corporate earnings. The Brooklyn Rapid Transit Company (which soon renamed itself the Brooklyn-Manhattan Transit Company, or BMT) entered bankruptcy in 1919.[32] As a result of inflation, the IRT's and BMT's preferentials consumed nearly all of the revenue, rather than just a fraction, as originally intended. By 1922 the municipality had not received any funds to cover its interest and sinking fund requirements, and was forced to pay for the interest charges on its bonds—over $10 million annually—out of the tax budget. This debacle strengthened press opposition to the IRT and the BMT and gave Mayor Hylan ammunition for his fight against the two companies.[33]

Hylan put his own stamp on rapid transit by building his own subways. In 1924, the state government transferred the power to develop subways to a new municipal agency, the Board of Transportation. Hylan intended a separate, municipally operated system that would rival the IRT and BMT and be "built, planned and operated to accommodate the transportation needs of the people . . . and not solely for the financial advantage of the operating companies."[34] This Independent Subway System (IND), the third and last major stage of underground construction, was completed in 1940.

As a separate system that would have to compete with the IRT and BMT, the IND's routes were primarily restricted to built-up areas that already had heavy traffic. Except for the Queensboro line, the IND did not extend to the outskirts; indeed, its Sixth Avenue, Eighth Avenue, and Fulton Street routes paralleled IRT and BMT elevateds. Unlike the first two stages of subway construction, the IND had little impact on residential expansion. One result of this changed locational pattern was that rapid transit began to lose a key constituency, the real estate developers who had supported the earlier subways in order to kindle property expansion. The failure of the IND to spur significant residential growth, along with the dual contracts' continuing drain on the City budget, prompted businessmen to reassess the importance of subways.[35]

To Mayor John F. Hylan also belongs the credit for making the five-cent fare a supreme political issue in New York City. With his refusal to grant the subway companies an increased fare, Mayor Hylan found a popular position that carried him to victory in his 1921 reelection campaign and begat an article of faith so sacred that no mayor risked raising it until 1948. "The five-cent fare is . . . not likely to be increased in the immediate or distant future," the U.S. Works Progress Administration's (WPA) famed *New York City Guide* observed in 1939. "The New Yorker is extremely sensitive on this point."[36]

The nickel fare made the 1920s and 1930s a golden age for subway passengers. The low fare enabled millions of poor New Yorkers to take full advantage of the city by traveling to City College, WPA jobs, or inexpensive concerts at Town Hall. The problem with the nickel fare, however, was that it deprived the private companies of income that was badly needed to maintain service standards, and that there was no corresponding effort to put new revenue into the system through direct municipal subsidies. By the 1920s, a nickel was no longer worth what it had been in 1904. The real value of the nickel fare dropped to 2.6 cents in 1919 and to 2.25 cents in 1920. The IRT and BMT remained in poor financial condition during the 1920s.[37]

The Great Depression crushed the Interborough and the Brooklyn-Manhattan. From 1928 to 1939, the rapid transit traffic of the BMT declined 23 percent and that of IRT fell 25 percent. In 1932, the IRT declared bankruptcy. By the early 1930s, the survival of the Interborough and Brooklyn-Manhattan as private companies, along with the physical integrity of the subway system itself, was in jeopardy.[38]

After entering City Hall in January 1934, Fiorello H. LaGuardia sought to reorganize the subways. To LaGuardia, reorganization was primarily an instrument for restoring the solvency of the City, which was in the midst of a severe financial crisis in 1934. He believed that the unification of the subways under direct public control would save millions of dollars by eliminating the dual contract preferentials and that the combination of the three separate systems into a single, more efficient network would put the subways on a self-sustaining basis. This conception of unification was critical. At a time when the municipality was no longer self-sufficient and when the national government was taking responsibility for urban functions such as relief, public housing, and highway construction, LaGuardia proposed to bring a rapid transit system that was losing money under City operation. Moreover, LaGuardia retained the existing definition of the subways as an enterprise that had to support itself, rather than formulating a new understanding of rapid transit as a vital municipal service entitled to government subsidy. Largely due to its history as a profit-making business, the subway continued to be perceived differently than the schools, water, fire, police, and sanitation.[39]

The LaGuardia administration's talks with the IRT and BMT were delayed by the intricacies of corporate ownership as well as by friction with Tammany Democrats on the state level who retained formal authority over unification. Finally, in June 1940, the City of New York acquired the properties of the Brooklyn-Manhattan and the Interborough for $326 million. The Board of Transportation then began direct operation of the largest transit system in the world, a huge network of nearly 1,200 track miles of railways and of 80 miles of bus routes that carried over two billion passengers per year.[40]

But unification did not cure the subways' fiscal ills or end the political battles over transit. In 1940, a progressive Republican lawyer, Paul Windels, initiated a drive to eliminate municipal operation. Alarmed by the rise of big government and determined to cut public spending, Windels founded several civic organizations that were supported by realtors and other businessmen who favored lower property taxes. Their chief target was the subway, which by 1944 required an annual debt service of $37 million and constituted the single biggest drain on the municipal treasury.[41]

Windels claimed that the transit imbroglio could be solved through the creation of a public authority. A transit authority would be independent of the other branches of government, and it would be run by efficiency-minded technocrats who could cut the deficits. Windels' model was perhaps the most successful special district ever established, the Port of New York Authority. Created by the states of New York and New Jersey in 1921 to rationalize the region's chaotic harbor facilities and originally limited to ports and terminals, the Port Authority gained financial strength due to its control of the Holland Tunnel's revenues. It used its solid bond ratings to become—according to Michael N. Danielson and Jameson W. Doig—"the most influential public development institution in the New York region."[42]

Paul Windels had served as assistant counsel of the Port Authority from 1930 to 1933, and he deeply admired it. Contrasting the Port Authority's success with the Board of Transportation's supposed failure, Windels argued that the practice of deciding weighty issues in an open forum jeopardized the public interest by putting the subways at the mercy of shortsighted politicians who played to the fickle crowd. Windels intended to put a stop to the convulsions over the nickel fare, the IND, and unification that had shaken New York ever since Hylan's tenure by stripping the subways from the mayor and the city council.[43]

Liberals protested that Windels' proposal was undemocratic. But the liberal opposition was compromised by the LaGuardia administration's prior definition of the subways as a business that was expected to support itself, rather than as a municipal service. When the New York City Transit System's operating deficits climbed from $1.2 million in 1950 to an alarming $24.8 million in 1952, the pressure mounted for Windels' transit authority. In March 1953, the Republican-dominated state government established the New York City Transit Authority.[44]

One critic, however, had already questioned Windels' claim that a transit authority would be a panacea for the subways. In a scathing 1949 memo, master builder Robert Moses argued that the subways could not generate enough revenue for a transit authority to be genuinely independent. "We believe that the 'authority' method of financing is valid in several fields of public construction and management," Moses asserted, "but that gold bricks wrapped up as bullion will kill this device." He concluded that "such an authority is not practical" for the subways and that a transit authority would not repeat the successes of the Port Authority or his own Triborough Bridge Authority.[45]

Moses was right. The Transit Authority's formal powers were negated when the inflationary wave of the 1960s and 1970s led to mammoth operating deficits. Ill-suited to the political environment created by these losses, the Transit Authority could not avert the physical deterioration of the subways.[46]

Halfway through the twentieth century, New York's subways had finally acquired a modern political structure. Yet, underground rapid transit had already lost its social function as a spearhead of metropolitan spatial expansion and remained mired in deficits. Ironically, the Transit Authority was established just in time to preside over the subways' decline.

Notes

1. Paul Barrett, *The Automobile and Urban Transit: The Formation of Public Policy in Chicago, 1900–1930* (Philadelphia: Temple University Press, 1983, pp. 3–10.
2. Ira Rosenwaike, *Population History of New York City* (Syracuse, NY: Syracuse University Press, 1972), pp. 16, 36, 58–59, 63; Kenneth T. Jackson, "The Capital of Capitalism: The New York Metropolitan Region," in Anthony Sutcliffe, ed. *Metropolis, 1890–1940* (Chicago: University of Chicago Press, 1984), p. 326.
3. Statistics for New York pertain to the greater city. New York State Public Service Commission for the First District, *Report, 1919*, vol. 2 (Albany, NY: n.p., 1920), pp. 12–17; U.S. Department of the Interior, Census Office, *Report on Transportation Business in the United States at the Eleventh Census: 1890*, Part 1, *Transportation By Land* (Washington, DC: Government Printing Office, 1895), pp. 683–685.
4. Abram S. Hewitt, "Message to the Board of Aldermen" (January 31, 1888), pp. 5, 15, 19, 27, 35.
5. Ibid, p. 37.
6. Ibid, pp. 31–32.
7. New York State, *Laws of the State of New York, 1891* (Albany, NY: Banks and Brothers, 1891), pp. 3–19; David C. Hammack, *Power and Society: Greater New York at the Turn of the Century* (New York: Russell Sage Foundation, 1982), pp. 235–241.
8. Chamber of Commerce of the State of New York, *Thirty-sixth Annual Report* (New York: Press of the Chamber of Commerce, 1894), pp. 84–89.
9. New York State, *Laws of the State of New York, 1894*, vol. 2 (Albany, NY: J. B. Lyon Company, 1894), pp. 1873–1874; James Blaine Walker, *Fifty Years of Rapid Transit, 1864–1917* (New York: Law Printing Company, 1917), pp. 138–161.
10. New York City Board of Rapid Transit Railroad Commissioners, *Contract for Construction and Operation of Rapid Transit Railroad* (New York: n.p., 1900), pp. 25–47.
11. Bion J. Arnold, *Reports upon the Interborough*, Report No. 4, *The Capacity of the Subway of the Interborough Rapid Transit Company of New York City* (New York: M. B. Brown, 1908), p. 3. In addition to the Contract No. 1 line, a second route, known as Contract No. 2, was then being built to Brooklyn.

12. *Real Estate Record and Builders Guide* (June 10, 1906); Jill Stone, *Times Square: A Pictorial History* (New York: Collier Books, 1982), pp. 23, 33–42.

13. Robert Coit Chapman, *The Standard of Living Among Workingmen's Families in New York City* (New York: Charities Publication Committee, 1909), pp. 75–84; New York City Tenement House Department, *Report for the Years 1912, 1913, and 1914* (New York: n.p., 1915), p. 121.

14. Cities Census Committee, Inc., *Population of the City of New York, 1890–1930* (New York: Cities Census Committee, Inc., 1932), pp. 51–53, 83–84.

15. New York State Transit Commission, *Ninth Annual Report: 1929* (Albany, NY: J. B. Lyon Company, 1930): pp. 86–87; Arnold, *Reports upon the Interborough,* Report no. 4, *The Capacity of the Subway:* p. 7.

16. New York City Board of Rapid Transit Railroad Commissioners, *Report 1905* (New York: n.p., 1906), pp. 179–197; *New York Herald* (March 24, 1905); *Brooklyn Standard-Union* (April 21, 1905); *New York Times* (December 27, 1905).

17. Adna F. Weber, "Rapid Transit and the Housing Problem," *Municipal Affairs* 6 (Fall 1902): 408–417; John DeWitt Warner, "Municipal Ownership Needed to Correlate Local Franchises," *Municipal Affairs* 6 (Winter 1902–1903): 516; Jackson, "The Capital of Capitalism," p. 326; Moses Rischin, *The Promised City: New York's Jews, 1870–1914* (Cambridge, MA: Harvard University Press, 1962), pp. 76–90.

18. *New York Times* (March 28, April 5, May 6, 7, and 15, 1907).

19. New York State Public Service Commission for the First District, *Annual Report, 1910,* vol. 1 (Albany, NY: J. B. Lyon Company, 1911): 49; *New York Evening Post* (January 2, 1908).

20. New York State Public Service Commission for the First District, *Annual Report,* vol. 1 (Albany, NY: J. B. Lyon Company, 1908), p. 13.

21. Ray Stannard Baker, "The Subway 'Deal,'" *McClure's Magazine* 24 (March 1904): 33–34. Warner, "Municipal Ownership Needed," p. 516.

22. August Belmont to Gardiner M. Lane, May 24, 1909, Confidential Letterbook 4a, Belmont Family Papers, Rare Book and Manuscript Library, Butler Library, Columbia University, New York, NY.

23. William Gibbs McAdoo to William R. Willcox, November 18, 1910, in New York State Public Service Commission for the First District, *Annual Report, 1910,* vol. 1, pp. 50–53; *New York Evening Post* (November 10, 1910).

24. William Gibbs McAdoo to William R. Willcox, December 15, 1910, in New York State Public Service Commission for the First District, *Annual Report, 1910,* vol. 1, pp. 60–63.

25. New York State Public Service Commission for the First District, *Contract No. 3* (New York: J. W. Pratt, 1913), pp. 65–77; New York State Public Service Commission for the First District, *Contract No. 4* (New York: J. W. Pratt, 1913), pp. 59–70.

26. Vincent F. Seyfried to Clifton Hood, May 20, 1986, letter in author's possession; *Jackson Heights News* 9 (August 21, 1925), pp. 1–12; Rosenwaike, *Population History,* pp. 55–60, 90–98, 133; Daniel Karatzas, *Jackson Heights: A Garden in the City* (New York: n.p., 1990), pp. 9–35.

27. Daniel L. Turner, "Rapid Transit Development," in New York City Board of Estimate and Apportionment, Committee on City Plan, *Development*

and Present Status of City Planning in New York City (New York: n.p., 1914), pp. 50–51; New York State Transit Construction Commissioner, *Proceedings of the Transit Construction Commissioner, June 1 to December 31, 1919,* vol. 2 (New York: n.p., 1920), pp. 916–934.

28. Mark S. Foster, *From Streetcar to Superhighway: American City Planners and Urban Transportation, 1900–1940* (Philadelphia: Temple University Press, 1981), pp. 38–45; John Ihlder, "The Automobile and Community Planning," *The Annals of the American Academy of Political Science and Social Science,* vol. 116 (Philadelphia: American Academy of Political and Social Science, 1924), pp. 200–204.

29. John F. Hylan, *Autobiography of John Francis Hylan* (New York: The Rotary Press, 1922), pp. 14–24; William Bullock, "Hylan," *American Mercury* 1 (April 1924): 444.

30. New York State Public Service Commission, *Contract No. 3,* pp. 65–77; New York State Public Service Commission, *Contract No. 4,* pp. 59–70; *New York Times* (January 6 and 7 and August 10, 1918).

31. New York State Transit Commission, *Report of the Special Counsel to the Transit Commission, Metropolitan Division, Department of Public Service of the State of New York, on the Definitive Plan and Unification Agreement, Proposed for the Acquisition and Control of Rapid Transit Railroads and Related Power Properties in the City of New York, dated June 22, 1936, together with Alternative Recommendations and Memorandum of Law* (New York: n.p., 1937), pp. 36–37.

32. *New York Times* (January 17, 1919); New York City Board of Transportation, *Transit Record* 20 (August 1940): 2–4.

33. New York City Board of Transportation, *Transit Record* 20 (August 1940): 2–4; *New York Times* (May 7, 1922); Cornelius M. Sheehan, *The Subway Contracts: What They Are, and Who Put Them Over, How the City is Affected By Them and the Remedy* (New York: n.p., 1925), pp. 2–5; John F. Hylan to voters, August 27, 1925, John F. Hylan Correspondence File, Box A-20, Citizens Union Collection, Rare Book and Manuscript Library, Butler Library, Columbia University, New York.

34. *Mayor Hylan's Plan for Real Rapid Transit* (New York: n.p., 1922), p. 6.

35. Daniel L. Turner, "Memorandum for Chairman McAneny Re. Transit Commission New Subway Lines" (January 11, 1927), Transit 1927 Folder, Box 35, George McAneny Papers, Seely G. Mudd Manuscript Library, Princeton University, Princeton, NJ; Merchants' Association, Committee on City Transit, *Subway Consolidation Necessary for Adequate Service and Economy* (New York: n.p., 1927), p. 5.

36. U.S. Works Progress Administration, Federal Writers Project, *New York City Guide,* American Guide Series (rev. ed., New York: Random House, ca. 1939; reprint ed., 1982), p. 407.

37. *New York Times* (December 16, 1989); *New York Sun* (May 12, 1922); Interborough Rapid Transit Company, *Annual Report, 1920–1930.*

38. New York State Transit Commission, *Nineteenth Annual Report, 1939* (Albany, NY: Williams Press, 1942), pp. 233–235.

39. Barrett, *The Automobile and Urban Transit,* pp. 3–10; Citizens Committee for the Re-election of LaGuardia, McGoldrick and Morris, *Speaker's Handbook: Eight Years of the LaGuardia Administration* (New York: n.p., 1941), pp. 3, 20–24, 32–36; "Suggested Outline: 'City of Tomorrow' by Mayor LaGuardia," Box 24B1, Folder 17, Fiorello H. LaGuardia Pa-

pers, LaGuardia and Wagner Archives, LaGuardia Community College, CUNY, Long Island City, NY.

40. *New York Times* (January 2 and 7, 1934); New York State Transit Commission, *Plan and Agreement of Unification and Adjustment for the Acquisition and Unification under Public Ownership and Control of Rapid Transit and Surface Railroads and Related Power Properties and Omnibus Lines of the Brooklyn-Manhattan Transit System in the City of New York* (New York: n.p., 1939), pp. 5–19; New York State Transit Commission, *Proposed Plan and Agreement of Unification and Readjustment for the Acquisition and Unification, Under Public Ownership and Control, of Rapid Transit Railroads and Related Properties in the City of New York of the Interborough and Manhattan Transit Systems* (New York: n.p., 1939), pp. 8–25; Thomas Kessner, *Fiorello H. LaGuardia and the Making of Modern New York* (New York: McGraw-Hill, 1989), pp. 459–461; Joshua Freeman, *In Transit: The Transport Workers Union in New York City, 1933–1966* (New York: Oxford University Press, 1989), pp. 191–220.

41. "The Reminiscences of Paul Windels" (1950), The Oral History Collection of Columbia University, New York, NY; *New York Times* (December 16, 1967) p. 112; Committee of Fifteen, *Recommendations to Civic, Labor, Business, Civil Service and Taxpayer Groups for a Fiscal Program for New York* (New York: n.p., 1943), pp. 1–4; Citizens' Transit Committee, *The Subways of New York* (New York: n.p., 1944), pp. 20–21.

42. Michael N. Danielson and Jameson W. Doig, *New York: The Politics of Urban Regional Development* (Berkeley, CA: University of California Press, 1982), p. 40; Erwin Wilkie Bard, *The Port of New York Authority* (New York: Columbia University Press, 1939), pp. 3, 17, 49; *New York Times* (December 16, 1967).

43. *New York World-Telegram* (April 21, 1948); John C. Bollens, *Special District Governments in the United States* (Berkeley, CA: University of California Press, 1957), p. x; *New York Times* (February 11, 1945).

44. New York City Board of Transportation, *Transit Record* 30 (September 1950), p. 1; *Transit Record* 31 (September 1951), p. 1; *Transit Record* 32 (September 1952), p. 1; New York State, *Laws of the State of New York*, vol. 1 (Albany, NY: n.p., 1953), pp. 746–759.

45. Robert Moses, George V. McLaughlin, and Charles G. Meyer to William O'Dwyer, October 7, 1949, Board of Transportation, September-October 1949 Folder, Box 974, William O'Dwyer Papers, Municipal Archives, New York City Department of Records and Information Services, New York.

46. Two measures of this decline are the frequency of car breakdowns and on-time performance. The average distance a subway car traveled between breakdowns decreased from 34,294 miles in 1964 to 9,000 miles in 1984; the on-time performance of subway trains fell to 70 percent in 1983, after having been above 95 percent in the 1940s. *New York Times* (February 6, 1970; February 15, May 17, and June 30, 1984).

9

Sweatshop Migrations: The Garment Industry Between Home and Shop

Nancy L. Green

A visit to Manhattan is like a course in urban archaeology. What strikes the newcomer is not only the postmodern skyline but also the mélange of new and old, of glass and steel with brick and stone, of skyscrapers and tenements. Yet, while the soaring buildings tower in height and imagination in representing the city, the point of this chapter is to show why the pregentrified loft still merits a symbolic place on the New York postcard.

The garment industry is perhaps one of the best reminders that not every New York building is a brownstone or a high-rise. One of the last manufacturing sectors to remain in the urban core, it provides the link between past and present. Indeed, for some analysts, the apparel trade's transformed sweatshops are the economic model of flexibility for the twenty-first century.[1] We can examine the ways in which the industry and its workers have shaped the New York landscape and have been shaped by it. The joint needs of light industry, of manufacturers, and of a largely immigrant work force have interacted with the urban environment for over a century. Whereas certain sectors of the industry as well as successive immigrant groups have moved out of the city center, an important part of the garment trade has remained downtown.

We need to look first at the development of the industry, its space needs, its relationship to New York City, and its relocation within the city. In the second part of this chapter, we will then examine the urban geography of the industry's immigrant work force and discuss the relationship between industrial structure and immigrant labor, and between home and shop.

The Geography of Garment Making

Two forces characterize the urban geography of the New York apparel industry in the twentieth century: a centrifugal motion and a constant redefinition of an inner core of urban production. These two movements are contradictory only at first sight. The movement outward, to escape Manhattan, is but one stage in the process of redefining the urban industry, its specific needs, and the reasons for its particular location.

Concentration in New York City

By the late nineteenth century, New York City had become the fashion capital of America. The growth of ready-to-wear during the century—first for men's wear, then for women's wear—meant a relative centralization of garment production. Sewing migrated from the local tailor shop and rural outworker to urban factories and shops. Home-made clothes gave way to store-bought ones, and sewing became the occupation of industrial homeworkers instead of individual homemakers. By 1890, 44 percent of all readymade clothes in the United States were produced in New York City.[2] But the city already specialized in women's wear; 53.3 percent of all women's garment industry workers in the United States worked there in 1899. In 1904, that figure rose to 65 percent, dropping back to a still healthy 57.3 percent by 1925.[3] New York's position was even more marked in terms of product value: 65 percent of the total value of American-made women's wear came from the city in 1899 and 78 percent in 1925, far exceeding the role played by any other city. (Chicago, although one of the major manufacturing centers for men's wear, employed only 5.2 percent of the nation's women's wear workers and produced only 4 percent of that sector's value in 1925.[4])

The concentration of style in New York City occurred largely because it was a capital of other things: a financial and manufacturing center, a cosmopolitan harbor, and the first port of arrival both for the immigrants who made up the majority of the work force and for Parisian patterns. Nevertheless, as ready-to-wear spread, so did the decentralization of production. The current debate and despair over the loss of jobs in this sector must not be seen as purely conjunctural. We must turn to industrial restructuring from the 1920s on in order to understand the origins of Manhattan's relative decline as a garment center.

Centrifugal Motion

Early ready-to-wear manufacturers hoped that premade, serial production of clothing for the anonymous figure would both regulate production and render it more efficient. Standardization meant concentration of production and increased space needs. Those items that were able to become increasingly standardized moved out of town. Men's wear rather than women's wear, work clothes rather than fashion items, underwear rather than outerwear were product lines best able to take advantage of mass production in larger factories. A veritable "exodus" of men's wear occurred in the 1920s, along with a relocation of women's housedresses, uniforms, and aprons.[5]

The specter of decline has thus been with the city's apparel industry since the interwar period. Growth began slowing in the early 1920s. The Depression worsened but did not cause this trend (indeed, heavy industry was hit much harder than light manufacturing). And despite the return to industrial prosperity during World War II, the theme of decline has been a recurrent issue for most of this century.[6]

Decline is both a real and relative notion. Although New York City remained until recently the predominant center of garment production in the United States, industrial reports began noting early on, with varying degrees of alarm, that other centers were growing and challenging New York's hegemony. Men's garment manufacturing, as we have indicated, left New York City in the 1920s. After World War II, California began to compete seriously in women's wear. From 1947 to 1954, the United States garment work force increased by 7.8 percent nationwide, but only 1.8 percent in the New York–New Jersey Standard Metropolitan Area. Chicago had lost 20.1 percent of such employment, whereas the Los Angeles region had made a spectacular gain of 30.5 percent.[7]

At the same time, movement to outlying boroughs constituted a microcosm of this centrifugal motion. Whereas Brooklyn accounted for less than 6 percent of New York City's women's wear production in 1899, the growth of contracting shops there increased its share to 14.6 percent in 1937 and to 17.8 percent by 1954. Although Manhattan lost 14,858 employees from 1947 to 1954, Brooklyn gained 4,241, the Bronx 2,853, and Queens 1,293. In Brooklyn as well as in Queens, this outward movement also corresponded to somewhat larger shops.[8] The highest priced dress lines remained closest to the fashion core, but in 1945 only 28 percent of the cheapest dresses were still made in Manhattan.

Thus, well before the current trend in overseas manufacturing, and after the initial period of ready-to-wear growth and concentration in New York City, the industry has been moving outward from the city center. To the outlying boroughs and suburbs of Manhattan, across the river to New Jersey, to Pennsylvania, to upper-state New York and beyond, the garment industry then shifted westward, to the Midwest, and then on to the Southwest, one step before heading toward Taiwan.

Space was not the only factor in these successive movements "off-shore" (from the island of Manhattan). Labor costs and union avoidance were paramount in the setting up of "runaway" shops. New York labor is expensive, and the precocious development of the garment unions made it all the more so. An inexpensive and noncombative labor force has been as much a clothing industry imperative as the desire to standardize production. At the same time, clothing manufacturers looked with a dim eye on labor and housing legislation. In this respect, the New York garment landscape has been shaped by two competing tendencies. Progressive reformers, labor leaders, and state legislators pushed through laws to better conditions within that landscape, while manufacturers threatened that too many constraints would make that landscape disappear altogether.

City Lights and the Limits of Dispersion

Two major factors, however, have limited an absolute dispersal of garment production: the advantages of concentration and the imperatives of fashion. The city's very reputation has served as a powerful stimulus along with its noted concentration of skilled labor (higher productivity offsetting the higher wages) and skilled management. Concentration itself has acted as a positive magnet, offsetting the much decried congestion which is its corollary.[9] The centralization of showrooms for out-of-town buyers, the concentration of design decision making for manufacturers, the clustering of support industries from button makers to sewing machine repairmen, and modeling agencies are all aspects of the economic advantages of congestion. Although dress racks moving samples and merchandise at a snail's pace through the streets may be aggravating to taxi drivers, they symbolize the raison d'être of a centralized location.

Furthermore, fashion itself has limited the centrifugal movement and reinforced the urban industry. For items highly sensitive to style trends, only close-in production sites can execute styles quickly enough to respond to the season's latest craze. Those garments necessitating rapid shifts in production, short production schedules, and fast deliveries have hung on with particular tenacity to the urban core. Housedresses may have gone, but silk dresses stayed. More style-oriented, made of more expensive material, needing greater skill and supervision, these were the goods that made Seventh Avenue's reputation in the interwar period. (In 1939, almost one-half of the New York garment industry was devoted to unit-priced dresses.[10]) It has been these high-fashioned women's garments that have kept manufacturers together in the urban center, bemoaning the inscrutability of female whims and the impossibility of foreseeing fashion trends, yet clinging together in order to defy and define those trends.

Intra-urban Migration:
The Garment Industry Moves to Midtown

This simultaneous history of outward movement and inward concentration within the fashion capital is the tale of over a century of ready-to-wear, as seen from New York City. Concomitant to it is the story of the industry's migration within the city. As space and specialization needs changed, so did location within Manhattan. In the 1920s, the industry moved northward, creating the present-day Garment District of Seventh Avenue (see Figure 9.1), which has since become a short-hand symbol for the New York Garment District, for the women's wear industry, and often for the American garment industry in general. Several factors explain this intown reshaping of the garment industry landscape.

First, the garment industry followed the general relocation of the shopping district further north (to Madison Avenue) that occurred in the 1920s. The opening of Penn Station at Seventh Avenue and Thirty-fourth Street (in 1910) had already led many garment wholesalers to move in that direction to be closer to the buyers' new point of arrival.

A second, related factor was the restructuring of industrial production itself. The rise of the jobber in the 1920s exacerbated the cutthroat competition endemic to the industry. Jobbers pitted contractors against each other and further consecrated a growing separation between production and sales. Whereas the pre–World War I manufacturer had assumed every aspect of garment production from design to cutting, sewing, finishing, and sales, the interwar jobber directly supervised cutting and perhaps finishing, but subcontracted out the sewing. Their small cutting shops and showrooms became increasingly concentrated in the midtown Garment District, while the sewing was sent out to lower Manhattan, the outlying boroughs, and over

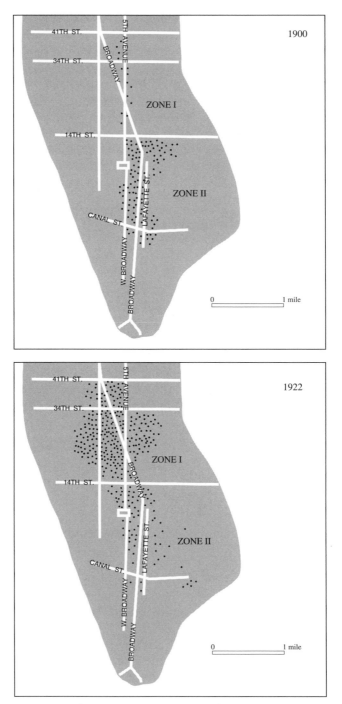

Figure 9.1 Location of Women's Garment Production, 1900, 1922. *Source:* Derived from Magee, *Trends in Location*, Maps 4, 10, and 11, pp. 74, 80–81.

state borders. Overnight hauling defined the perimeter of contractors' shops out to New Jersey, Pennsylvania, and Connecticut.

Nonetheless manufacturers, too, moved northward, especially those small firms that could not afford the overhead of a split personality between sales and production sites. By the early 1950s, approximately 65 percent to 80 percent of garment manufacture in Manhattan took place in the area bounded by Thirtieth and Forty-second streets, from Tenth to Fifth avenues.[11] In a microcosm of the nationwide model of apparel geography, the "center" became increasingly consolidated within a context of decentralizing production.

Third, space availability and urban renewal helped draw the industry northward. While overcrowding and state laws helped "push" the industry out of the tenement district, as we will see, the construction of newer loft buildings in midtown "pulled" the industry in that direction in the 1920s and 1930s. According to the embittered version of the Fifth Avenue Association, the overbuilding of office space had led owners to entice cloak and suit manufacturers into their vacant space.[12] But the newer steel-framed buildings above Fourteenth Street had their own appeal: they were better fireproofed and had more floor space than the older cast-iron structures below Houston Street. And some of the larger and lighter loft buildings were constructed by successful coat and suit manufacturers and other Jewish builders who began turning to real estate investment.[13] These lofts not only provided more space but could also be subdivided into smaller units (familiarly called "Coney Island shops," after the summer bathhouses). The move also enabled manufacturers to overhaul their operations and replace foot-activated treadle machines with electric-powered ones. By the end of the 1920s, a shortage of space led to taller and taller loft buildings—from the sixteen-floor norm of 1920, to buildings of eighteen and twenty floors, and "monsters" of thirty floors.[14]

The geography of garment making has thus been one of industrial migration and of concentration and dispersion, both within New York City relative to the United States and within Manhattan relative to the New York metropolitan region. However, the story of relocation within Manhattan also corresponds to the movement of the immigrant work force around the city. The intra-urban migration of the New York immigrant garment workers is the story of the rise and demise of tenement manufacture and the twentieth century separation of home and work space.

The Geography of Immigrant Settlement

The construction of "Seventh Avenue" was as much a commercial, industrial, and architectural endeavor on the part of manufacturers and jobbers as a reflection of the intra-urban migrations of its immigrant work force.

Just as earlier immigrants settled on farm or lumber camp sites integral to their work, so the urban immigrants of the late nineteenth century took up residence near prospective employment or took up occupations near their place of residence.[15] Proximity to ports, the availability of low-cost housing and of jobs were important in the creation of immigrant neighborhoods. The nearness of home to work, characteristic of the nineteenth century, remained an important trait of the immigrant neighborhoods, especially where light industry provided jobs.

Garment making has always been conducive to this trend. Whether in factories, workshops, or tenement homes, garment production, at the turn of the century, was primarily located in lower Manhattan where most of the women's garment workers lived.[16] Shops and factories were more often than not within walking distance for those who worked outside the home. For those women or immigrant families working in their own tenement, home and shop were identical. Homework for women (then as now) meant being close to (whimpering?) children and (boiling?) pots, but it also provided a solution for those whose cultural norms frowned upon work outside the home. Ethnic workshops also provided easy job entry and minimal language barriers, and could be the first step to upward mobility for immigrant entrepreneurs.[17]

This nearness of home and work meant that rather than the worker going to work, the work had to come to the worker. With contractors, manufacturers, and workers all located in and near the immigrant neighborhoods, a geographically close, integrated network served everyone's interests. Bundles carried by men, women, and children—the garment "schleppers"—through the streets were a characteristic sight of the early twentieth century New York landscape.

If we can understand the symbiotic relationship between immigrant neighborhoods and light industry, and particularly between tenements and the garment industry, why the decline of the tenement workshop and the shift northward in the 1920s? Three factors beyond the changing geography of the industry seen above affected the geography of the immigrants' work and home place: the reform movement, state and federal legislation, and the internal transformation of immigrant neighborhoods.

Reformers and health inspectors began a steady campaign against conditions in the sweatshops in the late nineteenth century. Tenement homework in particular caught the progressives' imagination as a symbol of all that was dangerous to both workers and consumers.

Graphic images of garment bundles used as bedclothes and breeding vermin spread along with fears of contagion. Consumers' leagues worried that garments could transmit smallpox, whereas labor leaders castigated the effects of tenement manufacture on workers' health, and working and living conditions.[18]

State and federal laws began regulating homework and tenement production. The New York State Factory Act of 1892 set up a licensing procedure for tenement production, which the 1901 Tenement House Law sought to strengthen. In 1911, the State Factory Investigating Commission Report suggested complete abolition of tenement work, but then (only) recommended reinforcement of existing licensing laws.

Nonetheless, a number of factors militated against the effective abolition of homework. For all of its faults, the system did, to a certain extent, suit workers and manufacturers/contractors alike. Manufacturers protested that severe regulation would drive wages up and business out of town. Others argued that women's place was in the home, and that forcing them out to the shop would only cause hardship. In a telling example, the Industrial Commission dramatically contrasted a female shop worker with one who worked at home. The woman obliged to leave her children alone all day virtually abandoned them "with absolutely no one to look after them or keep a fire to warm them." The three-year-old child of the homeworker, on the other hand, may have had to help its mother fix trimmings, but was thus "never out of her sight and is where the mother could attend to its wants and allay its fears and suffering."[19] In any case, inspectors had difficulty in tracking down tenement production. Perhaps, as one report stated, this was because conditions were so bad that the inspectors themselves hated to penetrate the foul atmosphere.[20] But mostly, the state simply never had enough money or manpower to enforce the rules. Variability in fashion and flexibility of production were mirrored by instability of the labor force. Faced with "the nomads of the tenements," the inspection force often felt helpless.[21]

In 1933, the National Industrial Recovery Act (NIRA) established codes to regulate homework. As Lazare Teper and Nathan Weinberg commented, antisweating legislation to protect the consumer had finally given way to antihomework regulations to protect the worker. Ninety-four percent of homeworkers were taken into factories after the code was adopted.[22] However, this new deal was short-lived. The Supreme Court declared the codes unconstitutional, and homework reappeared, as strong as ever. A 1936 study found that 194 New York manufacturers were sending work out to 1,661 homeworkers in 16 states and Puerto Rico.[23] Other attempts were made at the industry, state, and federal levels to control conditions in garment production.

221

An industry-run National Coat and Suit Recovery Board was set up in 1935 to try and police contracting competition. A 1935 New York State law set up a mechanism for strictly controlling industrial homework with a view toward eliminating it entirely. In 1938, the federal Fair Labor Standards Act (FLSA), known as the "Wage and Hour Law," set minimum standards for factories and homework alike. As in the earlier period of regulation, the years 1936 to 1940 saw a greater relative consolidation of big inside shops and a decrease (by 26 percent) in the number of contracting shops.[24] In 1945, further restrictions were extended to all other industries, and it is estimated that between 1935 and 1955 the number of homeworkers in New York State dropped from 500,000 (in all fields) to less than 5,000.[25]

Beyond tenement manufacture, all eyes turned in horror to conditions in the nearby factories when fire broke out at the Triangle Shirtwaist factory on March 25, 1911. The shirtwaist workers' "Uprising of the 20,000" the previous year had included demands for greater safety precautions. But it took the fire in the ten-year-old, ten-story Asch building and the widely reported images of young girls jumping to their death to focus attention on other work and health hazards of the lower Manhattan infrastructure.[26]

However, it was not only reformers, state intervention, and urban renewal that caused the great garment migration uptown. The immigrant neighborhoods in which early garment manufacture was located were themselves being transformed and joining the decentralization of the city. As the Heckscher Plan razed blocks of tenement buildings and realtors pressed own-your-home campaigns, first- and second-generation garment workers moved to Brownsville, East New York, Coney Island, Bensonhurst, Van Cortlandt Park and northern New Jersey.[27] Immigrants dissatisfied with their areas of first settlement sought more space and more light in other parts of town. As Donna Gabaccia and Deborah Dash Moore have shown, Jews and Italians began moving from the Lower East Side well before World War I. Intra-urban migration was related to new housing as well as job opportunities.[28] Whereas the law increasingly discouraged work at home, and as shops moved away from the immigrant neighborhoods of first settlement, the immigrants and their children were themselves moving "offshore" to the outer boroughs and suburbs of Manhattan. Patterns of sociability were transplanted and transformed there, while new garment shops re-created the proximity of home and shop for some.

Immigrants followed jobs and jobs followed workers. But the 1920s were increasingly characterized by a growing separation of home and shop. Production was shifting from residence to factory, from downtown to midtown, and out of town. Already by 1917, 68.6 percent of the women's garment workers worked in the midtown garment district, compared to only 17.5 percent in lower Manhattan.[29] A 1925 survey estimated that some 53,000 of the women's garment workers (40 percent of those employed in Manhattan) now lived in Brooklyn and the Bronx and another 15,000 to 16,000 had settled in upper Manhattan.[30]

The 1920s thus saw a triple phenomenon of spatial relocation within the industry: the concentration of activity in the new garment district; the dispersion of the work force both due to the move northward of the industry and the move out of town of the immigrants; and the quantitative and geographic growth in contracting. All of this meant a greater separation of home and workplace for many garment workers along with a greater separation between sales and manufacture for the industry. For some workers, in contractors' shops in the new neighborhoods, this could still mean walking to work, but for the bulk of the work force it meant dependence on urban transportation.

By the early 1950s, three-quarters of the metropolitan area apparel jobs were still in Manhattan, although only one-quarter of the work force lived there. Furthermore, about half of all jobs were located between Fourteenth and Forty-second streets, where only one-half of 1 percent of the workers lived. Garment workers thus commuted from northern Manhattan and the Lower East Side as well as from Brooklyn and the Bronx. Garment manufacturers now living on the posh Upper West Side had a direct link to Seventh Avenue via the IRT. Brooklyn was the only other county with significant employment as well as residence. (See Figures 9.2 and 9.3.)

If the garment industry took part in the general movement of urban dispersion out to the boroughs, it was thanks to the subway. Clifton Hood has shown how the IRT and the BMT had an impact on residential expansion.[31] And as Emanuel Tobier has pointed out, the fact that the IND line did not reach the Lower East Side until the 1930s left that neighborhood at a relative disadvantage compared to the newer working-class areas of Brooklyn, the Bronx, and upper Manhattan.[32]

The subways provided the new link between home and shop, and the concentration around Seventh Avenue took on a new meaning for the workers. In response to a survey concerning possible decentralization of the Garment District in the early 1950s, apparel workers were adamant. They had become accustomed to the central location of the midtown district and were against any move elsewhere. The labor market was conveniently concentrated there; employers only had to put up a sign, and job seekers only had to canvass a relatively circumscribed area to look for work. The convenience of public transportation

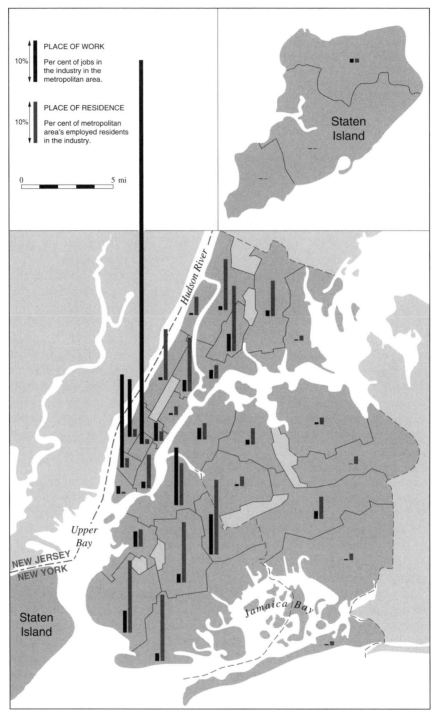

PLACE OF WORK

10% Per cent of jobs in
the industry in the
metropolitan area.

PLACE OF RESIDENCE

10% Per cent of metropolitan
area's employed residents
in the industry.

0   5 mi

Staten
Island

Hudson River

Upper
Bay

NEW JERSEY
NEW YORK

Staten
Island

Jamaica Bay

Figure 9.2 Home and Shop Locations, New York City, 1950. *Source:* Derived from Larry Smith, *Garment District Study*, 2:36.

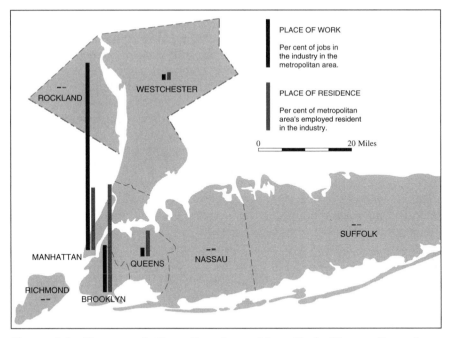

Figure 9.3 Home and Shop Locations, New York Metropolitan Area, 1950. *Source:* Derived from Larry Smith, *Garment District Study,* 2:37.

was an important factor. As one manufacturer commented, "Workers are particular, they want to avoid excessive fares and train changes." Some said they would never work below Thirtieth Street; others, on the IRT line, refused to go west of Eighth Avenue because it would mean paying a crosstown fare. Finally, workers refused to give up their friends. Seventh Avenue meant a social network to them that they did not want to see dispersed.[33]

But if the development of the Garment District meant subways for the workers, it meant increased reliance on trucking for the Seventh Avenue manufacturers. To get piece goods and finished goods to and from the subcontractors in the boroughs or beyond, the bundles on backs now had to be motorized. Trucking filled the new space between production and sales and permitted this evolution, and truckers in turn encouraged geographic expansion of the industry. For better or for worse, they became the lifeline between in-town manufacturers and out-of-Manhattan contractors and workers, linking the center to the periphery.[34]

Fifth Avenue Versus Seventh Avenue

Industrial migration and work force relocation thus went hand in hand, consecrating a new, twentieth century vision of the metropolis in which sales and production, home and work would become physically separate entities. The consolidation of the Seventh Avenue Garment District nonetheless represented a compromise between nineteenth and twentieth century views of the city: the tenacity of the garment lofts represents this link between past and present.

While sweatshop reformers tried to propel the garment industry out of the lower Manhattan tenements, central business district planners tried to preserve their domain for commerce. Early twentieth century planners and midtown merchants envisaged a commercial city free from the mess of manufacturing. Their discourse was infused with a language of separation and "segregation" (of commerce from industry), to counter the "invasion" of the sewing machines. The "tragic consequences" of factory "encroachment" were not only a "menace" to individual retail property owners, but also a "threat" to the common good. "Public welfare" was at stake, and not simply that of Fifth Avenue. It would be a "public calamity" for the city and even the nation if the country's greatest retail district were destroyed.[35]

From 1913 to 1916, the Fifth Avenue Association of retail merchants and hotel and other property owners tried to impose their view of a loft-free retail environment.[36] Ultimately, however, the locational needs of light industry prevailed. Thriving on congestion around a central locus of fashion, the garment industry forswore the decentralization of design, and trucks became the lifeline between the garment industry's inner and outer zones.

Nevertheless, the creation of the Seventh Avenue Garment District can be described as a compromise to the extent that the showrooms and lofts settled there rather than on Fifth Avenue itself. The Fifth Avenue merchants kept their street manufacturing free, but no planner was able to keep the lofts out of Manhattan altogether. The twentieth century use-segregated city was fashioned but two avenues away from a more nineteenth century mixed-use model.

Conclusion

The persistence of the loft, even when gentrified, is still testimony to the integrated, commercial, and manufacturing city of the nineteenth century. Not only is there a physical continuity to New York's lower skyline, but much of that space is being used as it was in the last century. The resurgence of immigration combined with "new" old forms of production have given new life to the urban industry. Asian

Figure 9.4 Manhattan's Garment District at Rush Hour. Note the Absence of Women on the Street. *Source:* WPA Collection, Municipal Archives, New York City Department of Records and Information Services.

immigrants have once again settled in the cheap, rundown buildings of the immigrant neighborhoods of yesteryear, which no one ever got around to redeveloping.[37] Jobbers on Seventh Avenue or Broadway send work to contractors' shops in Chinatown, north Manhattan, the Bronx, and Queens. Light industry, which planners in 1916 complained was "scattered indiscriminately over the entire city throughout the business and residential sections,"[38] still shows an amazing adaptability of space usage, from converted storefronts to basements to dilapidated lofts.

I would argue that a certain continuity in the urban cityscape from the nineteenth century to the present is due to the very structural elements described above. The urban landscape continues to have pockets of rundown buildings, cheap enough for the "first family" to rent and for others to follow. The dynamics of immigrant neighborhoods, language difficulties, and traditional attitudes about women's work encourage the persistence of small immigrant contracting shops and homework. Industrial needs and space availability interact with immigrant needs for cheap housing and the reproduction of the "urban village."

The new immigrants from Asia, Latin America, and the Caribbean have picked up where the early twentieth century immigrants left off. While they are moving into the ever-expanding service "industry," the new immigrants are also maintaining a New York "tradition" in the urban light industrial sector. It is a mixed tradition, indeed. If the proximity of work and residence has remained strong in lower Manhattan, it also recalls other aspects of nineteenth century conditions: high turnover, poor working conditions, low margins for contractors, and low pay for employees.

Many aspects of the New York physical and working landscape have changed, and city planners and developers continue to reshape the skyline in their image. Bundles have moved off backs onto trucks. Workers have gone underground in order to get to work. But elements of continuity persist. The Garment District is as congested as ever. The basic structure of the apparel industry, with its heavy reliance on subcontracting, remains intact. When the printing presses leave the city altogether, the International Ladies' Garment Workers' Union may be the sole representative of urban industry still marching down Fifth Avenue on Labor Day.

Notes

1. Roger Waldinger and Michael Lapp, "Back to the Sweatshop or Ahead to the Informal Sector?" (unpublished, 1989). See Michael J. Piore and Charles F. Sabel, *The Second Industrial Divide* (New York: Basic Books, 1984), pp. 263–264.
2. New York State Department of Labor, *Annual Report* (1901): 1:119.
3. Mabel A. Magee, *Trends in Location of the Women's Clothing Industry* (Chicago: University of Chicago Press, 1930), p. 39. According to Roy

Helfgott, there were only 33 women's-wear manufacturing plants outside of New York City in 1900, although by 1922, there were 524. Roy B. Helfgott, "Women's and Children's Apparel," in Max Hall, ed., *Made in New York: Case Studies in Metropolitan Manufacturing* (Cambridge: Harvard University Press, 1959), p. 56. See also B. M. Selekman, Henriette R. Walter, and W. J. Couper, *The Clothing and Textile Industries in New York and Its Environs* (New York: Regional Plan of New York and Its Environs, 1925), p. 18.

4. Magee, *Trends in Location*, p. 39. See Wilfred Carsel, *A History of the Chicago Ladies' Garment Workers' Union* (Chicago: n.p., 1940).

5. By 1942, only 14 percent of the country's housedress makers were still at work in New York City. Leonard A. Drake and Carrie Glasser, *Trends in the New York Clothing Industry* (New York: Institute of Public Administration, 1942), pp. 58, 83. The correlation of more standardized production and larger factory space, and the difference between women's wear and men's wear, can be seen by comparing figures for New York and Chicago. In 1921, for example, New York's garment establishments averaged 17.9 workers, whereas Chicago had 22.1; Cleveland (home of Brooks Brothers) had a high of 47.8 workers per establishment. Louis Levine, *The Women's Garment Workers: A History of the International Ladies' Garment Workers' Union* (New York: B. W. Huebsch, 1924), p. 521. For a fuller comparison of Chicago's manufacturing and New York City's contracting systems, see *Reports of the Immigration Commission*, 42 vols. (Washington, DC: Government Printing Office, 1911), vol. 11, Part 6. Differences can also be seen with regard to seasonal fluctuations in employment. New York charted much greater volatility in employment patterns than Pennsylvania, Indiana, or Ohio, for example. Gertrud Greig, *Seasonal Fluctuations in Employment in the Women's Clothing Industry in New York* (New York: Columbia University Press, 1949), charts II and IIIA, pp. 44–45. See Helfgott, "Women's and Children's Apparel," pp. 41–42.

6. See, for example, Magee, *Trends in Location*; Drake and Glasser, *Trends in New York*; Larry Smith and Company, *Garment District Study*, 2 vols. (New York: Larry Smith and Company, 1957); Helfgott, "Women's and Children's Apparel."

7. In absolute numbers, these figures are much less dramatic: New York's small growth represented an increase of over 6,400 workers, not that far from the more than 7,800 new employees added to the Los Angeles work force during this period. Larry Smith, *Garment District Study*, 1:10; Charles S. Goodman, *The Location of Fashion Industries with Special Reference to the California Apparel Market* (Ann Arbor, MI: University of Michigan Press, 1948).

8. For an average of nineteen and twenty-one employees per establishment in Manhattan in 1947 and 1954, Brooklyn had twenty-four, then twenty-six; and Queens, twenty-seven and twenty-eight people per firm. (The Bronx shops remained smaller, with only an average of seventeen employees in 1947 and twenty-two in 1954.) Drake and Glasser, *Trends in New York*, p. 50; Larry Smith, *Garment District Study*, 1:13.

9. Larry Smith, *Garment District Study*, passim. See also Roger D. Waldinger, *Through the Eye of the Needle: Immigrants and Enterprise in New York's Garment Trades* (New York: New York University Press,

1986); Edgar Hoover and Raymond Vernon, *Anatomy of a Metropolis* (New York: Doubleday, 1959); Helfgott, "Women's and Children's Apparel."

10. According to the 1939 U.S. Census of Manufacture, 48.5 percent; see table in Greig, *Seasonal Fluctuations*, p. 60.

11. Larry Smith, *Garment District Study*, 1:22, 31–32; see the more concentrated definition—from Thirty-fourth to Fortieth streets and from Ninth to Sixth avenues—of Helfgott, "Women's and Children's Apparel," p. 22. Joel Seidman, *The Needle Trades* (New York: Farrar and Rinehart, 1942), p. 7, defined "the greatest garment producing center in the world" from Fourteenth to Forty-first streets and from Eighth to Fifth avenues. It is impossible to establish fixed boundary definitions for the "center." See also Waldinger and Lapp, "Back to the Sweatshop," pp. 57–58. According to their study, although 63.1 percent of women's outerwear jobs in Manhattan were still located in the Garment District in 1969, this figure dropped to 39.8 percent in 1988. At the same time, jobs in women's wear shops in Chinatown grew from 12.8 percent to 38.2 percent of the Manhattan jobs over the period.

12. City of New York Board of Estimate and Apportionment, Committee on the City Plan, *Final Report* (June 2, 1916), p. 110 (statement by Bruce M. Falconer, attorney for the Fifth Avenue Association).

13. See the chapter on the Jewish architect Ely Jacques Kahn in Robert A. Stern et al., *New York 1930* (New York: Rizzoli International, 1987), pp. 550–563. Kahn found that the self-made and often self-taught men of the Garment District gave him greater freedom to experiment.

14. Larry Smith, *Garment District Study*, 1:23, 24; Levine, *Women's Garment Workers*, p. 171; Stern, *New York 1930*, p. 556. On the general development of lofts, see Chester Rapkin, *The South Houston Industrial Area* (New York: City Planning Commission, 1962); Charles R. Simpson, *Soho: The Artist in the City* (Chicago: University of Chicago Press, 1981); Sharon Zukin, *Loft Living: Culture and Capital in Urban Change* (Baltimore: Johns Hopkins University Press, 1982).

15. On the relationship between home and workplace, see, for example, Olivier Zunz, *The Changing Face of Inequality: Urbanization, Industrial Development, and Immigrants in Detroit, 1880–1920* (Chicago: University of Chicago Press, 1982); Ira Katznelson, *City Trenches: Urban Politics and the Patterning of Class in the United States* (New York: Pantheon, 1981); David Ward, *Cities and Immigrants: A Geography of Change in Nineteenth-Century America* (New York: Oxford University Press, 1971); Donna Gabaccia, *From Sicily to Elizabeth Street* (Albany, NY: SUNY Press, 1984).

16. In 1900, 82 percent of the women's garment workers worked below Fourteenth Street, near to where most of them lived. Magee, *Trends in Location*, p. 104. According to Selekman et al., *Clothing and Textile Industries*, 67 percent of all factory employment and 70 percent of the women's garment workers were located below Fourteenth Street in 1906 and 1900, respectively. See Emanuel Tobier, "Manhattan's Business District in the Industrial Age," in John H. Mollenkopf, ed., *Power, Culture and Place: Essays on New York City* (New York: Russell Sage Foundation, 1988), pp. 87–88.

17. See, for example, Eileen Boris and Cynthia R. Daniels, eds., *Homework: Historical and Contemporary Perspectives on Paid Labor at Home* (Urbana, IL: University of Illinois Press, 1989); Boris, "Regulating Industrial Homework: The Triumph of 'Sacred Motherhood,'" *Journal of American History* 71:4 (March 1985): 745–763; Nancy L. Green, *The Pletzl of Paris: Jewish Immigrant Workers in the Belle Epoque* (New York: Holmes and Meier, 1986); idem., "Quartier et travail: Les immigrés juifs dans le Marais et derrière les machines à coudre, 1900–1939," in Christian Topalov and Susanna Magri, eds., *Villes Ouvrières, 1900–1950* (Paris: L'Harmattan, 1989), pp. 83–92; and Waldinger, *Through the Eye of the Needle.*

18. For example, Elizabeth Sergeant, "Toilers of the Tenements: Where the Beautiful Things of the Great Shops Are Made," *McClure's Magazine* 35 (July 1910): 3 (reprinting a report of the Consumer's League of the City of New York).

19. *Reports of the Industrial Commission*, 19 vols. (Washington, DC: Government Printing Office, 1900–1902), 15:372.

20. *Report of the Committee on Manufactures on the Sweating System* (1893), cited in *Report on the Garment Industry in New York State* (New York: New York State Department of Labor, 1982), p. 7.

21. Ibid., p. 11; in 1903, 10,000 licenses were surrendered or canceled due to change of residence.

22. Lazare Teper and Nathan Weinberg, *Aspects of Industrial Homework in the Apparel Trades* (New York: ILGWU Research Department, 1941), pp. 23–30.

23. Ibid., p. 34.

24. Florence S. Richards, *The Ready-to-Wear Industry, 1900–1950* (New York: Fairchild Publishers, 1951), p. 27; Teper and Weinberg, *Aspects of Industrial Homework*, pp. 34–37.

25. New York State, *Report on the Garment Industry* (1982), p. 14.

26. Leon Stein, *The Triangle Fire* (Philadelphia: Lippincott, 1962); *Preliminary Report of the Factory Investigating Commission* (Albany, NY, 1912); *Second Report of the Factory Investigating Commission* (Albany, NY, 1913).

27. New York City, Board of Education, *Vocational Survey*, GIV, p. 105.

28. See Chapter 10 by Donna Gabaccia and Chapter 11 by Deborah Dash Moore in this volume.

29. Magee, *Trends in Location*, p. 104. See Selekman et al., *Clothing and Textile Industries*, who give more conservative figures: 70 percent of the women's garment workers worked below Fourteenth Street in 1900, only 10 percent in 1922; only 5 percent of those employees worked between Twenty-third and Forty-second streets in 1900, but 36 percent in 1922. Tobier, "Manhattan's Business District," p. 88.

30. Cited in New York City, Board of Education, *Vocational Survey*, GIV, p. 107.

31. See Chapter 8 by Clifton Hood in this volume.

32. Tobier, "Manhattan's Business District," p. 91.

33. Larry Smith, *Garment District Study*, 2:35.

34. Truckers began lowering their costs in the interwar period in order to encourage out-of-town production, which was good business for them. (The International Ladies' Garment Workers' Union attempt to organize

the truckers, in Local 102, was not very successful.) By the 1980s, however, the trucking lifeline had become a veritable stranglehold on both jobbers and contractors, "married" to racketeering truckers. Trucking companies provide financial backing to start up shops and arrange work for them, but they also charge inflated rates. Senator Franz S. Leichter denounced organized crime in the garment industry in his report, "The Return of the Sweatshop" (unpublished, 1979–1982), Parts 2 and 3. Just recently, however, a garment industry "sting" operation led to the indictment of several organized crime leaders for having imposed a "mob tax" on garment trucking. *New York Times* (October 19, 1990).

35. *Statement of the Fifth Avenue Association on the Limitation of Building Heights to the New York City Commission and the Testimony of the Association's Representatives at a Conference* (June 19, 1913); City of New York Board of Estimate and Apportionment, *Report of the Heights of Buildings Commission* (December 23, 1913); idem., Committee on the City Plan, *Final Report* (June 2, 1916). I would like to thank Marc Weiss for communicating these documents to me.

36. See Chapter 2 by Keith Revell, Chapter 3 by Marc Weiss, and Chapter 5 by Robert Fishman in this volume; on the sense of "invasion," see Chapter 13 by Daniel Bluestone. See also Tobier, "Manhattan's Business District."

37. See Peter Kwong, *The New Chinatown* (New York: Hill and Wang, 1987).

38. Committee on the City Plan, *Final Report*, p. 17.

Part V

FIGHTING
FOR IDENTITY

10

Little Italy's Decline:
Immigrant Renters and Investors
in a Changing City

Donna Gabaccia

Three-quarters of New Yorkers in the Progressive Era were immigrants and their children. As in most industrial cities at that time, they lived in a few densely settled and highly visible central city neighborhoods. In 1890 over half of New York's Italians lived in just three wards bordering on Canal Street in lower Manhattan.[1] The size and apparent permanence of neighborhoods like theirs frightened native-born Americans, and inspired the more socially concerned among them to agitate for stricter regulation of housing, industrial workplaces, and immigration from abroad. Many of these native-born reformers soon began to call for the dispersal of industry and industrial workers out of the central city.[2]

By 1930, neighborhoods like these seemed about to disappear: the population of Little Italy (defined here as Manhattan's Fourteenth Ward) had declined by half; only a third of its tenements were fully occupied; a quarter were totally abandoned. Although the Italian population of New York continued to increase until 1930, new arrivals and longtime settlers now sought homes outside Manhattan in Brooklyn, Queens, and the Bronx (see Figure 10.1). In doing so, however, they created new *Italian* neighborhoods. Much like the Jewish New Yorkers of Deborah Dash Moore's chapter in this volume (Chapter 11), New York's Italians did not abandon their desire for territories of their own within the expanding city. To this day, segregation of European ethnic groups, although continuing to decline, is still more characteristic of New York than of other American cities.[3]

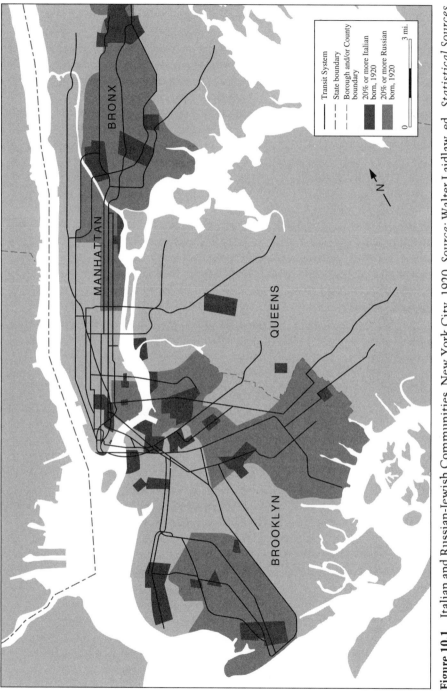

Figure 10.1 Italian and Russian-Jewish Communities, New York City, 1920. *Source:* Walter Laidlaw, ed., *Statistical Sources for Demographic Studies of Greater New York, 1920* (New York: The New York City 1920 Census Committee, 1920), and idem., *Population of the City of New York, 1890–1930* (New York: Cities Census Committee, 1932), pp. 85, 95, 110, 256–257.

The decline of Little Italy—and of neighborhoods like it throughout urban America—was neither the straightforward fulfillment of reformers' dreams nor the inevitable consequence of immigration restriction and Americanization. Instead, it is best viewed as the result of complex changes in investment that separated work and residence while reconnecting the two with extensive new systems of transportation. The essays in this volume identify the many New Yorkers—from reformers and urban planners to loft manufacturers, mayors, and professional real estate investors—who politically and financially created this new pattern of investment and urban life. Few were foreigners. But this does not mean that immigrants were uninterested in either investment or their place in New York's transformation. A focus on the development and decline of Little Italy uncovers investments and a real estate market almost completely unconnected to those of the native-born professionals discussed in Keith Revell's and Marc Weiss's essays (Chapters 2 and 3 in this volume), and thus a new perspective on immigrant renters and investors and their choices.[4]

The advantages Little Italy had initially offered—housing near immigrant workplaces—could not remain unaffected as the city around it changed. And with limited political and financial resources, immigrant renters and modest property owners suffered significant losses in the creation of New York's landscape of modernity. Perhaps it was the sense of loss associated with Little Italy's demise that reinforced Italian New Yorkers' preference for a territorially based ethnicity as they moved to new homes in the outer boroughs.

Little Italy as Real Estate Market

Although little is known about investment in real estate in nineteenth century New York, it is obvious that humble, and often immigrant, investors initially developed this part of the city, constructing tenements and workplaces close together.[5] Once developed, the construction of new housing became more expensive, requiring a strong rental market to sustain it; commercial use also kept local land prices high. Eventually, this excluded small investors from construction, but they remained interested investors in existing housing for many more years.

Beginning around 1830, the Fourteenth Ward became a typical walking city neighborhood, mixing working-class residence, commerce, and industry. German and Irish immigrants occupied the 700 barracks tenements hastily constructed before 1870. Factories, shops, schools, and workplaces covered another 700 lots. Open spaces were limited to streets and to warrenlike rear yards hidden inside city blocks.[6]

By any urban standard, barracks tenements were inadequate: Water supply and toilets were in rear yards, sometimes with no sewer connection; most inner rooms had no windows. Concern with public health first inspired housing reformers to seek improved construction standards. By 1880, new regulations resulted in the era of the "dumbbell" tenements. Their hallway toilets, apartment sinks, and windows in inner rooms were improvements; but they remained firetraps, and reformers continued efforts to replace them with tenements similar to the model dwellings built by philanthropists. Model tenements were built on wide lots, with internal courts and a toilet in each apartment. A new law of 1901 required such construction.[7]

Because regulation of new construction could not touch the older tenements housing most Manhattanites, reformers also worked for municipal condemnation and the evacuation of rear tenements. The new law of 1901 required installation of sinks, toilets, fire escapes, and inner windows in existing tenements. But frustrated by the slow pace of such strategies, reformers after 1900 increasingly turned toward zoning, the relocation of industry, and cheap public transportation—in a word, toward planning—to improve urban housing. Although reformers had often identified "the real estate interests" as their enemies, most real estate professionals came to share the reformers' vision of a Manhattan with neither immigrant workplaces nor crowded tenements. These real estate interests were not important investors in areas like Little Italy.

It was mainly small-scale investors, many of them immigrants, who had to respond to the reformers' changing initiatives in aging Manhattan neighborhoods. Most early builders of tenements were modest investors. In the 1870s, barracks could be built in the Fourteenth Ward for $11,000 to $12,000, and most builders were local German or Irish residents. About half were building craftsmen; most of the rest were grocers and saloon keepers building to accommodate business ventures and acquire rental income. Most builders erected only one tenement.

Regulation of tenement construction did not initially discourage such investment. Sixty barracks were built in the Fourteenth Ward in the 1870s; fifty dumbbells were built there in the 1880s, and another twenty during the economic depression of the 1890s. Even under the much more restrictive new law, thirty-seven tenements were constructed between 1901 and 1913. Instead, it was rising building costs that pushed out the modest investors.

By 1880, the cost of building a dumbbell was $18,000; by 1900 (with no significant change in requirements), it reached $34,000. Builders of the most expensive tenements increasingly lived outside the Fourteenth Ward, and some erected large blocks of dumbbells. Although they could have done so, no builders followed philanthropic examples. A few of the larger builders during the dumbbell era were former residents of the ward, but more were *rentier* owners or the administrators of their estates. By the 1890s, the most active builders were contracting companies organized by Jewish immigrants on the nearby Lower East Side. Italian companies soon competed with them.

As long as small investors had controlled building, speculation was rare. When the builders of the 1870s moved out of the Fourteenth Ward (usually within ten years), they held on to their properties. But the partnerships and corporations of the 1890s often speculated— purchasing land, loaning money to contractors, and selling properties for an average profit of 15 to 20 percent.[8] These practices became common after 1900.

Experts on New York's low-end real estate agreed that tenement construction was a good investment, returning 10 to 12 percent annually. Model tenements returned 5 percent at best. This was because dumbbells had more rooms per floor and thus provided higher rental incomes. (Thus, in tenement building, too, form followed finance.) Small builders especially needed high rates of return to meet their large short-term mortgage obligations.[9]

As they were excluded from building, small investors continued to purchase standing tenements, although this was a riskier investment. Prices for prewar brick tenements changed little in the 1870s and 1880s as Irish and Germans left the ward; at the same time, other parts of the city enjoyed a real estate boom.[10] Fewer than thirty tenements sold annually during the 1890s. Purchasing was a more sensible investment when the rental market was strong; prices rose again by about two-thirds once the depression was over and new Italian renters began arriving.

Small investors dominated among tenement owners. There were few slumlords in the Fourteenth Ward, although these few received disproportionate attention from housing reformers like Jacob Riis. Most tenement owners held only a single tenement, and a sizable percentage of owners were elderly, widowed, and retired persons. Only about 15 percent of the tenements were owned by large-scale *rentier* owners or their estates.

Still, in 1900, only the small number of Italians who had purchased tenements actually lived in them or elsewhere in the ward. Three-quarters of all tenements had absentee owners. With the absentee owner came the agent, who managed buildings and collected rents. As Italians moved into the Fourteenth Ward, grocers, bankers, business owners, and a surprising number of women became agents. Reformers portrayed agents as indifferent to law, overcrowding, and filth; real estate professionals concurred.[11] For Italian immigrants, however, work as an agent was a first step into ethnic real estate; every twentieth century Italian builder, realtor, and owner of multiple tenements in the ward had worked previously as a building agent.[12]

Between the Civil War and the passage of the New York Tenement House Act of 1901, then, neither reformers' initiatives nor population turnover radically changed the character of the Fourteenth Ward. Commercial and industrial investment in the area continued, encouraging new immigrants to move in as older ones moved out. Residential investment remained surprisingly small-scale and local. Although tenement construction was beyond the means of small-scale investors by century's end, local speculators were also replacing outside investors. Both investment in existing tenements and owner occupancy increased as Italians repopulated the ward. After 1900, all tenement purchasers were Italians; most invested in homes for themselves in a neighborhood they viewed far less negatively than the reformers.

Italian Renters: Their Homes and Neighborhood

The attitudes of Italians toward property, residence, and sociability helps explain why so many Italian renters tried to become tenement owners in Little Italy. Most Italian immigrants were middling peasants and artisans, recently arrived from southern Italy. Although men outnumbered women, Little Italy was a community of families, not a boardinghouse gathering of sojourners. As an area of first settlement, population turnover was rapid, but some newcomers also stayed for many years. Even in 1905, Little Italy housed a stable contingent of prospering families with child wage earners, held to the area by the great diversity of nearby workplaces.[13]

Italian peasants were already familiar with the density of urban life; few had lived in rural free-standing homes.[14] Their houses had been physical expressions of their families, since any space occupied by a family became its house—its boundaries perfectly visible to the community. Because the simplest houses provided little living or working space, Italians were comfortable sharing space outside their houses but concerned to preserve privacy for family sleeping and eating.[15]

The major appeal of Little Italy for Italian renters was the availability of many nearby workplaces, which allowed immigrants to achieve housing ideals for the first time. In Italy, the workplaces of peasants were far away; only higher-status artisans and shopkeepers worked close to home. In Little Italy in 1905, half of all working men were unskilled laborers employed nearby in the construction of buildings, bridges, streets, tunnels, subways, or on the docks; practically all employed women worked in the local garment industry. The neighborhood was crowded because immigrant renters chose to live near their work.

In other important respects, however, Little Italy's tenements poorly met the needs of arriving immigrants. Even the largest apartments were far smaller than artisans' homes in Italy. Worse, Little Italy offered only rental dwellings; in Italy home ownership had been common, even among the poor.

In New York, rents equaled one-third to one-half the wages of unskilled laborers.[16] Paying this rent was a monthly challenge. Some renters identified enemies in the struggle, reportedly dumping hot grease down drainpipes to avenge themselves on agents in disfavor.[17] More frequently, observers reported Italians as tractable tenants.[18]

To reduce housing costs, Italians both limited the amount of space they rented and sought to increase household income. Critics charged that immigrants had no living standards whatsoever.[19] But linking census listings to tenement floor plans suggests that larger households rented larger apartments, primarily to segregate the sleeping of older sons and daughters in different rooms.

Young families with no wage-earning children had the strongest incentives for crowding. Almost half of young couples and one-third of families with young children formed joint "partner households," according to the New York State census of 1905. Married siblings formed most partner households; within them, the kitchen was shared like a courtyard, while each family had its own "house" in an adjoining bedroom or front room. Partner households were most common in dumbbells, both because of their higher rents and because entrance to all rooms in their apartments was through the kitchen.

Increasing the number of wage earners also helped pay rents. Families too large to live in two rooms took boarders into three-room apartments; the boarders slept with older sons in the kitchen.[20] Boarding also allowed immigrant wives to earn by working at home. The partner household freed other wives for wage earning: one worked in nearby garment shops, while the other cared for the children of both. Tenement apartments were regularly transformed into workshops, with wives and children contributing their pittances to the monthly rent payments.[21]

Jobs, not class or status, determined which families lived in Little Italy. In Italy, poor, skilled, and professional lived in close proximity. In Little Italy, they often lived in the same tenements, albeit in differing types of households. Italian renters moved often—forming and reforming households as friends and relatives arrived, and as families changed in size and composition. But improved economic circumstances alone did not always provoke a move away from Little Italy, as Italian tenement purchases reveal. In Italy, the successful often bought up property around their original homes, creating a grander house. Thus housing symbolized status for Italians, but it did so most effectively when displayed within a known community.

As a setting for family and community life, the tenements differed significantly from Italian towns, which had developed horizontally, with public spaces immediately outside each doorway. In New York, instead, people lived stacked "like drawers in a bureau";[22] public areas were on the roof above or in the yard and street below (see Figure 10.2). This arrangement of space created differing options for sociability among men, women, and children, and colored each group's satisfaction with tenement life.

Immigrant women had to use considerable ingenuity to find space for their domestic social worlds, especially because Italians had taken mothers' supervision of children for granted.[23] In New York, fire escapes were transformed for play, but eventually children escaped to yard and street, a source of some anxiety. Women made airshafts into telephones in their efforts to keep track of children and each other in the building and rear yard.[24] The woman at the window became a local fixture as women avoided constant trips on the dark, steep stairs.[25] Within partner households, they found easy sociability at their doorstep, as in Italy. And in old tenements with backyard water supplies, housework itself remained an occasion for sociability.[26]

Dense tenement housing provided mobile children and men with rich opportunities for socializing outside the apartment. *Paesani* clustered in a few tenements or along a single block.[27] Kin formed partner households, or lived in adjoining apartments or buildings. Children took over the yards and streets.[28] Men gathered in the many groceries, cafés, and saloons of the ward, or simply met friends in small knots on street corners.

Predictably, Italians' attitudes toward the tenements were ambivalent. They did not like the airless tenements, and they certainly resented their rents. But even women liked Little Italy and its social world, and all valued its proximity to jobs. When asked, many stated a preference for remaining in the neighborhood.[29] For Italian immigrants, the challenge was to improve their rental housing or find housing to purchase without giving up the convenience of location or the familiarity of friends and kin nearby. Those goals could not easily be achieved in Little Italy in the twentieth century.

Figure 10.2 A Backyard Scene in an Italian Neighborhood. *Source:* Mrs. Helen Campbell, *Darkness and Daylight or Lights and Shadows of New York Life* (Hartford, CT: Hartford Publishing Company, 1891), p. 197.

Little Italy's Demise

Little Italy's decline began around 1910, just as the number of Italians entering New York came to its peak. Both before and after that date, Italians remained surprisingly interested in investing in Little Italy housing. Their investments were not well rewarded, however. While New York's Italian population continued to grow, Little Italy's rental market first slumped, then collapsed. Immigrant renters' decisions to live elsewhere in the city were the immediate cause of Little Italy's demise. Their decisions, in turn, can only be explained through reference to large-scale changes occurring in the city as a whole.

Figure 10.3 Street Scene in Little Italy. *Source:* Mrs. Helen Campbell, *Darkness and Daylight or Lights and Shadows of New York Life* (Hartford, CT: Hartford Publishing Company, 1891), p. 402.

After 1901, the new tenement law again raised construction costs modestly. Still, new building continued in Little Italy. New construction was the domain of a few prosperous investors, mainly local Italian bankers and businessmen. In fact, Italian builders abandoned construction only when World War I doubled construction costs.[30]

Critics had warned housing reformers that new-law tenements would not be economically feasible because their rents were beyond the reach of low-income renters.[31] But this had already been true of dumbbell construction in Manhattan. Like all New York builders, Italian investors in Little Italy were building for the better off. In the Fourteenth Ward, that meant building for skilled workers, professionals, and older families (with wage-earning children) that wanted to remain in the area. In 1905, these two groups were almost half the population of the Fourteenth Ward; their numbers increased somewhat over the next two decades, despite Little Italy's generally declining population.

New-law tenements remained fully occupied throughout the 1920s. In contrast, where no new residential construction occurred (on the southern blocks of Little Italy, for example) renters' flight had begun before 1900.[32] It was the poorer immigrants, not the more prosperous ones, who were most likely to seek homes beyond Little Italy.[33] To use Jane Jacobs' terminology, Little Italy seemed on the verge of "unslumming."[34]

Here, too, may be an explanation for immigrants' enthusiasm for purchasing tenements. By 1925, Italians owned half the tenements of Little Italy. Prices of old-law tenements declined 12 percent from 1900 to 1920 and another 25 percent during the 1920s.[35] Initially, this allowed ever humbler investors—small businessmen, garment workers, even day laborers—to buy tenements. Purchasers generally lived in and sometimes operated a business from the tenements they bought, much like the builders of the 1870s. Many had good financial reasons too for buying a tenement. Although tenement prices began at $10,000—with down payments from $3,000—it was easier for a small investor to purchase an income-generating tenement than a cheaper one-family house.[36] But without a strong rental market, slumping tenement prices eventually threatened disaster.

Nor did investment stop with tenement purchase. Italian landlords generally worked to improve their property, probably because they lived and worked there. Most complied with the new law, investing up to a thousand dollars in sewer connections, sinks, toilets, ventilating windows, and fire escapes. They also responded to a weakening rental market by installing steam heat, gas stoves, and electricity.[37]

Owners like these were very hard pressed by the 1920s. With renters disappearing, tenement values declining, and tax rates on assessed values doubling, rates of foreclosure more than doubled. Some owners hoped the city would condemn and purchase their empty buildings; other owners demolished aging tenements, hoping to attract a commercial developer.[38]

But no new commercial developers appeared—and their disinterest was intimately linked to renters' choices. By the twentieth century, jobs followed commercial and industrial investment to other parts of the city. The origins of New York's transformation were—of course— complex, and are addressed in many essays in this volume. Both reformers and large-scale investors (in the garment industry, downtown skyscrapers, and outlying housing developments) argued for municipal policies that fundamentally reshaped the city. Reformers and their old enemies, "the real estate interests," had actually come to share a roughly common vision of the future: both supported zoning and investment in mass transit to banish unsightly industry and working-class housing from the central city.[39] Both dreamed of a grandiose elite "downtown" in Manhattan, and either profits or better housing in outlying boroughs. Relocation of jobs and local demolition quickly eliminated Little Italy's appeal for many renters.

City government invested in Little Italy during these years, but its building projects regularly required demolition—and significant disruption of area social life. The construction of a school, a bridge approach, and a new street destroyed 1,500 Little Italy apartments (a quarter of existing housing) after 1901. It is striking that city projects leveled no new-law tenements and only a few dumbbells. However unintentionally, the city was clearing the worst of old housing as it built new systems of transportation: reformers routinely praised construction that accomplished this goal.[40]

Private investment in new tenements (1,400 new apartments) almost kept pace with the demolitions but could not eliminate the demolitions' impact on local socializing. Italian social networks were extremely localized. Displaced families often wanted to, and tried to, move in groups,[41] but rarely could they succeed. Since a satisfying social life had helped hold ambivalent renters, demolition surely tipped the balance against Little Italy, independent of other influences.

Of even greater significance was city support of rapid transit and the northward migration of the garment industry to the area south of Penn Station. Between 1900 and 1910, the first subways to northern Manhattan and to Brooklyn opened, and a third East Side bridge improved travel to Brooklyn. The garment industry had reasons of its own for seeking new production sites nearer the rail terminals in New Jersey. Reformers and businessmen interested in encouraging elite and corporate use of Manhattan also actively sought to segregate and re-move factories from lower Manhattan with the zoning plan of 1916.

The construction of rapid transit and garment industry relocation eliminated the important advantage Little Italy had offered poorer renters. Since Italian laborers dug the subways, and preferred to settle close to jobs, many new Little Italys clustered along developing sub-way lines in Brooklyn, the Bronx, and Queens (see Figure 10.1). The Manhattan subway tunnels, by contrast, skirted Little Italy, as they did much of the Lower East Side. The result? By 1925, a working girl could travel to garment factories more quickly from Brooklyn than from Little Italy.[42]

If we believe literary accounts, the immigrants who left neighbor-hoods like Little Italy did so with some regrets.[43] Like the Bostonians displaced by later urban renewal projects, some grieved for their lost homes.[44] Italians generally acquired better housing by moving, but at considerable cost: only one-fifth purchased their own homes; the majority instead paid rents 50 percent higher than in Manhattan.[45] Fewer could keep home and work close together: by the 1930s over half the working residents of some Brooklyn Little Italys were already commuting more than an hour daily.

From builders of tunnels and bridges, Italian residents of New York were becoming what Manhattan sophisticates today disparage as "bridge and tunnel people"—residents of the outer boroughs. Ac-cording to the formulators of the Regional Plan in the 1920s, as Robert Fishman's essay (Chapter 5 in this volume) indicates, that is where they—and their jobs—were believed to belong.

And what of Manhattan's Fourteenth Ward, Little Italy? New York-ers think of Mulberry Street as the Italian center of the city. The area's symbolic ethnic identity has held firm in part because Little Italy developed no clear new function in the modern city. Perhaps because it was poorly served by public transport, Little Italy never became part of Manhattan's "ultimate downtown." Lacking clear integration into the modern landscape, it became a district of parking lots, older Italian businesses, and half-inhabited tenements. Most of the next generation of new New Yorkers, from the South and from Puerto Rico, passed it by.

If we judge the demise of Little Italy a mixed blessing for the Italian renters who chose to leave it, their gains must still be balanced against the losses. Not the least of these were incurred by Little Italy's many modest investors. Dependent on a good rental market, their invest-ment strategy left them with few ways of responding to renters' flight. The tenement law of 1901 made it illegal for owners to rebuild rental housing on their narrow lots; they could not borrow to rehabilitate.[46]

In short, "unslumming" could not occur. A century of small immigrant investment in Manhattan real estate had closed. Losses extended beyond these immigrant small investors to the much larger group of New Yorkers who had hoped to enjoy a modernized Manhattan business district. Without new investment in neighborhoods like Little Italy, Manhattan would remain incompletely transformed. Its several downtowns were mere bright spots of modernity separated by threatening and underused reminders of an earlier city where the immigrant poor and their jobs had dominated the urban life of Manhattan.

Notes

1. A good starting place on New York's Italians remains Nathan Glazer and Daniel Patrick Moynihan, *Beyond the Melting Pot: The Negroes, Puerto Ricans, Jews, Italians and Irish of New York City* (Cambridge: The MIT Press, 1963). See also Thomas Kessner, *The Golden Door: Italian and Jewish Immigrant Mobility in New York City, 1880–1915* (New York: Oxford University Press, 1977); Donald Tricarico, *The Italians of Greenwich Village: The Social Structure and Transformation of an Ethnic Community* (Staten Island, NY: Center for Migration Studies, 1984); Donna Gabaccia, *From Sicily to Elizabeth Street: Housing and Social Change Among Italian Immigrants, 1880–1930* (Albany, NY: State University of New York Press, 1984).

2. Roy Lubove, *The Progressives and the Slums: Tenement House Reform in New York, 1890–1917* (Pittsburgh, PA: University of Pittsburgh Press, 1962); Anthony Jackson, *A Place Called Home, a History of Low-Cost Housing in Manhattan* (Cambridge: The MIT Press, 1976); David Ward, *Poverty, Ethnicity, and the American City, 1840–1925, Changing Conceptions of the Slum and Ghetto* (Cambridge: Cambridge University Press, 1989).

3. Elsewhere, migration within expanding cities produced ethnically mixed class-specific neighborhoods. Humbert S. Nelli, *Italians in Chicago, 1880–1930; a Study in Ethnic Mobility* (New York: Oxford University Press, 1970); Olivier Zunz, *The Changing Face of Inequality: Urbanization, Industrial Development, and Immigrants in Detroit, 1880–1920* (Chicago: The University of Chicago Press, 1982).

4. For Detroit, Zunz identifies this as a "dual housing market," *Changing Face of Inequality*, pp. 161–175.

5. Elizabeth Blackmar, *Manhattan for Rent, 1785–1850* (Ithaca, NY: Cornell University Press, 1989).

6. Housing and population sources for all tenements between Canal and West Houston streets, and from the Bowery to Baxter/Center/Elm streets were linked. Tenements are identified in George W. and Walter S. Bromley, *Atlas of the City of New York, Borough of Manhattan* (Philadelphia, PA: Bromley's, 1891, 1902, 1915, 1922), and Charity Organization Society, Tenement House Committee, "Disease and Poverty Maps" (New

York Historical Society, 1896). Floor plans and building records are found in "Block and Lot Records," New York City Bureau of Buildings, City Hall. Standard floor plans are in Robert de Forest and Lawrence Veiller, eds., *The Tenement House Problem* (New York: Macmillan, 1903). Plans, costs, and names of builders for new construction and renovation are in *Real Estate Record and Builder's Guide*. Ownership and leasing on lots containing tenements can be traced in New York City in "Conveyance Ledgers, 1890–1916 and 1917–1930" (New York City Hall of Records). The names of builders, owners, and agents can be traced in City Directories for five-year intervals. *Real Estate Record and Builder's Guide* also contains information on sales, prices, leases, mortgages, and assessed values. Additional prices for the 1920s are from *Bollettino della Sera*. Information about households and families come from New York State Manuscript Census Records in the New York County Clerk's Office, for 1905, 1915, and 1925.

7. See Lubove, *The Progressives and the Slums*; Jackson, *A Place Called Home*; Ward, *Poverty, Ethnicity*; the Reports of the New York City Tenement House Department (1903–1931); James Ford, *Slums and Housing*, vol. 2 (Cambridge: Harvard University Press, 1936).

8. Jackson, *A Place Called Home*, p. 121.

9. Ibid., pp. 82–83; *Real Estate Record and Builder's Guide* (May 5, 1885): 517.

10. *Real Estate Record and Builder's Guide* (May 1, 1880): 410.

11. *Real Estate Record and Builder's Guide* (February 9, 1895): 204–205.

12. See biographies in Italian American Directory Company, *Gli Italiani negli Stati Uniti* (New York: Italian American Directory Company, 1906).

13. Gabaccia, *Sicily to Elizabeth Street*, Chapters 2, 4, and 5.

14. Anton Blok, "South Italian Agrotowns," *Comparative Studies in Society and History* 11 (1969): 121–135.

15. Lidia Sciama, "The Problem of Privacy in Mediterranean Anthropology," in Shirley Ardener, ed., *Women and Space, Ground Rules and Social Maps* (London: Croom Helm, 1981), pp. 89–111.

16. De Forest and Veiller, *The Tenement House Problem*, Appendix IX.

17. *Real Estate Record and Builders Guide* (February 9, 1895): 205.

18. Jacob Riis, *Ten Years War* (Boston: Houghton Mifflin, 1900), p. 61.

19. Compare *Real Estate Record and Builder's Guide* (February 9, 1895): 202; Riis, *Ten Years War*, p. 24.

20. Lillian Betts, "Italian Peasants in a New Law Tenement," *Harper's Bazaar* 38 (1904): 807; New York State Factory Investigating Commission, *Second Report*, vol. 4 (Albany, NY: Argus Company, 1912), pp. 1547, 1549.

21. Cynthia R. Daniels, "Between Home and Factory: Homeworkers and the State," in Eileen Boris and Cynthia R. Daniels, eds., *Homework: Historical and Contemporary Perspectives on Paid Labor at Home* (Urbana, IL: University of Illinois Press, 1989), pp. 14–19.

22. Richard Watson Gilder, "The Housing Problem—America's Need of Awakening," *The American City* 1 (1909): 34.

23. Elizabeth H. Pleck, "A Mother's Wages: Income Earning Among Married Italian and Black Women, 1896–1911," in Michael Gordon, ed., *The*

American Family in Social-Historical Perspective (New York: St. Martin's Press, 1978), p. 505

24. Thomas Jesse Jones, *The Sociology of a New York City Block*, Columbia University Studies in History, Economics and Public Law, 21 (New York: Columbia University Press, 1904), p. 34.

25. Dorothy Reed, "Leisure Time of Girls in a 'Little Italy,' " Ph.D. diss. (Columbia University, 1932), p. 33; Elizabeth Watson, "Home Work in the Tenements," *Survey* 25 (1911): 777; Antonino Marinoni, *Come ho 'Fatto' l'America* (Milan: Athena, 1932), p. 139.

26. Donna Gabaccia, "Housing and Household Work, Sicily and New York, 1890–1910," *Michigan Occasional Papers in Women's Studies* (1981); Caroline F. Ware, *Greenwich Village, 1920–1930* (Boston: Houghton Mifflin, the Riverside Press, 1935), p. 104.

27. Robert E. Park and Herbert A. Miller, *Old World Traits Transplanted* (New York: Harper and Brothers, 1921), map on p. 148.

28. New York City Tenement House Department, *First Report* (New York: Martin B. Brown Press, 1903), p. 114; Irvin L. Child, *Italian or American, the Second Generation in Conflict* (New Haven, CT: Yale University Press, 1943).

29. Harry M. Shulman, *Slums of New York* (New York: Albert and Charles Boni, 1938), p. 195; Fred L. Lavanburg, *What Happened to 386 Families Who Were Compelled to Vacate Their Slum Dwellings to Make Way for a Large Housing Project* (New York: Fred L. Lavanburg Foundation, 1933), p. 5.

30. *Real Estate Record and Builders Guide* (July 9, 1927).

31. See Ernest Flagg's letter to I. N. Phelps Stokes in Ford, *Slums and Housing*, p. 884.

32. Compare block populations for 1896 (in Charity Organization Society, "Disease and Poverty Maps"), 1900 (in New York City Tenement House Department, *First Report*), and census figures for 1905. Eleven southern blocks peaked before 1905.

33. The proportion of unskilled Italian laborers in Brooklyn in 1905 was actually higher than in Manhattan. Kessner, *The Golden Door*, Table 24.

34. Jane Jacobs, *The Death and Life of Great American Cities* (New York: Random House, 1961), Chapter 15.

35. On the general fate of the Lower East Side, see Leo Grebler, *Housing Market Behavior in a Declining Area: Long Term Changes in Inventory and Utilization of Housing on New York's Lower East Side* (New York: Columbia University Press, 1952), p. 100.

36. Ware, *Greenwich Village*, p. 30; Grebler, Ibid., p. 233.

37. Grebler, Ibid., p. 180; *Real Estate Record and Builder's Guide* (March 8, 1919).

38. Grebler, Ibid., pp. 180–181.

39. Ward, *Poverty, Ethnicity*, pp. 136–138. On *Real Estate Record and Builder's Guide*'s long-standing support for rapid transit, see February 20, 1875, and March 3, 1900. With some trepidation, it later noted "Heart of City Almost Free from Manufactories" (January 4, 1919).

40. "Avenue of Travel to Be Created by Williamsburgh Bridge," *New York Times* (February 8, 1903): 20.

41. Lavanburg, *What Happened to 386 Families*, p. 5.

42. Grebler, *Housing Market Behavior*, p. 112.
43. Mario Puzo, *The Fortunate Pilgrim* (New York: Lancer Books, 1964), p. 288.
44. Marc Fried, "Grieving for a Lost Home," in Leonard J. Duhl, ed., *The Urban Condition* (New York: Basic Books, 1963), pp. 151–171; Grebler, *Housing Market Behavior*, pp. 126–127.
45. Ware, *Greenwich Village*, p. 30.
46. Jacobs (*Death and Life*, p. 303) claimed that the Lower East Side was "blacklisted" by banks; I assume this means "red-lining."

11

On the Fringes of the City: Jewish Neighborhoods in Three Boroughs

Deborah Dash Moore

In 1902, when Hutchins Hapgood published his evocative account of the Lower East Side, *The Spirit of the Ghetto,* he captured the symbolic moment of the immigrant Jewish world.[1] By the middle of the Depression, a decade after Congress decisively restricted immigration in 1924, images of the Lower East Side summoned nostalgia among many New York Jews.[2] In the intervening years, they had left the area in the heart of lower Manhattan[3] (see Figure 10.1, p. 236). Finding homes on the fringes of the city in neighborhoods of second and third settlement in the Bronx, Brooklyn, and upper Manhattan, immigrants and their children created Jewish ethnic alternatives to the Lower East Side. For Jews, the shift from immigrant enclave to ethnic neighborhood marked the transition into the urban landscape of modernity. Though hardly the major shapers of the modern city, as the other essays in this volume show,[4] Jews did contribute to the physical forms of their urban world as well as to the emerging spirit of the neighborhood. In the city spaces they inhabited, they integrated cultural and religious resources, social organizations and networks, with class and ideology, and encoded these upon the landscape.

The movement from immigrant ghetto to ethnic neighborhood paralleled a move from tenement house to apartment building. Jews followed the evolution of the apartment house, from its tenement origins to the height of art deco luxury during the Depression. Tenements, defined as multifamily dwellings without separate baths or elevators, housed the immigrant poor. Flats, with separate baths in walk-up buildings, provided homes for the middle classes, while apartment

252

houses, consisting of suites of rooms with private baths in elevator buildings, catered to the upper classes. In the 1920s, builders began designing apartment houses for the middle classes, enabling those living in walk-ups to rent apartments in elevator buildings. "The demand for modern, comfortable apartments emanated from the growing ranks of immigrant New Yorkers who were rising in economic status into the emerging middle class and were consequently leaving the city's tenements."[5] The sociologist Marshall Sklare called the apartment house "the emblem of the Jews' love affair with the city."[6] Multifamily dwellings provided a sufficient concentration of Jews for ethnic group activity. The public space of lobbies, hallways, rooftops, stairways, and elevators allowed for controlled social action among tenants and mediated the encounter with what Jews perceived as the American world of the streets.[7] Though some Jews invested in single family homes in Brooklyn, most remained renters.[8] Renting facilitated mobility, and Jews moved often from one apartment to another, depending upon their changing fortunes. Thus, they learned how to interpret the view from the kitchen window as a measure of their class position.

Jews came to accept the notion that where you lived told the world who you were.[9] To move to a new neighborhood—to change the view from the kitchen window—meant to exchange an old ethnic identity for a new one, to abandon tradition for modernity. Jews living on the Lower East Side looked out onto narrow, densely crowded streets, often filled with pushcarts. Washing hung from clotheslines strung across the rear yards. Yiddish and English signs adorned the tenement facades, advertising the coexistence of workplace and residence. By contrast, Jews who moved to the Bronx saw from their windows wide, clean streets, filled with the crisscrossing patterns of fathers traveling to and from work, children heading to school or at play, and women making the rounds of shopping in local stores. Striped awnings covered windows in the summer, laundry often hung on the roof to dry, and pushcart markets cluttered only a handful of streets.[10] For Jewish immigrants, this was the urban landscape of modernity.

Like other New Yorkers, Jews reckoned their ethnicity as part of the common coin of urban discourse and as an aspect of the urban landscape. Those who grew up in the city, especially the children of immigrants, quickly learned to decode the messages of the streets.[11] Unlike newcomers, who often made mistakes, children grasped the relative concepts of neighborhood and turf as they navigated the patterns of daily life, walking from home to school, running errands at local stores, visiting relatives, playing games, meeting fathers returning from work at the subway or elevated stations. Occasional trips outside of the neighborhood reinforced through contrast a sense of the familiar. New Yorkers also understood the relativity of ethnicity: It depended upon the angle of vision. Immigrants served as reference groups for each other, helping to define what they shared as New Yorkers and how they differed. Where each group chose to settle inevitably influenced its comparative perceptions.[12] The enormous mobility of the New York population during the first three decades of the century constantly reshuffled the ethnic composition of the city's neighborhoods.[13] The process enlarged New Yorkers' notions of ethnicity, extending the ethnic label to include second-generation residential areas as well as immigrant sections.[14] In the popular imagination, New York City came to embody the ethnic and the foreign, serving as a yardstick with which to measure either the authentic ethnicity or, by contrast, the genuine Americanness of other cities.[15] New York's landscape of modernity embraced the contrary images of corporate capitalism and ethnic particularism, of mass culture and cultural pluralism. Jewish expressions of ethnicity encoded on the modern landscape influenced the city's image of itself and the nation's perception of New York.

Immigrant and second-generation Jews shaped New York's landscape of modernity first through their role in the building industry. Jews participated in both aspects of the dual housing market: as small-scale immigrant entrepreneurs who built one to four houses and as ambitious speculators in the highly risky end of the formal housing market.[16] During the 1920s, New York City accounted for 20 percent of new residential construction in the United States. Apartment buildings, only 39 percent of new residential construction in 1919, soared to 77 percent in the peak year of 1926.[17] In a period of rapid expansion, the boundaries between the formal and informal housing markets remained fluid. Jewish immigrants entered the housing field after starting out in the garment industry, or in construction as plumbers, carpenters, or trimmings men. As self-taught and self-made men, they had no preconceived notions of architectural beauty.[18] They engaged architects, whom they often treated as hired hands, and left design considerations to them. The architects, many of them Jews closed out of the social world of architects and its commissions, accepted the speculative work and designed buildings to meet the aspirations of their upwardly mobile clients.[19] In Brooklyn and the Bronx, Jewish builders working in the informal housing market constructed thousands of tenements and flats, and one- and two-family houses in sections that subsequently housed immigrant workers.[20] Other Jewish builders in these boroughs and in Manhattan entered the speculative housing market and built apartments to appeal to the rising middle and upper middle classes. These quintessential "background build-ings" defined New York's modern cityscape.[21]

But art deco architecture, the style of geometric forms that best expressed modernity, was designed by Jewish architects and built by Jewish builders only for the middle class.[22] Those Jews who built and designed tenements and flats for the working class eschewed the exu-berance of art deco architecture, due to financial constraints. Those who designed and built for the upper class catered to a taste for opulent solidity.[23] Escalating land values in Manhattan dictated a massiveness of form rather than theatrical gestures on a more modest scale. And those Jews who built hundreds of one- and two-family houses in Brooklyn for the lower middle class emphasized internal amenities rather than external physical features.[24]

If Jewish architects and builders set the stage—a stage they built for various New Yorkers, not just for Jews—Jewish residents produced the play. They chose to live in certain neighborhoods, and not in oth-ers.[25] They then created in these city spaces an environment that fos-tered ethnic cultural pluralism. The political, social, economic, and cultural life of the streets, and of the organizations located in the area, rebounded off the buildings until the physical character of the neighborhood appeared to acquire a persona. Despite their different physical characteristics, Jewish neighborhoods on the fringes of the city shared a common ethnic "language" of cultural pluralism. New York Jews came to inhabit a modern ethnic world whose plural land-scapes spoke to and reflected Jewish cultural assumptions.

There were important constraints on the expression of these values. Economic variables narrowed the type of housing that could be built for a profit, a significant restraint on Jewish builders of the modern tenements and flats in Brownsville. Those who constructed housing for wealthy Jews were restricted by discriminatory real estate cove-nants that limited where they could build.[26] However, residential dis-crimination also gave Jewish builders a captive audience, as it were. Because many second-generation Jews faced employment discrimina-tion in white collar work, the location of such key industries as the garment center and its accessibility via mass transit influenced where Jews chose to live.[27] Jewish neighborhoods belonged to New York City's landscape, yet they often appeared to their inhabitants and to outsiders to be a separate world linked only through mass transit with the "real" city of corporate Manhattan.

The transition from immigrant city to ethnic metropolis occurred during a period of enormous urban growth.[28] Continuing, albeit re-duced, immigration retarded the decline of immigrant slums and pre-

served the skyline of the tenements, making it more difficult to perceive the alternative emerging ethnic landscape. The new Jewish
geography required decoding, since it did not depend upon Yiddish
street signs and the hallmarks of urban poverty for its identity. Nonetheless, through their daily activity, Jews gave the local cityscapes
ethnic Jewish rhythms that identified them as urban Jewish milieus. A
brief examination of selected Jewish neighborhoods in three boroughs
suggests how variations in ethnicity, class, and even ideology registered in city spaces during the first four decades of the twentieth
century.

In its spatial and social dimensions, Brownsville in Brooklyn represents a Jewish immigrant alternative to the Lower East Side. Its history
suggests how the complex interplay of residential migration, ethnic
entrepreneurship, and urban growth produced an ethnic landscape.
Brownsville was an ethnically and physically homogeneous neighborhood of the immigrant working class. In Brooklyn and the Bronx, contrasting ideologies of second-generation Jews, middle and working
class, also found expression in the urban landscape. Boro Park developed in Brooklyn as a neighborhood of individual homeowners whose
commitment to Jewish religious tradition influenced the rhythms of
the street. By contrast, a handful of cooperative apartment houses built
and tenanted by left-wing secular Jews shaped the character of neighborhood life in Pelham Parkway, the Bronx. Yet, Jews in both sections
shared a common vision of a desirable urban community. Treelined
streets, spacious parks, houses on a modest scale with light, air, and
yards, easy access to public transportation, convenient shopping, and
good, new public schools characterized these neighborhoods. Neither
contained, however, the modern art deco architecture found in the
middle class, second-generation neighborhood of the Grand Concourse. The Grand Concourse's physical reality exuded an urbane modernity that also flourished within other Jewish sections with less
distinguished housing styles. Finally, a look at the Upper West Side,
the East European Jews' "gilded ghetto," indicates how even this
wealthy area shared common ethnic features of the modern urban
landscape.

Brownsville grew rapidly during the first decades of the twentieth
century.[29] In 1884, Gilbert Thatford, a large property owner in that
section of Brooklyn, convinced Aaron Kaplan, a Jewish real estate
agent who summered in Brownsville, to buy thirteen lots. Another
decade passed before he, in turn, persuaded his fellow vacationer, Elias
Kaplan, to move his garment factory to Brownsville. The factory's
relocation awaited the provision of mass transit facilities, but not such
other urban amenities as paved streets, lighting, gas, and electricity.

In the early days Brownsville residents who ventured out at night ran the risk of falling into unfinished cellars; and when it rained, residents claimed that there were puddles large enough to drown a horse. The first houses clustered near the factories. As the price of lots skyrocketed from $300 to $1,000 by the turn of the century, the percentage of tenements built increased from 58 percent in 1891 to 88 percent in 1904. Three years later, 96 percent of the new buildings were tenements, as lot prices rose to $14,000 by 1910. Friction with the Irish in East New York and with Protestant Americans in East Flatbush constricted Brownsville's expansion, so Jewish builders built taller and taller structures. The most popular buildings were multifamily brick dwellings, many with commercial space on the ground floor. Despite the individuality and diversity of Brownsville's Jewish builders—64 percent of them constructed only one to four houses—the neighborhood developed a homogeneity that reflected the tastes and pocketbooks of its future residents.[30] Most of the houses, though new, were modest, drab, brick buildings faced with fire escapes, few taller than six stories. Builders interspersed residential, commercial, and industrial buildings.

The builders and real estate speculators promoted Brownsville in the Yiddish press. Rather than stressing modern housing, they advertised the "fresh open spaces of the suburbs."[31] These open spaces, largely undeveloped lots, included a handful of working farms. Brownsville did not abut any large park; in fact, the area included only one modest park. Trees did grow in the backyards, however, and during World War I there was vacant land available for students to plant liberty gardens.[32] Brownsville did not boast any wide avenues, but it developed a major commercial street, Pitkin Avenue—nicknamed "the Fifth Avenue of Brooklyn"—as well as an open-air peddlers' market on Belmont Avenue (see Figure 11.1). Jewish merchants and peddlers, respectively, dominated each street. Brownsville came close to resembling a modern, densely populated, overly large *shtetl*.[33] A vibrant street-corner life developed. Often, children knew only those who lived in adjoining blocks.[34] Although religious and radical Jews supported a wide array of organizations, they erected few prominent institutional buildings. Religion and politics most often flourished on the street and in the kitchen.

By 1905, with paved streets, water, electricity, sewage, and rapid transit to Manhattan, Brownsville's Jewish population soared; but so did its non-Jewish population. In 1905, approximately 49,000 Jews lived in Brownsville, roughly 80 percent of the neighborhood's residents. There were also at least twenty synagogues and four Hebrew schools.[35] By 1925, over 200,000 Jews lived in Brownsville, but their

Figure 11.1 Brownsville's Show Street—Pitkin Avenue. It had 372 stores on the fourteen blocks from Stone to Ralph Avenue. *Source:* WPA Collection, Municipal Archives, N.Y.C. Department of Records and Information Services.

proportion of the district remained a constant 80 percent of the total. The number of synagogues had also increased to over eighty. Brownsville grew into an exclusively working class section. The successful entrepreneurs who owned the many stores on Pitkin Avenue and the manufacturers who profited from Brownsville's garment shops lived in the adjacent neighborhood of Eastern Parkway.[36] The majority of Brownsville's Jewish immigrants were skilled workers, with the largest percentage employed in the needle trades, most of them in local garment shops. These included a larger proportion of men's relative to women's clothing factories than existed in Manhattan, suggesting that the decision to relocate was made selectively by firms who followed

Kaplan's lead. The building trades employed the second-largest number of Brownsville's immigrant workers, followed by the printing trades. Brownsville's immigrant population also included many recent arrivals; by 1910, Jews leaving Ellis Island often came directly to Brownsville without tarrying for several years on the Lower East Side. Of the males in Brownsville in 1910, 43 percent had lived in the United States less than five years.[37] Brownsville lacked not only socioeconomic diversity but also ethnic variety, and the absence of both registered in the plain sameness of its streets. Most of Brownsville's Jews came from Russia. Few Galicians, Rumanians, and Hungarians chose to settle in the neighborhood.

During the years that Russian Jews filled up Brownsville's brown brick tenements, well-off immigrant entrepreneurs and second-generation Jews moved into single family homes in Boro Park along tree-lined streets.[38] Initially developed by the politician William Reynolds and the builder Edward Johnson, Boro Park grew into a residential neighborhood along the streetcar lines that carried its residents to work in Manhattan. After the turn of the century, Jewish builders discovered the area and built extensively in Brooklyn's building boom during the 1920s. The decade-long boom produced over 118,000 new houses for the borough and a "whole array of streets that sprang up almost overnight."[39] The Chanin brothers, Henry and Irwin, got their start during Brooklyn's boom with a $7,000 frame house. By the decade's end, they were completing a $15 million art deco office building in the heart of Manhattan.[40] In Boro Park "utterly new blocks of homes have arisen and hitherto grass-covered tracts of land bloomed into dwellings, without radically changing its physiognomy."[41] By 1925, 60,000 Jews had settled in Boro Park, many of them purchasing single- and two-family houses, often built by Jewish builders. The neighborhood's population more than doubled during the decade.[42]

Although they made up only half of the total local population, the Jews of Boro Park quickly established the religious patterns of the neighborhood. Observant Jews' need to walk to the synagogue on the Sabbath and the synagogue's accessibility for weekday morning and evening prayers reinforced the compactness of the Orthodox neighborhood. The synagogue buildings attested to the prosperity of the residents; many required their officers and clergy to wear formal dress on the Sabbath and holidays. The sociologist Egon Mayer observed that "there were no structures built by competing religions or secular organizations to detract from the impressive shadow cast over the community by these early Jewish organizations."[43] Israel Schorr, rabbi of the Orthodox Temple Beth El, recalled that the members were not interested in *"arbeiter yidn."* Indeed, few Jewish workers could afford to live in the neighborhood above Forty-sixth Street, which boasted a median annual family income of $4,000 in 1930. Less religious Jews also avoided Boro Park. The shadow cast by the impressive synagogues and large communal religious schools discouraged the aggressively secular from settling in the district.[44] The streets reflected the rhythm of Jewish observance; Sabbaths and holidays were times for family strolls and visits to neighbors. Boro Park's suburban landscape within the urban milieu—mothers pushed baby carriages on the streets, children walked to school, fathers used public transit to ride to work— suggested the middle-class prosperity of its residents, as its synagogues and Hebrew schools indicated its religious sensibilities. More homogeneous than Brownsville, Boro Park catered largely to one ideological segment of New York Jews. It offered homeownership, treelined streets, Jewish religious facilities—including a handful of commercial streets with kosher butchers, bakers, and delicatessens—urban conveniences and American, non-Jewish neighbors in a residential neighborhood.[45] The city's rapid growth and ethnic entrepreneurship encouraged such segregation along class and ideological lines in place of concentration based on immigrant origins.

Religious Jews were not alone in building exclusively residential neighborhoods that emphasized a mix of urban compactness with suburban amenities. Left-wing Jews used their garment unions and fraternal organizations to acquire some of the perquisites of light, air, trees, and gardens that appealed to the middle class.[46] However, they turned to the Bronx, rather than Brooklyn, to realize their dreams of a better life. Jewish workers employed in the garment and fur industries followed the transit lines and moved to the Bronx in the decade preceding World War I. The Bronx was "the country." In fact, the Bronx contained more park land than any other borough, although it also supported a variety of industries along its southern waterfront. Radical Jewish immigrants first moved to the East Bronx, an ideologically and socioeconomically diverse neighborhood that held approximately 130,000 Jews by 1930. From the densely populated immigrant East Bronx approximately 29,000 moved into the Pelham Parkway section; some residents came from Harlem or even directly from the Lower East Side. Yiddishists, socialist Zionists, communists, and the socialist Amalgamated Clothing Workers Union each built large cooperative apartment houses in the late 1920s. Most were located near the parks, either the eastern edge of Bronx Park or the southern rim of Van Cortlandt Park.

Jewish builders, committed to some form of socialism and to the virtues of consumer cooperatives, constructed these apartment houses. The builders tailored the houses to the desires of their future tenants.

To provide light and air, each room contained a window and the apartments had two exposures. The buildings offered the latest plumbing advances. They were centrally heated with electricity. In response to the union's request, Springsteen and Goldhammer, who designed both the Amalgamated houses on Grand Street in Manhattan and the cooperatives in the Bronx on Sedgwick Avenue and Gunhill Road, laid out the apartments with halls so that no circulation existed through the rooms.[47] The privacy of each room, with its own entrance, distinguished middle-class apartments from working-class tenements, which usually had interior bedrooms reached only by walking through another room.[48] In addition, rather than using the ground floor for commercial space, the houses contained community rooms to be used for meetings and social occasions, a cooperative library, and a kindergarten. The siting of the buildings allowed for a courtyard with grass, bushes, flowers, and trees, and play areas for the children to mediate the transition from the street. These public spaces complemented the accessible parks and provided an alternative for children to play on the streets. However, the six-story buildings did not have elevators, distinguishing them from the "ritzy" apartment buildings in the west Bronx. Nor did the architecture flaunt the art deco style of the Grand Concourse apartments whose modernity proclaimed the middle-class American status of their residents. Instead, the cooperatives harked back to Europe, employing a version of Tudor architecture[49] (Figure 11.2).

The Jews who moved into the cooperatives found that their new environment nourished an intense ideological fervor that spilled over into the neighborhood. In the communist Workers Cooperative Colony, "the most important day of the year was neither Yom Kippur nor Christmas but May Day," recalled one resident.[50] The cooperatives often set the tone for the residential neighborhood, embedding ethnicity, class, and politics in a residential urban landscape of English-styled apartment buildings, large public parks, and small stores.

However, the Bronx Jewish neighborhood whose physical reality came to embody the landscape of modernity was not Pelham Parkway but its bourgeois contemporary in the west, the Grand Concourse. During the 1930s Jewish builders constructed modern, six-story, art deco elevator apartments along the broad treelined boulevard itself and on adjoining streets. The art deco styling appealed to "new money"—those more conscious of being fashionable and up-to-date.[51] A handful of architects who embraced the modern geometric style made an enduring impact that extended beyond the Concourse to the entire neighborhood (Figure 11.3). Jacob Felson, a designer of many of the early movie houses in New York City, drew the plans for nine

Figure 11.2 Housing the Working Class. The International Workers Order cooperative houses on Allerton Avenue in the Bronx, between the park and the candy store. *Source:* WPA Collection, Municipal Archives, N.Y.C. Department of Records and Information Services.

buildings on the Grand Concourse alone that were built between 1935 and 1939.[52] Together with Horace Ginsbern and Hyman Feldman, Felson covered many blocks with yellow brick, curving apartments that flaunted geometric motifs, recessed entrance ways with precast concrete panels, corner windows and roof lines with metal railings.[53] The buildings exuded an enthusiasm suggestive of the Broadway stage, a love of the theatrical, and mass culture. The shining metal doorways, colored brick ornamentation, and the dramatic, indirectly lit lobbies spoke powerfully of modernity. The lobbies' theatrical flair claimed tenants' attention on entering the building and may have encouraged a friendly familiarity as appropriate behavior to such public space.[54] Interior public spaces were ornamented with mosaic ceilings, tiled floors, incised elevator doors, and metal reflecting radiator covers. The

Figure 11.3 Art Deco Splendor. At 161st Street in the Bronx, 888 Grand Concourse, designed by Emery Roth, 1937. The eighty-four apartments had sunken living rooms, a bath for each bedroom, and five to six closets for a three room apartment. *Source:* Emery Roth and Sons.

rooftops often boasted sun decks and play spaces for children instead of the clotheslines associated with tenements and flats.

Inside the apartments the architects gave middle-class Jewish tenants the latest amenities. Steven Ruttenbaum, the biographer of the Jewish architect Emery Roth, credits Roth with the innovation of the central foyer or gallery, an interior room near the entrance that elimi-

263

nated long hallways and allowed for a more efficient use of space. With a foyer, the sleeping rooms could be clustered and set apart from the entertaining rooms, thus preserving privacy for the family. Roth also learned to place windows in relation to the rooms' interiors and their furniture, rather than in a uniform pattern on the facade.[55] By the 1930s, most architects had adopted these features in designing apartments for the middle class. The Grand Concourse art deco apartments also contained aspects that suggested luxury for those who had lived in tenements: sunken living rooms for entertaining, spacious bedrooms with private, tiled bathrooms, generous closet space, and kitchens with dining alcoves (Figure 11.4). Separate dining rooms, once a mark of apartment living along with servants' rooms, disappeared as space itself became a luxury and smaller apartments were built for the middle class. Despite its striking physical appearance, the Grand Concourse neighborhood did not differ significantly from other non-ideological middle-class Jewish sections. In its pretensions, however, it aspired to rival Manhattan's "gilded ghetto."[56]

Not only did working-class and middle-class, immigrant and second-generation Jews create modern ethnic neighborhoods in New York City, even upper-class Jews chose to settle in their own district, thus contributing another variation to the urban Jewish landscape. On the Upper West Side of Manhattan, from 79th Street north to 110th Street west of Central Park, wealthy East European and upper-middle-class German Jews fashioned yet another alternative ethnic urban neighborhood.[57] Unsympathetic observers labeled it "the gilded ghetto" and mocked the "alrightniks" who made their homes in its fancy, massive apartment houses.[58] In fact, the Upper West Side represented less of a "ghetto" in terms of the proportion of its residents who were Jewish than did the Grand Concourse neighborhood. Despite its reputation, the Upper West Side did not constitute a substantial Jewish residential concentration. In the Grand Concourse, Jews were approximately 70 percent of the total population, but they were only a third of the Upper West Side's residents.

The physical character of the Upper West Side contributed to the perception of Jewish ethnic concentration. The large elevator apartment buildings, twelve to fifteen stories high, dominated the wide streets—Central Park West, West End Avenue, Riverside Drive, Broadway, and the major cross streets—while brownstones nestled on the side streets and tenements stood beside the elevated train on Columbus Avenue. Jews lived almost exclusively in the luxury apartment buildings, especially those built after World War I. Irish lived in the tenements, and a mixed population of native-born white Protestants and second-generation Germans lived in the brownstones. Although

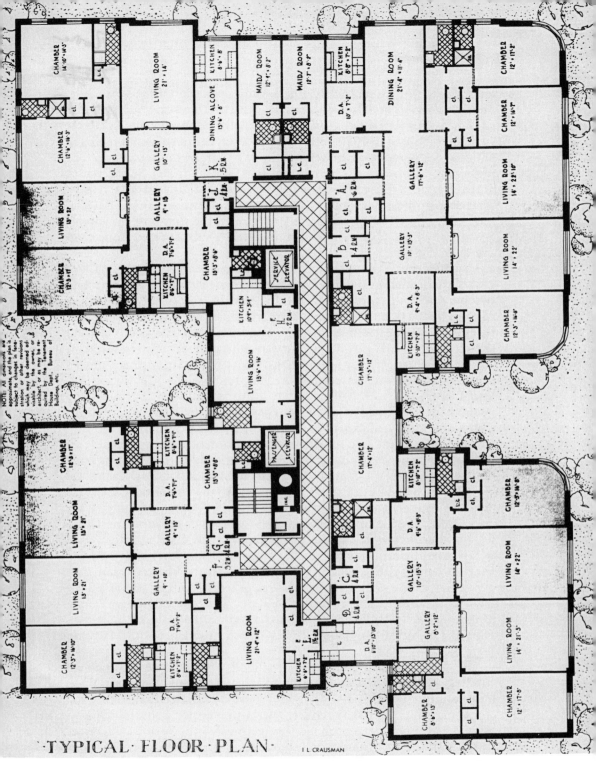

TYPICAL · FLOOR · PLAN ·

I L CRAUSMAN

Figure 11.4 Typical Apartment House Floor Plan, by I. E. Crausman who designed over 300 buildings in the 1920s. *Source:* In exhibit by Brian Danforth and Donald Sullivan at Hunter College in 1976 called "Bronx Art Deco Architecture: An Exposition." Department of Urban Planning, CUNY.

Jews shared the streets with other ethnics on the Upper West Side, their synagogues standing opposite an array of Protestant and Catholic churches, they less often shared their lobbies. Of the seventeen largest apartment houses in 1930, Jews were 100 percent of the tenants in one building, 75 percent of the tenants in two, half of the tenants of four more, and a third of the remaining ten. The historian Selma Berrol noted that "the most homogeneously Jewish buildings were tenanted by East European Jews and located furthest north on West End Avenue," the street Ruttenbaum calls a "formidable masonry canyon."[59] Second-generation German Jews more often lived dispersed along Central Park West.

Jews first moved across Central Park in the years before World War I, at a time when the Upper West Side had already grown through two previous building booms that had set the pattern of its housing. Although Jewish builders tore down a number of the row houses and tenements to construct apartment buildings after the war, they did not alter the mixed character of the neighborhood.[60] The pioneers of the Jewish neighborhood were wealthy East European garment manufacturers and second-generation Jewish professionals. They were followed after the war by the more affluent Russian, German, and Hungarian Jews who abandoned Harlem as its African American population grew and expanded. Attracted by the extension of the subway down the west side to the new center of the garment industry on Seventh Avenue, clothing manufacturers moved to the area in large numbers. By 1925, a sample of Jewish neighborhood households revealed over half to be garment manufacturers, a remarkable increase over the 3 percent in this occupation in 1915. Rents of $100 to $200 per month attested to the affluence of the Jewish tenants who chose to rent apartments in a densely populated urban district, rather than to buy single family homes in the suburbs. These Jews also used the neighborhood's public spaces, its parks and streets, for recreation. The physical attributes of the upper-class neighborhood they fashioned catered to their sense of urbanity and style, while its ethnicity, visible in the solid synagogues, kosher butcher shops, bookstores, delicatessens, and bakeries, nourished a sense of cohesion and security despite their minority status.

The diverse Jewish ethnic neighborhoods shared some common attributes, as did the Jews who built and lived in them. Most contained multifamily dwellings and, in many, these dominated not merely the corner plots but the large avenues. Jews also retained a common vision of the ideal urban neighborhood that permeates the various imperfect manifestations constructed on the streets of New York City. This improved urban environment included wide, preferably treelined streets and access to parks, public spaces to allow for the easy intercourse that sustained a sense of neighborhood and community. New York Jews did not abandon the city streets for private pleasures, even when they acquired the affluence to support such privacy.[61] In fact, they continued to endow the streets with ethnic attributes, even boldly claiming a whole neighborhood like the Upper West Side as their own when they constituted only a sizable fraction of its population. Jews sought out and built neighborhoods with easy access to schools, transportation, and shopping. They evidenced less concern to segregate residential buildings, although middle-class Jews preferred to assign the ground floors of apartment buildings for professional instead of commercial purposes.

Jews were not alone, of course, in their ability to transform the gridiron into an ethnic mosaic. Most ethnic groups placed their stamp upon the city. Indeed, the distinctiveness of Jewish urban landscapes can best be seen in comparison with the spatial choices of other groups. Jewish immigrants and their children developed an array of urban environments that encouraged physical mobility not only as an expression of social mobility and acculturation, but also of ideological preference. These neighborhoods partook of New York's landscape of modernity; they constituted the ethnic city, the cultural pluralist alternative.

The Jews who lived in this urban world did not always perceive their space as part of the city, despite their embrace of modernity. Was Brownsville the nurturing neighborhood, the *shtetl* modernized, or was it the streetscape of criminality, the breeding ground of Murder, Inc.? Was the Grand Concourse the epitome of urbane style, expressing the appeal of the theatrical, or was it just another bourgeois ethnic enclave, provincial and smug? It all depended on one's point of view, where one stood at the time, what one saw from the kitchen window. Together with other New Yorkers, Jews encoded their ethnic choices on the city's landscape and learned to interpret with great subtlety the meaning of the view from the kitchen window.

Acknowledgments

I want to thank Professor Arthur A. Goren for his critical eye and persistent enthusiasm that improved successive versions of this essay. I am also indebted to the members of the Committee on New York City of the Social Science Research Council for their constructive suggestions and to the participants (many of them authors of chapters in this volume) at two conferences on "The Landscape of Modernity" for their critical responses. The conferences provoked an intellectual interchange that enhanced the theoretical and substantive contexts of the essay.

Notes

1. Moses Rischin, "Introduction," in Hutchins Hapgood, *The Spirit of the Ghetto* (Cambridge: Belknap Press of Harvard University Press, 1967), p. vii.
2. For example, Zalmen Yoffeh, "The Passing of the East Side," *The Menorah Journal* (December 1929): 264–275.
3. In 1930, 77 percent of New York's Jewish population lived in the Bronx and Brooklyn. Morris C. Horowitz and Lawrence J. Kaplan, *The Estimated Jewish Population of the New York Area* (New York: Federation of Jewish Philanthropies, 1959), p. 22.
4. See especially Chapter 2 by Keith Revell, Chapter 3 by Marc Weiss, Chapter 6 by Gail Fenske and Deryck Holdsworth, and Chapter 7 by Carol Willis in this volume.
5. Steven Ruttenbaum, *Mansions in the Clouds: The Skyscraper Palazzi of Emery Roth* (New York: Balsam Press, 1986), p. 42, quote on p. 65.
6. Marshall Sklare, "Jews, Ethnics, and the American City," *Commentary* (April 1972): 72.
7. Elizabeth Collins Cromley, *Alone Together: A History of New York's Early Apartments* (Ithaca, NY: Cornell University Press, 1990), p. 211.
8. Rentals also allowed Jews to use their capital for business investment or to invest in education for their children.
9. Louis Wirth, "The Ghetto," in Albert J. Reiss, Jr., ed., *Louis Wirth on Cities and Social Life* (Chicago: University of Chicago Press, 1964), p. 94.
10. Bathgate Avenue in the Bronx supported a lively pushcart market. Some garment shops moved to the Bronx, but many Jewish workers took mass transit to the new center of garment manufacturing on Manhattan's west side. In 1919, the Bronx had 213 garment shops and 4,068 garment workers. The Bronx Board of Trade, *The Bronx* (New York, 1923), p. 5. (The figures derive from the Federal Census of Manufactures.)
11. The wealth of memoir literature by second-generation New York Jews attests to this. For example, Alfred Kazin, *A Walker in the City* (New York: Harcourt, 1951), and Norman Podhoretz, *Making It* (New York: Random House, 1967), on Brownsville; Jerome Weidman, *Fourth Street East* (New York: Random House, 1970), and Charles Reznikoff, *Family Chronicle* (New York: C. Reznikoff, 1963), on the Lower East Side; Kate Simon, *Bronx Primitive* (New York: Viking Press, 1982), and Irving Howe, "A Memoir of the Thirties," *Steady Work* (New York: Harcourt Brace Jovanovich, 1966), pp. 349–364, on the east Bronx; Ronald Sanders, *Reflections on a Teapot* (New York: Harper & Row, 1972), on Flatbush.
12. See Chapter 10 by Donna Gabaccia in this volume.
13. Thomas Kessner documents the mobility of Irish and German immigrants in the decades before the turn of the century as well as the physical mobility of Italians and Jews. Thomas Kessner, *The Golden Door: Italian and Jewish Immigrant Mobility in New York City 1880–1915* (New York: Oxford University Press, 1977), pp. 140–141, 143–156. For changes in distribution of borough population from 1900 to 1970, see Ira Rosenwaike, *Population History of New York City* (Syracuse, NY: Syracuse University Press, 1972), pp. 92–93, 133. Rosenwaike also notes that New York City increased its drawing power for immigrants in the 1920s, pull-

ing one out of four, and thus remained an immigrant and second-generation city throughout the interwar decades in contrast to other American cities, which saw a growth in their population of native born of native parentage (third generation).

14. Even in 1980, New York's white ethnic groups maintained patterns of residential segregation in higher-class neighborhoods characterized as "good examples of the American Dream realized for first and second and even later generations of ethnic New Yorkers." William Kornblum and James Beshers, "White Ethnicity: Ecological Dimensions," in John Hull Mollenkopf, ed., *Power, Culture and Place: Essays on New York City* (New York: Russell Sage Foundation, 1988), p. 204, quoted on p. 213.

15. Kathleen Neils Conzen, "Immigrants, Immigrant Neighborhoods, and Ethnic Identity: Historical Issues," *Journal of American History* 68 (1979): 603–608.

16. On the concept of a dual housing market, see Olivier Zunz, *The Changing Face of Inequality: Urbanization, Industrial Development, and Immigrants in Detroit, 1880–1920* (Chicago: University of Chicago Press, 1982), pp. 161–171.

17. Ruttenbaum, *Mansions in the Clouds*, pp. 66–67.

18. Robert A. M. Stern, Gregory Gilmartin, and Thomas Mellins, *New York 1930: Architectural Urbanism Between the Two World Wars* (New York: Rizzoli, 1987), p. 553.

19. Ruttenbaum, *Mansions in the Clouds*, pp. 7, 50.

20. Leon Wexelstein, *Building Up Greater Brooklyn* (New York: Brooklyn Biographical Society, 1925).

21. Ruttenbaum, *Mansions in the Clouds*, pp. 7, 67.

22. The best examples can be found in the construction of art deco apartments during the 1930s in Washington Heights in Manhattan and on the Grand Concourse in the Bronx. Steven Lowenstein, *Frankfurt on the Hudson* (Detroit, MI: Wayne State University Press, 1989), and Donald Sullivan and Brian Danforth, *Bronx Art Deco Architecture: An Exposition* (New York: Hunter College, 1976).

23. Compare Emery Roth's elegant art deco apartment at 888 Grand Concourse with the many buildings he designed on the Upper West Side of Manhattan. Ruttenbaum, *Mansions in the Clouds*, pp. 67–73, 169–171.

24. Eleanora Schoenebaum mentions appliances, stoves, parquet floors, refrigerators, and tiled baths in connection with houses built in Flatlands and Sheepshead in the 1920s. She argues that these interior amenities were incentives designed to induce renters to buy. Eleanora Schoenebaum, "Emerging Neighborhoods: The Development of Brooklyn's Fringe Areas, 1850–1930." Ph.D. diss. (Columbia University, 1977), p. 241.

25. The relative paucity of Jewish builders in Queens prior to World War II contributed to the absence of significant concentrations of Jewish population and of Jewish neighborhoods in the borough. Franklin Sherman chronicles the biographies of only 31 Jews out of 165 builders of Queens, and several of the 31 are lawyers and building-supply owners, not builders. Franklin J. Sherman, *Building Up Greater Queens Borough* (New York: Brooklyn Biographical Society, 1929).

26. Each borough had restricted areas, for example, along Fifth and Park avenues in Manhattan, the Riverdale section in the Bronx, parts of Jack-

son Heights and Forest Hills in Queens, and Prospect Heights and parts of Flatbush in Brooklyn. Such restrictions encouraged ethnic groups' tendency to cluster. Heywood Broun and George Britt, *Christians Only: A Study in Prejudice* (New York: Vanguard Press, 1931); Ronald Bayor, *Neighbors in Conflict* (Baltimore, MD: Johns Hopkins University Press, 1978).

27. See Chapter 9 by Nancy Green in this volume.
28. Immigrants crowded into the city in such numbers that New York's population doubled from 3,437,000 to 6,930,000 between 1900 and 1930. Rosenwaike, *Population History of New York City*, pp. 90–92. As a result, in 1930 as in 1900, over 80 percent of all white household heads in New York were immigrants and their children, the second generation.
29. The account of Brownsville draws on Alter F. Landesman, *Brownsville: The Birth, Development and Passing of a Jewish Community* (New York: Bloch Publishing Company, 1969); the statistics, unless otherwise indicated, derive from Max Halpert, "Jews of Brownsville 1880–1925." Ph.D. diss. (Yeshiva University, 1958).
30. Schoenebaum, "Emerging Neighborhoods," pp. 104–106, 117–120, 141.
31. Quoted in Halpert, "Jews of Brownsville," p. 15.
32. Stephen Brumberg, *Going to America, Going to School* (New York: Praeger, 1986), p. 94.
33. Alter Landesman, who spent his life working in Brownsville as the director of the Hebrew Educational Society, characterized it as "an isolated corner, a provincial world removed from the crosscurrents of the metropolitan city." Landesman, *Brownsville*, p. 375.
34. Gerald Sorin, *The Nurturing Neighborhood: The Brownsville Boys Club and Jewish Community in Urban America, 1940–1990* (New York: New York University Press, 1990), pp. 13–15.
35. Schoenebaum, "Emerging Neighborhoods," p. 125.
36. Alter F. Landesman, "A Neighborhood Survey of Brownsville," Report for Members of the Society (Brooklyn, NY: Hebrew Educational Society, n.d.), pp. 4a, 5–9. Although a 1925 survey of housing costs in Brownsville disclosed some new postwar buildings renting for as much as $19 per room—significantly higher than the older houses, which rented for $5 to $6 per room, prices competitive with or lower than the Lower East Side—the families paid the higher rents by pooling the income of three or four members.
37. Schoenebaum, "Emerging Neighborhoods," p. 153.
38. The account of Boro Park draws on Egon Mayer, *From Suburb to Shtetl: The Jews of Boro Park* (Philadelphia: Temple University Press, 1979).
39. Wexelstein, *Building Up Greater Brooklyn*, pp. xv–xvii. Wexelstein chronicles the biographies of close to two hundred Brooklyn builders, most of them Jewish, who changed the physical face of the borough after World War I. Many of them built sections that became Jewish neighborhoods. Schoenebaum also notes the connection between the builders and the future residents of a neighborhood. She contrasts the eighteen and eleven builders of houses on East Eighty-fifth and Eighty-sixth streets, respectively, in Canarsie, who were all Italian, with the twenty-two of twenty-seven builders on Flatlands Avenue, east of Ninety-second Street, who were Jewish. The subsequent ethnic distribution of Italians and Jews

in Canarsie largely reflected the builders' respective ethnic backgrounds. Schoenebaum, "Emerging Neighborhoods," p. 292. Sherman similarly observes: "It is a truism that what sets the tone . . . of any given locality is, primarily, the character of the builder who builds it. . . . The builder determines the size, appearance and the manner of the structure; this is obvious. But it is *not* so obvious that he determines thereby the class of people who would seek to live on his property." Sherman, *Building Up Greater Queens*, p. 62.

40. Paul Goldberger, "Style Moderne—Kitsch or Serious—Is in Vogue, ART DECO," *New York Times* (January 31, 1974).
41. Wexelstein, *Building Up Greater Brooklyn*, p. xxxi.
42. *Brooklyn Market Survey* (Brooklyn, NY: 1936), p. 14.
43. Mayer, *From Suburb to Shtetl*, p. 27.
44. A handful of Yiddish schools were established in the lower-middle-class section.
45. Retail stores were largely limited to the retail streets: Fort Hamilton Parkway, New Utrecht Avenue, and Eighteenth Avenue.
46. There are no studies of Jewish neighborhoods of the Bronx. For documentation and sources, see Deborah Dash Moore, *At Home in America* (New York: Columbia University Press, 1981), Chapters 2 and 3.
47. Stern, Gilmartin, and Mellins, *New York 1930*, pp. 421, 488.
48. Cromley, *Alone Together*, pp. 159–160.
49. The Jewish architect Albert Goldhammer, together with Leo Stillman or George Miller, also designed half a dozen art deco apartment buildings in the west Bronx between 1936 and 1940. His choice of a less flamboyant style for the cooperatives probably reflected the unions' desires as well as financial constraints. Sullivan and Danforth, *Bronx Art Deco Architecture*, pp. 51, 53–54, 57–58. The Work Projects Administration criticized the Amalgamated's houses' facade as "decorated with incongruous details derived from English Cottage designs." WPA, *New York City Guide* (1939; reprint, New York: Pantheon, 1982), p. 525.
50. Quoted in Calvin Trillin, "U.S. Journal: The Bronx," *The New Yorker* (August 1, 1977): 50.
51. Ruttenbaum, *Mansions in the Clouds*, p. 144.
52. See *New York Times* obituary for Felson (October 19, 1962). Sullivan and Danforth documented most of the architects of the art deco buildings in the Bronx. *Bronx Art Deco Architecture*, pp. 47–55.
53. Feldman designed over 9,000 apartment buildings in New York City, many of them in the Grand Concourse neighborhood. He also designed such buildings as the Pierrepont Hotel in Brooklyn and Schwab House on Riverside Drive. See his obituary in the *New York Times* (January 27, 1981). Albert Berger, an architect who designed several apartment buildings on the Grand Concourse and neighboring Jerome Avenue with M. Henry Sugarman, also designed the Garment Center Building in Manhattan. Sullivan and Danforth, *Bronx Art Deco Architecture*, pp. 49, 56.
54. Cromley, *Alone Together*, p. 151.
55. Ruttenbaum, *Mansions in the Clouds*, pp. 44, 48–49.
56. Ruth Glazer, "West Bronx: Food, Shelter, Clothing," *Commentary* (June 1949): 578–585.

57. This account draws on Selma Berrol, "The Jewish West Side of New York City 1920–1970," *Journal of Ethnic Studies* 13:4 (1986): 21–45.
58. Aaron M. Frankel, "Back to Eighty-Sixth Street," *Commentary* (August 1946): 169–170.
59. Berrol, "Jewish West Side," p. 31; Ruttenbaum, *Mansions in the Clouds,* p. 58.
60. Ruttenbaum, Ibid., p. 67.
61. Schoenebaum argues that "for the average individual the suburb of the twenties had become internalized; he moved not to a community, but to his own modern dwelling." Schoenebaum, "Emerging Neighborhoods," p. 266.

12

Cities of Light,
Landscapes of Pleasure

David Nasaw

In the year 1900, two remarkable novels were published about mid-western farm girls who left "gray" homes with "gray" families to journey to cities blazing with light, color, and irrepressible gaiety.

Home and family were not havens of warmth and affection for Dorothy and Carrie. Dorothy's Uncle Henry, we are told in the first few pages of *The Wizard of Oz*, "never laughed. He worked hard from morning till night and did not know what joy was." Aunt Em "was thin and gaunt, and never smiled." Their home in Kansas was surrounded by the "great gray prairie. . . . The sun had baked the plowed land into a gray mass. . . . Once the house had been painted [but now it] was as dull and gray as everything else."[1]

Theodore Dreiser, the author of *Sister Carrie*, uses similar adjectives to describe his heroine's first home in Chicago: damp, gray, lonely, silent, subdued, cold, narrow, humdrum. Carrie's sister, with whom she boarded, "carried with her much of the grimness of shift and toil." Carrie's brother-in-law "slopped about . . . in a certain solemnity of countenance." Their flat was "a narrow, humdrum place . . . interest and joy lay elsewhere."[2]

For each of these authors, it is not the home, but the downtown city with its restaurants, shops, and theaters that welcome with a "blaze of lights." It is not the home fires, but "the artificial fires of merriment" that raise our spirits when "the chill hand of winter lays upon the heart."[3]

Both Dreiser and Baum describe the magical cities their heroines escape to in terms of merriment and light, often conflating the two. Carrie in visiting downtown Chicago and Dorothy on entering Oz are "dazzled by the brilliancy of the wonderful city [where] everyone seemed happy and contented and prosperous."[4] These images were not plucked from thin air. *Sister Carrie* and *The Wizard of Oz* were written in 1900, when electric lighting was wondrously turning night into day and providing what would come to be a central metaphor for the delights of modern life in the American city.

The first central power stations and isolated generators had been built in the early 1880s to furnish electric current to fashionable homes (more properly, mansions) and scattered downtown streets, shops, hotels, and theaters. Marshall Fields installed its first electric lights in 1882. In 1883, Haverly's theater in Chicago bought two dynamos from Edison, generating enough power to light sixty-three incandescent lamps, including a chandelier and separate lights in the vestibules and dressing rooms.[5] By the 1890s, electricity was beginning to power the city's streetcars and factories, while electric interior lighting and exterior displays had become "essential to competition" for downtown theaters, restaurants, hotels, and department stores. By the first decade of the new century, American cities large and small were lighting their major shopping and entertainment streets with electric lamps. New York City "took an early lead as the most brightly lighted urban center," though cities from Wichita and Cincinnati to New Haven and Philadelphia emulated it in constructing their own "Great White Ways."[6] The American cities were far ahead of their European counterparts in this development. By 1903, New York City alone had almost 17,000 electric street lamps. Chicago had only half that many, but its 8,000 was twelve times greater than the total for Berlin.[7]

In his marvelous book on the history of street lighting, Wolfgang Schivelbusch recounts how earlier eighteenth and nineteenth century municipal lighting systems based on kerosene and oil had not lit up the street as much as provided markers for individual houses and a small degree of protection for those who had no choice but to be out after dark. The switch to gas street lamps in the mid-nineteenth century increased the amount of artificial light projected, but not enough to turn night into day. The eye continued to see "as it did at night, with retinal rods." Only with electric lighting would it see "as it did during the day, that is, with the retinal cones."[8] Electric street lamps were so bright, it was said, one could read the newspaper by them. They illuminated not simply the lamppost beneath, but both sides of the street with a clear, bright, white light, not the sooty gray of the gas lamps.[9]

The streets of the downtown entertainment districts that Dreiser described realistically and Baum fantastically were by 1900 literally bathed in electric light. Unlike gas, which was highly flammable, electric lamps could be kept on all night, drawing attention to window displays in department stores or attracting customers to the amusements that catered to the habitués of a new nightlife. While the street lamps banished darkness from the streets, the commercial lights of restaurants, shops, and theaters added the merry twinkle that gives the "nocturnal round of business, pleasure and illumination . . . we think of as night life . . . its own special atmosphere." "The illuminated window as stage, the street as theatre and the passers-by as audience—this is the scene of big-city night life."[10]

The lighting of the city's downtown shops and streets stood in sharp contrast to its residences, the vast majority of which were still not wired for electrical current. The contrast between flats partially lit by gas and streets blazing with light could not have been greater. Richard Harding Davis, who in 1892 was commissioned to write the chapter on "Broadway" for a book on *The Great Streets of the World*, graphically described the impact of the new streetlights on the city's working people. For the working girl like Carrie, who felt trapped inside her dimly lit flat, Broadway "at night, when all the shop-fronts are lighted, and the entrances to the theatres blaze out on the sidewalk like open fireplaces" presented a new kind of public space. Here the "girl bachelor, who is either a saleslady or a working-girl, as she chooses to call herself . . . can and does walk alone . . . at night unmolested, if she so wishes it. . . . She has found her hall bedroom cold and lonely after the long working day behind a counter or at a loom, and the loneliness tends to homesickness . . . so she puts on her hat and steps down a side-street and loses herself in the unending processions on Broadway, where, though she knows no one, and no one wants to know her, there is light and color, and she is at least not alone."[11]

The darkness and shadows that had hidden the city's sporting men and lower classes as they pursued their illicit pleasures had given way to what Dreiser called the "gushes of golden hue" that welcomed and protected the decent people of the city. No longer would the "thick veil of night," as George Foster wrote in 1850, cover "the fearful mysteries of darkness in the metropolis—the festivities of prostitution, the orgies of pauperism, the haunts of theft and murder, the scenes of drunkenness and beastly debauch and all the sad realities that go to make up the lower stratum—the underground story—of life in New York." The electrical lights of the city would pierce the "thick veil of night," banishing "the fearful mysteries of darkness." The newly lit city—and its nighttime amusements—could now be opened to respectable folk, women and men, who feared the shadows and welcomed the light.[12]

The lights symbolized the new safety, decency, and welcoming warmth of the city after dark. In an editorial extolling the virtues of the new electrically lit signs, *The Four-Track News* (published by the passenger department of the New York Central and Hudson Railroad) warned that without its lights the city "would become as cheerless and cold as a country road, instead of being, as it is now, the one place on earth where, with night turned into day, the friendless stranger feels at home, and that lonesome, homesick sensation has no place."[13]

It was taken for granted that the city's lights removed much of the danger that had once lurked in the dark. A 1912 article in *The American City* listed first among "the advantages accruing from ornamental street lighting," a decrease in "lawlessness and crime. . . . Regarding street lighting as a preventative of crime, there comes to mind an old saying that 'A light is as good as a policeman.' . . . A criminologist of worldwide fame, and one who is considered an authority, says that he would rather have plenty of electric lights and clean streets than all the law and order societies in existence." Whether the electric lights truly led to a decrease in criminality, we cannot say, but there can be no doubt that they made the city's nighttime workers, revelers, and visitors feel more secure.[14]

The city's lights served other purposes as well. They were attractions in their own right, sights to be seen, witnessed, and enjoyed. As Rand, McNally's *Bird's-Eye Views and Guide to Chicago* proclaimed in 1893 under a separate heading, "Beautiful Lights at Night," "It is literally true that the genius of Edison has added a thousand beauties to the night. The visitor from the country can scarcely fail to be impressed by the brilliancy of an evening in town." Broadway in New York City illuminated for more than twenty blocks by street lamps and electric advertisements was by 1910 one of the country's primary tourist attractions.[15]

Electricity was not simply a source of power to light the urban landscape. It provided a central metaphor for the city it illuminated. Electrification, as David Nye reminds us in his brilliant new book, "was both a process and an attribute, and Americans understood the new technology in both ways. They regularly shifted from seeing electricity in terms of technical change to a metaphorical level where it meant novelty, excitement, modernity, and heightened awareness." Electrifying, for example, meant both "charging with electricity" and "intensely exciting," as in an "electrifying performance."[16]

Electric lighting reconfigured the urban landscape into a fairyland of illuminated shapes, signs, and brightly colored, sometimes animated messages and images—40-foot green pickles, gigantic pieces of chewing gum, Roman chariots racing on top of a hotel. The lights of the city created "a new kind of visual text," a new landscape of modernity. They foregrounded the city's illuminated messages, its theaters, tall buildings, hotels, restaurants, department stores, and "Great White Ways," while erasing its "unattractive areas and cast[ing] everything unsightly into an impenetrable darkness. If by day poor or unsightly sections called out for social reform, by night the city was a purified world of light, simplified into a spectacular pattern, interspersed with now-unimportant blanks."[17]

After dark, the city's residences, offices, and factories receded into darkness. The lighting of the lights signaled that the workday was over and the time for play at hand. "It is an old, old theme, and an oft told tale—but when the lights are on, and the season is in full swing, as it is now, any evening . . . when Broadway is really itself, it is a continuous vaudeville that is worth many times the 'price of admission'—especially as no admission price is asked. Where else is there such a free performance—such a festive panorama of gay life as Broadway 'puts up' when the lights are on."[18]

The landscape of pleasure that was silhouetted in electric lighting advertised the popular amusement centers of the turn-of-the-century city. Mid-nineteenth century music academies, opera houses, and legitimate theaters had blended into the street, rather than standing out from it, in part because their owners were reluctant to advertise a product many still regarded as sinful. The new theaters, on the contrary, employed electrical displays, signage, and marquees to call attention to themselves and blaze a welcome onto the street. Though the apotheosis of display would only be attained with the movie palaces, from the turn of the century onward, legitimate theaters, vaudeville halls, nickelodeons, neighborhood movie theaters, and amusement parks all relied on the magic of electrical lighting to attract customers like "moths in endless procession [come] to bask in the light of the flame."[19]

In 1895, Oscar Hammerstein illuminated his own name and that of his new theater, the Olympia, in electrical lights strung over its entrance on the east side of Broadway, between Forty-fourth and Forty-fifth streets. In 1905, Frederic Thompson ventured one step further by employing electric lighting not as ornament or signage, but as an integral design feature in the facade of his Hippodrome Theatre on the east side of Sixth Avenue, between Forty-third and Forty-fourth streets.

Thompson had served his show business apprenticeship at world's fair midways and at Luna Park on Coney Island, which he had designed. In these locations, he had learned that the first step in selling a ticket was to capture the attention of the passerby—and the best attention-getters were light bulbs by the hundreds. Electric signs with the theater's name and the current attraction were installed at either side of the entrance. At the building's corners, twin towers rose from the roofline supporting "glittering globes outlined in electric lights." Although the electric signs on the Hippodrome were too high to focus the gaze of the pedestrian below, they served as a perpetual advertisement of the theater and the show.[20]

Thompson, like Hammerstein before him, could afford to promote his theater and his show literally over the heads of passersby to the city at large because most of his tickets were sold in advance. Vaudeville and moving-picture proprietors without large advance sales had to focus their electrical displays more narrowly on the pedestrians who passed in front of the proprietors' houses.

The city's vaudeville houses garishly ornamented their classical exteriors with hundreds of light bulbs that illuminated the entrance, decorated the canopy, and spelled out in block letters the name of the theater. The nickelodeons, with no advance sales, abandoned all restraint in their pursuit of the pedestrian's attention. The message their electrical signs and twinkling lamps shouted was a simple one. Passengers were encouraged to abandon their workaday lives and detour from the street and their chores or shopping into the nickelodeon. The gaudily ornamented facades advertised the distance between the gaiety within and the drab routine on the outside by radiating with visual delight. Hundreds, sometimes thousands of electric lights "shone from the front of every theater, outlining the architectural or sculptural forms, spelling the name of the theater, or simply forming geometrical patterns."[21]

The Bijou, which opened its doors in March 1908 in Providence, Rhode Island, was housed in a converted storefront with a huge false front. "In style, this facade can best be described as 'High Coney Island.' It was elaborate in the extreme, painted white, and contained 2,000 light bulbs. These were not in a sign but were actually mounted on the woodwork and traced the curves, arches, and parapets in brilliant relief for the benefit of evening crowds."[22]

If the facade with its twinkling arches drew the gaze of passersby to the theater, it was the exterior box office that directly focused attention on the business within. Live theaters—vaudeville, musical comedy, legitimate, and cheap stock—had stationed their box offices inside the outer lobby or vestibule. The nickelodeons moved theirs outside, decorated them lavishly, strung them with garlands of electric lights, and displayed vividly their 5 cents or 10 cents admission price.[23]

The nickel-show box office was more than a place to buy tickets. It became, as the *Motion Picture News* explained, "the emblem of the motion picture theater"; a "sales medium," and the signal to pedestrians that all that was required for entrance was a simple cash transaction. The nickelodeon facade, with its massive entry arches, electric lights and signs, and exterior vestibules and box offices was, as Charlotte Herzog has written, "its most important part."[24] It was the face of the amusement. Its wide-open grin spelled out one simple message: All decent folk—women, men, and children—are welcome within.

The movie palaces of the 1910s and 1920s achieved the ultimate in nighttime display. Theater owners spent hundreds of thousands of dollars on the wildly exotic atmospheric interiors and exteriors that lit up the sky. Quantity generated its own particular qualities: the more bulbs, the more light, the more spectacular the entryway, the greater the expectations for the show inside. The Saxe Brothers' Princess Theatre, which opened in December 1909, boasted "a forty-foot facade with an ornamental arch over the entrance and 1,500 incandescent light bulbs to attract the eye."[25] Clune's Broadway Theatre in Los Angeles, built in early 1911, used 2,000 tungsten lamps to light its sign out front.[26] In Denver in 1913, where seven moving-picture and vaudeville houses were lined up on Curtis Street between Sixteenth and Eighteenth streets, a total of 10,387 lamps with more than 51,500 candlepower lit up the street. The Paris Theatre alone had over 4,000 lamps "in a variety of colors, red, blue, and purple, arranged to give a very pleasing effect." The Isis Theatre, which had 2,200 lamps, was adding another 2,000.[27] As the theaters got bigger and more luxurious through the 1920s, more and more lights, in more spectacular exterior designs and interior "atmospherics," were added. When the Roxy Theatre opened on Broadway in 1927, it was prominently advertised that the theater by itself consumed enough electricity to power a city of 25,000.[28]

The crowning glory of the mature movie palaces was their brilliantly lit marquees, which extended onto and colonized the sidewalk by covering it with a ceiling studded with hundreds of light bulbs. The marquees served practical as well as display functions. They roofed the entryway, providing shelter and incentive for pedestrians to examine the posters and billboards; they publicized the names of the movies and their stars; and, in bright, bold electric lights, they "blazed a trail to the theater from great distances."[29] The only way to avoid passing under the marquees and into the theater's entryway was to step off the sidewalk into the street.

The larger palaces had additional vertical marquees climbing up their sides, shouting their names for blocks in every direction. "These massive electric marquees could be seen for miles by those riding on trolleys; signs flashing multicolored messages towered several stories in height."[30] They projected their light far beyond the theaters, illuminating the darkness and involuntarily focusing the gaze of residents and visitors on the city's nighttime pleasures.

The amusement park entrances were as spectacular as the movie palaces'. They too signaled to passersby that a new and extraordinary world, entirely separate from the mundane spheres of home and work, was at hand. The first and most primitive of the Coney Island amusement parks, Steeplechase Park, had attracted and then channeled visitors inside "through entrances marked by triumphal arches of plaster accumulations of the iconography of laughter—clowns, pierrots, masks." The Luna Park gateway was flanked on either end by electrically lit towers topped with fully illuminated globes and framed by four levels of electric signage, each larger than the one beneath it. Visitors to Dreamland entered the park through a monumental archway formed by the outspread wings of a barebreasted sculpture entitled "Creation."

The amusement parks were the first "totally synthetic" environments, fabricated dream worlds where, in the words of Frederic Thompson, all was "bizarre and fantastic—crazier than the craziest part of Paris—gayer and more different from the everyday world." Visitors were greeted by towers and minarets, domes and spires, massive statuary, castles, lagoons, ballrooms, pavilions, roof gardens, and electric lights, one-quarter million in Luna Park, over one million in Dreamland.[31]

The exterior designs and electrical lights of the new theaters, vaudeville houses, nickelodeons, movie palaces, and amusement parks established and advertised their distinct personalities. Like the playgrounds described by Johan Huizinga in *Homo Ludens*, these electrically illuminated amusement spaces were "temporary worlds within the ordinary world, dedicated to the performance of an act apart."[32] Their exterior design and ornamentation accentuated their separation from the everyday "gray" worlds of home and work.

The illuminated palaces of amusement were the central institutions of the new urban nightlife. Their electrically ornamented exteriors "marked" the city after dark as an "attraction" and called attention to the particular delights for sale within.

A new public world of entertainment opened its doors in the early years of this century as city folk, rich and poor alike, left home to join the crowds in vaudeville halls, popular-priced theaters, movie palaces, and amusement parks. "So popular, indeed, have commercial amusements become, that their patronage may be said to be universal," observed Richard Henry Edwards in 1915. "One has only to watch the night life of any city as it moves in and out past the box offices, to see young, middle aged, and old, men, women, and children, of every occupation and station in life, all intent on finding 'a good time.' "[33]

The new commercial entertainments were both cheap and accessible to most city residents. The amusement parks were only a trolley ride away and charged no more than fifteen cents for admission. By 1919, there were some 1,500 of them at the edges of cities across the country. Kansas City had three, which together drew over 1,600,000 customers in 1911. Cleveland's two major parks drew over 2,250,000. Coney Island, of course, far surpassed these figures. Attendance there was estimated at 20 million for the 1909 season.[34]

The cheap theaters were even more accessible—and more popular. Whereas the first vaudeville and moving-picture theaters had been built on the entertainment and shopping streets of the central business districts, there were, by the early years of the new century, theaters on the secondary shopping streets as well, within walking distance of the immigrant and working-class districts, and on the metropolitan fringe and in the suburbs where an emerging middle class of native-born and immigrant families was settling.

It is difficult to know how many theaters there actually were at any given moment or what percentage of the population was actually attending them. Michael Davis's *The Exploitation of Pleasure* listed 400 licensed moving-picture theaters in New York City in 1911; 201 were in Manhattan. John Collier of the People's Institute and the National Board of Censorship of Motion Pictures, speaking in 1912, put the number of picture shows in the city at 800. In October 1913, J. Stuart Blackton was quoted in *Motography* as saying that there were "400 moving picture shows in Brooklyn alone, and about 1,500 in the Greater City."[35]

The actual numbers are less important than the fact that by the second decade of the twentieth century, there were moving-picture theaters within walking distance of most city residents. According to Russell Merritt, by 1910, the picture shows were attracting some 26 million Americans every week, a little less than 20 percent of the national population. In New York City alone, between 1.2 and 1.6 million people (or more than 25 percent of the city's population) attended movies weekly.[36]

As the public for cheap amusements expanded almost geometrically in the decades before and after the turn of the century, show businessmen had to work hard to assure their customers that the wildly heterogeneous audience they had assembled included no ruffians, foul-mouthed youth, mashers, or "ladies of the night." Admission would be reserved for those who were, as Henry James had described the clientele of the American hotel, "presumably 'respectable' . . . that is, not discoverably anything else."[37]

To make their audience feel welcome and safe, the show business-men fashioned environs of pleasure that drew on the life of the street and its myriad pedestrians, but did not merge with it. The street, as Robert Gutman has written, functions "instrumentally" as a road con-necting places and "expressively" as a site "for casual social interac-tion including recreation, conversation, and entertainment."[38] As a passageway, the street belonged to the quotidian world and thus had to be removed from the theater. As a "site," the street existed as a self-enclosed, self-defining space with a citizenry and life all its own. But those citizens (including streetwalkers, newsboys, peddlers, and vagrants) and that "life" were too overflowing, too chaotic, and too threatening for the many passersby that the show businessmen hoped to bring into their theaters. To maintain their magical quality as "play-grounds" or "worlds apart," the entertainment centers had to be sepa-rated from the street and the mundane worlds it fronted, connected, and represented.[39]

Massive gateways, portals, and arches set off the interior space of the theaters and palaces, marking the threshold where street and amusement met *and* were separated. One entered most theater audito-riums and amusement parks only after passing by a box office, through an entry door, and into and out of a series of intermediate buffer zones. Lobbies, vestibules, and the tunnel-like entrances of the amusement parks all shielded and sheltered the interior "playgrounds" from the street outside. The separation of amusement and street defined the space inside as secure from the world without. It also helped to assure those inside that they had nothing to fear from the crowd of strangers with whom they shared their space. As Erving Goffman has written, "engagements of the unacquainted" can only succeed where there is "the assumption of mutual regard and good will." The gates, arches, and vestibules filtered out the disharmonious and dangerous aspects of the street and, in so doing, sustained this "assumption of mutual regard and good will."[40]

The lower the admission price, the more care the show businessmen had to exercise to assure their audiences that all who entered would obey the rules of the establishment. The nickelodeons were architec-turally set off from the street, their entrances recessed or pulled back about six feet from the sidewalk. The movie palaces went a step fur-ther, separating their auditoriums from the street by "a breathtaking group of lobby spaces," foyers, stairways, and promenades. The amusement parks with their nominal admission fees (5 to 15 cents) and expansive acreage had to be totally fenced off from the outer world. George Tilyou, the father of Coney Island, created the first modern park when he enclosed his scattered attractions in the "undulant iron tracks" of the Steeplechase ride he had imported from England, thereby excluding the "rowdy element" and providing a safe haven for decent folk with money in their pockets.[41]

The larger entertainment centers employed armies of ushers and usherettes, street men, doormen, page boys, footmen, ticket takers, attendants, "attachés," guides, and floor managers, to guarantee that the temporary residents of the interior "playgrounds" would behave in accordance with the rules of the establishment. The larger and more heterogeneous the audience, the greater the need for ushers to maintain order within. The vaudeville palaces clothed their attachés in pseudomilitary dress suits. The movie palaces, located downtown with prices so low that almost anyone could afford them, relied on their "uniformed staff" to symbolize and maintain public order. As *The Moving Picture World* reminded exhibitors in 1911, "The presence of a uniformed attendant at a moving picture house, whether outside or inside, symbolizes order, in that the public at large recognizes that he is the representative of the proprietor of the house and is there to keep order."[42] In some of the larger movie palaces, ex-Marines were hired to drill the ushers weekly, pushing the citizen/soldier metaphor a bit further. Each one of the ushers at the Rialto on Forty-second Street and Broadway carried "a swagger stick with mother-of-pearl tips that lit up in the dark. The Head Usher carried a bugle."[43]

The public for the new nighttime entertainments was, as we have seen, simultaneously drawn from and distinct from the population of the street and the city at large. It was a public self-defined by a common need to be entertained in a crowd of strangers, a willingness to pay (usually small sums) for that entertainment, and a tacit and voluntary acceptance of the rules of the establishment.

This nighttime public was larger than any individual audience. It included all those who visited, if only for a few hours each week, the city's theaters, parks, and pleasure palaces; those who saw first-run Broadway shows for $2 and last year's hit from 10-cent gallery seats; those who cheered Al Jolson at the prestigious Winter Garden and small-time vaudeville in the Bronx; those who witnessed the magic of moving pictures at luxurious downtown "palaces" and local nickel dumps.

The illuminated nightlife of the turn-of-the-century city defined, if not created, new urban spaces and social groups outside the everyday spheres of home, family, work, and workplace. It afforded residents of a divided city the momentary experience of belonging to a social grouping that was totalizing rather than divisive or, to borrow anthropologist Victor Turner's terms, generous rather than snobbish, inclusive rather than exclusive.[44]

In going out into the city of lights, individuals did not experience an extension or transformation of their everyday identities, but a momentary departure from them. The Carries and Dorothys who stepped out into the gaily lit streets of the city left behind the gray worlds of urban flat and farmhouse. They fled their particular locations in a social world defined by class, culture, ethnicity, and occupation, to merge into an undifferentiated public of pleasure seekers, that "ordinary American crowd," as journalist Edwin Slosson would call it at Coney Island, "the best natured, best dressed, best behaving and best smelling crowd in the world."[45]

Notes

1. L. Frank Baum, *The Wizard of Oz* (Closter, NJ: Sharon Publications, 1981), pp. 2–3.
2. Theodore Dreiser, *Sister Carrie* (New York: Penguin Books, 1981), pp. 11, 30, 34.
3. Ibid., pp. 43, 90–91.
4. Baum, *Wizard of Oz*, pp. 90–91.
5. Susan Strasser, *Satisfaction Guaranteed: The Making of the American Mass Market* (New York: Pantheon, 1989), p. 209.
6. David E. Nye, *Electrifying America: Social Meanings of a New Technology, 1880–1940* (Cambridge, MIT Press, 1990), pp. 49, 56–57.
7. Jon C. Teaford, *The Unheralded Triumph: City Government in America, 1870–1900* (Baltimore, MD: Johns Hopkins University Press, 1984), p. 230.
8. Wolfgang Schivelbusch, *Disenchanted Night: The Industrialization of Light in the Nineteenth Century*, Angela Davis, trans. (Berkeley: University of California Press, 1988), pp. 81–134; quotations on p. 118.
9. See, for example, for Paris, Eugen Weber, *France: Fin de siècle* (Cambridge: Harvard University Press, 1986), p. 73.
10. Schivelbusch, *Disenchanted Night*, pp. 142, 148. I have taken the liberty of rearranging Schivelbusch's phrases in constructing the first quotation.
11. Richard Harding Davis, "Broadway," in *The Great Streets of the World* (New York, 1892), p. 26.
12. Dreiser, *Sister Carrie*, p. 76; George G. Foster, *New York by Gas-Light*, cited by John F. Kasson, *Rudeness and Civility* (New York: Hill and Wang, 1990), p. 78.

13. *The Four-Track News* VI (March 1904): 195–196.
14. John Allen Corcoran, "The City Light and Beautiful," *The American City* VII:1 (July 1912): 46–47.
15. Rand, McNally and Company, *Bird's-Eye Views and Guide to Chicago* (Chicago, 1893), pp. 108–109.
16. Nye, *Electrifying America*, p. x.
17. Ibid., pp. 50–51, 60.
18. *The Four-Track News* VI (February 1904): 121.
19. Dreiser, *Sister Carrie*, p. 46.
20. Robert A. M. Stern et al., *New York 1900: Metropolitan Architecture and Urbanism 1890–1915* (New York: Rizzoli, 1984), p. 209.
21. Charlotte Herzog, "The Archaeology of Cinema Architecture: The Origins of the Movie Theater," *Quarterly Review of Film Studies* (Winter 1984): 13; Craig Morrison, "From Nickelodeon to Picture Palace and Back," *Design Quarterly* 93 (1974): 7, 9.
22. Roger Brett, *Temples of Illusion* (Bristol, RI, Brett Theatrical, 1976), p. 154.
23. On box offices, see "The Boxoffice: A Collection of Boxoffice Portraits," *Marquee* 6:1 (1974): 4–5.
24. Herzog, "Archaeology of Cinema Architecture," p. 13.
25. Larry Widen, "Milwaukee's Princess Theater," *Marquee* 17:2 (Second Quarter, 1985): 20.
26. *Moving Picture World* 8:6 (February 11, 1911): 296–297.
27. "Illumination of Denver's Picture Theaters: Effect on Civic Activity," *Motography* IX:2 (January 18, 1913): 41–43.
28. Maurice Kann, "A House Built on Merit," in Ben M. Hall, *The Best Remaining Seats: The Golden Age of The Movie Palace* (New York: DaCapo, 1988), 88; David Naylor, *American Picture Palaces: The Architecture of Fantasy* (New York: Prentice Hall, 1981), 110. Naylor puts the size of the city at 250,000, but cites no reference.
29. Charlotte Herzog, "The Movie Palace and the Theatrical Sources of Its Architectural Style," *Cinema Journal* 20:2 (Spring 1981): 17–18.
30. Douglas Gomery, "The Movie Palace Comes to America's Cities," in Richard Butsch, ed., *For Fun and Profit: The Transformation of Leisure into Consumption* (Philadelphia, PA: Temple University Press, 1990), p. 142.
31. Rem Koolhaas, *Delirious New York: A Retroactive Manifesto for Manhattan* (New York: Oxford University Press, 1978), pp. 29–30; Frederic A. Thompson, "The Summer Show," *The Independent* 62 (June 20, 1907): 1461; Albert Bigelow Paine, "The New Coney Island," *Scribner's* 68 (August 1904): 535, 538; Frederic Thompson, "Amusing the Millions," *Everybody's* XIX (September 1908): 385.
32. Johan Huizinga, *Homo Ludens: A Study of the Play-Element in Culture* (Boston: Beacon Press, 1955), p. 10.
33. Richard Henry Edwards, "Public Recreation," in *Bulletin* of the University of Wisconsin, Serial No. 709, General Series No. 513 (Madison, 1915), p. 14.
34. Gary Kyriazi, *The Great American Amusement Parks* (Secaucus, NJ: Citadel Press, 1978), p. 98; "Survey of Commercial Recreation of Kansas City, Mo." by Fred F. McClure, Superintendent of the Recreation Department, Board of Public Welfare, in *Second Annual Report of the Recre-*

ation Department of the Board of Public Welfare (1911–1912); Cleveland Foundation, *Cleveland Recreation Survey: Commercial Recreation* (Cleveland, 1920), pp. 115–117; *New York Times* (October 24, 1909): 5:7.

35. Michael M. Davis, *The Exploitation of Pleasure: A Study of Commercial Recreations in New York City* (New York: Russell Sage Foundation, n.d.) p. 21; John Collier, "Leisure Time, The Last Problem of Conservation," Address before the Economic Club of Providence, RI, March 1912, reprinted in National Recreation Association of America, "Publication No. 99," 13; *Motography* X:8 (October 18, 1913): 264.

36. Russell Merritt, "Nickelodeon Theaters, 1905–1914: Building an Audience for the Movies," in Tino Balio, ed., *The American Film Industry*, rev. ed. (Madison: University of Wisconsin Press, 1985), p. 86.

37. Henry James, *The American Scene* (Bloomington, IN: Indiana University Press, 1968). p. 103.

38. Robert Gutman, "The Street Generation," in Stanford Anderson, ed., *On Streets* (Cambridge: MIT Press, 1986), p. 250.

39. I borrow the phrase, "worlds apart," to describe the theater from Jean-Christophe Agnew's work, *Worlds Apart: The Market and the Theater in Anglo-American Thought, 1550–1750* (New York: Cambridge University Press, 1986).

40. Erving Goffman, *Behavior in Public Places: Notes on the Social Organization of Gatherings* (New York: Free Press, 1963), p. 136.

41. On the movie palace, see Naylor, *American Picture Palaces*, pp. 34–36. On the amusement parks, see Russel B. Nye, "Eight Ways of Looking at an Amusement Park," *Journal of Popular Culture* XV (Summer 1981): 65–66; Robert E. Snow and David E. Wright, "Coney Island: A Case Study in Popular Culture and Technical Change," *Journal of Popular Culture* IX (1975–1976): 967.

42. "Uniformed Attendants," *Moving Picture World* VI (March 19, 1910): 417.

43. "Theatres: 'Ushers,' " clippings file and Scrapbook MFL 1523 Billy Rose Theater Collection, New York Public Library; Hall, *Best Remaining Seats*, p. 50.

44. Victor Turner, *From Ritual to Theatre: The Human Seriousness of Play* (New York: PAJ Publications, 1982), p. 51.

45. Edwin E. Slosson, "The Amusement Business," *The Independent* (July 21, 1904): 135.

13

"The Pushcart Evil"

Daniel Bluestone

In 1936, William Fellowes Morgan, Jr., New York's commissioner of the Department of Public Markets, proudly reported the successful "conversion of the pushcart peddler to a small merchant with self respect and banking relations."[1] Morgan viewed his department's recent completion of an enclosed Park Avenue Market between 111th and 116th streets as an important "advancement of social progress." He hoped that enclosed markets would sound "the death knell of the pushcart, which long has outlived its usefulness in this day of modern, quick, sanitary distribution of foods."[2] The enclosed market simply represented the latest approach in a decades-old effort by various civic, political, and business interests to conquer the "pushcart evil," regulate street commerce, and extend progressive era crusades for a beautiful, clean, and efficient city. Reform optimism aside, the figure of the pushcart peddler who sold "almost anything . . . from a wedding ring to a loaf of bread"[3] faced the figure of the small merchant across a gulf much wider than the typical sidewalk—a gulf that separated burgeoning forms of middle-class commercial culture from an older and now largely working-class tradition.

As people debated the pushcart question, their different visions of urban commerce clashed, as did their different perspectives on the city, its people, and the proper uses of public space. Proposals for banning pushcarts favored a modern ideal of the street as the exclusive province of smoothly circulating "traffic." This vision anticipated not only the eradication of street buying and selling, but also the eclipse of earlier social uses of the street for political activity, gregarious socializing, and popular amusements. The narrow view of the street as a traffic artery resembled the broader specialization of urban space during the nineteenth century. Growing nineteenth century cities had tended to separate residences from workplaces. This pattern of physical separation was complemented by a sorting of the city by economic and social class; class and ethnic neighborhoods characterized the residential landscape, whereas white collar work concentrated in emerging downtowns and blue collar work moved increasingly to the periphery.[4] City streets, public conveyances, and public parks concentrated the cosmopolitan social diversity of the city to an extent rarely found in other parts of the urban landscape. In this context, pushcart bans aimed to erase the vestiges of an older and decidedly less refined tradition of urban commerce; at the same time, they sought to extend upper-class ideals of public decorum and social separation to one of the least ordered spaces of the modern city—the street.[5]

Nineteenth century urban developments spurred the centuries-old efforts by municipalities to regulate and control the business of street hucksters. The provision of public markets and the regulation of public commerce had been one of the earliest activities of municipal corporations. In 1691, a New York ordinance had forbidden street selling by hucksters until two hours after the public markets opened. In 1707, all street hawking was forbidden.[6] Officials used the public market system to regulate and license trade and to provide a clearly defined meeting place for urban buyers to meet rural sellers in a period when urban food supplies were far from assured. Street hucksters and peddlers challenged municipal control of the market and threatened to disrupt through forestalling and competition the provisioning of the city. The aims of these ordinances varied considerably over time. By the mid-nineteenth century the government directed little attention to the provisioning of the city; yet, the basic stance of municipal regulation and control of street selling continued unabated. Why did the regulations of street selling persist? Why did newer and more abstract rationales for regulation, like the right to free use of the street by city "traffic," emerge?

Despite the continuing regulation of street selling, sharply different urban contexts gave street regulation quite different meanings between the seventeenth and the early twentieth centuries. Late-nineteenth and early-twentieth century proposals for pushcart bans capped a long history in which many vital social and economic activities had been gradually removed from city streets. In short, the bans sought to accommodate a vision of streets as exclusive traffic arteries that simply would not have been conceivable in earlier cities. During the course of the nineteenth century, a whole array of novel commercial settings replaced the relatively unspecialized commercial spaces of the seventeenth and eighteenth century city. Assuming a variety of architectural forms, specialty shops, retail arcades, and department stores contributed to the ebbing of street life while both setting up the conditions of and the demand for the redefinition of the street itself as a traffic artery.

Specialty shops clustered along Broadway and other streets; the street itself simply provided the connecting link between new stores. Commercial exchange moved indoors in the midst of other retail developments. In 1827, for example, the New York Arcade, designed by John Haviland, placed exclusive retail shops along a skylight-covered corridor or "street," which crossed private property parallel to Broadway between Maiden Lane and John Street. The arcade protected well-to-do shoppers from the general nastiness of nineteenth century urban streets and from "the inclemency of the weather in the winter, and the burning rays of the sun in summer."[7] Starting with A. T. Stewart's Marble Palace, which opened in 1846, the rise of the department store continued the internalization of retail exchange; at Stewart's this development was dramatized architecturally by the ninety-foot-high domed rotunda and galleries that formed a "handsome promenade."[8] Department stores grew increasingly elaborate in the second half of the nineteenth century and featured an all-encompassing setting that included not only an abundance of goods but also restaurants, libraries, picture galleries, and highly embellished resting and writing rooms. The architects of these settings for bourgeois consumption designed alluring and sumptuous buildings with orderly and controlled interiors that promoted commerce by fostering the image that retail shopping was a cultivated pursuit. Central to this process were the sumptuous aisles and monumental stairs that replaced public streets as the essential connections between an expansive variety of retail goods.

Although not as dramatic in an architectural sense, the structures for the retail sale of food also altered significantly during the nineteenth century. Food distribution burst the bounds of the public market and filled private specialty shops and grocery stores. As in the case of retail goods, a host of entrepreneurs, both wholesale and retail, came to fill the links between producer and consumer.[9] Despite the elaboration of retail systems and architecture in the nineteenth century, the volume and expansiveness of street selling did not necessarily decline. As middle- and upper-class shoppers withdrew from street markets, the streets were left to the growing ranks of the poor in the expanding urban populations.

In 1870, when *Scribner's Monthly* profiled "The Street-Venders of New York," it settled primarily on "picturesque" individuals engaged in "tedious" work, many of whom were enveloped by "a certain air of humility and unconscious pathos." The pushcart dealers made up a "humbler class" of street merchants, operating somewhere between the peddlers who worked with baskets and small portable stands and the "richer" merchants who sold from four-wheeled, horse-drawn wagons. *Scribner's* found that Nassau Street was a "favorite haunt" of vendors, whereas Printing House Square presented a "curious colony of venders." Nevertheless, the street peddlers were portrayed primarily as individuals and as wanderers.[10] They did not appear to have sufficient force of numbers or actual presence in the landscape to create what came to be known as the "pushcart evil."

In New York, the pushcart rose to prominence in urban commerce in the final quarter of the nineteenth century, when formerly peripatetic peddlers started gathering daily at specific locations to form street markets. Hundreds of thousands of poor immigrants familiar with European street markets and anxious to buy as cheaply as possible patronized thousands of peddlers. The extremely high residential densities in certain New York immigrant neighborhoods permitted many pushcart peddlers to stop pushing their carts and to start selling continuously from single locations. One student of New York's pushcart markets traces their origin to 1886, when four vendors took up adjacent positions along Hester Street on the city's Lower East Side. They were soon joined by other pushcart peddlers, and this informal market system spread to Ninth Avenue (1887), Grand Street (1893), Orchard Street (1898), Rivington Street (1898), and East Monroe (1901).[11]

Between the 1880s rise of pushcart street markets and their nearly complete abolition in the 1930s, pushcart commerce passed through four distinct but overlapping periods of development. During this period, the dominant view of the street moved from a socially diverse pluralistic conception toward a modern unitary reality. The first phase was that of the illegal street market. Early pushcart markets established after the Hester Street market were illegal; they violated city ordinances against peddling at one spot for extended periods (longer than fifteen or thirty minutes). In 1913, the city inaugurated a second phase of pushcart markets by designating the areas underneath the approaches to the Manhattan, Williamsburg, and Queensboro bridges as pushcart market areas. The idea was that peddlers resorting to such areas would be able to escape from selective "charges and persecution" by city officials and the police; in these areas they would be "out of the way and are unmolested."[12] This represented the first firm step in dealing with the "pushcart evil" by enclosing it—reining in its threatening boundlessness. A third phase started in the period around World War I, when food shortages, distribution problems, and efforts to buttress the least expensive means of selling food prompted another reorientation of the pushcart system. Following decades of official hostility, New York legalized and expanded numerous pushcart street

markets. It also attempted to phase out licenses for "itinerant" peddling in the hope of confining all pushcarts to designated streets. Between 1920 and 1924, twenty-three city street markets were officially
sanctioned. In the early 1930s, sixty markets operated around the city.
Finally, in the fourth phase of pushcart marketing, during the 1930s,
the LaGuardia administration abolished nearly all existing street markets and, at the same time, built several enclosed market buildings for
the use of pushcart peddlers.

There was not much question that in pushcart markets poor people
sold food and merchandise to other poor people (Figure 13.1). In fact,
the vast majority of vendors and their customers were repeatedly identified as both poor and "foreign." A 1906 survey of New York's pushcart system recognized that proposed regulations would have "serious
consequences to the great mass of the poorer people of the city."[13] A
1912 article in *Outlook* reviewed pushcart commerce under the title

Figure 13.1 Pushcart Banana Peddler, New York City, c. 1900. *Source:*
Courtesy of the Library of Congress.

"The Markets of the Poor."[14] In 1928, Thomas F. Dwyer, commissioner of the Department of Public Markets, reported that "The fact that these markets are located on crowded streets in the poorer sections of the city is because they are where the need for them is greatest. The pushcart is the poor man's market."[15] Municipal regulation and action was directed at the thousands of pushcart vendors who worked outside of the bounds of middle-class commercial patterns, selling goods unfreighted by the overhead of rent, taxes, and utilities.

New York's emerging late-nineteenth century pushcart markets were tended largely by European immigrants who crowded into the ghetto neighborhoods of New York. Irish, Italians, and Greeks stood out in the ranks of pushcart peddlers. Jewish immigrants from Russia, Poland, Rumania, and elsewhere also turned to pushcart peddling in large numbers. In the early 1890s, the Baron de Hirsch Fund survey of 23,801 Jewish families in New York's Seventh, Tenth, and Thirteenth Wards on the Lower East Side found that peddling was the second largest occupation, behind tailoring, with over 2,440 peddlers identified.[16] By 1925, among New York City's fruit and vegetable peddlers, 63 percent were Jewish immigrants, whereas 32 percent were Italians; in the field of merchandise 95.7 percent of the peddlers were Jewish.[17]

The neighborhood-based pushcart markets gave recent immigrants a familiar cultural and linguistic setting in which to earn a living. In reviewing the vocational possibilities for new immigrants, one urban chronicler wrote in 1899, "For those who had no handicraft there was but one resource—peddling."[18] In 1898, the *Tribune* reported that "Recently landed immigrants are advised by their friends to take a pushcart until they can establish themselves in some business."[19] However, there is some evidence that peddlers did not necessarily gain quick mobility into other lines of work. In 1925, for example, researchers found that fruit and vegetable peddlers spent an average of 10 years in the pushcart trade; those peddlers selling other merchandise worked the streets for an average of 5.9 years. In 1898, the *Tribune* noted that many people who found themselves out of work, like tailors and mechanics, worked temporarily as pushcart peddlers until they found new employment in their trade.[20] Peddlers could rent pushcarts from garage owners, and thus with only modest resources and skills could work the streets, where their native languages often served as the dominant language of the market.[21] Beyond their economic utility, pushcart markets provided immigrants with a free social space unburdened by the financial costs paid by wealthier city people both for larger private residences and for semipublic places constructed for social gatherings and amusement. In pushcart markets, social space as well as food was available without the overhead costs attached to the uses of private property.

The ease of entry into pushcart peddling certainly did not match the conditions of the work. An 1899 observer remarked succinctly, "It is a hard life." The men and women who peddled worked very long days in the most adverse weather conditions—"under broiling sun, in torrents of rain, in desperate cold, and in the midst of swirls of snow. . . . For what? For the most beggarly pittance—not enough, scarcely, to live on." Besides difficult weather and modest compensation, peddlers found themselves enmeshed in an official legal system shot through with potential for corruption and exploitation. The city licensed pushcart peddlers, but made it illegal for them to stand at single locations where they found a ready market. This opened the way for property owners and the police to extort money from the peddlers as the price for not being hauled into the magistrate's court where they could be fined and/or deprived of time to sell their goods.[22]

Pushcart markets stood in striking contradiction of what many economic and civic leaders viewed as the essence of urban modernity— novel commercial forms such as specialty shops, department stores, skyscrapers, and transportation systems planned for the free circulation of traffic and commodities. In relation to novel commercial forms, one critic insisted in 1930 that "The pushcart markets are as characteristic a part of the New York pageant as the skyscrapers."[23] Some observers of the urban landscape viewed pushcart markets as picturesque places steeped in urban cosmopolitanism. However, for many reformers, the coexistence of pushcarts and skyscrapers evidenced a disquieting polarization of urban life between poverty and progress. Various reform efforts to curb the pushcart markets went hand in hand with xenophobic Americanization and immigration restriction campaigns directed at working-class immigrants. Efforts to bar pushcart commerce from the streets aimed to conform working-class patterns to more middle-class norms. This effort was particularly acute during the 1930s, when pushcarts represented to many civic and political leaders just another uncomfortable reminder of the instability and failure of national economic life.

Beyond the divergent visions of commercial culture, advocates of pushcart restrictions often presented their cause as a conflict between the commercial and the noncommercial use of the streets; in doing so they obscured the competing economic interests bound up in the issue. In 1906, for example, conflict between pushcart vendors and Mayor McClellan presented the question in just these terms. The East Side Push Cart Peddlers' Association wrote to the mayor, "The members of our Association are a poor and miserable lot, and if you will not grant us our little privileges in order to make a living for ourselves and our families, you will drive us to desperation. Please give this your immediate attention, as otherwise we will be compelled to march ourselves, our wives and little children down to the City Hall, and will wave *black* banners to show to this metropolis how its poor are treated by the Mayor of the City."[24] McClellan promised "the fullest and most careful consideration"; however, he insisted that the peddlers "should remember that they have not a vested right to use the streets for the purpose of trade, that the streets are highways and are intended solely for that purpose, and that the city and its citizens have rights in the streets which must also be fully protected."[25]

In twentieth century New York, the free use of streets by citizens had important commercial implications. Pushcarts competed directly with retail stores occupying private property; however, in the case of arguments related to congestion, the realm of competition was much broader. Here working-class pushcart commerce opposed the "commerce" of realty and increasing densities on Manhattan island. Pushcarts crowded streets which, if given over only to transit, would raise the possibilities of higher density and higher real estate values. In the 1920s, traffic and congestion obsessed the researchers working on the Regional Plan of New York and Its Environs; having assigned dollar figures to the cost of congestion, the Regional Plan determined that pushcarts were "inconsistent with the proper use of traffic ways" and advocated a complete ban on pushcart commerce.[26]

Combating congestion increasingly served as a central goal of wealthy commercial interests and the nascent profession of city and regional planning. This was not because of some abstract notion of the rights of citizens, but rather because increased circulation helped generate higher densities and land values. Reviewing efforts to banish pushcarts from the streets in 1912, one writer noted that in earlier years, when the city had been smaller, few people had seen any harm in street peddling; however, "with the changed conditions that have resulted because of the increase of tall buildings and the more concentrated housing of persons, both in their homes and in their places of labor, the congestion of the streets has increased with great rapidity. At the present time there are few problems confronting the city authorities more difficult of a solution than the traffic problem."[27] Large merchants, in particular the proprietors of modern department stores, also joined forces with realty interests to combat traffic congestion. The department store owners absolutely depended upon the relatively unfettered circulation of customers and goods for their high volume, high turnover businesses. They also made heavy use of the streets to fulfill their alluring promises of free home delivery of their customers' purchases. In a battle between pushcart street commerce and the modern commerce related to higher densities and large mercantile interests, municipal officials tilted toward the modern.

Blaming pushcarts for New York's congestion involved a certain amount of abstraction and exaggeration. Streets with pushcarts lining the right-of-way were undoubtedly crowded and hard to pass through quickly. However, the pushcart markets predominated on streets in high-density working-class neighborhoods like the Lower East Side, which did not have much through traffic (Figure 13.2). In 1925, Earl R. French, the author of one of the most comprehensive studies of New York's pushcart markets, pointed out that since pushcarts generally lined side streets or very broad thoroughfares, they did not really interfere with traffic to the degree often asserted by many reformers. French insisted that the pushcarts did pose a "certain nuisance" during peak business hours and the holiday season, when "congestion reaches the point of irritation."[28] In a city increasingly overwhelmed by traffic, invoking the congestion issue broadened the impetus for restriction. Pushcart markets undoubtedly looked congested, and their elimination would offer some appearance of headway against congestion without disturbing more powerful commercial interests. When reformers asserted that pushcarts caused congestion, they rarely specified which traffic flows were interrupted or what precise conditions could be remedied with the elimination of pushcarts.

Pushcart debates took on a much more tangible form when they moved from abstractions related to citywide traffic congestion to focus on neighborhood real estate values and retail trade. Here the concern was twofold. First, many people argued that pushcarts competed directly with local stores and thus made the property less valuable for both rental and sale. Second, many advocates of pushcart restrictions believed that the presence of pushcarts in certain streets would stigmatize entire neighborhoods, reducing real estate values generally. In the case of commercial competition, the arguments were made frequently and vociferously. In 1896, for example, a supporter of Street Commissioner Col. George Waring's effort to suppress the Hester Street pushcart market pointed to the problems this trade caused local retailers and property owners; he wrote that the municipal administration should bar street activity that

> interfere[s] with business men who occupy stores, as they pay heavy licenses & rents, and are prevented from carrying on their business by pushcarts standing in front of their doors, collecting crowds & giving such a disreputable appearance to the stores as to keep cus-

Figure 13.2 Street Market, Lower East Side, New York City, c. 1890–1901.
Source: Library of Congress.

tomers from entering. . . . If the nuisance is permitted to go on for any length of time a large number of property owners will be obliged to sell out at very low prices, as they cannot afford to pay taxes on empty property & it is impossible to let stores or carry on business.[29]

In 1911, storekeepers along Avenue C between Fifth and Eighth streets echoed these arguments in appealing to Mayor Gaynor to "abate a public nuisance" posed by pushcarts. The petitioners objected that "it is impossible for the ordinary customers to pass by our stores without being molested by the push-cart peddlers as well as hundreds of hawkers passing and standing in front of our stores and selling practically the same kind of merchandise that we have in our stores thus working a great hardship upon us."[30] Pushcart bans would effectively drive peddlers out of business or onto private property; higher overhead would temper their competitive edge over small merchants who by renting stores had adopted the rudiments of an assimilated middle-class commercial culture.

Pushcart peddlers and former pushcart peddlers themselves shared the keen sensitivity toward competition that led so many storekeepers to oppose pushcart markets. In 1912, delegates of the United Citizens Peddlers' Association, representing 5,000 licensed peddlers, met in conference and interrupted their deliberations with the unusual chant "Abolish the pushcart!" What they proposed was the setting aside of specific streets and squares in the city for open-air markets, with fixed stands rented by the month, and the banning of pushcarts from city streets. The Peddlers' Association criticized the municipal administration for crowding all the pushcart peddlers into the Lower East Side and for failing to rid the streets of an estimated 22,000 unlicensed vendors who evaded municipal license fees and regulations and "who were making the life of the minority, who had licenses, unbearable."[31] A similar change of consciousness was apparent when, in 1938, the members of the Park Avenue Open Air Retail Merchants Association, those who had given up pushcarts for stands in the enclosed municipal market, complained to Mayor LaGuardia about the fact that peddlers still operated on the streets around the market, posing unfair competition to those inside.[32] Thus, not only prosperous storekeepers but also poorer former pushcart peddlers, working stands in public markets, proved themselves anxious to call on the power of the state to regulate the market, to promote their own parochial interests, and to enforce middle-class patterns of internalized commerce and street decorum. Such efforts pervaded all campaigns and proposals for pushcart restriction, and have a familiar ring today.

Beyond the direct clashing of commercial interests between store merchants and pushcart peddlers stood a more generalized and pervasive conflict. Many observers thought of pushcarts as an agent of neighborhood deterioration. Once middle- and upper-class urban residents identified pushcarts as central to immigrant and working-class life, they often viewed the arrival of a pushcart market in a neighborhood as tangible evidence of undesirable demographic and social change. Despite the apparent enthusiasm of some people for patronizing street markets, pushcarts could be viewed as a form of neighborhood blight—a harbinger of unsettling change.

Objections concerning the supposed blighting effects of the pushcart spanned the decades of its commercial prominence. In 1896, for example, David Bartlett Gould, a physician and resident of Hester Street, complained to Mayor Strong about local "streets infested with pushcarts & peddlers." Gould ended his letter by writing, "In concluding I may say I have lived almost 15 years on Hester Street."[33] Gould was a Scottish immigrant who had moved to the United States in 1865; despite his long residence on Hester Street, he moved within a year of complaining to the mayor about the local pushcart market. Gould moved with his wife and daughter to an apartment on West Fifteenth Street between Seventh and Eighth avenues where he settled in a building occupied primarily by native-born New Yorkers, many of Irish parentage. In sharp contrast, Gould's former residence was soon occupied by ten Russian immigrants, two German immigrants, and five children born in New York to immigrant parents. The new residents of Gould's former home included a tailor, a peddler, and a paperstand operator.[34] One Hester Street peddler observed, "What difference does it make if we take up the street with our carts? There is nobody in this neighborhood but Russians, and I am sure none of them complain."[35] It is clear that the Hester Street pushcart market was only one of the more obvious manifestations of neighborhood transition. In 1916, a petition by the Yorkville Citizens' Committee termed the pushcart business an "undesirable institution" that "unless checked . . . will grow to such large proportions that it will tend to become a fixed institution not only in the districts on the Lower East Side but in the new districts which it tries to invade."[36] In the late 1920s, the Harlem Board of Trade, which had led an organized opposition to African-American settlement in Harlem, orchestrated a campaign for the "complete elimination" of open-air pushcart markets.[37] In 1938, the *Real Estate News* reported that the "deterioration and debasement of so-called pushcart districts and the utter decline of property values abutting open-air markets have been disastrous to thousands of owners, who have been helpless to stay the hand of extreme financial depreciation. . . . Investments in these stigmatized areas have vanished into thin air."[38] Numerous other neighborhood-based civic and business groups mounted similar campaigns. City officials, as collectors of property taxes, often lent support as interested parties in these debates.

The metaphorical use of terms like "invasion" to characterize the proliferation of pushcarts carried a particular resonance in the 1910s in relation to New York real estate, municipal regulation, and commerce. In 1916, New York codified in formal zoning statutes decades of efforts by New York's middle and upper classes to stabilize real estate values and to prevent the intrusion of "incompatible" land uses on elite enclaves. In particular, zoning aimed to protect the elite Fifth Avenue shopping district from the disagreeable intrusion of factories and workers; it also barred apartment house and commercial construction from single family neighborhoods. In the nineteenth century, the trend toward specialization of land use represented one of the most important developments of the urban landscape. The middle and upper classes promoted specialized residential neighborhoods that provided an important mark of elite social refinement and cultivation. Zoning extended and protected this system. The 1916 zoning deliberations included an open critique of pushcarts and their contribution to both street congestion and neighborhood deterioration.[39] However, zoning ordinances regulating private development did little to protect a neighborhood from itinerant pushcart peddlers. This problem required other regulations.

The peddlers' unbounded movement through, and settlement in, city streets threatened just the sort of sudden change in neighborhood character that had spurred restrictive covenants and zoning legislation. Beyond real estate values, many neighborhood residents found that street peddlers offended their sense of decorum and public propriety. In 1938, Deputy Mayor Henry H. Curran complained to the chief city magistrate that

> A band of flower peddlers infests my neighborhood along Fifth Avenue from 8th Street to 12th Street. They are dirty, defiant, unlicensed peddlers, and the flowers they sell last about twenty minutes. . . . I hear many complaints from people who live about there and whose passage along the sidewalk is actually blocked by these peddlers thrusting their wares upon the passers-by. . . . And I don't know what contagious diseases these peddlers carry around with them. . . . At first there was only one peddler, but now there are seven or eight, each one dirtier than the other.[40]

Curran also sought police help in chasing away pushcart peddlers who sold candy and "infest the same neighborhood."[41] Mayor LaGuardia's concurrent ban on organ grinders embodied a similar revulsion, a distaste acquired, according to one LaGuardia biographer, in childhood, due to the ridicule suffered at the hands of other children because his father gave an itinerant Italian organ grinder, visiting his army post, an excessively cordial and warm reception.[42] In 1938, when a representative of several pushcart peddlers wrote to LaGuardia complaining of the "high handed practices of the police" in enforcing city ordinances, LaGuardia referred him to Curran. LaGuardia was no more sympathetic than Curran. He directed his deputy mayor to "Please confer with Mr. Krantz in the matter, but make it clear that we have got to get rid of these peddlers."[43]

It was not easy to get rid of pushcarts in New York. From their concentrated development on the Lower East Side they had moved to far-flung parts of the city. Many former residents of dense slum areas who moved to the outlying areas of the city often petitioned for the right to establish pushcart markets in their new neighborhoods. One observer reported in 1930 that "the markets have spread over the town as the neighborhoods have changed. When the first exodus began from Delancey Street the markets moved north. When gaunt new apartment buildings in the Bronx welcomed families which had lived along Allen Street there was immediate demand for the familiar curbside stores. When miles of frame houses in Queens offered light and air to crowded tenement dwellers petitions went to the Municipal Building that persuasive peddlers might anchor their carts at the front doors."[44] In 1938, the Kings Highway Board of Trade complained to Mayor LaGuardia that pushcart peddlers selling "poor and inferior merchandise" had unlawfully taken up the most prominent corners along Kings Highway—"one of the finest suburban shopping streets around the City."[45] The most common proposal for remedying the pushcart nuisance short of a total ban was for the city to set aside areas for pushcart markets. In the 1890s, while suppressing the Hester Street market, Street Commissioner Waring proposed separate enclosed markets for pushcarts. In the late 1890s, the Social Reform Club proposed a pushcart fish market in the Hester Street Park in a building that would be cleaned and dedicated to park and community purposes each afternoon.[46] In 1904, despite the strenuous objections of shopkeepers and complaints concerning traffic congestion and sanitation, Commissioner James B. Reynolds opposed a ban on pushcarts. Instead, Reynolds recommended a series of steel and glass public markets in Manhattan, accommodating about 800 pushcarts each. In Reynolds' view, the "streets would be cleared, public markets maintained, no injustice would be done, and public sanitation would be vastly facilitated."[47]

In 1906, Mayor McClellan's Push-Cart Commission, chaired by Lawrence Veiller, undertook an early and systematic consideration of New York's pushcart business. The existing ordinances that permitted vendors to remain in a single spot for only thirty minutes or less had proven notoriously difficult to enforce (many vendors merely moved their pushcarts a few feet to comply with the ordinance). The Push-Cart Commission began its work with a stance that mixed tolerance with condescension. The commission reported that pushcarts added to the "picturesqueness of the city's street and impart[ed] that air of foreign life which is so interesting to the traveler, lending an element of gaiety and charm to the scene which is otherwise lacking." Nevertheless, the familiar problems of congestion and sanitation had led many people to call for abolition of the pushcart industry "if it may be dignified by that term." The commission set out not to abolish pushcart peddling, but rather to define a workable system of regulation. As Veiller contemplated the possibility of 100,000 immigrants arriving in New York from Russia during 1906, he thought it especially important to scrutinize the entire issue of street peddling.[48]

The Veiller Commission's plan for pushcarts paralleled the conclusions embodied in Veiller's 1901 draft of New York's tenement house legislation; in connection with both studies, Veiller proposed strong municipal regulation, disdained direct government involvement beyond regulation, and aimed to lower the concentration of the poor by promoting decentralization. The Push-Cart Commission sought to lower the density of pushcarts in the street by providing for their even spacing around the city. Hoping to do away with the spectacle of one hundred pushcarts or more lining a single block, the commission recommended limiting the number of pushcarts on any one block to four. The four pushcart positions would be firmly established twenty-five feet back from each of a block's four corners. In the "restricted" area bounded by Fourteenth Street, Brooklyn Bridge, Broadway, and the East River, peddlers would purchase licenses at an annual auction for a specific corner on a specific block. In the remainder of the city, peddlers could only set up their pushcarts on blocks where one of the four locations was open.

The 1906 Push-Cart Commission rejected the notion of establishing a few specific market areas for pushcarts; it reported, "We can see no reason why the City of New York should go into the business of providing shop space for dealers in any class of supplies, at a large annual loss, nor why taxpayers should be called upon to bear such a burden."[49] Furthermore, the four-to-a-block rule would effectively reduce objections related to congestion and sanitation while banning the heavy concentrations of peddlers that stood at the center of reformers' construction of the "pushcart evil." The dispersion of pushcarts would also mitigate fears concerning the adverse effect of pushcart markets on local real estate values.

The Veiller Commission proposals for pushcart dispersal failed. At the conclusion of the commission's deliberations, Veiller had written, "As I have worked very hard over this subject [and] given much thought to it, I am very anxious that our recommendations should be enacted into law, especially as they will completely solve the present problem and without working any hardship to the Push-Cart Peddlers."[50] In fact, after discussing the commission's approach and proposals with Sigmund Schwartz, president of the United Citizens Peddlers' Association, Veiller had thought that Schwartz was "entirely in sympathy with these recommendations."[51] It turned out that he had misjudged the peddlers' position. Schwartz, a Rumanian immigrant and father of six children who worked as both a peddler and as an undertaker, helped organize massive protest meetings in the wake of the Push-Cart Commission report. Responding to the proposal to disperse an economically profitable and socially congenial pattern of concentration, the street peddlers threatened a three-day boycott, which they felt would bring the powerful support of the wholesale fruit dealers to their aid.[52] The boycott never took place, but the Push-Cart Commission regulations were never acted upon by the city.

With the demise of the Veiller Commission recommendations, the selective official prosecution and harassment of peddlers continued (Figure 13.3); this tended to concentrate rather than disperse pushcart trading because some areas of the city were carefully policed while others were not; particularly notable was official tolerance of pushcart markets on the Lower East Side. Pushcart reform proposals made in a 1912 aldermanic committee, a 1915 plan of the Manhattan borough president, and the reports of mayoral commissions in 1913 and 1917 were all directed toward delimiting specific spots in the city as market areas and the simultaneous banning of transient pushcart street vending. Establishing the legal markets under the approaches to the Manhattan, Williamsburg, and Queensboro bridges had proved relatively easy because they stood on city-owned land. However, a thoroughgoing system of market areas located off from the streets proved more problematic; it would, in many cases, involve the costly condemnation and public purchase of land. Nor could such a plan effectively deal with the sudden disruption of food distribution outlets arising around World War I. In this period, the Board of Aldermen established another course by legalizing and expanding the existing pushcart street

Figure 13.3 Flower Peddlers, Union Square Looking North Toward Broadway and Seventeenth Street, New York City, c. 1904. *Source:* Library of Congress.

markets. By the 1930s, sixty such markets operated in New York (Figure 13.4).

The Board of Aldermen voted to establish each pushcart street market. Thus, ward politics defined the legal bounds for the operation of pushcarts within the city. Aldermen and local interests mediated the relation between the city's neighborhoods and pushcart selling. The view of pushcarts as representing an advantage or a blight often depended upon one's economic class and culture and where one lived. The rapid development of open-air markets suggested the pushcarts'

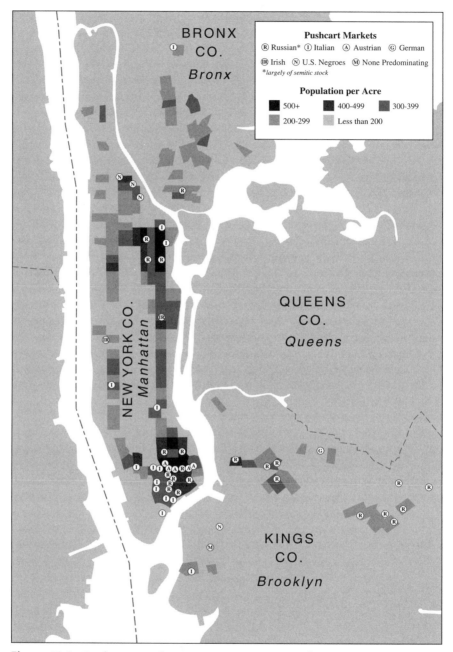

Figure 13.4 Pushcart Market Location Versus Population Density, Greater New York City, c. 1925. *Source:* Earl R. French, *Push Cart Markets in New York City (1925)* (United States Agricultural Economics Bureau, mimeographed report).

continuing popularity in many parts of the city. The new street market plan permitted the political system to arbitrate conflicting visions of the city, its commerce, and the uses of the streets.

Politicians did more than simply respond to public demands for pushcarts and mediate competing neighborhood interests. Aldermen had long granted licensing favors, such as special permission for individuals to sell during holiday periods, in exchange for political support. When Mayor LaGuardia set out to abolish pushcarts, he acted out of a distaste for the politics surrounding pushcart commerce as well as their economic and cultural aspects. In 1938, when LaGuardia responded to the complaints of the Kings Highway Board of Trade concerning pushcarts, he wrote, "You know a peddler system has developed in this city through systematized political graft during the past administrations. . . . I am glad to have your cooperation and hope you will continue in the helpful activity toward the elimination of the peddler nuisance."[53] Markets Commissioner Morgan engaged in a protracted administrative struggle to gain control of the street markets, which he insisted had been operated by "fixers" and district leaders connected with the local political clubhouses. In his view, the pushcart street markets offered "a complete picture of a broken down system of government in the hands of professional politicians."[54] LaGuardia and his markets commissioner attacked this "broken" system through a system of executive and administrative centralization—portrayed as a triumph of modern politics and efficiency over a corrupt politics of tradition.

Yet, numerous other people and interests beyond clubhouse politicians, peddlers, and their customers supported pushcart markets. Many charity and philanthropic workers supported the open-air markets. In 1915, John L. Elliott, for example, wrote to Mayor Mitchel to say that his work at the Hudson Guild, which brought him into "daily contact with the people of the tenement houses," had convinced him of the importance of pushcarts in providing the poor with cheaper and better quality food.[55] In 1930, the New York Civic Conference commissioned the noted model-housing architect Andrew J. Thomas to turn his attention to designing a model pushcart market for 600 to 700 peddlers. Thomas' plan placed the pushcart market in the center courtyard of a block-long perimeter block building. Drawing on diverse elements of the contemporary reform urban-planning agenda, he topped the market with a playground, built model working-class apartments and industrial lofts in the building itself, and designed basement truck ramps for an uncongested system of freight delivery and garbage removal. Further, the building's sidewalk frontage would be lined with stores that would provide rents to subsidize the entire project.[56] Had it been built, the Thomas project would have hidden the pushcarts from the street, accommodated regular stores, and fostered the ideal of harmony between pushcart commerce and the city's broader mercantile and realty interests.

Beyond the support of charity and settlement workers, the editors of numerous Jewish newspapers also advocated a system of pushcart markets, as did outspoken religious leaders in the Jewish, Italian, Irish, and African American neighborhoods. In the mid-1920s, it was estimated that pushcart peddlers sold nearly fifty million dollars' worth of food and merchandise annually. More importantly, growers and wholesalers of fruits and vegetables also lobbied in favor of pushcart peddling. The California Fruit Exchange, the American Cranberry Exchange, the Washington State Apple Growers Association, and the California Pear Growers all lobbied in favor of New York's pushcart peddlers. Some distributors estimated that between 25 and 40 percent of fresh fruit and produce in New York was sold from pushcarts.

In 1938, when a western grower of Hilly Billy pears objected to pushcart restrictions, he drew upon cultural as well as economic arguments. He wrote to Commissioner Morgan: "I understand the purpose of this action is to get your streets clean for the World's Fair, but I am sure the uniqueness of these peddlers would be colorful to the visitors who attend rather than to dispense with your push carts and make New York just like any other city."[57] The solicitousness over New York's image in the face of the World's Fair involved the cultural assessment on the part of municipal officials that pushcarts did not comport with the officials' desired image of a clean, dignified modern, commercial metropolis. Pushcarts were "daily more oppressive to the retail merchants," said the Yorkville Chamber of Commerce, and such a scene should not collect along East Eighty-sixth Street—"one of the gateways of the World's Fair."[58] During the Depression, the future of New York seemed to hang in the balance. On the one side stood the modern world of refined commercial pursuits presented in modern skyscrapers, department stores, and at the fair. On the other side was a city mired in deep poverty.

For the boosters of the World's Fair and its rosy scenarios of the future, the sight of pushcarts encompassed more distress than an admirable ideal of picturesque cosmopolitanism. In the eyes of many, including some peddlers and their advocates, pushcart peddling was only a step removed from begging and charitable relief. In 1906, peddlers who petitioned Mayor McClellan for assistance declared themselves "poor people" who if denied the "right to peddle" would "fall burden to the City and to the charitable institutions."[59] One pushcart customer who complained of LaGuardia's pushcart restrictions wondered what the municipal officials wanted peddlers to do: "Beg—steal or go on relief instead of earning an honest living by peddling."[60] Another advocate of the pushcart peddlers' cause in the 1930s asked rhetorically, "What are peddlers, and what is it they are doing? They are common folk out of employment, mostly with empty cupboards at home, trying to *earn* a few cents in a manner which to them seems moral and lawful . . . in these days of unprecedented unemployment."[61] The concentration of pushcarts palpably manifested pervasive poverty, an impression that people interested in promoting "modern" New York and "modern" commerce found troubling. The approach of the World's Fair and mounting concerns over the image of the city helped crystallize the cultural and economic dimensions that had long characterized the pushcart reform cause. LaGuardia's markets commissioner sanguinely included a section titled "The Life and Death of the Pushcart" in his department's World's Fair exhibit.[62]

In August 1938, an ill-tempered LaGuardia vigorously debated the New York Good Humor man. They confronted each other at a public hearing on an ordinance to restrict the use of city streets by pushcart vendors and peddlers. George A. Spohr, Jr., representing Good Humor, called the proposed restrictions an "arbitrary and capricious exercise of police power." LaGuardia asserted that "If I can get cooperation from the City Council I'm going to abolish all itinerant peddling from the streets. . . . I have to protect the city. . . . This whole thing of pushcarts has been abused. . . . Now Good Humor will simply have to adjust itself to doing business under the conditions demanded by a city of seven million people; that's all there is to it. . . . You can adjust yourself to these conditions by putting up attractive little stores in the neighborhoods. There is no objection to that." Pushcarts and attractive stores opposed each other in the same manner as the peddlers and merchants did. Despite the fact that Good Humor was a substantial corporate entity with 92 automobiles and 255 bicycles distributing its products, its sales techniques rendered it liable to restrictions directed primarily at independent, working-class vendors.[63]

Proceeding on the assumption that pushcart commerce was "a bad practice, unworthy of the reputation of this great City," the LaGuardia administration succeeded in drastically reducing its presence in the streets of New York. Year after year the administration persisted in closing and consolidating pushcart street markets. In 1937, it closed eighteen markets; by the end of 1939 only seventeen markets remained of the sixty that had operated in 1934. The number of pushcart licenses declined from 7,000 to just over 1,000. Political opposition to this policy was overcome by the insistence that enclosed markets would take the place of street markets. When representatives of the

Brownsville, East New York and East Flatbush Street Peddlers' Organization complained to Mayor LaGuardia of the "vicious attempt of police and magistrates to drive us from the streets and deprive us of our living," they were informed that it was "the policy of this administration . . . to provide covered markets in sections where they are needed." The mayor's secretary told the peddlers to go and visit the Park Avenue enclosed market in order to see what the administration was doing to "help the pushcart peddlers."[64] The administration built nine enclosed markets that accommodated only a fraction of the peddlers displaced from forty street markets. But the strategy proved politically workable. For many peddlers and their customers, the enclosed market still provided food at prices unencumbered by overhead. Merchandise peddlers were less lucky, as the administration set out to exclude them from the public markets. LaGuardia insisted that they should move into stores located on private property. People who worried about the image of the city preferred enclosed markets that helped hide poverty and obscure the contrasts of conflicting commercial cultures.

Only a vestige of the pushcart street market system survived into the 1940s. In 1946, ten of New York's open air markets still operated—five in Manhattan and five in Brooklyn. In Manhattan, two street markets remained on the Lower East Side, two in Harlem, and one in Greenwich Village. The enclosure movement worked so successfully that the image of the pushcart peddler rebounded in the 1960s as a cherished figure in urban myth and memory. In 1964, Markets Commissioner Albert S. Pacetta pointed to the six remaining street markets and declared benignly: "There is a strong nostalgic attachment on the part of many of our citizens for these markets. They date back to the early days of this city's history and are a reminder of changes and growth which have occurred. Also, the pushcart and open air stands tend to reflect a continental atmosphere, since in European cities these are familiar scenes and reflect a common method of shopping." The 1960s also saw a sharp rise in the number of licensed peddlers working the streets of New York and again stirred some complaints, according to Commissioner Pacetta, from "store-keepers, home owners, civic groups and others."[65] However, the suppression and restriction of the 1930s and 1940s had largely purged these figures of their threat to bourgeois patterns of consumption. Nostalgia tends to predominate over complaints in contemporary views of street peddlers. The proof is in the streets. Commercial developers of modern festival marketplaces have brought the peddler back to enliven their slick assemblages of merchants and stores.

From the proposals of progressive era reformers it took decades to suppress the pushcart trade. The government's regulatory efforts clearly favored a modern, rationalized, efficient system of commerce that would serve higher realty values, higher urban densities, and the unrestricted circulation of people and store-bought commodities. However, city officials had to contend with a massive constituency of poor residents who bought and sold from pushcarts daily and voted annually. In the end it was the Depression crisis—the weakness, not the strength of the modern economic system—that most effectively removed working-class pushcart commerce from the streets. Government public works programs and expanded regulatory power overcame earlier municipal resistance to the construction of public markets. The LaGuardia pushcart ban tightly regulated city streets at precisely the time when a more heterogeneous group of people found themselves on the streets for both social and economic reasons.

Acknowledgments

I have benefited greatly from the incisive comments of "The Landscape of Modernity" conference participants, as well as those of Elizabeth Blackmar and Barbara Clark Smith. An earlier version of this paper appeared in the *Journal of Urban History* 18 (November, 1991): 68–92.

Notes

1. William Fellowes Morgan, Jr., *The City of New York Department of Public Markets, Weights and Measures, Annual Report for the Year 1935* (New York: F. Hubner, 1936), p. 5.
2. Ibid.
3. *New York Times* V (July 14, 1912): 9.
4. Sam Bass Warner, Jr., "The Public Invasion of Private Space and the Private Engrossment of Public Space," in Swedish Council for Building Research, *Growth and Transformation of the Modern City. The Stockholm Conference September 1978, University of Stockholm* (Stockholm: Swedish Council for Building Research, 1979), pp. 171–177.
5. On changing uses of city streets, see Stanley K. Schultz, *Constructing Urban Culture. American Cities and City Planning, 1800–1920* (Philadelphia, PA: Temple University Press, 1989), pp. 176–177; François Bedarida and Anthony R. Sutcliffe, "The Street in the Structure and Life of the City: Reflections on Nineteenth-Century London and Paris," *Journal of Urban History* 6 (1980): 379–396; Christine Stansell, "Women, Children, and the Uses of the Streets: Class and Gender Conflicts in New York City, 1850–1860," *Feminist Studies* 8 (Summer 1982): 309–335; Daniel Bluestone, "From Promenade to Park: The Gregarious Origins of Brooklyn's Park Movement," *American Quarterly* 39 (Winter 1987): 529–550. On questions of class and urban form and space, see Elizabeth

Blackmar, *Manhattan for Rent, 1785–1850* (Ithaca, NY: Cornell University Press, 1989); Roy Rosenzweig, *Eight Hours for What We Will* (New York: Cambridge University Press, 1983).

6. Richardson Wright, *Hawkers & Walkers in Early America* (Philadelphia, PA: J. B. Lippincott, 1927), pp. 233–234.

7. *The Picture of New-York and Stranger's Guide to the Commercial Metropolis of the United States* (New York: A. T. Goodrich, 1828), pp. 425–426.

8. *New York Herald* (September 18, 1846); see also M. Christine Boyer, *Manhattan Manners: Architecture and Style, 1850–1900* (New York: Rizzoli, 1985), pp. 43–129.

9. Chester H. Liebs, *Main Street to Miracle Mile: American Roadside Architecture* (Boston: Little, Brown, 1985), pp. 117–135.

10. "The Street-Venders of New York," *Scribner's Monthly* 1 (December 1870): 113–129.

11. Earl R. French, *Push Cart Markets in New York City* (U.S. Department of Agriculture, Agricultural Economics Bureau and the Port of New York Authority, March, 1925), p. 7.

12. Manhattan Borough President to John Purroy Mitchel, n.d., ca. September 1914, Mayor John P. Mitchel Papers, Box 215, New York City Municipal Archives; see also R. A. C. Smith et al., *To The Honorable The Mayor William J. Gaynor, A Report by a Committee Appointed by Him to Study and Recommend a Solution of the Pushcart Question, March 26, 1913* (New York: Clarence S. Nathan, 1913).

13. *Report of the Mayor's Push-Cart Commission. The City of New York, 1906* (New York: F. Hubner, 1906), p. 15.

14. "The Markets of the Poor," *Outlook* 101 (August 3, 1912): 750.

15. *The City of New York Department of Public Markets, Weights and Measures, Annual Report for the Year 1928* (New York: F. Hubner, 1929), p. 8.

16. Lloyd P. Gartner, "The Jews of New York's East Side, 1890–1893, Two Surveys by the Baron de Hirsch Fund," *American Jewish Historical Quarterly* 53 (March 1964): 264–285.

17. French, *Push Cart Markets*, pp. 34–35.

18. E. Idell Zeisloft, *The New Metropolis* (New York: D. Appleton, 1899), p. 530.

19. *New York Daily Tribune* (September 15, 1898); see also Abraham Cahan, *The Rise of David Levinsky* (New York: Grosset & Dunlap, 1917), p. 105.

20. *New York Daily Tribune* (September 15, 1898).

21. *Eighteenth Annual Report of the Bureau of Labor Statistics of the State of New York, for the Year 1900* (Albany, NY: James B. Lyon, 1901), p. 292.

22. Zeisloft, *The New Metropolis*, pp. 548–553; James B. Reynolds, Commissioner, Bureau of Weights and Measures, Licenses and Marshals, "[Report to Mayor Seth Low,]" *City Record* (January 21, 1904): 401.

23. *New York Times* V (March 30, 1930): 30.

24. East Side Peddlers' Association to Mayor George B. McClellan, November 14, 1906, MGB–117.

25. Mayor George B. McClellan, "Statement with Regard to the Push-Cart Situation," June 6, 1906, MGB–117.

26. *New York Times* (October 25, 1930): 19.

27. *New York Times* V (July 14, 1912): 9; see also Reynolds, "[Report to Mayor Seth Low,]" p. 401.
28. French, *Push Cart Markets*, pp. 28–29.
29. David Bartlett Gould to Mayor William L. Strong, March 15, 1896 (Mayor William L. Strong Papers, Box 38, New York City Municipal Archives; hereafter, Strong Papers, NYCMA).
30. "Petition," in Samuel H. Kunstlich to William F. Gaynor (Mayor William F. Gaynor Papers, Box 92, New York City Municipal Archives).
31. *New York Times* (July 1, 1912): 22.
32. Louis Dorfman to Fiorello H. LaGuardia, October 3, 1938 (Mayor Fiorello H. LaGuardia Papers, Box 3713, New York City Municipal Archives; hereafter, LaGuardia Papers, NYCMA).
33. Gould to Mayor Strong (Strong Papers, NYCMA).
34. "12th United States Census (1900), New York City Manuscript," Enumeration District 114, reel no. 1085; Enumeration District 153, reel no. 1087.
35. Quoted in *New York Times* (July 30, 1893).
36. Brief filed by Yorkville Citizens' Committee in support of Ordinance No. 191, December 8, 1916, New York City Municipal Reference Library.
37. "Would Oust Pushcarts from City Streets," *Harlem Magazine* (April–May, 1930): 4–5.
38. J. J. Berger, "Pushcart Markets Defile Public Streets," *Real Estate News* (May 1938): 161.
39. City of New York, Board of Estimate and Apportionment, Committee on the City Plan, *Commission on Building Districts and Restrictions, Final Report, June 2, 1916*, see Figures 102, 103, 104.
40. Henry H. Curran to Jacob Gould Schurman, Jr., February 23, 1938 (LaGuardia Papers, NYCMA).
41. Henry H. Curran to Captain Charles L. Lewis, March 21, 1938 (LaGuardia Papers, NYCMA).
42. Lawrence Elliott, *Little Flower: The Life and Times of Fiorello LaGuardia* (New York: William Morrow, 1983), pp. 27–28.
43. Arnold A. Krantz to Fiorello H. LaGuardia, March 5, 1938; Fiorello H. LaGuardia to Henry H. Curran, March 7, 1938 (LaGuardia Papers, NYCMA).
44. *New York Times* V (March 30, 1930): 30.
45. H. G. McNeil to Fiorello H. LaGuardia, March 13, 1938 (LaGuardia Papers, NYCMA).
46. *New York Daily Tribune* (September 15, 1898).
47. Reynolds, "[Report to Mayor Seth Low,]" pp. 401–404.
48. *Report of the Mayor's Push-Cart Commission, The City of New York, 1906* (New York, 1906), pp. 15, 200, 201.
49. Ibid., p. 75.
50. Lawrence Veiller to Hon. James C. Meyers, September 11, 1906 (Mayor George B. McClellan Papers, Box 89, New York City Municipal Archives; hereafter, McClellan Papers, NYCMA).
51. Lawrence Veiller to William A. Willis, March 30, 1906 (McClellan Papers, NYCMA).
52. *New York Times* (September 24, 1906).
53. Mayor Fiorello H. LaGuardia to H. G. McNeil, April 19, 1938 (LaGuardia Papers, NYCMA).

54. William Fellowes Morgan, Jr., Commissioner, *Annual Report [for] 1934, Department of Public Markets, Weights and Measures, City of New York*, p. 31.

55. John L. Elliott to John Purroy Mitchel, January 6, 1915 (Mayor John Purroy Mitchel Papers, Box 218, New York City Municipal Archives).

56. "Model Pushcart Market Suggested. Andrew J. Thomas, Noted Architect, Prepares a Plan at Suggestion of New York Civic Conference on Pushcart Markets," *Harlem Magazine* (November 1930): 9, 16; *New York Times* (November 7, 1930).

57. L. J. Hamilton to William F. Morgan, Jr., June 30, 1938 (LaGuardia Papers, NYCMA).

58. Charles W. Ferry to Fiorello H. LaGuardia, August 18, 1938 (LaGuardia Papers, NYCMA).

59. East Side Push Cart Peddlers' Association to George B. McClellan, October 31, 1906 (McClellan Papers, Box 117, NYCMA).

60. Samuel Mayers to Fiorello H. LaGuardia, May 12, 1938 (LaGuardia Papers, NYCMA).

61. Joseph S. Weinberger to Jacob G. Schurman, Jr., May 13, 1938 (LaGuardia Papers, NYCMA).

62. "Department of Markets" (LaGuardia Papers, Box 3638, NYCMA).

63. Transcript of Public Hearing on "Proposed Local Law C. No. 211, No. 222," August 16, 1938 (LaGuardia Papers, Box 3713, NYCMA).

64. Brownsville, East New York, and East Flatbush Street Peddlers' Organization to Fiorello H. LaGuardia, May 26, 1938; Stanley H. Howe to Brownsville, East New York, and East Flatbush Street Peddlers Organization, May 27, 1938 (LaGuardia Papers, NYCMA).

65. Commissioner Albert S. Pacetta, *New York City Department of Markets, Annual Report for Year Ending 30 June 1964*, pp. 43, 44.

Part VI

COMPLETING
THE LANDSCAPE

14

Fiorello H. LaGuardia and the Challenge of Democratic Planning

Thomas Kessner

The Depression of the 1930s put an abrupt end to national dreams of permanent prosperity, confronting the United States with an economic catastrophe of surpassing proportions and throwing New York City into fiscal turmoil. At the same time, precisely because this was an emergency that the federal government could not ignore for long, the Depression initiated an era of federal involvement in relief, public works, and economic planning that made possible a wide-reaching transformation for the aging industrial metropolis.

Depression acquainted New Yorkers with bank failures, industrial meltdown, curbside apple sellers, bread lines (what Heywood Broun called the "worm that walks like a man"), and hopelessness. So deep was the gloom, the sense of worse times impending, that working people applied for assistance *in anticipation* of unemployment. "I wish there were war again," a jobless worker told Louis Adamic. And natives from the Cameroons sent a contribution of $3.77 to feed "the starving" of New York.[1]

With relief expenses soaring and tax collections plummeting, the city budget fell into deep arrears. Jimmy Walker's insouciant minimalist government had been enough in the twenties, when New Yorkers were satisfied with a stylish mayor who went about the business of serving Tammany faithfully. But bad times required leadership to help the growing number of needy, and to secure a shaky public order. In the face of fiscal disaster, a style of governing designed to "make good Democrats" was overmatched.

Mayor Jimmy Walker recognized as much, going hat in hand to the bankers, who allowed themselves to be persuaded to help the city stave off bankruptcy—for a good price. A humiliating "bankers' agreement" ceded control over city finances to its creditors. The bankers dictated new taxes and secured a veto over spending; tax revenues were expressly committed to paying off loans before meeting any other obligations; and the city placed $50 million in escrow in the event that tax revenues proved insufficient. The city would be able to pay back its loans; left unanswered, however, was how the city would be able to continue to operate.[2]

City governments are not reshaped in good times. When the free market provides jobs and basic services for the large majority, insurgent candidates find it hard to sell the electorate on reform. In 1929, Congressman Fiorello LaGuardia ran for mayor after a career as an outspoken critic of unregulated profit-motive economics and pinchpenny social policy. The incumbent Jimmy Walker defeated him by the largest margin in the city's history. LaGuardia's strident charges of corruption and insistence on reform threatened to make a serious thing of government. In 1929, New Yorkers still preferred Beau James and unregulated good times.[3]

New York's 322 square miles represented perhaps the most densely packed and complexly divided cityscape in the world. Commerce, industry, and a surging residential population competed for limited space. Growing in a relentlessly uncharted fashion, the city's business districts projected a titanic quality. The 56-story Chanin Building and the 77-story Chrysler, both completed in 1929, prepared the midtown skyline for the 102-story Empire State Building. While these soaring masterpieces, built upon private initiative, had profoundly public effects, their developers were assigned no larger responsibility for the congestion and safety problems that they brought on than meeting minimal zoning requirements.

Unlimited skyscraper construction was just one symbol of New York's unguided growth, of a metropolis lacking the municipal will and public intelligence to shape its own evolution. Here was a world-class city where no mayor or public official conceived of a master plan or even thought in such terms. Lineaments for future growth were instead proposed by the privately organized Regional Plan Association of New York (RPA) and paid for by the Russell Sage Foundation.[4]

Throughout the 1920s, this group carried out a study of the New York metropolitan region, publishing its agenda for growth and orchestrated development in a ten-volume "Plan for the New York Region and Its Environs." This pioneering document outlined a comprehensive policy to protect harbors, zone industrial use, and organize regional transportation and recreational space with some concern for civic beauty and aesthetic grace. Published between 1929 and 1931, the plan was presented to the public at a time when the city was perched on the edge of fiscal collapse. The comprehensive reconstruction of its infrastructure seemed like the last thing that it could undertake amidst the immediate crisis of unemployment and widespread immiserization. In addition to money, the task demanded creativity, imagination, and a large conception of public responsibility; and all New York had was Jimmy Walker and his band of bossed aldermen.

Beset by economic crisis and political paralysis, New Yorkers were further stunned by the Seabury investigations, which disclosed how extensively the bosses had corrupted the city. The genial practitioners of honest graft had focused their limited political intelligence and imagination on "seein' my opportunities and takin' 'em," on sacking the municipality they had been pledged to serve. Little wonder that they had failed to develop a government appropriate to New York's size and complexity. Jimmy Walker's New York was not merely corrupt, it lacked the freshness and vision with which to meet the challenge of modern times.[5]

The Seabury inquiries forced Walker from office on September 1, 1932, and the following year Fiorello LaGuardia, who had been retired from Congress in the New Deal landslide in 1932, was elected as New York's ninety-ninth mayor on a Fusion ticket. Written history has often overplayed the impact of individuals on large forces. Yet, it is difficult to write the history of modern New York without paying proper attention to the role of Fiorello LaGuardia. Before LaGuardia, the city was run by mayors who conceived of their jobs in the narrowest terms possible. They played politics with relief, ran a corrupt and wasteful municipal shop, and, even in these days of generous federal grants, were frozen out of competition for Washington's dollars. There was just no assurance that they would make honest and efficient use of the funds.[6]

Jimmy Walker and his successors Joe McKee and John O'Brien saw the Depression as calamity; LaGuardia saw it as an opportunity for himself and for the municipality that he aimed to serve. For all the money and thinking that went into the RPA's plans and for all the effect that the Port Authority had, it was LaGuardia and his three administrations that remade New York in its modern image. Max Weber wrote that the art of politics is the "knowledge of influencing men . . . of holding in one's hands a nerve fiber of historically important events." The larger structural forces prepared New York for its modern era, but it was LaGuardia who lifted the city's politics to new levels of possibility by marshaling the political will and intelligence to confront the critical public issues of the time.[7]

LaGuardia broke with the past to lay out a new agenda. He brought into office five goals: (1) restore the city's fiscal health and win back its political independence from the bankers' consortium; (2) develop a policy of humane and financially prudent relief; (3) clean out corruption; (4) establish a merit-based civil service; and (5) rebuild New York into a modern, aesthetically pleasing, efficiently laid out city. The key to achieving his plans lay in a new relationship with Washington.

The crash, LaGuardia told Congress a few weeks after taking over City Hall, had put "every municipality to the wall," and the states were not able to be of much help. What Fiorello meant to do, New York City Chamberlain Adolf A. Berle, Jr., wrote to his friend President Franklin Roosevelt, "is to navigate New York City into a friendly cooperative basis with both the state and National Administrations."[8]

Historically, cities had been viewed as wards of their states, and it was to the states that they turned for assistance. Mayors negotiated with governors and aldermen, not with presidents and cabinet secretaries. But LaGuardia aimed to involve Washington. He had worked with the New Deal as a member of the House of Representatives, and public works chief Harold Ickes welcomed his election. "His career in Congress," Ickes wrote about LaGuardia, "shows that he has real ability and high courage. . . . He ought to give New York a great administration." Nonetheless, when the mayor-elect first came to Washington to discuss federal assistance for his strapped municipality, Ickes sent him home with a blunt message: "Go home and balance your budget, your credit is no good."[9]

Within its first one hundred days the new Fusion government pushed through an Economy Bill that trimmed the budget and pared down the municipal work force. As a congressman, LaGuardia had attacked Herbert Hoover for proposing a federal sales tax and had led the fight to defeat the regressive excise. But now he saw things differently. Relief costs had to be placed on a pay-as-you-go basis, or they would jeopardize the budget with huge and unpredictable debt, making it impossible to secure loans or grants. So LaGuardia took Ickes' admonition to heart and signed into law a 2 percent sales tax.

He also put the other elements of the Fusion agenda into place, establishing a humane relief policy, launching a wide-ranging attack on corruption, and expanding the merit basis of the civil service. This done, he turned to his ambitious program for the federally assisted reconstruction of New York.

LaGuardia assembled groups of engineers, architects, and other experts and put them to work planning new projects. "I want help from the people who know something," he told the pleased professionals, "rather than from the politicians." Even before he was sworn into office, LaGuardia presented Washington with a laundry list of proposals for subways, bridges, airports, slum clearance, street repair, and public housing. Each project was carefully detailed with a firm price tag and a prudent projection for the use of relief labor. And each promised to leave a public monument to the New Deal upon its completion.[10]

At LaGuardia's suggestion, relief czar Harry Hopkins appointed Wall Street attorney Travis Harvard Whitney as New York's Civil Works administrator. Whitney called newspaper columnist Heywood Broun one day soon after taking office to ask for a list of laid-off reporters he could put to work. Broun came by Whitney's office that day, but said it would take some time to compile the names. "That won't do at all," rebuked Whitney. "You don't understand. This is a rush job, every day counts." Within weeks tens of thousands of the unemployed were put to work. After less than a month the fifty-eight-year-old Whitney collapsed at his desk and died. "Killed in action," wrote an admiring Heywood Broun.[11]

In Chicago, Detroit, and San Francisco, federal money went into useless boondoggles or to buy votes. So completely did Massachusetts State Treasurer Charles Hurley control Civil Works Administration appointments that the press referred to CWA as Charlie's Workers Administration. Little wonder that Hopkins and Ickes took LaGuardia seriously. His way of governing was different from the regular crowd. Within weeks of his election, LaGuardia brought home an allotment of 200,000 federally funded jobs, 20 percent of the entire CWA program. The new administration initiated 4,000 separate projects, ranging from the construction of covered municipal markets and refurbishing of city parks to developing shelters for the homeless and clearing slums. Just a few weeks into Fusion, national studies described LaGuardia's management of federal projects as the most honest and effective in the country, and a state report concluded that "New York City is remarkably free from political control or influence."[12]

Historian Bernard Fay had remarked in the twenties that New York was the only city wealthy enough to rebuild itself every ten years. It was no longer rich enough, but LaGuardia envisioned a program of new bridges, airports, public housing projects, health stations, hospitals, and beaches that would enhance the quality of city life and provide hundreds of thousands of jobs. It was the thirties, tough times, when most mayors were begging to get a school or a bridge, and he insisted that he wanted to make urban life into a "great living adventure, with playgrounds, parks, museums, libraries, and parkways," to match the grand aesthetic spirit of the European cities he had known as a youth.[13]

"You know," LaGuardia once mused to Paul Kern, "I am in the position of an artist or a sculptor. . . . I can see New York as it should be and as it can be, but now I am in the position of a man who has a conception that he wishes to carve or paint, who . . . hasn't a chisel or a brush." It was to Washington that he turned for the chisels and brushes, and it was to the globally renowned developer Robert Moses that he assigned the primary responsibility for putting these chisels and brushes to creative public use.[14]

To get the stormy forty-five-year-old president of the Long Island State Parks Commission to accept the appointment, LaGuardia consolidated the five separate borough parks departments and placed them under Moses' control; he also threw in the chairmanship of the Triborough Bridge Authority. Once in office, Moses corralled the best engineers and architects and rammed his projects to successful completion. A hard-bitten taskmaster who ridiculed do-gooders, Moses had the charmed gift of spinning the gossamer of exalted higher purpose over his undertakings. In less than a year, he poured 26 million federal dollars into the city's parks and increased their number by a third.[15]

Years before, during the twenties, New York City had created an authority to negotiate a loan and build a colossal complex of four bridges linking together Manhattan, the Bronx, and Queens, as well as two East River islands. Tammany characteristically converted this $50 million Triborough project into a patronage trough for designing politicians, leading the federal government to shut off funding. With LaGuardia's new standing in Washington, the credit tap was reopened. Moses streamlined the plans, added approach roads, parkways, the East River Drive, vast recreation areas on Ward's and Randall's islands, and converted the Triborough project into New York's brood mare of public works.

Then, less than two months into the new administration, suddenly the federal money stopped coming, and it was put to LaGuardia that he would have to choose between his master builder and the president who held the chisels. Years before, Moses had made an enemy of Franklin Roosevelt, and now the president made it clear to a shaken LaGuardia that no more money would be available for the Triborough or other major projects unless he got rid of his commissioner.

Moses was an extremely gifted builder, but he came to represent more than that. If LaGuardia was to succeed in his ambitious plans for the city, he needed Washington. But he also needed to state the basis of the relationship, to keep the city's independence and its right to manage its own programs and policies. Over the next months, as LaGuardia painstakingly developed a scheme that satisfied Roosevelt while saving Moses' position, the mayor was able to achieve two things: He gained the personal trust and respect of the president, and he won a measure of control over his autocratic parks commissioner.[16]

LaGuardia understood one fundamental point with regard to cities: The time of the self-sufficient, wholly independent city had passed. New York could not pay for relief, social services, *and* new parks and bridges. The money had to come from the well-financed federal experiments in pump priming and social welfare assistance, and LaGuardia managed to make his city into the New Deal's favorite laboratory for urban and social initiatives. "He has a confidential relationship with President Roosevelt enjoyed by no Democrat," reported the *Albany Times Union.* "The doors of the White House open at his radiant approach, and the President is never too busy to sit down and have a chat with him." Roosevelt himself said of his foxy friend: "Our Mayor is the most appealing man I know. He comes to Washington and tells me a sad story. The tears run down my cheeks and tears run down his cheeks and the first thing I know he has wangled another $50 million." The CWA, WPA, and PWA alone spent more than $1.1 billion in New York during Fusion's first five years.[17]

None of the thousands of federal projects promised to have a broader effect than the movement to clear the slums and replace them with subsidized housing. To say today that New York was a pioneer in public housing recalls little of the boldness that went into this effort in the thirties. But in those days, the battle to clear the slums seemed to offer promise, not only for improving the terrible situation in these poor neighborhoods, but also to battle the crime, disease, and defeat that it produced. For a brief moment in the thirties, then, housing represented a different dream. Slum clearance and public housing would work a reform not only on the cityscape but also on its inhabitants, reinforcing sobriety, thrift, cleanliness, and civic virtue. It would reduce crime, uplift the poor, and provide jobs.

Not in that order.

Perhaps public housing deserved to be treated as a reform in its own right, but Depression politics dictated that the only lever for large-scale federal funds was the promise of creating jobs to put the unemployed to work. And so the housing program, like so many New Deal projects, developed backward out of a search for projects that would absorb federal money. The goal was jobs, not houses. For the moment this did not make much of a difference. First Houses, Williamsburg Houses, and Harlem Houses quickly went up, providing more than 1,200 working-class families with new accommodations, but there were important long-range implications for basing a policy on the shifting sands of the federal relief program.[18]

With its initial projects underway, the New York City Housing Authority turned to a long-range plan for comprehensive urban renewal. NYCHA Chairman Langdon Post conceived a $2 billion program for a "real new deal" in slum clearance and public housing. At the same time, LaGuardia commissioned Nathan Straus to study the European public housing experience and make recommendations for the city.[19]

Straus brought back from his travels a proposal for an even more far-reaching approach than Post's. He recommended that New York forget about rebuilding slum areas. The new projects would only be swallowed up by their loathsome surroundings. He advocated quarantining entire city sections, declaring the old housing unfit, bulldozing the rookeries, and replacing them with parks and playgrounds. To prevent the growth of other slums, he wanted strong zoning laws that would limit density and require adequate light, air, and space for all new construction. The plan called for panoramic planning and massive allocations, the cost to be shared by the city and the federal government.[20]

LaGuardia received the report, praised Straus' unstinted efforts, and buried it. He could not pay for new housing, and Franklin Roosevelt had already indicated to Post his disinterest in a program that carried nine figures on the bottom line and a ten-year turnaround. Instead, LaGuardia allowed the housing reformers their enthusiasms, exploited their commitments, and picked their brains; but New York's housing program was limited to building what it could with the chisels and brushes that it got from Washington.[21]

Here was the single best chance for housing reform in American history, but even for a Fusion administration comprehensive reform was out of the question. Piecemeal was better than no meal at all, and the best that LaGuardia could do was take the hopeful plan for large-scale public housing and shrink it to the politically possible: a few housing developments and several thousand families in better surroundings than they had ever dreamed possible.

But so long as only a small portion of the virtuous poor (to be accepted, applicants were required to have jobs, some insurance, and at least a modest bank account) were rehoused, the premise of rehabilitating the socially unfit through sunshine and private toilets was never really tested. And with the pioneering public housing program conceived primarily as a means for providing work relief, the entire undertaking was placed on the unsteady foundation of anti-Depression largesse.

Langdon Post was unwilling to accept so shrunken a dream, and, by LaGuardia's second term, the disillusioned commissioner was clashing openly with PWA chief Ickes. LaGuardia, who quickly tired of reform commissioners defining their own agendas, accepted Post's resignation. When Post lamely pointed out that he had not submitted it and intended to stay in office until a successor was appointed, LaGuardia immediately swore in his press secretary. Easing himself away from the warm language of caring, dreaming, and hoping, LaGuardia was steering toward what was reasonable and could be sold to Washington. Housing, he said now, was too important to leave to the reformers; it had become a "big business proposition."[22]

By 1938, Robert Moses understood just how big a business proposition even a limited housing program was going to be. As allocations for bridges and parkways were being cut, Moses aimed to make housing his new domain. First, he sought to prepare the ground by criticizing existing policy. Then, he began attacking the incumbent commissioner, sending him abusive letters about his stupidity and ignorance, while he peppered the mayor with memos and suggestions about housing policy.[23]

Finally, Moses was ready. He had secretly put his own architects to work creating an ambitious plan for slum clearance and public housing. A select audience of housing reformers, builders, realtors, and friendly journalists were invited to the Museum of Natural History to hear an address on "housing and recreation" on November 22, 1938. What Moses had in mind for this talk was much more. He handed out lavishly illustrated brochures that detailed a $245 million slum clearance and housing program.

The speech aimed to establish a comprehensive set of principles for a new housing program under Moses. The proposals were precise to the exact dimensions of the houses and their locations. It was a bold effort to overwhelm those present and the large radio audience that was expected to be listening to the talk over WNYC.

But no one listening to WNYC that night heard Moses. Someone had tipped off LaGuardia, and he pulled the plug on the broadcast. The next day, he explained that technical considerations had prompted WNYC to cancel coverage, but his message to his power-hungry parks commissioner could not be more clear. LaGuardia ridiculed Moses' housing plan as a beautiful printing job while privately instructing his Housing Committee to make sure that not one of Moses' ideas was adopted.[24]

Early in his administration, LaGuardia had protected Moses from Roosevelt because he valued Moses' skills and considered him an important symbol of the city's independence. He also respected Moses' rare gifts as a planner and builder, but LaGuardia had no intention of arming his power-hungry commissioner with any more planning authority than he already had. For, unlike Moses, LaGuardia had come to understand that he had to balance city growth with other municipal imperatives. He also came to appreciate the profoundly disturbing effect that Moses-type programs could have on city populations.

Moses' audacious plans and radical reconception of the city represented a strong city-planning ethos. He welcomed the idea of imposing his vision on vast slabs of urban territory, on assembling properties and converting them into magnificent parks and spanning the waters with world-class bridges in the name of larger public purpose. Ultimately, of course, modernization programs—whether for parks, bridges, or highways—in a city as tightly settled as New York means assigning choices between competing uses, between people and businesses, cars and trains, growth and shrinkage, the present and the future.

Moses viewed the cityscape as fluid, ever alterable, something for him to mold into an efficiently integrated whole. Once the experts agreed on the guiding principles, the rest was a question of raising the funds and engineering. He could understand that pressure groups, guided by their own blinkered interests, might try to obstruct modernization, but he had no sympathy for them. They must learn, he used to say, that you can't make omelets without cracking eggs, that you could not build a better city without disturbing established arrangements.

LaGuardia initially supported comprehensive planning as a way to harness expert architects and engineers to the exciting job of creating a better city, and reclaiming urban growth from the primitive chaos of laissez-faire thinking. The new 1938 charter, in the words of Wallace Sayre and Herbert Kaufman, charged the City Planning Commission "with the adventurous responsibility for introducing innovation and rationality into the political processes of a city long accustomed to opportunistic bargaining among vested political and economic interests of great strength." LaGuardia did not trust Moses with this much power over New York's planning process, passing over the mercurial commissioner to appoint New Deal brain truster Rexford Guy Tugwell as chairman of the City Planning Commission. Tugwell believed that the city should be steered toward long-term stability instead of growth. He called for interspersing generous green belts between residential areas to add beauty and a sense of human scale to the massive metropolis. With his commission, Tugwell spent more than a year and a half dividing the city into residential, manufacturing, and commercial sectors, and designing detailed land-use maps to guide city growth into the next decade. But while the charter assigned the commission broad responsibilities (preparing a master plan, zoning regulations, a capital budget, and a five-year capital program), it granted no authority to implement these plans.[25]

Like all plans that make choices between conflicting possibilities, between jobs and beauty, between clean air and efficiency, between sunlight and profits, between individual freedom and the "commonweal," Tugwell's work raised strong objections. Real estate and commercial interests pressed LaGuardia to modify the plan. Only a fully committed LaGuardia could clear the way for Tugwell, and because ultimately the ethic of the planner conflicts with the ethic of the democratic politician, LaGuardia was far from committed. Without LaGuardia's protection, Tugwell's plan was eviscerated.

Fed up with his impossible task and LaGuardia's fading support, Tugwell accepted a White House offer to serve as the appointed governor of Puerto Rico. *That* was the sort of power a planner needed. Eighteen months of finely detailed work and a strong planning point of view went with him. The new commission that replaced Tugwell's group limited itself to imposing restrictions on building heights and residential concentrations.[26]

Planners and social critics may criticize Moses, Tugwell, or LaGuardia, but if they are to be taken seriously, they must answer this: How much control can a municipality cede to planners to fasten their own long-range vision upon the city outside the checking limits of democratic politics? LaGuardia flourished in the hothouse of the present, the push and pull of elective politics. He learned that planning, like much else in urban government, involves municipal priorities and is open to debate and political wrangling. Ultimately, LaGuardia was not prepared to assign this power to master builders or brilliant technicians.

Walter Lippmann once said that LaGuardia took the human sympathy that had been the abiding strength of Tammany and infused it into the tradition of good government. He upgraded New York into a more modern city, a more honest city, a more humane city, a city that got out from under the thumb of the state to develop its own relationship with Washington. By undertaking a comprehensive program of federally funded renovation, LaGuardia influenced the city's built environment in ways no other mayor had. He brought his city wonderful things—hundreds of parks, pools, and playgrounds, thousands of new public housing units, dozens of new medical facilities, world-class tunnels, bridges, and airports, and even a World's Fair—but they were products of a political moment, when the Depression and LaGuardia's relationship with FDR opened new, but limited, possibilities for cooperation between Washington and New York. Ultimately, however, these projects were designed in an atmosphere that focused on fighting an economic emergency, not on charting fundamentally new urban policy.[27]

When World War II put an end to these projects, LaGuardia realized that the city was on a treadmill. It could not pay for maintaining its own infrastructure, much less plan its continued growth, without steady infusions of new federal funding. While the war was being won, LaGuardia readied detailed plans for a peacetime program of $1.25 billion in federally funded public improvements for his city.

Again his plans were designed to meet an immediate need. It took him a long time to accept the idea that businesses were moving out of the city, that industry was declining, that growth could reach a strangulation point. His plans reflected none of this; they demonstrated instead the immediate needs of assuring jobs and houses and parks and police protection to the city's people. But the federal government was not prepared to spend as much in good times as it had spent during the Depression. And when the special era that had been cemented by an unusual personal relationship between the Fusion mayor and the New Deal president passed, the city was left with a style of expensive progressive government to which it had become accustomed, but which it would only now have to get used to supporting largely on its own.[28]

When LaGuardia left office, Rexford Tugwell, who once described Fiorello as one of the few men of his generation of truly presidential mettle, was disappointed in the state of the city. The budget was unbalanced, the streets were dirty, and the schools were crowded. "The whole of the City's machinery," he wrote, "was breaking down from sheer lack of funds." In the end, planners and realists both had to contend with the problem of limits, of how much the citizens of the city, whose service ultimately legitimized the efforts, were willing to pay for better futures for themselves and their children.[29]

Many of the other essays in this volume focus on structural change. Well into the third decade of the "new social history," it is not necessary to state the argument that plain people and large processes need to be factored into any serious historical equation. But there are times when the historical context is swiftly altered, opening up broad opportunities for individual salience. The Depression was such a time. It created opportunities for sweeping change both on the federal and local level. It took a Franklin Roosevelt to make a New Deal of the national opportunity, and it took a Fiorello LaGuardia to reshape New York.

Herbert Hoover and Jimmy Walker could not have done it. And once LaGuardia's second administration completed the initial agenda for progressive reform, even he could not sustain the level of transforming activity.

But between 1934 and 1939 with the hopes of the people focused on him, with his open access to Washington, with his ability to attract the best and the brightest to city government, with his audacious politics and insistent will, LaGuardia was able to use the moment to permanently alter the scope of municipal government. And unlike the mayors who followed him, he was also able to use Robert Moses and control him, to make the most of this moment.

Notes

1. Edward R. Ellis, *Epic of New York City* (New York: Coward McCann, 1966), p. 524; Gene Fowler, *Beau James: The Life and Times of Jimmy Walker* (New York: Viking, 1949), pp. 256–259; George Walsh, *Gentleman Jimmy Walker: Mayor of the Jazz Age* (New York: Praeger, 1974), pp. 210, 214; Robert A. Caro, *The Power Broker: Robert Moses and the Fall of New York* (New York: Vintage, 1974), p. 323; Lillian Brandt, *An Impressionistic View of the Winter of 1930–31 in New York City* (New York: Welfare Council of NYC, 1932), pp. 6–8; *New York Times* (November 28, 1930); Irving Bernstein, *The Lean Years: A History of the American Worker* (Boston: Houghton Mifflin, 1960), pp. 293–295.
2. *Fusion Handbook* (New York: LaGuardia Campaign Headquarters, 1933), p. 26; *New York Times* (June 12, September 1, 29, October 4, November 16, 1933; January 25, 1934); Leonard Chalmers, "The Crucial Test of LaGuardia's First One Hundred Days: The Emergency Economy Bill," *New-York Historical Society Quarterly* 57 (1973): 239–240.
3. Lowell Limpus and Burr W. Leyson, *This Man LaGuardia* (New York: E. P. Dutton, 1938), pp. 291–292, 295; Howard Zinn, *LaGuardia in Congress* (Ithaca, NY: Cornell University Press, 1959), p. 174; Arthur Mann, *LaGuardia: A Fighter Against His Times, 1882–1933* (Philadelphia, PA: J. B. Lippincott, 1959), p. 278; Thomas Kessner, *Fiorello H. LaGuardia and the Making of Modern New York* (New York: McGraw-Hill, 1989), pp. 159–164.
4. Kessner, ibid., pp. 199–209; Frederick Shaw, *The History of the New York City Legislature* (New York: Columbia University Press, 1954), pp. 31, 78. On the Regional Plan, see Chapter 5 by Robert Fishman in this volume.
5. On the Seabury investigation, see Herbert Mitgang, *The Man Who Rode the Tiger: The Life and Times of Judge Samuel Seabury* (Philadelphia, PA: J. B. Lippincott, 1963), pp. 219–243.
6. Kessner, *LaGuardia and Modern New York*, pp. 209–232.
7. H. H. Gerth and C. Wright Mills, *From Max Weber: Essays in Sociology* (New York: Oxford University Press, 1946), p. 115.

8. Mark I. Gelfand, *A Nation of Cities: The Federal Government and Urban America, 1933–1965* (New York: Oxford University Press, 1975), p. 28; Adolf A. Berle, Jr., to Franklin D. Roosevelt, January 9, 1934 (FDR Library, Hyde Park, NY; hereafter, FDR Library).

9. Harold Ickes, *The Secret Diary of Harold Ickes*, vol. 1 (New York: Simon & Schuster, 1953), p. 126; Chalmers, "Crucial Test of LaGuardia's Economy Bill," pp. 239–240.

10. *New York World-Telegram* (November 29, 1933); *New York Times* (November 30, 1933).

11. Edward R. Ellis, "Nation in Torment," *New York Times* (November 23, 1933); Edward R. Ellis, *A Nation in Torment: The Great American Depression 1929–1939* (New York: Capricorn, 1971), p. 500.

12. Barbara Blumberg, *The New Deal and the Unemployed: The View from New York City* (Lewisburg, PA: Bucknell University Press, 1979), p. 32; Joseph Verdicchio, "New Deal Work Relief and New York City: 1933–1938," Ph.D. diss. (New York University, 1980), pp. 104, 115–117; Roger Biles, *Big City Boss in Depression and War* (De Kalb, IL: Northern Illinois University Press, 1984), p. 77; Charles Trout, *Boston, the Great Depression and the New Deal* (New York: Oxford University Press, 1977), pp. 148–151; *New York Times* (April 21, 1936).

13. Bernard Fay, quoted in Bayrd Still, *Mirror for Gotham: New York as Seen by Contemporaries from Dutch Days to the Present* (New York: New York University Press, 1956), p. 297; *New York Times* (November 30, 1933); August Heckscher, *When LaGuardia Was Mayor: New York's Legendary Years* (New York: W. W. Norton, 1978), p. 68.

14. Caro, *Power Broker*, p. 358.

15. Kessner, *LaGuardia and Modern New York*, pp. 300–309.

16. Ibid., pp. 306–319.

17. *Albany Times Union* (June 28, 1935); *New York Times* (October 29, 1940).

18. Peter Marcuse, "Public Housing in the United States in the 1930s: The Case in New York City." Paper delivered before Conference on Public Housing in New York, Columbia University, October 12–14, 1984. Langdon Post, "Memorandum on a Comprehensive Housing Program" January 18, 1935 (New York Housing Authority Papers, LaGuardia Archives; hereafter, NYCHA Papers); *New York Daily News* (November 28, 1933).

19. Post, ibid.; Post to FDR, January 21, 1935 (NYCHA Papers).

20. Nathan Straus, "Low Cost Housing Here and Abroad, Report to Mayor LaGuardia" (NYCHA Papers).

21. *New York Times* (October 21, 1935).

22. Kessner, *LaGuardia and Modern New York*, pp. 430–431.

23. Robert Moses to Fiorello LaGuardia, August 29, 1938 (LaGuardia Papers, Box 35, New York Municipal Archives; hereafter, LaGuardia Papers, NYMA); Moses to Alfred Rheinstein, November 18, 22, 1938; July 1, 7, September 18, 1939 (NYCHA Papers).

24. Caro, *Power Broker*, pp. 611–612; *New York Times* (November 24, 25, 1938; June 24, 1939).

25. Kessner, *LaGuardia and Modern New York*, pp. 404–406, 554; Wallace Sayre and Herbert Kaufman, *Governing New York City* (New York: Russell Sage Foundation, 1960), p. 372. My view of the relationship between Moses and LaGuardia is in *LaGuardia and Modern New York*, pp. 316–

319, 411–415, 428, 452–459; but Caro's *Power Broker* is proof enough. After explaining in dramatic fashion that Moses had made LaGuardia understand that he was LaGuardia's equal (this conclusion is rather perversely offered after Moses loses his fight to build a Brooklyn Battery Bridge), Caro cannot prove his assertion of Moses' dominance and is reduced to changing the topic with a little scandalmongering about Moses' relationship with his wife and his brother. Indeed, this leaves a serious gap in the book's narrative account of Moses' career. Despite its more than 1,200 pages, Caro can find little evidence of major accomplishments (except for some evidence of Moses' spite work) for the years between 1938 and 1945, when LaGuardia capped Moses' urge for power. Caro, *Power Broker*, pp. 577–688.

26. Kessner, *LaGuardia and Modern New York*, pp. 554–555.
27. *Oakland Daily News* (November 4, 1937).
28. "New York Opens Its Post War Exhibit," *The American City* (May 1944): 5; Fiorello LaGuardia, "Vast Public Works Program Essential to Full Time Production," *The American City* (September 1945): 101; *New York Times* (December 20, 1940). See also LaGuardia to FDR, February 9, 1943 (LaGuardia Papers, NYMA); FDR to LaGuardia, September 23, 1945 (FDR Library); Henry A. Wallace to LaGuardia, August 16, 1944 (Wallace Papers, FDR Library).
29. Citizens Budget Commission, *Annual Report* (1945), p. 9; Rexford G. Tugwell, *The Art of Politics as Practiced by Three Great Americans: Franklin Delano Roosevelt, Luis Munoz Marin, and Fiorello H. LaGuardia* (Garden City, NY: Doubleday, 1958), pp. 28–30.

Selected References

Bacon, Mardges, *Ernest Flagg: Beaux-Arts Architect and Urban Reformer* (New York and Cambridge: Architectural History Foundation and MIT Press, 1986).

Bayor, Ronald H., *Neighbors in Conflict: The Irish, Germans, Jews, and Italians of New York City, 1929–1941* (Baltimore: Johns Hopkins University Press, 1978).

Bell, Daniel, *The Coming of Post-Industrial Society: A Venture in Social Forecasting* (New York: Basic Books, 1973).

———, *The End of Ideology: The Exhaustion of Political Ideas in the Fifties* (Glencoe, IL: Free Press, 1960).

Bellush, Jewel, and Dick Netzer, eds., *Urban Politics: New York Style* (Armonk, NY, and London: Sharpe, 1990).

Bender, Thomas, *New York Intellect: A History of Intellectual Life in New York, from 1750 to the Beginnings of Our Own Time* (New York: Knopf, 1987).

Berman, Marshall, *All That Is Solid Melts into Air: The Experience of Modernity* (New York: Simon & Schuster, 1982).

Berrol, Selma, "The Jewish West Side in New York City, 1920–1970," *Journal of Ethnic Studies* 13 (Winter 1986): 21–45.

Billington, David P., *The Tower and the Bridge: The New Art of Structural Engineering* (New York: Basic Books, 1983).

Birch, Eugenie, and Deborah Gardner, "The Seven-Percent Solution: A Review of Philanthropic Housing, 1870–1910," *Journal of Urban History* 7 (August 1981): 403–439.

Blackmar, Elizabeth, *Manhattan for Rent, 1785–1850* (Ithaca, NY: Cornell University Press, 1989).

Bluestone, Daniel, *Constructing Chicago* (New Haven, CT: Yale University Press, 1991).

Blumberg, Barbara, *The New Deal and the Unemployed: The View From New York City* (Lewisburg, PA: Bucknell University Press, 1979).

Blumin, Stuart, "Explaining the Metropolis: Perceptions, Depiction, and

Analysis in Mid-Nineteenth Century New York," *Journal of Urban History* 11 (November 1984): 9–38.

Bogart, Michele Helene, *Public Sculpture and the Civic Ideal in New York City, 1890–1930* (Chicago: University of Chicago Press, 1989).

Boyer, M. Christine, *Dreaming the Rational City: The Myth of American City Planning* (Cambridge: MIT Press, 1983).

———, *Manhattan Manners: Architecture and Style, 1850–1900* (New York: Rizzoli Press, 1985).

Boyer, Paul, *Urban Masses and Moral Order in America, 1820–1920* (Cambridge: Harvard University Press, 1978).

Bridges, Amy, *A City in the Republic: Antebellum New York and the Origins of Machine Politics* (New York: Cambridge University Press, 1984).

Butsch, Richard, *For Fun and Profit: The Transformation of Leisure into Consumption* (Philadelphia, PA: Temple University Press, 1990).

Cardia, Clara, *Ils ont construit New York: Histoire de la métropole au XIXème siècle*, with a preface by Marcel Roncayolo (Geneva: Georg Ed., 1987).

Caro, Robert A., *The Power Broker: Robert Moses and the Fall of New York* (New York: Knopf, 1974).

Chandler, Alfred D., Jr., *Scale and Scope: The Dynamics of Industrial Capitalism* (Cambridge: Belknap Press of Harvard University Press, 1990).

———, *The Visible Hand: The Managerial Revolution in American Business* (Cambridge: Belknap Press of Harvard University Press, 1977).

Cheape, Charles W., *Moving the Masses: Urban Public Transit in New York, Boston, and Philadelphia, 1880–1912* (Cambridge: Harvard University Press, 1980).

Clark, Kenneth, *Dark Ghetto: Dilemmas of Social Power* (New York: Harper & Row, 1965).

Clark, William C., and J. L. Kingston, *The Skyscraper: A Study in the Economic Height of Modern Office Buildings* (New York: American Institute of Steel Construction, 1930).

Cohen, James K., "Structural versus Functional Determinants of New York's Fiscal Policies Towards Metropolitan Transportation, 1904–1990," *Social Science History* 15 (Summer 1991): 177–198.

Commission on Building Districts and Restrictions, *Final Report* (New York: Board of Estimate and Apportionment, Committee on the City Plan, 1916).

Committee on the Regional Plan of New York and Its Environs, *Regional Plan of New York and Its Environs*, vol. I, *The Graphic Regional Plan* (New York: Regional Plan of New York and Its Environs, 1929).

———, *Regional Plan of New York and Its Environs*, vol. II, *The Building of the City*, by Thomas Adams, assisted by Harold M. Lewis and Lawrence M. Orton (New York: Regional Plan of New York and Its Environs, 1931).

————, *Regional Survey of New York and Its Environs*, vol. I, *Major Economic Factors in Metropolitan Growth and Arrangement*, by Robert Murray Haig, in consultation with Roswell C. McCrea (New York: Regional Plan of New York and Its Environs, 1927).

————, *Regional Survey of New York and Its Environs*, vol. IA, *Chemical, Metal, Wood, Tobacco, and Printing Industries* (New York: Regional Plan of New York and Its Environs, 1928).

————, *Regional Survey of New York and Its Environs*, vol. IB, *Food, Clothing, and Textile Industries, Wholesale Markets and Retail, Shopping and Financial Districts* (New York: Regional Plan of New York and Its Environs, 1928).

————, *Regional Survey of New York and Its Environs*, vol. II, *Population, Land Values, and Government*, prepared by Thomas Adams, Harold M. Lewis, and Theodore T. McCroskey (New York: Regional Plan of New York and Its Environs, 1929).

————, *Regional Survey of New York and Its Environs*, vol. III, *Highway Traffic*, by Harold M. Lewis (New York: Regional Plan of New York and Its Environs, 1927).

————, *Regional Survey of New York and Its Environs*, vol. IV, *Transit and Transportation*, by Harold M. Lewis, William J. Wilgus, and Daniel M. Turner (New York: Regional Plan of New York and Its Environs, 1928).

————, *Regional Survey of New York and Its Environs*, vol. V, *Public Transportation*, by Lee F. Hammer (New York: Regional Plan of New York and Its Environs, 1928).

————, *Regional Survey of New York and Its Environs*, vol. VI, *Buildings, Their Uses and the Spaces Around Them*, by Thomas Adams, Wayne D. Heydecker, and Edward M. Bassett (New York: Regional Plan of New York and Its Environs, 1931).

————, *Regional Survey of New York and Its Environs*, vol. VII, *Neighborhood and Community Planning*, by Clarence Arthur Perry, Wayne D. Heydecker, Ernest P. Goodrich, Thomas Adams, Edward M. Bassett, and Robert Whitten (New York: Regional Plan of New York and Its Environs, 1929).

————, *Regional Survey of New York and Its Environs*, vol. VIII, *Physical Conditions and Public Services*, by Harold M. Lewis (New York: Regional Plan of New York and Its Environs, 1929).

Condit, Carl W., *The Port of New York* (Chicago: University of Chicago Press, 1981).

Connelly, Harold X., *A Ghetto Grows in Brooklyn: Bedford Stuyvesant* (New York: New York University Press, 1977).

Conzen, Kathleen Neils, "Immigrants, Immigrant Neighborhoods, and Ethnic Identity: Historical Issues," *Journal of American History* 66 (December 1979): 603–615.

Conzen, Michael, ed., *The Making of the American Landscape* (Boston: Unwin Hyman, 1990).

Cromley, Elizabeth Collins, *Alone Together: A History of New York's Early Apartments* (Ithaca, NY: Cornell University Press, 1990).

Cronon, William, *Nature's Metropolis: Chicago and the Great West* (New York: W. W. Norton, 1991).

Danielson, Michael N., and Jameson W. Doig, *New York: The Politics of Urban Regional Development* (Berkeley: University of California Press, 1982).

Davies, James Clarence, *Neighborhood Groups and Urban Renewal* (New York: Columbia University Press, 1966).

Davies, Robert Bruce, *Peacefully Working to Conquer the World: Singer Sewing Machines in Foreign Markets, 1854–1920* (New York: Arno Press, 1976).

DeForest, Robert, and Lawrence Veiller, eds., *The Tenement House Problem* (New York: Macmillan, 1903).

Doig, Jameson W., "Coalition-Building by a Regional Agency: Austin Tobin and the Port of New York Authority," in Clarence N. Stone and Heywood T. Sanders, eds., *The Politics of Urban Development* (Lawrence: University Press of Kansas, 1987).

———, " 'If I See a Murderous Fellow Sharpening a Knife Cleverly . . .': The Wilsonian Dichotomy and the Public Authority Tradition," *Public Administration Review* 43 (July/August 1983): 292–304.

———, *Metropolitan Transportation Politics and the New York Region* (New York: Columbia University Press, 1966).

———, "Politics and the Engineering Mind: O. H. Ammann and the Hidden Story of the George Washington Bridge," in *Yearbook of German-American Studies* (Lawrence: University Press of Kansas, 1991).

———, "Regional Conflict in the New York Metropolis: The Legend of Robert Moses and the Power of the Port Authority," *Urban Studies* 27 (April 1990): 209–219.

Domosh, Mona, "The Symbolism of the Skyscraper: Case Studies of New York's First Tall Buildings," *Journal of Urban History* 14 (May 1988): 321–345.

Duffy, John, *A History of Public Health in New York City, 1866–1966* (New York: Russell Sage Foundation, 1974).

Fenske, Gail, " 'The Skyscraper Problem' and the City Beautiful: The Woolworth Building." Ph.D. diss. (MIT, 1988).

Fishman, Robert, *Urban Utopias in the Twentieth Century: Ebenezer Howard, Frank Lloyd Wright, and Le Corbusier* (New York: Basic Books, 1977).

Ford, James, *Slums and Housing: With Special Reference to New York City* (Cambridge: Harvard University Press, 1936).

Freeman, Joshua, *In Transit: The Transport Workers Union in New York City, 1933–1966* (New York: Oxford University Press, 1989).

Gabaccia, Donna, *From Sicily to Elizabeth Street: Housing and Social Change Among Italian Immigrants, 1880–1930* (Albany: State University of New York Press, 1984).

———, *Militants and Migrants: Rural Sicilians Become American Workers* (New Brunswick, NJ: Rutgers University Press, 1988).

———, "Sicilians in Space: Environmental Change and Family Geography," *Journal of Social History* 16 (Winter 1982): 53–66.

Gelfand, Mark I., *A Nation of Cities: The Federal Government and Urban America, 1933–1965* (New York: Oxford University Press, 1975).

———, "Rexford G. Tugwell and the Frustration of Planning in New York City," *Journal of the American Planning Association* 51 (Spring 1985): 151–160.

Gibbs, Kenneth Turney, *Business Architectural Imagery in America, 1870–1930* (Ann Arbor, MI: UMI Research Press, 1984).

Giedion, Sigfried, *Space, Time, and Architecture: The Growth of a New Tradition* (Cambridge: Harvard University Press, 1941).

Gifford, Bernard, "New York City and Cosmopolitan Liberalism," *Political Science Quarterly* 93 (Winter 1978–1979): 559–584.

Gilbert, James, *Perfect Cities: Chicago's Utopias of 1893* (Chicago: University of Chicago Press, 1991).

Girouard, Mark, *Cities and People: A Social and Architectural History* (New Haven, CT: Yale University Press, 1985).

Glazer, Nathan, and Mark Lilla, eds., *The Public Face of Architecture: Civic Culture and Public Spaces* (New York: Free Press; London: Collier Macmillan, 1987).

Glazer, Nathan, and Daniel Patrick Moynihan, *Beyond the Melting Pot: The Negroes, Puerto Ricans, Jews, Italians, and Irish of New York City* (Cambridge: MIT Press, 1963).

———, eds., *Ethnicity: Theory and Experience* (Cambridge: Harvard University Press, 1975).

Gottman, Jean, *Megalopolis: The Urbanized Northeastern Seaboard of the United States* (New York: Twentieth Century Fund, 1961).

———, "Why the Skyscraper?" *Geographical Review* 56 (April 1966): 190–212.

Grebler, Leo, *Housing Market Behavior in a Declining Area: Long Term Changes in Inventory and Utilization of Housing on New York's Lower East Side* (New York: Columbia University Press, 1952).

Green, Nancy L., "Immigrant Labor in the Garment Industries of New York and Paris: Variations on a Structure," *Comparative Social Research* 9 (1986): 231–243.

———, *The Pletzl of Paris: Jewish Immigrant Workers in the Belle Époque* (New York: Holmes & Meier, 1986).

Gurock, Jeffrey, *When Harlem Was Jewish, 1870–1930* (New York: Columbia University Press, 1979).

Gutman, Herbert, *The Black Family in Slavery and Freedom, 1750–1925* (New York: Pantheon Books, 1976).

Haber, Samuel, *Efficiency and Uplift: Scientific Management in the Progressive Era, 1890–1920* (Chicago: University of Chicago Press, 1964).

Hall, Ben M., *The Best Remaining Seats: The Golden Age of the Movie Palace* (New York: C. N. Potter, 1961).

Hall, Max, ed., *Made in New York: Case Studies in Metropolitan Manufacturing* (Cambridge: Harvard University Press, 1959).

Hall, Peter, *Cities of Tomorrow: An Intellectual History of Urban Planning and Design in the Twentieth Century* (Oxford: Basil Blackwell, 1988).

Hammack, David C., *Power and Society: Greater New York at the Turn of the Century* (New York: Russell Sage Foundation, 1982).

Hapgood, Norman, and Henry Moskowitz, *Up from the Streets: Alfred E. Smith: A Biographical Study in Contemporary Politics* (New York: Grosset and Dunlap, 1927).

Harris, Richard, "American Suburbs: A Sketch of a New Interpretation," *Journal of Urban History* 15 (November 1988): 98–103.

Hartog, Hendrik, *Public Property and Private Power: The Corporation of the City of New York in American Law, 1730–1870* (Chapel Hill: University of North Carolina Press, 1983).

Harvey, David, *The Condition of Postmodernity: An Enquiry into the Origins of Cultural Change* (Oxford: Basil Blackwell, 1989).

Haskell, Thomas, ed., *The Authority of Experts: Studies in History and Theory* (Bloomington: Indiana University Press, 1984).

Hays, Forbes B., *Community Leadership: The Regional Plan Association of New York* (New York: Columbia University Press, 1965).

Hays, Samuel P., "The Politics of Reform in Municipal Government in the Progressive Era," *Pacific Northwest Quarterly* 55 (October 1964): 157–169.

Heffer, Jean, *Le port de New York et le commerce extérieur Américain, 1860–1900* (Paris: Publications de la Sorbonne, 1986).

Heiman, Michael, *The Quiet Evolution: Power, Planning, and Profits in New York* (New York: Praeger Books, 1988).

Heinze, Andrew R., *Adapting to Abundance: Jewish Immigrants, Mass Consumption, and the Search for American Identity* (New York: Columbia University Press, 1990).

Hine, Lewis W., *Men At Work: Photographic Studies of Modern Men and Machines*, 2nd ed. (New York: Dover Publications, 1977).

Hines, Thomas S., *Burnham of Chicago: Architect and Planner* (New York: Oxford University Press, 1974).

Hoover, Edgar, and Raymond Vernon, *Anatomy of a Metropolis: The Changing Distribution of People and Jobs Within the New York Metropolitan Region* (Cambridge: Harvard University Press, 1959).

Howe, Irving, *World of Our Fathers* (New York: Harcourt Brace Jovanovich, 1976).

Huthmacher, J. Joseph, *Senator Robert F. Wagner and the Rise of Urban Liberalism* (New York: Atheneum Books, 1968).

Huxtable, Ada Louise, *The Tall Building Urbanistically Reconsidered: The Search for a Skyscraper Style* (New York: Pantheon Books, 1985).

Irish, Sharon, "A 'Machine That Makes the Land Pay': The West Street Building in New York," *Technology and Culture* 20 (April 1989): 376–397.

Jackson, Anthony, *A Place Called Home: A History of Low-Cost Housing in Manhattan* (Cambridge: MIT Press, 1976).

Jackson, John Brinckerhoff, *Discovering the Vernacular Landscape* (New Haven, CT: Yale University Press, 1984).

Jackson, Kenneth T., "The Capital of Capitalism: The New York Metropolitan Region," in Anthony Sutcliffe, ed., *Metropolis, 1890–1940* (Chicago: University of Chicago Press, 1984).

———, *Crabgrass Frontier: The Suburbanization of the United States* (New York: Oxford University Press, 1985).

Jacobs, Jane, *The Death and Life of Great American Cities* (New York: Random House, 1961).

Johnson, David A., "The Emergence of Metropolitan Regionalism: An Analysis of the Regional Plan of New York and Its Environs." Ph.D. diss. (Cornell University, 1974).

Kasson, John F., *Amusing the Millions: Coney Island at the Turn of the Century* (New York: Hill & Wang, 1978).

———, *Rudeness & Civility: Manners in Nineteenth Century Urban America* (New York: Noonday, 1990).

Katznelson, Ira, *City Trenches: Urban Politics and the Patterning of Class in the United States* (New York: Pantheon, 1981).

Keller, Morton, *The Life Insurance Enterprise, 1885–1910: A Study in the Limits of Corporate Power* (Cambridge: Harvard University Press, 1963).

———, *Regulating a New Economy: Public Policy and Economic Change in America, 1900–1933* (Cambridge: Harvard University Press, 1990).

Kessner, Thomas, *Fiorello H. LaGuardia and the Making of Modern New York* (New York: McGraw-Hill, 1989).

———, *The Golden Door: Italian and Jewish Immigrant Mobility in New York City, 1880–1915* (New York: Oxford University Press, 1977).

Kouwenhoven, John A., *The Columbia Historical Portrait of New York: An Essay in Graphic History* (New York: Harper & Row, 1972).

Lawson, Ronald, ed., *The Tenant Movement in New York City, 1904–1984* (New Brunswick, NJ: Rutgers University Press, 1986).

Lippmann, Walter, *Drift and Mastery: An Attempt to Diagnose the Current Unrest*, with an introduction by William E. Leuchtenburg (Englewood Cliffs, NJ: Prentice-Hall, 1961).

Lowi, Theodore J., *At the Pleasure of the Mayor: Patronage and Power in New York City, 1898–1958* (New York: Free Press of Glencoe, 1964).

Lubove, Roy, *The Progressives and the Slums: Tenement House Reform in New York, 1890–1917* (Pittsburgh, PA: University of Pittsburgh Press, 1962).

McCraw, Thomas K., *Prophets of Regulation: Charles Francis Adams, Louis D. Brandeis, James M. Landis, Alfred E. Kahn* (Cambridge: Belknap Press of Harvard University Press, 1984).

Makielski, Stanislaw J., *The Politics of Zoning: The New York Experience* (New York: Columbia University Press, 1966).

Melosi, Martin V., *Garbage in the Cities: Refuse, Reform, and the Environment, 1880–1980* (College Station: Texas A & M University Press, 1981).

Moehring, Eugene P., *Public Works and the Patterns of Urban Real Estate Growth in Manhattan, 1835–1894* (New York: Arno Press, 1981).

Mollenkopf, John H., "City Planning," in Charles Brecher and Raymond Horton, eds., *Setting Municipal Priorities, 1990* (New York: Russell Sage Foundation, 1989).

———, *The Contested City* (Princeton, NJ: Princeton University Press, 1983).

———, ed., *Power, Culture, and Place: Essays on New York City* (New York: Russell Sage Foundation, 1988).

Mollenkopf, John H., and Manuel Castells, eds., *Dual City: Restructuring New York* (New York: Russell Sage Foundation, 1991).

Moore, Deborah Dash, *At Home in America: Second Generation New York Jews* (New York: Columbia University Press, 1981).

———, "The Construction of Community: Jewish Geography and Ethnicity in the United States," in Moses Rischin, ed., *The Jews of North America* (Detroit, MI: Wayne State University Press, 1987).

———, "The Ideal Slum," *American Jewish History* 73 (December 1983): 134–141, 185–204.

Moses, Robert, *Public Works: A Dangerous Trade* (New York: McGraw-Hill, 1970).

Mujica, Francisco, *History of the Skyscraper* (Paris: Art and Archeology Press, 1929).

Naylor, David, *American Picture Palaces: The Architecture of Fantasy* (New York: Van Nostrand Reinhold, 1981).

Nye, David E., *Electrifying America: Social Meanings of a New Technology, 1880–1940* (Cambridge: MIT Press, 1990).

Osofsky, Gilbert, *Harlem, the Making of a Ghetto: Negro New York, 1890–1930* (New York: Harper & Row, 1966).

Perry, Clarence, *The Rebuilding of Blighted Areas: A Study of the Neighborhood Unit in Replanning and Plot Assemblage* (New York: Regional Plan Association, 1933).

Plunz, Richard, *A History of Housing in New York City: Dwelling Type and Social Change in the American Metropolis* (New York: Columbia University Press, 1990).

Porter, Glenn, *The Rise of Big Business, 1860–1910*, 2nd ed. (Arlington Heights, IL: Harlan Davidson, 1992).

Pratt, Edward Ewing, *Industrial Causes of Congestion of Population in New York City* (New York: Columbia University Press, 1911).

Pred, Allan, "The Intrametropolitan Location of American Manufacturing," *Annals of the Association of American Geographers* 54 (June 1964): 165–180.

Regional Plan Association, *The Economic Status of the New York Metro-politan Region in 1944* (New York: Regional Plan Association, 1944).

Relph, Edward, *The Modern Urban Landscape* (Baltimore, MD: Johns Hopkins University Press, 1987).

Report of the Heights of Buildings Committee to the Committee on the Height, Size, and Arrangement of Buildings to the Board of Estimate and Apportionment of the City of New York (New York, 1913).

Reports of the Immigration Commission, 42 vols. (Washington, DC: U.S. Government Printing Office, 1911).

Reports of the Industrial Commission, 19 vols. (Washington, DC: U.S. Government Printing Office, 1900–1902).

Riis, Jacob. *Ten Years War* (Boston: Houghton Mifflin, 1900).

Rischin, Moses, ed., *Grandma Never Lived in America: The New Journalism of Abraham Cahan* (Bloomington: Indiana University Press, 1985).

———, *The Promised City: New York's Jews, 1870–1914* (Cambridge: Harvard University Press, 1962).

Robbins, Sidney M., and Nestor E. Terleckyj, *Money Metropolis: A Locational Study of Financial Activities in the New York Region* (Cambridge: Harvard University Press, 1960).

Rodgers, Cleveland, *Robert Moses: Builder for Democracy* (New York: Henry Holt, 1952).

Rosenwaike, Ira, *Population History of New York City* (Syracuse, NY: Syracuse University Press, 1972).

Rosenzweig, Roy, *Eight Hours for What We Will* (New York: Cambridge University Press, 1985).

Rosner, David, *A Once Charitable Enterprise: Hospitals and Health Care in Brooklyn and New York, 1885–1915* (New York: Cambridge University Press, 1982).

Ruttenbaum, Steven, *Mansions in the Clouds: The Skyscraper Palazzi of Emery Roth* (New York: Balsam Press, 1986).

Sayre, Wallace, and Herbert Kaufman, *Governing New York City: Politics in the Metropolis* (New York: Russell Sage Foundation, 1960).

Schaffer, Daniel, ed., *Two Centuries of American Planning* (Baltimore, MD: Johns Hopkins University Press, 1988).

Schiesl, Martin J., *The Politics of Efficiency: Municipal Administration and Reform in America, 1880–1920* (Berkeley, CA: University of California Press, 1977).

Schoenebaum, Eleanora, "Emerging Neighborhoods: The Development of Brooklyn's Fringe Areas, 1850–1930." Ph.D. diss. (Columbia University, 1977).

Schultz, Stanley K., *Constructing Urban Culture: American Cities and City Planning, 1800–1920* (Philadelphia, PA: Temple University Press, 1989).

Scott, Mel, *American City Planning Since 1890: A History Commemorating the Fiftieth Anniversary of the American Institute of Planners* (Berkeley: University of California Press, 1969).

Shanor, Rebecca Read, *The City That Never Was: Two Hundred Years of Fantastic and Fascinating Plans That Might Have Changed the Face of New York City* (New York: Viking Press, 1988).

Sharpe, William, and Leonard Wallock, eds., *Visions of the Modern City: Essays in History, Art, and Literature* (Baltimore, MD: Johns Hopkins University Press, 1987).

Simpson, Michael, *Thomas Adams and the Modern Planning Movement: Britain, Canada, and the United States, 1900–1940* (London: Mansell, 1985).

Skowronek, Stephen, *Building a New American State: The Expansion of National Administrative Capacities, 1877–1920* (New York: Cambridge University Press, 1982).

Smith, Robert G., *Ad Hoc Governments: Special Purpose Transportation Authorities in Britain and the United States* (Beverly Hills, CA: Sage Publications, 1974).

Stansell, Christine, *City of Women: Sex and Class in New York, 1789–1860* (New York: Knopf, 1986).

Starr, Roger, *The Rise and Fall of New York City* (New York: Basic Books, 1985).

Starrett, Paul, *Changing the Skyline* (New York: McGraw-Hill, 1938).

Starrett, William A., *Skyscrapers and the Men Who Build Them* (New York: Charles Scribner's Sons, 1928).

Stein, Leon, *The Triangle Fire* (Philadelphia, PA: J. B. Lippincott, 1962).

Stern, Robert A. M., Gregory Gilmartin, and John Massengale, *New York 1900: Metropolitan Architecture and Urbanism, 1890–1915* (New York: Rizzoli Press, 1983).

Stern, Robert A. M., Gregory Gilmartin, and Thomas Mellins, *New York 1930: Architectural Urbanism Between the Two World Wars* (New York: Rizzoli Press, 1987).

Strasser, Susan, *Satisfaction Guaranteed: The Making of the American Mass Market* (New York: Pantheon Books, 1989).

Susman, Warren, *Culture as History: The Transformation of American Society in the Twentieth Century* (New York: Pantheon Books, 1984).

Sutcliffe, Anthony, *Towards the Planned City: Germany, Britain, the United States, and France, 1780–1914* (Oxford: Basil Blackwell, 1981).

Tarr, Joel E., and Gabriel Dupuy, eds., *Technology and the Rise of the Networked City in Europe and America* (Philadelphia, PA: Temple University Press, 1988).

Taylor, William R., ed., *Inventing Times Square: Commerce and Culture at the Crossroads of the World* (New York: Russell Sage Foundation, 1991).

Teaford, Jon C., *The Municipal Revolution in America: The Origins of Modern Urban Government, 1650–1825* (Chicago: University of Chicago Press, 1975).

———, *The Unheralded Triumph: City Government in America, 1870–1900* (Baltimore, MD: Johns Hopkins University Press, 1984).

Toll, Seymour I., *Zoned America* (New York: Grossman, 1969).

Trachtenberg, Alan, *Brooklyn Bridge: Fact and Symbol* (Chicago: University of Chicago Press, 1979).

Tricarico, Donald, *The Italians of Greenwich Village: The Social Structure and Transformation of an Ethnic Community* (Staten Island, NY: Center for Migration Studies, 1984).

Tyack, David B., *The One Best System: A History of American Urban Education* (Cambridge: Harvard University Press, 1974).

Van Leeuwen, Thomas A. P., *The Skyward Trend of Thought: The Metaphysics of the American Skyscraper* (Cambridge: MIT Press, 1988).

Vernon, Raymond, *Metropolis, 1985: An Interpretation of the Findings of the New York Metropolitan Region Study* (Cambridge: Harvard University Press, 1960).

Waldinger, Roger D., *Through the Eye of the Needle: Immigrants and Enterprise in New York's Garment Trades* (New York: New York University Press, 1986).

Walker, James Blaine, *Fifty Years of Rapid Transit, 1864–1917* (New York: Law Printing Company, 1918).

Wallock, Leonard, ed., *New York: Culture Capital of the World, 1940–1965* (New York: Rizzoli Press, 1988).

Walsh, Annmarie H., *The Public's Business: The Politics and Practices of Government Corporations* (Cambridge: MIT Press, 1978).

Ward, David, *Cities and Immigrants: A Geography of Change in Nineteenth-Century America* (New York: Oxford University Press, 1971).

———, ed., *Geographic Perspectives on America's Past: Readings on the Historical Geography of the United States* (New York: Oxford University Press, 1979).

———, *Poverty, Ethnicity, and the American City, 1840–1925: Changing Conceptions of the Slum and Ghetto* (Cambridge: Cambridge University Press, 1989).

Weisman, Winston, "New York and the Problem of the First Skyscraper," *Journal of the Society of Architectural Historians* 12 (March 1953): 13–21.

Weiss, Marc A., "Richard T. Ely and the Contribution of Economic Research to National Housing Policy, 1920–1940," *Urban Studies* 26 (February 1989): 115–126.

———, *The Rise of the Community Builders: The American Real Estate Industry and Urban Land Planning* (New York: Columbia University Press, 1987).

Wiebe, Robert H., *The Search for Order, 1877–1920* (New York: Hill & Wang, 1967).

Wilkins, Mira, *The Emergence of International Enterprise: American Business Abroad from the Colonial Era to 1914* (Cambridge: Harvard University Press, 1970).

Willis, Carol, "Zoning and Zeitgeist: The Skyscraper City in the 1920s,"

Journal of the Society of Architectural Historians 45 (March 1986): 47–59.

Wilson, Richard Guy, *McKim, Mead & White, Architects* (New York: Rizzoli Press, 1983).

Wilson, Richard Guy, Dianne H. Pilgrim, and Dickran Tashjian, *The Machine Age in America, 1918–1941* (New York: Brooklyn Museum, in association with Abrams, 1986).

Wood, Robert C., *1400 Governments: The Political Economy of the New York Metropolitan Region* (Cambridge: Harvard University Press, 1961).

WPA Guide to New York City (New York: Pantheon Books, 1939).

Zukin, Sharon, *Loft Living: Culture and Capital in Urban Change* (Baltimore, MD: Johns Hopkins University Press, 1982).

Zunz, Olivier, *The Changing Face of Inequality: Urbanization, Industrial Development, and Immigrants in Detroit, 1880–1920* (Chicago: University of Chicago Press, 1982).

———, *Making America Corporate, 1880–1920* (Chicago: University of Chicago Press, 1990).

Index

Boldface numbers refer to figures and tables.